Hiring the Black Worker

Timothy J. Minchin

The

University

of North

Carolina

Press

Chapel Hill

and London

Hiring the Black Worker

The Racial Integration of the Southern Textile Industry, 1960–1980

© 1999 The University of North Carolina Press

All rights reserved

Designed by April Leidig-Higgins

Set in Minion by Running Feet Books

Manufactured in the United States of America

The paper in this book meets the guidelines for
permanence and durability of the Committee on
Production Guidelines for Book Longevity of the
Council on Library Resources.

Library of Congress Cataloging-in-Publication Data

Minchin, Timothy J.   Hiring the black worker: the
racial integration of the Southern textile industry,
1960–1980 / by Timothy J. Minchin.

p. cm.   Includes bibliographical references and index.

ISBN 0-8078-2470-4 (cloth : alk. paper)

ISBN 0-8078-4771-2 (pbk. : alk. paper)

1. Discrimination in employments—Southern States
—History—20th century.   2. Textile workers—Southern
States—History—20th century.   3. Race discrimination
—Southern States—History—20th century.   4. Trade-
unions—Afro-American membership—Southern States
—History—20th century.   I. Title.

HD4903.3.T42U66 1999   331.6'396073—dc21

98-30146 CIP

Portions of chapters 4 and 8 previously appeared in
Timothy J. Minchin, " 'Color Means Something': Black
Pioneers, White Resistance, and Interracial Unionism
in the Southern Textile Industry, 1957–1980," *Labor
History* 39, no. 2 (May 1998): 109–33. Used by
permission.

03 02 01 00 99   5 4 3 2 1

contents

illustrations

tables

acknowledgments

This book was researched and written while I was Mellon Research Fellow at Cambridge University. I wish to acknowledge the financial assistance of the Mellon Fund that allowed me to undertake several extended research trips to the United States. I also wish to acknowledge the support provided by Sidney Sussex College in Cambridge, where I was a fellow between 1995 and 1998. The college provided a wonderful research environment that helped a great deal in the writing of this book. I would also like to thank St. Andrews University for allowing me time to add the finishing touches to this book before I started my teaching duties with them.

I owe a great debt to my friend and colleague, Jim Leloudis. Jim helped arrange for me to be a visiting scholar at the University of North Carolina in 1996, and he was supportive and helpful throughout. I am also grateful to other members of the Leloudis family, of a wide variety of ages, who looked after and entertained me while I was in the United States. Especially I thank Dianne, James, and Virginia for their hospitality and friendship. Other friends in the United States helped me in many ways. I especially wish to express my thanks to my friends Rick and Hatsy Nittoli, George Waldrep, and Richard and Claire Zieger, who all helped me a great deal while I was living in North Carolina. Many people were kind enough to put me up while I was on my travels, and in this regard I especially wish to thank Norris and Alice Tibbetts, Laura Ann Pope, and Bob and Gay Zieger.

Various members of the Union of Needletrades, Industrial, and Textile Employees (UNITE!) helped me in setting up and carrying out interviews. On many occasions, UNITE! members allowed me to use their union halls for interviews, and I thank them for this. I owe a special thanks to UNITE! joint board managers who helped me locate many of the people I needed to see, especially Reese Boulware in Columbus, Georgia; Sammy Glover in Andalusia, Alabama; James Johnson in Andrews, South Carolina; Clyde Bush in Roanoke Rapids, North Carolina, and Sydney Young in Rock Hill, South Carolina. UNITE! organizer Nick Atkins assisted me in carrying out interviews in the Columbus, Georgia, area. Former organizer Bob Freeman was a great help with interviews in Kannapolis, North Carolina. UNITE!'s southern regional director, Bruce Raynor, also helped me a great deal when I was carrying out my interviews across the South. In Andrews, South Carolina, Laura Ann Pope was of enormous assistance. I wish to thank all those whom I interviewed for providing me with such an enjoyable and memorable experience, and especially for being so hospitable and helpful.

I also wish to thank several archivists who were particularly helpful. I am especially grateful to Bob Dinwiddie at the Southern Labor Archives for allowing me to use several important record collections before they had been fully processed. I also wish to thank the staff at the Federal Records Center in East Point, Georgia, who looked after me very well during my prolonged visits to their archives. The editors at the University of North Carolina Press deserve thanks for all their support and help in seeing this project to publication, especially Lewis Bateman, Mary Laur, and Ron Maner. The manuscript also benefited from the skillful copyediting of Mary Reid.

My debts to academic colleagues and friends are also considerable. I want to give particular thanks to Tony Badger, who has consistently encouraged and supported my research ever since I began my Ph.D. under his supervision. I have benefited greatly from the way that Tony has advanced the profile of American History in Britain and Europe. I also wish to thank those who provided useful comments on drafts of this book, especially Tom Terrill and John Thompson. Gavin Wright provided valuable advice and guidance in the early stages of the project. Others whose advice I have benefited from include Howell Harris, Rick Halpern, Annette Cox-Wright, John Salmond, and Bob Zieger.

Finally, I wish to give thanks to my family, especially to my parents and to my wife, Olga, for all their support and love that helped make this book possible.

Hiring the Black Worker

There is little value in a Negro's
obtaining the right to be admitted
to hotels and restaurants, if he has
no cash in his pocket and no job.
—President John F. Kennedy

introduction

Although a vast amount of historical literature on the civil rights movement
has been written in the last twenty years, very little attention has been focused
on economic aspects of the civil rights upsurge, especially the impact that the
movement had upon southern workers. This neglect has occurred partly
because scholars have concentrated overwhelmingly on protest efforts, especially examinations of protest organizations and leaders during the "heroic
period" of activism from 1954 to 1968. Only very recently have historians
begun to explore some of the issues surrounding the impact of the civil rights
era upon southern workers and the southern labor movement.[1]

Investigation of the relationship between the civil rights movement and
southern labor is important because the struggle for economic equality was
recognized by the federal government as well as by black leaders as central to
achieving black equality. In the 1950s and 1960s, both politicians and civil
rights leaders repeatedly emphasized the centrality of economic equality to the
wider struggle for black rights. As President Lyndon Johnson wrote in 1966,
"Surely there is no more difficult, nor more important question in the field of
civil rights than that of opening up new job opportunities for Negro Americans, helping them to prepare for those opportunities, and assuring them fair
treatment at promotion time. Negroes feel, and I think rightly, that full participation in the American promise can never be theirs, until the job question is
settled and settled rightly." Vice President Hubert Humphrey echoed Johnson

1

when he told a White House Conference in 1965 that Title VII of the Civil Rights Act of 1964—which prohibited racial discrimination in employment—was "the heart of the Act." Humphrey explained that "nothing is more important to the Negro in his struggle to free himself from the circle of frustration than the ability to have and to hold a good job."[2]

The central importance of the employment issue was developed by civil rights leaders, who argued that the ability to enter a good job was the key to true black equality. Rev. Martin Luther King Jr. repeatedly spoke of the importance of economic equality to the civil rights struggle, especially in the later years of his life, and was an active supporter of organized labor. As King declared in 1964, "Of what advantage is it to the Negro to establish that he can be served in integrated restaurants or accommodated in integrated hotels, if he is bound to the kind of financial servitude which will not allow him to take a vacation or even take his wife out to dinner?"[3]

While black leaders such as King recognized the centrality of economic equality to the struggle for civil rights, they also realized that ending discrimination in employment was far more complicated and problematic than achieving legal or political equality. King himself recognized that whites would be more sympathetic to granting individual rights documented in the Constitution than to promoting group solutions to poverty. Thus, from the mid-1950s on, the civil rights movement had tried to tackle the problem of black poverty by attacking legal and political barriers to equality, hoping that voting rights would ameliorate economic problems. As political and legal equality were achieved, however, the importance of the problematic issue of economic equality was thrown into sharp relief. King himself wrote in 1966 that the issue of better jobs was the most important of the future but added, "The future is more complex. . . . Jobs are harder to create than voting rolls." Ironically, the struggle for economic equality was both the most important and, as President Johnson admitted, the most difficult to achieve.[4]

The reluctance of the civil rights movement to address the issue of economic equality—and the failure of King's belated effort in the mid-1960s to wage a "War on Poverty" in the North—has meant that scholars have often assumed that few economic gains were made by the civil rights movement. The movement indeed seemed to leave black poverty untouched. In 1969 nearly two out of every three blacks in the rural South lived below the poverty line. The discovery of black economic problems disillusioned civil rights workers. The civil rights movement has thus become defined by the "classic" period of protest from 1954 to 1968 and the struggle to end legal segregation and political exclusion.[5]

One area that has been particularly neglected is the breakthrough that African Americans made into employment in the southern textile industry in the 1960s and 1970s.[6] The textile breakthrough was especially significant because blacks made rapid gains in an industry that had traditionally excluded them. The textile industry was the South's largest industry and had previously been overwhelmingly white. In 1964, for example, less than 5 percent of mill workers in South Carolina were black; by 1976, nearly one in three textile workers in the state were black. African Americans made employment gains in the southern textile industry at a much greater pace than in most other American industries. Between 1960 and 1969, black employment in textiles increased four times faster than the national average for all manufacturing. In 1960, only 3.3 percent of textile workers were black, compared to 7.6 percent of manufacturing employees. By June 1978, African Americans had progressed slightly to hold 12 percent of all manufacturing jobs, but textile firms, by hiring African Americans at twice the rate for all employees, had increased minority participation to over 18 percent. In 1978, blacks held a quarter of all production jobs in the southern textile industry.[7]

Data from individual firms further illustrates the major strides in black employment that were made in the 1960s and 1970s. Cannon Mills, one of the largest textile companies, was located in the Kannapolis area of North Carolina, where the black population was around 18 percent. Although the company hired almost no blacks until 1964, by 1975, black employment in the mills exceeded the community level, and in the early 1980s around a quarter of the company's 22,000 workers were African American.[8] Between 1967 and August 1977, the number of African Americans working for the large J. P. Stevens Company increased by over 200 percent. At Stevens, as elsewhere, major gains in black employment were made in the 1970s. At the company's main facility in Roanoke Rapids, North Carolina, the number of blacks in the workforce grew from 19.4 percent in 1970 to 37.1 percent in 1975, a figure that roughly matched the percentage of blacks in the community.[9]

Thus, the southern textile industry, which had always been known for its lily-white character, had thoroughly integrated its workforce within fifteen years.[10] Historians have noted the scale and significance of the change. Richard Rowan, who studied the industry's moves toward black employment in the late 1960s, concluded in his 1970 study that "a change of the magnitude noted in the racial employment structure of textiles has probably never occurred before in southern industry."[11] Gavin Wright has called the entry of blacks into the southern textile industry "a genuine revolution, very deserving of a prominent place in the history of the civil rights movement."[12] Similar conclusions have also been made by Mary Frederickson.[13]

Study of the racial integration of the southern textile industry has been limited, however. Studies outlining the importance of black entry into textiles have not gone beyond this, failing to explore in detail the issue of how much discrimination remained in the mills. The attitudes of companies to integration have also not been examined at length.[14] The most detailed treatment of the subject, Richard Rowan's "The Negro in the Textile Industry" (1970) is dated and only covers the early years of the integration. Because major employment gains were made by African Americans throughout the 1970s, a complete picture of the racial integration of the industry must cover the 1970s as well as the 1960s. Rowan's study also fails to provide any information on what black workers themselves felt about integration. The voices of the subjects, the black workers who were hired into the industry in the 1960s, are completely missing.

This study will examine the racial integration of the southern textile industry in detail, a task that is made possible by the availability of a wide variety of original sources, including excellent written records that have not been used in previous studies. My main source is legal records, especially the detailed documentation provided by class action racial discrimination lawsuits filed under Title VII of the Civil Rights Act of 1964. In the 1960s and 1970s, virtually every large southern textile company was involved in major litigation alleging racial discrimination. The companies sued included Cannon Mills, Fieldcrest Mills, Cone Mills, Burlington Industries, J. P. Stevens, Dan River Mills, and many others. As Ed Rankin, public relations director of Cannon Mills, admitted in 1982, as Cannon settled a class action suit, "This type of suit has been initiated against every major textile company . . . so it's not the first of its kind."[15]

The records of these lawsuits, housed in federal records centers, are voluminous. Because many cases were class action suits that went on for several years, the records provide details of many aspects of the racial integration of the industry that have not been covered at length in the existing literature. The depositions of aggrieved African American textile workers describe in compelling detail the discrimination in the mills. Statistics based on company records and covering thousands of black textile workers provide a detailed quantitative picture of the amount of racial discrimination remaining in the industry after integration. The trial testimony of company officials reveals the arguments that companies used to resist racial change and to defend their industry against charges of discrimination and provides valuable insights into the attitudes of textile executives to black employment.

These written records are supplemented by a large body of interviews that I carried out with African American textile workers across the South. Many of those interviewed had been plaintiffs in the lawsuits, and their memories highlight the motives and bravery of the black workers who initiated and participated in litigation. These interviews are intended to supplement the written record by showing what integration meant for its participants. Many interviews were conducted with "pioneers," the men and women who were the part of the first wave of African American workers hired in the industry in the mid-to-late 1960s. The experience of the pioneers is an important, untold part of the story of integration, illustrating the techniques that companies used to start the integration of their plants, and revealing the relationship between black and white workers in the workplace.

After an opening chapter that outlines the history of black employment in the southern textile industry before 1964, the reasons that companies hired increasing numbers of blacks in the 1960s and 1970s will be discussed in Chapter 2. While earlier studies have suggested that racial integration of the textile industry was caused by a labor shortage, this account will argue that federal regulations were also a major cause.[16] Chapter 3 will analyze the way that textile executives reacted to the racial integration of the industry. Many textile executives held deep-seated fears about the integration of the industry and resented federal efforts to push the pace of black hiring. They wanted to maintain control of the hiring process and resisted federal efforts to implement affirmative action programs in the textile industry. Although textile companies hired African Americans in increasing numbers, many executives were reluctant to accept black employment in nontraditional jobs.

Chapters 4–6 examine the experiences of the first black workers hired into production positions. These chapters draw upon remarkable letters that black workers wrote to the Equal Employment Opportunity Commission (EEOC) in which they described in detail the discrimination they faced. Such letters were often written by groups of black workers and were responsible for initiating the lawsuits.

One of the most striking aspects of the racial integration of the textile industry was that the experiences of African American women differed greatly from those of men, especially in the type of discrimination faced. Black women came into the industry from a different background than black men, and they faced different problems. Unlike black men, who had a history of participation in the industry in nonproduction jobs, black women had rarely been hired. Throughout the 1960s and 1970s, the major problem for black women was getting hired, while for black men, it was being promoted. Thus, the experience of integration varied greatly according to gender. This is reflected in the lawsuits, in which black male plaintiffs sought promotions but black female plaintiffs protested against hiring discrimination. Chapter 5 explores the discrimination faced by black men, while Chapter 6 examines the unique experiences of African American women, using the excellent records provided by the lawsuits.

Two final chapters examine the role that civil rights organizations and labor unions played in the integration of the industry. Historiographical emphasis on the major civil rights protests has meant that little is known about the impact of the civil rights movement outside the Deep South. Most textile mills were located in small towns in the industrial Piedmont, communities that have generally not achieved a reputation for civil rights activity. Through the lawsuits and the records of civil rights organizations, however, it is possible to uncover civil rights activism in textile communities. National civil rights organizations targeted the textile industry for particular attention. In 1967–68, the National Association for the Advancement of Colored People (NAACP) and a variety of other organizations funded Textiles: Employment and Advancement for Minorities (TEAM), a major project aimed at increasing black employment in the textile industry of South Carolina. The records of TEAM illustrate the extensive efforts made by civil rights groups to improve employment opportunities for African Americans in the textile industry.

Although most textile mills were not covered by union contracts, labor unions played a significant role in the racial integration of the industry. The entry of blacks into the workforce brought with it optimistic predictions that increased unionization would follow. This did not occur, however, and it is important to find out why. In recent years, historians have also debated the extent to which black and white workers were able to cooperate within unions, and studying the influx of blacks into the textile industry provides an opportunity to further examine this question.[17]

The extensive records of the lawsuits are supplemented by a variety of other written sources, particularly records of civil rights organizations. TEAM was an important civil rights initiative that has not been studied before, and the records of the project are extensive and rich. The records of the American Friends Service Committee (AFSC) also provide a wealth of information on the integration of the industry. Between 1952 and 1965, the AFSC carried out a merit employment program aimed at persuading southern companies to hire African Americans into nontraditional positions. The AFSC made hundreds of plant visits to southern industrialists, including many textile mill owners. The records of these visits offer a fascinating look at the racial attitudes and fears of textile executives. Union records are another important source, providing valuable information on the role that unions played in the integration of the industry.

There Were No Blacks
Running the Machines

Black Employment in the Southern
Textile Industry before 1964

one

On March 18, 1953, twenty-six-year-old Johnnie Franklin Archie started working as a laborer at Rock Hill Printing and Finishing Company in Rock Hill, South Carolina. A small, bearded black man, Archie was to work at the mill for the rest of his working life. Interviewed in 1996, Archie recalled that all the blacks who were hired at the plant in the 1950s and early 1960s worked in non-production positions that were heavy, dirty, and frequently hazardous: "The only black women there cleaned the white women's restrooms, none on production. And the blacks that were there were on the lowest paid and most hazardous, worst-condition jobs of any human being—this was the black man's job." Archie went on to describe some of the jobs that African Americans carried out: "The trash truck for one, hauling garbage for one; and a place called the napping department, you'd walk in there and you had to wear a mask over your face. Lint was pulled off the cloth and put in a small bin to make bales out of it—a black man seen to that. Another hazardous job was out on the yard, in the rain and cold." Archie felt that black men "wouldn't have been there if it wasn't that we were doing the work that the white man didn't want to do. That's the only reason we were there."[1]

The experiences of black workers at Rock Hill Printing and Finishing Company were typical of those of black workers in the textile industry generally before 1964. Very few blacks were employed in the industry, and those who were hired worked in nonproduction positions, often outside of the mill. Because of the heavy nature of many of these jobs, the majority of black textile workers before 1964 were men; the few black women in the industry tended to work, as at Rock Hill, purely in cleaning positions. The type of jobs described by Archie were typical of those performed by black textile workers. In 1964, for example, the Textile Workers Union of America (TWUA) confirmed this picture in a report it compiled on black employment in the industry. This report concluded that "Negro employment in the southern textile industry has traditionally been restricted to work in yard and labor gangs. There have been a few plants in which Negroes have been engaged in production work but these are relatively rare."[2]

The entry of African Americans into production jobs in the textile industry is especially significant when it is compared to the opportunities available to black workers in the industry before 1964. Indeed, prior to the 1960s, the textile industry employed African Americans only in a very limited number of jobs. In 1940, only 2.1 percent of textile workers were black, a figure that rose slightly to 3.6 percent in 1950. A study of black employment in the industry carried out by Donald Dewey in 1950, for example, found that blacks were employed either "as laborers outside the plant or as janitors inside the plant." In contrast, most white workers were "employed in office or production positions inside the plant."[3]

Thus, employment opportunities for African Americans in the textile industry were extremely restricted before 1964. This employment pattern clearly had major implications for African Americans who lived in a region dominated by that industry.

The American Textile Industry

In the 1960s and 1970s, a number of factors made it important for blacks to secure more jobs in the textile industry. Overall, the industry was in a unique position to reduce black economic inequality and bring substantial economic gains to the African American community. Most significant was the fact that its cultural and political influence as the South's largest industry meant that any integration that occurred in the textile industry would be repeated in smaller industries. In addition, most of the jobs in the industry were unskilled or semiskilled and could easily be learned by inexperienced black workers.

Throughout the 1960s and 1970s, the textile industry was a major American industry, employing between 800,000 and 1 million workers. These employment levels ranked the textile industry as a primary employer on a par with other major American industries such as automobiles, steel, and paper. Although the industry was affected by industrial decline and plant closings in the

1980s and 1990s, most of the period between 1960 and 1980 was one of sustained growth and prosperity. Between 1965 and 1974, in particular, the textile industry experienced unprecedented levels of prosperity and employment. In December 1973, for example, the trade journal *Textile Hi-Lights* reported that "year-end 1973 finds the textile industry with record sales, increased profits, rising employment, and a leveling off of imports." Between June 1965 and December 1973, the number of people employed in the industry rose steadily from 922,000 to 1,028,000.[4] In the main textile state of North Carolina, employment in textile mills reached an all-time high of 293,600 in 1973.[5]

The growth that the industry experienced for most of the 1960s and 1970s is well illustrated in trade sources. In 1964, *America's Textile Reporter*, a "conservative trade publication not given to overuse of rose-colored glasses," reported optimistically that "textile earnings are on the rise and there is nothing on the horizon that would suggest a reversal of the trend in the months ahead."[6] In 1965, the large Fieldcrest Mills reported that sales and earnings in 1964 "reached new highs for the third consecutive year."[7] Many other textile companies also reported record sales in the mid-1960s.[8] In 1967, *Textile Hi-Lights* reported that 1967 was the fourth successive year of "intensified operations in the U.S. textile industry. Increased volume since 1963 is indicated by a 22 percent increase in shipments, 72,000 added employees and a 12 percent increase in operating spindle looms."[9]

By the 1960s, the vast majority of the American textile industry was located in the South. In 1961, for example, southern textile plants were responsible for about 89 percent of the nation's total textile production. By 1965, the southern states had over 18 million spindles, compared to only 756,000 in New England, the industry's birthplace. The South had achieved a position of dominance in the industry largely through lower costs in the form of labor, transportation, and taxes.[10]

To a large extent, textiles dominated the South. In 1973, it was by far the South's biggest industry, employing 697,500 workers in eight southern states.[11] A further 421,900 people worked in the related apparel industry. The South's third largest industry, food processing, only employed around 275,000 workers. In 1973, *New York Times* writer Henry P. Leiferman called mill workers "the bedrock of the Deep South's economy, religion, politics, industry." The industry's cultural and economic influence upon the South was considerable. As Leiferman pointed out, "The industry, from floor sweeper to chairman of the board, reaches everywhere in the South. Senators such as Strom Thurmond, Sam Ervin, Herman Talmadge, governors such as John West, Terry Sanford and Jimmy Carter started their campaigns with the mill vote." Evangelist Billy Graham started his career reaching out to "the souls of the mill hands." Mill owners such as Roger Milliken, who was Richard Nixon's finance chairman in

1968 and later became a strong supporter of Pat Buchanan, were themselves often powerful political figures in the region. Milliken, indeed, had long been the source of money and support for Strom Thurmond and other Republican politicians, and he is an important figure in understanding the revival of the Republican Party in the South.[12]

The textile industry's dominance of the southern economy was most pronounced in North and South Carolina, both states with large black populations.[13] In December 1966, the EEOC found that around 45 percent of all manufacturing jobs in the Carolinas were in textiles. More than 48 percent of all U.S. textile plants that employed over 500 persons were in these two states. As an EEOC report concluded, "The Carolinas, therefore, are the hub of the U.S. textile industry."[14]

The industry went through a small recession in late 1974 and 1975, and employment levels fell below the peak of 1973. This was the start of a long-term decline for the southern textile industry that was largely related to the flood of textile imports that came onto the American market after 1975. Indeed, textile imports nearly tripled in the decade between 1974 and 1984, leading to widespread plant closings in the late 1970s and 1980s. Between 1975 and 1985 more than 800 American mills closed down, and in North Carolina textile employment fell 28 percent between 1973 and 1986.[15]

Although the textile industry began to decline in the late 1970s, it remained a major industry that still offered significant employment opportunities to many southerners. As of June 1978, for example, the textile industry's employment had just dipped under a million workers, at 990,800.[16] Even after the recession of 1974–75, the industry continued to dominate the economy of the Carolinas. In October 1978, textile payrolls provided a living for more North Carolinians than any other industry. Textile plants were located in eighty-one of the state's one hundred counties, with a payroll of nearly $3 billion a year. In the early 1990s, the textile industry remained North Carolina's largest industrial employer, and there were more textile workers in the state than in any other.[17]

Throughout the postwar period, the textile industry experienced a process of consolidation, whereby the average size of companies grew through mergers. The industry had traditionally been characterized by small, individually owned companies, and mergers were an attempt to improve profits and achieve better control of product lines. Although the industry was increasingly dominated by a small number of large companies, it was still competitive in character. Thus, the fifteen largest companies in 1968 employed less than half of all workers in the industry in the same year. The largest, Burlington Industries, employed less than 10 percent of the industry's workers in that year.[18]

The records of the class action lawsuits offer a detailed look at the process of integration at these large textile companies. Indeed, the companies that feature heavily in this story were among the biggest in the industry. J. P. Stevens, involved in several large class actions in this period, was the nation's second largest textile company, employing 49,300 workers in 1968. Cannon Mills, another company involved in a great deal of litigation, was the eighth largest, employing 18,000 workers in its plants around Kannapolis, North Carolina. Dan River Mills, Cone Mills, and Fieldcrest Mills, all at the center of this study, were also top-fifteen companies. The largest company, Burlington Industries, employed 83,000 workers in 1968. Burlington also features in this study through several lawsuits which were filed against it.[19]

Entry into the textile industry was particularly important for African Americans because most of the jobs were unskilled or could be easily learned with no specialist training. In 1968, Richard Rowan's study found that 87 percent of all textile jobs were classified as blue-collar, with most of these being operative positions. Rowan concluded that "there is probably no other basic industry in the United States with more employees classified as operatives." Even in the 1960s, the industry retained a labor-intensive character, meaning that it was in a unique position to employ large numbers of relatively unskilled workers.[20]

The vast majority of production work in the textile industry was unskilled or semiskilled, with machine operators holding over one-half of all jobs. Most mills, moreover, used standard equipment in the production process, making it easy for workers to transfer their skills from mill to mill. Although most jobs were not skilled, jobs within the industry were graded according to how heavy or dirty the work was. African Americans had traditionally been hired at the start and finish of the production process, where work was arduous and less desirable, rather than in the central processes of spinning and weaving, which were considered cleaner, more prestigious jobs.

The first stage of the production process was the opening room, where bales of raw cotton were opened and fed into a machine that cleaned the fiber. This job was unskilled and heavy, requiring regular lifting of raw cotton bales. For this reason, black men had traditionally been hired in the opening room.

After opening, the cotton was transferred by machine to pickers for additional cleaning. The pickers formed the cotton into large rolls called laps, which weighed up to ninety pounds. These laps had to be manually lifted to the next machine, making the picking room an undesirable job where large numbers of African Americans were employed in the 1960s and 1970s.

Following picking, carding machines straightened and cleaned the fiber into long strands called card slivers that were mechanically coiled into cans for transfer to the next stage of the process. After carding, drawing reduced several loose slivers into a single, compact, uniform strand, while roving twisted the strands and wound them onto bobbins ready for spinning.

Spinning made up around 20 percent of a textile mill's employment and was usually carried out by women. Spinning was the final operation of yarn manufacture and was responsible for drawing strands out further and then twisting them to form yarn. Spinning was traditionally restricted to white women, and black women had to fight hard to get spinning jobs in this period.

In the 1960s and 1970s, most mills also wove their own cloth, and in these mills weaving made up around half of all jobs. Weaving involved mixing crosswise (filling) threads with lengthwise (warp) threads on a loom to form cloth. This work was more skilled than most textile work and was the most highly paid. Consequently, it was dominated by whites, especially men. The position of loom fixer, responsible for maintaining a weaver's looms and keeping them running, was particularly prestigious and difficult for blacks to break into. Loom fixer was the highest paid and most prestigious job in the textile industry without entering management.

After weaving, the cloth was finished through processes such as dyeing, bleaching, and preshrinking. This work involved extensive exposure to chemicals and heat and was often considered undesirable. Again, this was an area of the industry where black men had traditionally been employed, and companies such as Cone Mills and Dan River Mills used large numbers of black men in their bleachery and dyeing operations well before the 1960s.[21]

Black Employment before 1964

A mixture of state law and social custom ensured that no blacks worked on production jobs in the southern textile industry before the 1960s. In South Carolina, the Segregation Act of 1915 made it illegal for anyone "engaged in the business of cotton textile manufacturing . . . to allow . . . operatives . . . of different races to labor and work together within the same room." The law, which stayed on the books until 1960, had a separate clause that excluded many nonproduction jobs, establishing a tradition of black employment in these jobs. Other states followed similar patterns due to social custom.[22]

This exclusion of African Americans from production positions was a central feature of labor relations in the southern textile industry before the 1960s. As one recent study of the industry in the early twentieth century has concluded, "The most striking feature of the labor system in southern mills was the exclusion of blacks from 'production jobs.'"[23] The industry's exclusion of blacks even stood out when compared to other southern industries, and for many observers the textile industry was a symbol of the racist South. Dr. Vivian W. Henderson, president of Clark College in Atlanta and an economist, told the EEOC textile forum in 1967: "The textile industry in the South has an extremely poor record on Negro employment. The industry has a vicious history of outright exclusion and sheer discrimination regarding Negroes from the workforce in the various plants. The only manufacturing industry, in my judgement, that parallels the textile industry—and this can be supported by data—in terms of Negro exclusion from employment in the South is apparel, an allied industry." Henderson used EEOC data to show that in 1960 "textiles had the poorest record of Negro employment as a proportion of total employment of all manufacturing industries."[24]

The only opportunities for African Americans before the 1960s were thus in nonproduction positions. The industry employed some black men in service or janitorial positions; these workers were usually hired to sweep or clean areas of the mill where the white workers operated the machinery. The jobs were frequently dirty and menial. Theodore Suggs, a retired black mill worker from Tarboro, North Carolina, remembered clearly the demeaning nature of the job that he was first hired to perform in 1952: "I was taking care of the floors, buffing and sanding and sweeping. A lot of times they would spit on the floor and we had to go and scrub up that spit. It would get real bad, especially in the weave room; we'd have to scrape up all the cotton and stuff that was stuck to the floor."[25] At the Rosemary Mill in Roanoke Rapids, North Carolina, Sammy Alston was hired in the 1950s to clean the bathrooms and empty the spit trays that white workers used while they were on the job. Alston remembered that he was the only black person in the entire department where he worked: "I used to work up there at that mill. What I was doing was putting in spit trays, putting sawdust in it, and I was cleaning bathrooms. . . . They had some little spit trays, what they used to spit in. You put sawdust in it . . . keeps them from spitting on the floor. . . . I would always get them up, put new ones down, and I had bathrooms I had to clean up. Weren't black people working there and I was the only one to come through there, and it would be nothing in that card room but white people."[26]

This isolation from other black workers determined the way that the few black workers had to behave. Many black men who secured jobs inside the plants before the 1960s remembered that they had to perform their work quietly and unobtrusively, taking care to avoid any contact with whites, especially white women, who worked on the machines. Calvin Quarles was hired at the Eagle and Phenix Mill in Columbus, Georgia, in 1952. His job was to sweep the weave department where white men and women tended the machines. A soft-spoken, affable man, Quarles remembered that "I started sweeping in the weaving department, and back then it was where you wasn't even supposed to go down an alley where a white person was. You had to get out that alley when they come in, and then when they got out of the way, then go and sweep the alley." Quarles felt that he had only been successful in holding down his job because he worked hard and did not talk back.[27] Jacob Little, who started working at the Columbus Towel Mill in Columbus, Georgia, in the early 1960s, recalled similar experiences: "In the early '60s some of the problems facing you was if you walked down—you know, you have a row of looms with machinery—if you walked down the row with the machinery and a white woman started walking down it, you'd better get out of the alley, you know, let her pass, you'd better not pass in the alley. So that was some of the things, you know, down South. We went from being called boy, nigger, black, to our names."[28]

Besides working in cleaning jobs within white departments, black men also found employment in heavy jobs either outside of the mill or in segregated departments within the mill. Before the 1960s, many large southern textile companies hired blacks in their dyeing departments, where workers were exposed to heat, dust, and chemicals. Other companies that were not involved in the finishing of cloth employed blacks in yard or warehouse labor. Theodore Suggs remembered that the choice for blacks before the 1960s was either cleaning work or heavy yard work: "The only thing you could get was a cleaning job, clean the machinery and stuff like that, the floors, the bathroom, and then doing a lot of heavy work like out on the yard, cleaning the yards and handling the cotton by the bale, that's what blacks were doing."[29]

At Rock Hill Printing and Finishing Company, black men were hired in a variety of heavy nonproduction jobs long before the 1960s. A number of jobs at the plant, in fact, became identified as "black" jobs. General Manager Durwood Costner admitted in 1972 that "the laundry, the yard and the shipping department" were all-black jobs. Many black men were hired into the shipping department, where they performed a variety of heavy, laborious tasks. As Jake Boger, hired into the shipping department in 1953, remembered, "Yeah, mostly it was heavy. Either heavy or dirty.... We loaded all those trucks by hand.... Bales or boxes, whatnot, anything that came in there we had to load it by hand or unload it by hand." The formal complaint in *Ellison v. Rock Hill Printing and Finishing Company* described blacks' jobs as "the lowest and least desirable jobs ... being generally the jobs demanding the most strenuous and continuous physical exertion, often in an environment of extreme heat or extreme cold, dirt, dust, noise and duties hazardous to health or physical safety."[30]

African Americans who worked in the industry before the 1960s believed that textile companies hired black men for these jobs out of necessity. They felt that the jobs were heavy and undesirable and that whites would not be willing to carry them out. Joan Carter, whose father worked in the dyehouse at Fieldcrest Mills in Eden, North Carolina, in the 1940s and 1950s, remembered that "some of my family always worked in the mills, but it was the men, not the women." Black men were hired for these jobs because, as Carter explained, "Who else is going to go into the spinning room and do those dirty jobs? They worked in the finishing plant, they worked in the distribution centers and places like that. My father worked in the dyehouse. They would come and get him out of bed if he was late for his work; they would beg him to go in. . . . A friend of ours that lived in the community, they would send him if my dad didn't come to work—'Come on, we really need you'—because they couldn't get anybody else."[31]

Many who were hired felt that companies were most interested in physical strength and a deferential attitude. Frank Jackson, a lively, talkative man from a sharecropping family, was hired at Muscogee Mill in Columbus, Georgia, in 1951. He remembered that "you come off the farm, any of the white people would hire you. . . . Anytime that you come off the farm . . . 'Where you from, boy?' 'I come off the farm.' 'You want a job?' 'Yeah.' If you worked on a farm, you work anywhere. . . . You say you come off a farm, they hire you."[32]

Many black workers claimed that supervisors encouraged blacks to inform on each other as a way of making their jobs a little easier. Many African Americans who worked in the industry in the 1960s and 1970s complained that companies tried to divide blacks through promoting or favoring "Uncle Tom" figures. Indeed, in the 1950s and 1960s many felt that the only way for blacks to move up in the industry was by becoming an "Uncle Tom." As Frank Jackson recalled, "When I come in '51, another black man sees you move up, he calls that other black man 'Uncle Tom.' . . . If I moved up a little bit, he'd say, 'Hey, you've got to watch old Frank, old Frank will go and tell the white man everything going.'" Jackson remembered that supervisors would even slip dollar bills to blacks who told them what was going on in the plant. Some blacks who lived in the country gave their supervisors hams so that the supervisors would treat them as a "good nigger."[33] Sammy Alston similarly recalled that at the Rosemary plant of J. P. Stevens, "that's the ones they would hire . . . a brown-nose. . . . If they ever picked one it would be one that would go back and tell the boss man everything he wanted to know."[34] African American workers hired in the 1960s also remembered that companies continued to try and divide workers by promoting blacks who "carried coffee to the boss."[35] Reaffirming the industry's preference for safe blacks, many recalled that the only way to avoid harassment on the job was to pretend to be ignorant and deferential.[36]

The need to maintain a deferential attitude was part of the general injustice that black textile workers remembered having to endure before the 1960s. Jettie Purnell, who worked for J. P. Stevens in the 1950s, recalled that black workers were "supposed to have stayed in your place, whatever they called your place. . . . The mill, seemed like as long as we was in semislavery, they was pleased with it." Like other workers, Purnell deeply resented the need to use segregated facilities. He remembered that at Stevens's Rosemary Mill, blacks were not allowed to sit in the company cafeteria but had to go to a "little hole" at the bottom of the mill to eat. At Cannon Mills in Kannapolis, North Carolina, Robert Lee Gill was hired as a janitor in 1956. A small, talkative man, he remembered vividly the fact that he could not use the same facilities that he cleaned: "Back then they had two bathrooms. . . . They had the white and colored, water was the same. I'd clean up over in the weave room, at No. 7 spinning room, card room, supply room, and the office, but still yet I couldn't use one of them bathrooms. . . . If you had to urine or do something you had to walk way out of there, leave all your stuff over there, and go way down up under the waste-house at plant seven. . . . You wanted some water . . . even though you cleaned the fountains . . . you had to go down on the cotton platform. That was the only colored water was there, wasn't no colored water over in the mill." Gill remembered clearly the day that the "colored" sign came down shortly before the passage of the Civil Rights Act.[37]

Although their work was usually heavy and dirty, black men often carried out jobs that were of crucial importance to the production process as a whole. One of these occurred at the first stage of the production process in what was known as the opening room. Here blacks opened bales of cotton and fed them into a machine that loosened and cleaned the fiber. In 1968, the trade journal *Textile Industries* reported that "the traditional 'production' job for the Negro was, until a few years ago, that of feeding opening machinery. Even though this job is largely menial in nature, it has recently become regarded as one of great importance to the over-all operating efficiency of the mill. Management is becoming increasingly aware of the quality role played by blending."[38]

The amount of African American employment varied among different southern textile companies. One company that stood out was Cone Mills, a major southern textile company based in Greensboro, North Carolina. Cone Mills hired more African Americans in a greater variety of jobs than almost any other southern textile company before 1960. Scott Hoyman, a TWUA representative who had worked all over the South, told the AFSC in 1955 that he "does not know any textile plant in the South where Negroes work in as large a range of jobs as in the Cone Mills."[39] African Americans had gradually moved into some production jobs that were generally considered "white" jobs in the industry, especially in the carding department. The AFSC found that Cone had been able to make some progress on placing blacks in production jobs because "they never made an issue out of it." Rather, individual African Americans were moved up after a lengthy period learning a job while the white operator was on breaks or out sick. Both the card room and the dye room had been integrated in this way.[40]

Even at Cone Mills, however, African Americans were limited to lower-paying positions in the opening room, the card room, and the finishing department. The central production processes of spinning and weaving remained all-

A black worker feeding cotton. (*Textile Industries*, November 1968)

white. Hoyman admitted that, although blacks had come into new jobs, "most progress has been made in the most unpleasant jobs such as the hot and smelly dye department, and the lint-filled card room." The "basic job" of spinning was still "all women, all white." No meaningful integration had taken place in the weaving department.[41]

In other southern textile companies as well, any progress that African Americans made before 1960 occurred in finishing departments, in carding, and in the opening room, leaving the spinning and weaving jobs all-white. At Dan River Mills, for example, by 1955 blacks were reported to have been placed in the bleachery, the card room, and the picker room. No African Americans, however, had been hired into spinning or weaving jobs.[42]

The integration that occurred at Cone and Dan River before the 1960s provided a dress rehearsal for the way that many southern textile companies increased their hiring of African Americans in the 1960s and 1970s. In general, most companies integrated by hiring blacks into the least desirable areas, such as the card room and picking room. Although some integration did occur in the spinning and weaving departments, this took longer and was more fiercely resisted by whites.

Our Employees Would Walk Out

The refusal of textile companies to hire African Americans into production jobs before 1964 did not go unchallenged. Between 1953 and 1965, the AFSC operated a merit employment program in the South aimed at increasing black hiring in major southern industries. The records of this program offer valuable insights into the reasons for the textile companies' failure to hire blacks in greater numbers in the decade before the Civil Rights Act.

Starting in 1953, the AFSC's Merit Employment Program conducted visits to southern employers from its base in High Point, North Carolina. The aim of these visits was "confrontation with policy-making management to present the moral challenge of hiring on merit." The program was also involved in consultations with leaders in the black community to try to raise vocational aspirations and recruit qualified applicants for nontraditional positions. The AFSC program was a unique effort, as no other agency or organization in North Carolina worked full-time on the employment problems facing African Americans.[43]

In general, the AFSC records show clearly that the textile industry was one of the most resistant of all southern industries to integration. In 1962, an AFSC agent wrote that the industry had an "adamant position in the matter of upgrading and employing minority people in other than traditional jobs."[44] Most companies that the AFSC visited were reluctant to make any changes in their racial hiring practices. Rather than seeking to change racial attitudes, companies usually portrayed them as immutable and inflexible. After one visit to Southern Mills in Atlanta, AFSC agent Noyes Collinson wrote that "Southern Mills apparently does not wish to be in the forefront of concerns hastening the new day." The company's manager told Collinson that racial attitudes were impossible to change: "It is simply the way we are brought up and the way we think." He added that, as a result, "the southerner does not wish to be pushed too far too fast."[45]

The main reason for the racial conservatism of textile companies was their deep-seated fear about the consequences of integration. The fears expressed by textile companies tended to be fairly representative of those of business as a whole. In 1962, an AFSC report from Atlanta described how most employers used one of three defenses to justify their failure to hire African Americans; most of these were heard from textile companies. The first two defenses were "Well, I personally agree, but I'm afraid I would antagonize or lose my white employees" and "The community is not ready for it yet." The third was that there was a lack of qualified African Americans in the labor market. The argument that textile companies were least likely to use was that they were afraid of community pressure. Textile companies' isolation from customer pressure explains why this excuse was rarely used by mill owners.[46]

The excuse that white workers would never accept integration was used more than any other by textile executives. Throughout the 1950s and early 1960s, many textile executives portrayed segregation as something that they had to follow, that could never be changed. In 1955, a Charlotte, North Carolina, textile manufacturer insisted that segregation could never be changed because his white employees would never allow it to happen. He claimed that, in the two plants he owned, "if they were to employ one Negro, he was confident his entire personnel would walk out."[47] At United Mills in Mount Gilead, North Carolina, the personnel manager argued in 1953 that "this organization would have to be converted from the top to the bottom before anything could possibly be done about integration."[48]

Many other companies also claimed that they were being held hostage by white workers' racism. One textile manufacturer in High Point, North Carolina, for example, said in 1958 that there was "no question" that merit employment was "morally right." However, "he said his concern was about his employees accepting it. He felt sure his employees and others would not." Many textile companies flatly refused to consider integration, citing employee opposition. The general manager of Randolph Mills in Asheboro, North Carolina, for example, "had no hesitation in making his thinking clear. He would not give the first thought to integrating employment. His employees would walk out as fast as Negroes came in—and then they wouldn't stand for it."[49]

Employers in the hosiery industry, in particular, emphasized that any attempt to hire blacks in the production position of boarder would lead to strikes and violence by the unionized boarders. Charles L. Kearns of Crown Hosiery Mills in High Point, North Carolina, declared in 1955 that "if any plant attempted to use Negro boarders, the union would call a strike." The AFSC agent added, "All hosiery men I've talked to hold this opinion."[50]

The AFSC tried to counter this argument by informing executives that workers would generally defer to a firm management commitment to integrate, citing examples where companies had integrated decisively and it had been accepted by workers. Most textile executives refused to accept this argument, claiming that racism among white textile workers was much stronger than the AFSC realized. An executive of Cone Mills claimed that he agreed with the AFSC's policy of merit employment but added that this policy was impossible to implement: "You don't have to sell me. You don't understand the problem. Management of Cone Mills wants to employ and upgrade the best qualified applicants regardless of all other considerations, but we can only do what local conditions will allow us to do. . . . He disagreed with suggestion that employees would generally accept a fair and firm policy by management. He said that we didn't know textile workers, and that he wouldn't ram this policy down the throats of employees even if he could."[51]

In explaining why they could not possibly integrate, many textile executives painted a very negative picture of a racist white workforce. It is clear, however, that this picture was not always accurate. In many cases management themselves held prejudiced views and merely blamed workers for their own inaction. Some executives became angry and agitated when the topic of integration was brought up. Arthur Ross, the president of Tip Top Hosiery Mills in Asheboro, North Carolina, for example, was convinced that integration was impossible, claiming that blacks only wanted to work in "conventional jobs." When the AFSC representative tried to leave some reading material for Ross, he "almost lost his temper," and when the representative mentioned a prointegration survey undertaken by the Illinois Chamber of Commerce, Ross "started raving about outsiders meddling in our affairs." Overall, the AFSC representative wrote, this was "a most discouraging interview."[52]

Other executives who cited worker opposition to integration also revealed that they themselves were opposed to civil rights. The Randolph Mills executive who claimed that his workers would walk out, for example, went on to add that "the matter of integration in the schools is equally unthinkable" and expressed the opinion that "the country will come to its senses soon and overthrow the Supreme Court decision."[53] Some manufacturers were reported to be so racist that they did not even realize it. An AFSC report described one textile executive who had been visited in 1958 as "a man of about fifty or less. He is from S.C. He is definitely prejudiced and not sufficiently informed to realize it. He seemed to consider it his duty to give us the facts of life on Negroes and the race situation and kept doing this for about one and a half hours. It was the usual story with this type of person. It's no problem for them. They are not prejudiced. They have fair employment practices."[54]

In other interviews, however, AFSC representatives gained the impression that executives were not exaggerating workers' racism. At Cone Mills, for example, the AFSC was sympathetic to the company's claims that it wanted to integrate but was constrained by worker opposition. An AFSC report written after a 1958 visit to Cone claimed that it accepted the company's position that "local conditions" restricted merit employment: "Mr. Bagwell was very firm in this position, and didn't seem to be using it as an excuse."[55] At Jordan Spinning Company in Cedar Falls, North Carolina, the AFSC representative was shocked by the racism of the local white community and went as far as to recommend that "I would not want to see Negroes integrated into production in this area under present circumstances. I doubt if it would be safe." Like textile executives, the AFSC representative linked this racism to the low socioeconomic level of the area: "The socio-economic level of this area is far lower than I thought was possible among industrial white workers in N.C. . . . A correlation of the socio-economic level of communities of this type and their attitudes on race would be very revealing. It might shock some of our 'intellectual' segregationists."[56]

While AFSC representatives rarely questioned employers' arguments that white workers would strike if the mills were integrated, not all observers were willing to accept the companies' arguments about strike violence. During the EEOC textile forum held in 1967, Vivian W. Henderson, president of Clark College, criticized an EEOC report that had claimed that fear of strike violence largely explained the lack of blacks in the industry. Henderson also rejected the report's suggestions that mill towns' social isolation was responsible for the exclusion of blacks. For Henderson, these were excuses to conceal the real reason for the lack of blacks—racial discrimination: "I don't know about the strike violence; I don't know about the social cohesion; but I do know the town that I grew up in Bristol, Tennessee, there's no history of strike violence and cohesion was not that prominent. It was a sheer matter of racial discrimination."[57]

The AFSC's records also show examples of the argument that the community would not stand for integration. Some companies claimed that racial tension was too great in their communities for them to respond to the AFSC's efforts. They often cited current tension as a justification for upholding segregation. The personnel manager of one company explained that racial tension was very high because of a series of housebreakings "believed" to be perpetrated by blacks: "He said tension is so high that many are ready to shoot on sight if a Negro is seen crossing the corner of their yard after dark."[58]

Many mills also used the excuse that they were open to black employment but that blacks were not qualified enough to get jobs. As an AFSC representative reported from a visit with the personnel manager of the large J. P. Stevens Company in 1962, "He assured me that they had always had a policy of merit employment. It was unfortunate that the only Negroes who had applied to them for employment, he says, were not qualified and did not pass their tests."[59]

The "lack of qualified applicants" excuse came to be used repeatedly in the later years of the AFSC program. An overview report written in April 1964 concluded, "Employers respond positively in favor of merit employment but generally find a comfortable hiding place in what they refer to as 'a lack of qualified applicants.' Few have demonstrated more than lip service to the merit philosophy.... '[T]okenism' continues to be the stage at which industrial integration has reached and stopped."[60] A typical example of the "qualifications" excuse occurred at a visit to a Greensboro mill in August 1964. As AFSC agent William Allison wrote, the company's personnel manager "assured me that the company did hire on merit. He cushioned the scarcity of Negroes on the skills needed in various jobs.... He stressed particularly the difficulty in finding people with the dexterity required."[61]

The AFSC interviews reveal many other excuses that textile companies used to uphold segregation. Most manufacturers were adept at passing the buck and blaming their workers or unions for the failure to hire more blacks. Unions, in turn, blamed both companies and workers for segregation and argued that unions were powerless to tackle the forces of racism. Large companies claimed that they were too big and dispersed to initiate integration, while small companies argued that they lacked the market influence to do it. Large companies claimed that integration would be easier if they were small, and small companies argued that they would integrate if they were large.

In 1962, for example, Clarence E. Elsas, president of Fulton Cotton Mills in Atlanta, Georgia, declared, "Of course we don't want to be guinea pigs; let Burlington and some of the big fellows take the initiative."[62] Large companies such as Burlington repeatedly refused to take such a lead, however. A Burlington executive claimed in 1955 that a policy of equal employment opportunity would be "ill-advised as a method of procedure, since Bur-Mill's plants are so scattered, so various, and most of them so well established before Bur-Mill [even] bought them."[63] An executive with another large company with sixteen plants argued in 1954, "I am sure you understand that a small plant has a much easier job than we would." The reasoning was that workers in large companies were crowded together on machines, so small companies with more space would find it easier to integrate.[64]

It was common for employers and unions to blame each other for the failure of merit employment. In 1953, for example, AFSC representative Ralph Rose "mentioned that some employers tell him, 'I would like to integrate but my union will not permit it', and in talking to the representatives of the union of that same place, the union people say, 'We would like to integrate but the employer will not permit it.'"[65]

A variety of social factors also made textile manufacturers reluctant to be leaders in merit employment. In some cases, employers cited various personal reasons for fearing public disapproval. The AFSC reported in 1956 that T. R. Kramer, the manager of a textile plant in Hickory, North Carolina, "still does not want to be the first to move because he is a Jew." Only when the large plant near him agreed to change would Kramer agree that "he will follow."[66]

Textile companies were also able to embrace the racial status quo because of their isolation from consumers. Unlike retail stores, textile mills did not have to consider the reaction of their customers and were not influenced by consumer pressure to integrate. One mill owner, for example, told the AFSC in 1962 that "as a manufacturer, he has no reason to consider the attitudes of customers (retail). He said that the situation would be different if he, for example, were operating Woolworths or a supermarket." The AFSC reported in 1965 that consumer goods companies feared the impact of sales boycotts and were leading the move toward job integration as a result: "In numerous Southern cities it was this boycott that pried open the door to new jobs in bakeries, groceries and soft drink bottlers. Airlines and hotels are vulnerable to concerted Negro action, because a string of false reservations made by telephone could crowd out legitimate customers."[67]

The civil rights protests that occurred in the late 1950s and early 1960s made it even harder to promote the idea of black employment to textile executives. The AFSC found that the 1954 Supreme Court decision in *Brown v. Board of Education*, together with the start of civil rights protests in Montgomery, Alabama, the following year, made textile companies more resistant to integration. An overview report in 1958, for example, claimed that some progress was being made until racial tension increased over the school integration question. In 1954, the AFSC had hoped that the implementation of the decision would mean that "many employers who are now shackled will, with a little help, free themselves and practice employment on merit." In fact, however, the AFSC noted, "The 'shackles' have actually been tightened and employers have more excuses to follow traditional patterns. They are more conscious of public opinion and pressures." In February 1957, the AFSC reported, "Excitement and tensions caused by efforts of the Southern states to evade the Supreme Court's decision and decree concerning desegregation of public schools have crystallized much sentiment and fear on the part of employers. These sentiments and fears have caused many to decide that even Merit Employment is too hot an issue for them to touch at this time." Consequently, the Merit Employment Program made very little progress in the South between 1954 and 1958.[68]

Segregated Plants

A wide variety of historical accounts have described the efforts in the 1890s to set up mills that relied solely on black labor. The most notable attempts occurred in Charleston, South Carolina, and Concord, North Carolina. These efforts to run all-black mills failed, however, and mill owners turned to white labor, largely because they found a surplus of poor whites who had migrated from the Piedmont and neighboring mountain region to work in the mills. The promotion of mills as the salvation of poor whites and the cultural taboo against black men working near white women contributed to the exclusion of blacks from production jobs. With whites becoming the primary labor source, blacks were relegated to working in nonproduction jobs with little direct contact with white production workers.[69]

Scattered records indicate, however, that mills continued to experiment with the idea of using blacks in segregated plants even in the post–World War II period. While historians have concentrated on the failure of segregated plants in the 1890s, some were still running even as late as the 1960s. Very little is known about the history of these segregated plants in the postwar period.

Mill owners' conviction about the permanency of segregation helps to explain why many companies sought to give employment to blacks in separate plants. Many mill owners visited by the AFSC in the 1950s and early 1960s argued that it was impossible to run an integrated plant. They expressed an interest in setting up segregated plants so that they could hire blacks without antagonizing whites. Arthur Ross of Tip Top Hosiery Mills in Asheboro, North Carolina, for example, was convinced that blacks could not work in an integrated environment; therefore, "he thinks he would set up separate plants for Negro workers if there were enough Negro workers available." The president of United Mills in Mount Gilead, North Carolina, considered setting up a segregated plant in 1953 "in order to utilize fully the labor potential of their community."[70]

Some companies did set up such plants, which usually performed a particular operation with an African American workforce and white supervisor. The AFSC reported in 1953 that Cone Mills had "established a segregated plant with fifteen or twenty employees, hemming diapers. They have a white supervisor for this small operation and all of the workers are Negro."[71] In 1954, the AFSC found that the work of hemming diapers "is one of the most skilled jobs of the textile industry."[72] A segregated mill was also reported to be operated by the Adams-Millis Company in High Point, North Carolina, in the 1950s.[73]

The largest recorded example of a segregated plant occurred at Templon Spinning Mills in Mooresville, North Carolina, where the company opened a plant specifically for African Americans in 1961. Mill executive Rufus M. Dalton admitted that the company got the idea from observing other segregated plants in the textile industry, including a knitting plant in Henderson, North Carolina. The Templon plant employed around seventy-five black workers with a white supervisor. At the company's other two plants in Mooresville, a single janitor was the only African American employed. The *Mooresville Tribune* reported that the separate plant was "aimed at making more jobs available to colored people." As at other segregated mills, the Mooresville plant employed blacks in production jobs, a clear departure from white plants where African Americans were restricted to nonproduction jobs. Indeed, Dalton claimed that the jobs at Templon involved "operating productive equipment and will require considerable training."[74]

One of the most striking examples of a segregated plant was at a small textile mill in Rich Square, North Carolina, located in a remote area of Northampton County in northeastern North Carolina. Student Non-Violent Co-Ordinating Committee (SNCC) representatives reported in August 1965 that the plant "has a high wall down the middle of it separating the Negro workers from the white workers. Thus everything is segregated: rest rooms, drinking fountains, etc. The Negro workers believe they produce much more ... and are paid less." The layout of the plant came about after it was opened in 1953 with white labor. The company wanted to hire black workers as well, because of the large black labor pool. As a result, a 35,000-foot extension to the existing building went into operation in 1961, with the two groups separated by a wall.

In response to passage of the Civil Rights Act, the company hired one black woman and placed her on the white side of the wall in 1965, but this move was resisted by white workers: "When she got out of work she found that the seats of her car had been torn up. Since then she has been receiving threatening phone calls. This week two more Negro workers were hired and put on the white side. This is the only integration so far—the wall still remains." The other black workers hired on the white side also received "threatening and abusive telephone calls," and a variety of other incidents also occurred. For example, one black pioneer "found a wreath outside her door with a note attached saying, 'Watch—next will be death.'" SNCC reported that there was considerable fear among black workers in the plant because a resurgent local Ku Klux Klan was burning crosses "at homes of Negroes involved in integration."[75]

SNCC representatives Virginia and Joseph Tieger criticized the company for the way that it had carried out integration. They relayed the views of black workers that placing blacks on the white side without removing the wall altogether was "unwise" because it made the black pioneers "easy targets for harassment and invites intimidation." They claimed that integration was being hampered by a racist white supervisor whom they described as "typical of a 'poor white' person grasping for any sort of power . . . particularly over Negro employees." They also claimed that the company did not want to remove the wall because blacks were working much harder than whites. Despite the demands of black workers to either remove the wall or hire whites on the black side, neither of these changes were implemented. SNCC representatives complained that the company refused to help them in trying to improve the situation at the plant.[76]

Black Employment during World War II

Census data show that African Americans made very little progress into the textile industry before 1960; between 1900 and 1960, black employment levels never exceeded 4.5 percent.[77] By recording employment levels every ten years, however, census data could miss short periods when blacks were hired in greater numbers. There is some evidence, indeed, that African Americans were hired into production jobs during World War II as a way of meeting acute labor shortages. This influx of black workers would not be reflected in census data as companies were quick to rehire whites immediately after the war. In addition, records show that textile firms who hired blacks in nontraditional jobs were anxious to conceal the fact and may not have reported true levels of black employment.

The World War II period is significant because it exerted considerable influence on the arguments used by executives in the postwar years to justify segregation. In particular, many mill owners cited examples of strikes by white workers during World War II to justify their failure to integrate in the postwar years. The entry of blacks into some nontraditional jobs during World War II was also the only occasion when the barriers of segregation were breached to some extent, and some of the employment gains made by blacks during the war were maintained in the postwar period in certain companies.

Evidence of blacks being hired into nontraditional textile jobs during World War II comes from a survey carried out by the Southern Regional Council in 1945. The survey found that "some mills in Georgia are using Negroes not only in jobs and departments traditionally employing them, but in others as well and along side white women operatives." Mills in Columbus, Augusta, Macon, and Porterdale had "pretty thorough utilization of Negroes on all sorts of jobs and in departments with whites."[78] At Bibb Mill in Columbus, blacks had been hired into the card room for the first time during the war. Around 700 had received jobs in the department that had previously been run by whites. At Bibb Mill No. 1, it was reported that "Negro found in most every part of Mill working along with white." At Jordan Mill in Columbus, it was found that "in the card room, Negro women and white women run drawing frames side by side on two shifts."[79] At Riverside Mill in Augusta, "Negroes work at all work throughout the mill, spinning, doffing, weaving, with fixers and head doffers being Negroes. The superintendent says that Negroes are doing excellent work throughout the mill where they work 150 to 200 per shift, 3 shifts." Overall, the Southern Regional Council found around fifteen mills in Georgia where blacks had been hired into nontraditional jobs, and estimated that up to 5,000 jobs were being run by blacks.[80]

The Southern Regional Council continued its survey in Alabama and found further evidence of blacks being hired into nontraditional jobs. At the Lanett Mill of West Point Manufacturing Company, it was reported that "Negroes have been placed on all cleaning and blowing down jobs throughout the mill, jobs which before the war were exclusively given to whites. . . . In the card room Negroes for the first time are employed at card stripping." At the company's Riverview Mill, thirty black women had been hired into the towel packing room on jobs "given before the war to whites." Blacks had also been hired in greater numbers in the large Comer Mills chain.[81]

There were strict limits to the jobs that blacks were hired into. Many were placed in service or cleaning jobs, where the companies were finding it increasingly difficult to hire whites. Other mills hired blacks in greater numbers than before but still placed them within traditional "black" jobs in the opening or picker room. While some were hired into the carding department, where only white men were customarily employed, examples of blacks being placed near white women were rare. The Southern Regional Council reported that segregation was maintained in many cases by hiring blacks only as machine operators on the third shift, leaving the most desirable shifts all-white, and giving blacks the unskilled part of a machine operator's job, with the white machine operator given an enlarged assignment.[82]

The Southern Regional Council's study also showed that white workers did not always accept the entry of blacks into the workforce. Indeed, many strikes and other protests were documented when blacks were introduced. At Muscogee Mill in Columbus, it was reported that "there was a strike in this mill when Negroes were placed on the job as machine operators where they ran all machines and did the work."[83] At Fairfax Mill, part of the West Point Manufacturing Company in Alabama, the company hired blacks into production jobs during the war because "the labor situation was so acute." After "a day or two" of blacks being introduced into the card room, however, "the whites became indignant to the point of grouping up in the mill gates and threatening the Negroes as they came to work one morning. Immediately the mill company abandoned the plan for manning the card room by Negroes." There were also rumors that the hiring of the blacks in the mill was linked to an incident where "two Negroes were thrown into the river and drowned."[84]

During AFSC plant visits in the 1950s and early 1960s, countless companies cited past incidents to justify their fear of white reaction. Many relied on violent incidents that had taken place during World War II to justify their inaction. These records again suggest that blacks were placed in nontraditional jobs during the war, and that whites often resisted these changes. One executive recalled that "in 1940 in a small town in south Georgia his company brought a Negro into its employ. The white citizens of the area threatened to kill the Negro if the company continued his employment. Believing that the community would become violent, the man was discharged."[85] Another textile executive "went into great detail about his past experiences with Negro employees to prove that they could not work in an integrated situation." He claimed that blacks who had been placed in nontraditional jobs during World War II were "almost killed. He implied that any Negro employee would not be safe in an Asheboro plant in any other than conventional jobs."[86]

At Dan River Mills in Danville, Virginia, a large number of blacks were hired during World War II. Indeed, the number of black workers at Dan River rose from 751 in 1940 to 1,505 in 1946. The union's joint board manager, Emanuel Boggs, explained to the AFSC in 1955 that blacks had been hired in a wide variety of jobs, and they had stayed in most of these jobs. It was when African Americans were placed in the more prestigious job of spinner that resistance occurred. Boggs blamed the support of the CIO business agent for the success of a 1944 strike led by spinners. As he explained, "During the war these mills put on a number of Negro spinners. Immediately, all of the white spinners walked out on strike. . . . The CIO business agent then in charge backed up the strikers. The result was, the mill had to fire all the Negro spinners." Boggs felt that if the business agent had taken a firm stand, integration would have succeeded, because "every other integration which was made during the war period has continued."[87]

The example of World War II was continually cited by textile companies in the 1950s and 1960s.[88] The way that many companies described strikes by white workers showed how executives could use such incidents to justify their own reluctance to integrate. In general, when white workers protested against the introduction of blacks, management immediately backed down and acquiesced to their demands. Such strikes stand out in the southern textile industry because they were successful. When workers struck for union recognition, their efforts almost always met fierce management resistance and ended in failure. The textile industry seemed able to quell all forms of labor protest except strikes carried out by white workers in protest against the introduction of blacks. The Southern Regional Council interviewed one textile specialist who summed up how the introduction of blacks was sometimes expected to fail: "It was his feeling that the trial of introducing Negroes as mill workers in Dan River Mills, Danville, was over dramatic, probably at the invitation of both the management of the mill and the union. In other words management wanted the trial to end in failure." When the first two blacks were introduced and white workers stopped work, the black workers were immediately withdrawn.[89]

Targeting the Textile Industry

Although civil rights historians have largely ignored the textile industry, civil rights leaders and politicians focused particular attention on the industry throughout the 1960s and 1970s. They felt that the industry provided excellent employment opportunities for African Americans because most jobs could be easily learned by workers with no previous industrial experience. In January 1967, the EEOC held a forum to improve black employment prospects in the industry specifically because textiles could "serve as a training ground for Negroes in the future as it has for whites in the past . . . providing a medium through which workers can move from an agricultural to an industrial way of life." EEOC economist Donald Osburn emphasized that "it is important for Negroes to make employment gains in textiles" because "the industry teaches skills to workers previously engaged in agricultural production, and prepares them for higher skilled and higher paying jobs."[90]

Civil rights lawyers placed particular emphasis on the textile industry after the passage of the Civil Rights Act of 1964. Title VII of the act outlawed discrimination in employment, making it an unlawful practice "to fail or refuse to hire or to discharge any individual, or otherwise to discriminate against any individual with respect to his compensation, terms, conditions, or privileges of employment, because of such individual's race, color, religion, sex, or national origin." The Civil Rights Act created the EEOC to monitor and enforce compliance with the act. The commission was authorized to solve job discrimination complaints through "conference, conciliation, and persuasion." If the EEOC failed to achieve voluntary compliance within sixty days, however, it was required to notify the complainant that they were permitted, within the next thirty days, to bring civil action.[91]

Julius Chambers, the civil rights attorney who was responsible for bringing most of the lawsuits against textile companies, remembered that the industry's low skill basis made it a prime target for suits brought under Title VII: "The Civil Rights Act of 1964 really looked at the textile industry, the trucking industry, and mostly low professional areas because people felt that these jobs didn't require a high degree, amount of skill, and one could sort of apply general assumptions that most people would be able to operate a machine. . . . You could make some general assumptions that just about everybody would be able to do it." Lawyers such as Chambers were able to effectively attack the textile industry in the lawsuits because textile executives were unable to justify the exclusion of African Americans from most production jobs on the grounds of skills or qualifications needed to run the job.[92]

The textile industry was crucial because it could provide employment to thousands of African Americans who lacked academic or technical qualifications. Many black leaders pointed out that they were not concerned about black college graduates, as they could easily get jobs in the textile industry or elsewhere. It was blacks without such skills who really needed jobs. Black leaders described how the unemployment problem in black communities across the South was most acute among those without good qualifications. The textile industry was in a unique position to provide jobs for "thousands and thousands" of unemployed African Americans, helping to reduce the numbers on welfare. Kelly Alexander, president of the NAACP in North Carolina, claimed that opening up textiles could end the cycle of inherited poverty in black communities and stem out-migration to the north.[93]

Civil rights leaders and government officials also singled out the industry because it was the largest in the South. Emory Via of the Southern Regional Council told the EEOC forum that the textile industry was "uniquely qualified" to improve the economic opportunities available to African Americans in the South because it was the "predominant industry." Moreover, the industry was characterized by "important economic combinations in the form of chain manufacturing enterprises and manufacturing associations." Civil rights leaders recognized that the industry's cultural dominance and tendency to cooperate meant that it could eliminate employment discrimination if it wished. In 1967, EEOC head Stephen N. Shulman called the textile industry a "key spot" in his agency's efforts to end "across-the-board discrimination" in industry.[94]

The records of the Southern Regional Council show that the civil rights agency had selected textiles for particular attention as early as World War II. During the war, when the textile industry was affected by a labor shortage, the council had argued that more blacks should be hired to fill jobs. The council pointed out that most textile jobs required little training and added that the industry's traditional policy of not hiring black women meant that there was a vast surplus of black women who "would be glad to go into the mills."[95]

Throughout the 1960s, the textile industry continued to be singled out by civil rights leaders, the federal government, and many politicians. The industry's racial record made national headlines in February 1969, when Deputy Secretary of Defense David Packard awarded contracts totaling $9.4 million to three southern textile firms—J. P. Stevens, Dan River Mills, and Burlington Industries—on the basis of oral assurances that they would devise affirmative action programs, despite the fact that federal investigations had found discriminatory practices at all three companies. The move was criticized by many politicians, including Democratic senators Walter Mondale and Edward M. Kennedy. Indeed, the publicity given to the issue showed the importance it was accorded by liberal politicians and civil rights leaders. Highlighting the companies' records of racial discrimination, both Kennedy and Mondale stressed the importance of the federal government's taking a firm stand to improve job opportunities for blacks in the textile industry. A wide variety of civil rights groups also put pressure on the government to deny the contracts to the textile companies. In April 1969, eight black members of Congress wrote President Nixon, viewing with "grave concern" the award of contracts "to Southern textile mills practicing racial discrimination."[96] The New York Times reported that the decision to grant the contracts was of crucial importance in deciding the role that the federal government would play in attacking job discrimination: "In some respects the issue is even more important than school integration. It is an issue on which all the Negro and civil rights groups are united."[97]

The attack by Democrats brought a vigorous defense of the Defense Department's decision by leading Republican politicians. There were heated clashes between Republicans and Democrats, with an ill-tempered argument occurring at a Senate subcommittee meeting chaired by Senator Kennedy that approved the award of the contracts. One story in the New York Times called the March 28 meeting "the most politically explosive encounter on Capitol Hill since the President took office on January 20." Republican Everett Dirkson, for example, claimed that the EEOC was harassing textile companies and that he was "going to the highest authority in this Government and get somebody fired." Republican Strom Thurmond accused Mondale of "playing politics," to which Mondale replied, "There is no more important politics than assuring racial justice."[98]

Many politicians and federal agencies pinpointed the industry as crucial to black economic progress. Indeed, the federal government concentrated particular attention on the textile industry throughout the 1960s. The EEOC targeted the industry, and its January 1967 forum on employment discrimination in the industry provided the first hearings of their type and was widely publicized.[99] As a follow-up to the forum, the EEOC also funded a program with the North Carolina Good Neighbor Council aimed at plant visits and workshops to educate companies about equal employment.[100] In January 1968, the EEOC and the Department of Defense launched a special textile compliance program as part of an unusual attempt to coordinate federal and private agency programs to achieve equal employment opportunity. TEAM, made up of six private agencies, was established and cooperated with the federal agencies.[101]

In 1967, the Office of Federal Contract Compliance (OFCC) selected ten large textile companies for special attention as a test case of the government's efforts to eliminate discrimination among government contractors.[102] This move marked the first attempt by federal agencies to eliminate discrimination on an industrywide basis rather than simply working case by case. Senator Walter Mondale was an enthusiastic supporter of this move. In explaining the reasons for his support, Mondale summed up why civil rights leaders and politicians saw the textile industry as important: "The textile industry was chosen as a pilot project . . . because of its clear history of racial discrimination . . . because it had a labor shortage[,] because of its heavy involvement with Federal contracts . . . and because textile mills can offer jobs to unskilled, ex-farm workers. Moreover, the large roles textile companies play in the southern economy could, if employment patterns were changed, have a broad impact on job opportunity for minorities throughout the area."[103] Senator Kennedy supported the project for similar reasons.[104]

In several lawsuits, plaintiffs' counsel highlighted the crucial importance of opening up the textile industry to African Americans. This was especially apparent in *Lea v. Cone Mills*, a case involving a mill in Hillsborough, North Carolina, that refused to hire black women. The first page of the plaintiffs' main brief argued that "racially discriminatory hiring practices in a textile plant such as defendant's Eno plant in Hillsborough, North Carolina have a devastating effect on the employment opportunities of Negroes residing in the area. The textile industry is the cornerstone of the North Carolina economy. With the decreasing need for farm labor caused by automation, the textile industry is increasing in importance as an employer in the state." In many cases, plaintiffs' lawyers concentrated on the textile industry because they recognized that it could play a greater role than any other industry in raising the economic standard of living of African Americans in the South.[105]

The Impact of Black Entry into Textiles

Across the South, African Americans who were hired into textile production jobs in the 1960s and early 1970s saw their jobs as a great economic improvement for themselves and the black community as a whole. The positive reactions of black textile workers indeed confirmed why civil rights leaders and politicians placed such strong emphasis on the economic benefits of opening up the South's largest industry to African Americans.

The influx of African Americans into production jobs was a major shift in traditional employment practices. The opportunity to work in the mill represented a significant economic advance for blacks who had always been denied an industrial job. Previously blacks in textile communities had had very few employment alternatives. As Louise Peddaway, who was the first black hired into a mill in eastern North Carolina in 1964, explained, "It was a great improvement . . . because there weren't any jobs that really we could go on other than going in a cotton field or going in somebody's field for a job. There were plants, but it was a long time before they hired anybody black. They didn't hire anything but white."[106] Other black workers described the opening up of textile jobs as "a big plus" and "a great big step."[107]

EEOC records show that many blacks were able to earn around $90 a week in the mill; previously they had been averaging $25 a week in domestic work, and little more in the few other jobs available. In 1966, the average annual wage in the textile industry was $4,429, a figure that was approximately double the average income of African Americans in Piedmont counties. Mill work was thus a major economic improvement that allowed blacks to stay in their hometown, send their children to college, buy their own homes, and generally enjoy an unprecedented standard of living. Retired black mill worker William "Sport" Suggs, a towering man with a booming voice, was clear about the advantage that mill work offered over his previous jobs: "The mill job was definitely something that made my living better. The wages were much higher. . . . I was glad, and a whole lot of black people were pulled up, made their living a whole lot better. I bought this old house here. . . . I sent three of my children to college."[108]

Many other African American workers remembered how the standard of living in black communities increased as textile jobs became available in the late 1960s.[109] Roosevelt Broadnax was one of the first African Americans hired at the Eagle and Phenix Mill in Columbus, Georgia, when he started work in the napper room in January 1966. Broadnax remembered that as blacks entered the mill from agriculture or poorer paying work, "more began to buy houses and, you know, get better automobiles and have an improved lifestyle. . . . A lot of people, and I was among those, that I was able to buy me a house. . . . We were able to improve our lifestyle."[110]

Other black mill workers recalled that mill work had made it possible for them to stay in the South, whereas previously the only route to making a decent living was to migrate out of the region. Indeed, black employment in textiles played a major role in slowing migration from textile areas to other parts of the country in the late 1960s. In Rock Hill, South Carolina, Thomas Pharr remembered that the opening up of the Rock Hill Printing and Finishing Company mill reduced the need for young blacks to go north for work. As in many other textile communities, the annual exodus of young people after high school graduation had become a familiar ritual in Rock Hill. As Pharr recalled, "It's strange, prior to the Civil Rights Act passing, every summer here you have, after graduation of the high school students, you have this mass exodus of black people heading north. This train station right downtown, and all through the summer they'd just leave to go get better jobs up north, where they make more money, because really there was nothing here. The only decent paying job in the community was either a preacher or a teacher, and that was basically it. As far as getting employment in these plants in the same way as the white man, that was something unheard of. . . . That was a ritual— New York, Baltimore, Philadelphia, you know, wherever—you know, every year after graduation everybody loaded up and took off."[111]

Pharr, a large, imposing man who was one of the first African Americans hired at the mill in 1966, summed up what textile employment meant to the black community in Rock Hill: "Once the '60s came along the high school people, they stayed here. They became a more stable part of the community, they had better employment, they could encourage their children to go on to school, and they could pay for their education. And, you know, it improved things, it uplifted the whole community. . . . In this area textiles led the way as far as employing blacks into those jobs because a lot of them they weren't high-skilled jobs, so basically you could take somebody that's right out of school and put them right in on the job, and in a month's time they'd be trained and ready to go." Pharr felt that "textiles helped the South by employing blacks, and as a direct result of that it uplifted the whole community, but it should have been right in the first place." Higher textile wages represented "a step into the mainstream of America. . . . You had people buying homes, that was unheard of. I mean like, 'What! Where you working at?'"[112]

Press accounts confirm that textile integration played a key role in stopping

By the late 1960s, textile industry journals recorded the entry of African Americans, such as this quiller technician, into many production jobs. (*Textile Industries*, November 1968)

out-migration. In 1969, for example, the *Charlotte Observer* reported that "a reversal in textile industry hiring is helping to reverse the Carolinas' traditional loss of people to Northern ghettoes. Once lilywhite, the Carolinas textile industry now is hiring blacks in dramatic numbers. As a result, the industry is doing as much as anyone in the South to stem Negro out-migration."[113] Other press accounts reached similar conclusions.[114]

Stories in the press highlighted individuals whose own lives illustrated the economic improvement that textile work represented. The *New York Times* reported that the opening up of the textile industry meant that "the share-cropping cycle is broken" for southern blacks. They still might choose to leave the South, but the offer of decent textile jobs meant that they were no longer forced to. Describing the case of the black McDougald family in the textile town of Erwin, North Carolina, the *Times* wrote, "The three McDougald children who are still at home eventually may decide to move elsewhere, as thousands of young Negroes in Harnett County have done in recent years. But they, at least, will have a local choice worth thinking about." In contrast, the chil-

The 1960s saw the expansion of the carpet industry in the South, and many African American workers filled production jobs in carpet and rug mills. (*Textile Industries*, November 1968)

dren's father had only had a choice "to leave for other parts of the country or to stay at home with little hope of getting much beyond subsistence status."[115]

The black breakthrough in textiles was seen as a significant advance by African American workers despite the discrimination that they faced in the mill. Workers like Thomas Pharr and James Boone, indeed, were victims of discrimination and harassment and expressed frustration with the lack of opportunities for promotion in the industry. They were strong union supporters because of the experiences of racial discrimination that they witnessed in the textile industry. Others were also able to see the huge advance that textile jobs represented even though they were very critical of the industry's treatment of black workers.

As well as describing the significant economic progress that mill work represented for African Americans, the contemporary press also noted the massive social and cultural change represented by racial integration of the textile industry. Several articles exploring the integration of textiles in some detail appeared in the *New York Times*. Capturing the scale of the change, the *Times'* main article on textile integration was entitled "The Mill: A Giant Step for the Southern Negro." The *Times* pointed out that the hiring of African Americans broke the racial hiring practices that had prevailed in the industry since its birth after the Civil War.[116] In 1969, the *Times* noted that the industry "has hired more Negroes in the last five years than it had ever employed before, and will hire a great many more in the years ahead."[117] Trade papers such as the *Daily News Record* also followed the racial integration of the southern industry in detail. Capturing the significance of the hiring of blacks into production positions, the *Record* reported in 1965 that "Negroes are quietly moving over to the heretofore all-white production line in Southern textile mills . . . and the statistics are imposing." It termed this integration "a new cycle in the industrial revolution—not a black cycle but an integrated cycle."[118]

Discrimination: The Long-term Experience of Black Textile Workers

Although the entry of African Americans into production jobs represented economic advancement for the black community, blacks who came into the industry also faced continued discrimination. Numerous lawsuits testify to the massive discrimination that existed in the textile industry in the 1960s and 1970s. Indeed, almost every major textile company was involved in class action racial discrimination lawsuits in these years, including J. P. Stevens, Burlington Industries, Cannon Mills, Fieldcrest Mills, Cone Mills, and Dan River Mills. These lawsuits provide a detailed look into the racial employment practices of most of the major southern textile companies. In addition, many smaller companies were also involved in significant lawsuits.

The largest and most important textile case was *Sledge v. J. P. Stevens*. This case was brought in 1970 against Stevens facilities in Roanoke Rapids, North Carolina. Stevens was, after Burlington Industries, the nation's second largest textile company. It operated some eighty-five textile plants, the bulk of them located in small towns in North and South Carolina, and employed over 49,000 workers.[119] The Sledge case involved the company's main concentration of plants in Roanoke Rapids, a town in an area of northeastern North Carolina described by one journalist who visited it in 1979 as "90 miles from everywhere."[120]

Sledge v. J. P. Stevens was originally brought by thirteen plaintiffs on October 2,

1970, although the class was eventually expanded to include over 3,000 people. The broad nature of the complaints made in the case illustrate how widespread discrimination was at Stevens. The company was accused of discrimination in hiring, especially against black female applicants. If hired, the plaintiffs claimed, blacks were discriminated against further through assignment to "lower paying or otherwise less desirable jobs than their average white counterparts." Black workers became trapped in these jobs because the company lacked "objective standards for promotability." In addition, black workers complained that they were required to perform additional work without receiving higher pay, while white workers were not required to carry out such work. Black workers at J. P. Stevens also complained of discrimination in layoffs and discharge, and of being paid less for the same work as whites.[121]

J. P. Stevens was also involved in two other major employment discrimination cases in the 1960s and 1970s. The case of *Lewis v. J. P. Stevens*, which also involved allegations of hiring discrimination, was brought in 1972. This case affected a Stevens plant in Abbeville, South Carolina, where the company employed around 150 workers in a mill it had acquired in 1966. Brought by a group of black women who had repeatedly been denied jobs at the Abbeville plant, the *Lewis* case was one of a number of cases brought by groups of black women who had failed to get jobs in textile plants. Another case, *Sherrill v. J. P. Stevens*, was filed in 1973 and concerned a Stevens synthetic yarn plant in Stanley, North Carolina, which employed around 700 workers. The main complaint in that case was the harassment of a black worker, A. C. Sherrill, who had tried to become a supervisor.[122]

Throughout the 1960s and 1970s, J. P. Stevens was in the news because of the extensive campaign to organize the company carried out by the TWUA. The union targeted Stevens because it believed that large companies such as Stevens were part of a conspiracy to keep the South nonunion. The campaign became characterized by Stevens's bitter opposition and its willingness to fire workers who were union supporters. Indeed, by 1974 the company had paid out over $1.3 million to more than 280 workers who had been discharged for union activity. To the labor movement, Stevens's frequent involvement in racial discrimination lawsuits and its reluctance to settle cases quickly were an extension of the company's hostile attitude to workers' rights. The TWUA's attorney, Jonathan Harkavy, claimed in 1977 that "the first few cases in which Stevens has been involved in Title VII matters are strong evidence that it is adopting a 'massive resistance' stance to employment discrimination claims in the same fashion as it has done over the past decade with respect to labor relations claims."[123] The company, indeed, used the same attorney, Whiteford Blakeney, to represent it in both labor relations and civil rights cases.

Another major class action case in the textile industry was *Adams v. Dan*

River Mills, brought in 1969 by a large group of black workers at Dan River Mills in Danville, Virginia. Dan River employed 19,000 workers in 1968, the majority in a complex of plants at the company's headquarters in Danville, a town of around 40,000 people located on the Virginia–North Carolina border. The company had been operating continually in the town since 1882 and was by far the largest employer. Dan River finished its own cloth and employed large numbers of African American men in bleaching and dyeing the cloth well before the 1960s. The majority of these workers were employed in a small number of nonproduction jobs in the bleachery and dyehouse, with few opportunities for promotion. With the passage of civil rights legislation in the 1960s, black workers were determined to receive a better deal, and a group of workers from the dyehouse initiated the lawsuit.[124]

The plaintiffs in *Adams* brought no fewer than twenty-five charges of discrimination against Dan River. The complaints were similar to those brought in *Sledge*, including discrimination in hiring and layoff, together with "the exclusion of Negro employees from certain well-paid job categories and departments and the restriction to Negro employees of certain of the lowest paid job categories and departments." Many of the complaints specifically cited women, particularly the assignment of "arduous work" to black women that was not assigned to white women and the continued problems that African American women had getting jobs in the industry. Although the company's public line throughout the class action was to deny any discriminatory action, privately the company admitted that the workers' case was "persuasive."[125]

The case of *Ellison v. Rock Hill Printing and Finishing Company* also figures heavily in this account. Rock Hill was a small South Carolina town located just south of Charlotte, with a population in 1960 of around 26,000, of whom 6,000 were African American. Rock Hill Printing and Finishing Company was part of the large Lowenstein textile chain, a New York–based company that employed over 18,000 workers in the 1960s. The Rock Hill plant had opened in 1929 and was used by Lowenstein to finish cloth that was produced in other mills. By the 1950s, the bleachery, as it was known locally, employed nearly 3,000 workers and was the largest plant of its kind under one roof. As at Dan River, the company had employed significant numbers of black men since the 1940s in nonproduction jobs. Most black workers were grouped together in the shipping department, where they performed a variety of heavy and hazardous jobs. In 1972, a group of black workers in the shipping department, led by a local minister, Rev. Leroy Ellison, joined together to initiate a major lawsuit protesting against a departmental seniority system that prevented them from getting higher-paying production jobs in the plant. The plaintiffs also complained that they were paid less than whites on comparable jobs, were excluded from all supervisory and managerial jobs, and were forced to work in segregated positions that were "the lowest paid and least desirable jobs."[126]

These lawsuits contain detailed information on the grievances of black workers and show that African American textile workers felt that there was considerable discrimination in the industry. In general, it is clear that the lawsuits provide an accurate record of the racial discrimination existing in the textile industry. The companies were in fact found guilty of violating the law against employment discrimination in most of the cases. For example, U.S. District Judge Franklin T. Dupree Jr. ruled in *Sledge v. J. P. Stevens* in December 1975 that the company management in Roanoke Rapids had engaged at various times since 1969 in a series of discriminatory employment practices, including hiring on the basis of race, reserving clerical jobs for whites, discriminating against black males in job assignment, reserving for black employees the low-paying job of warehouseman, and discriminating against blacks in layoffs and recalls. In finding the company guilty of discrimination, the court cited the plaintiffs' statistical evidence as the main reason for its decision.[127]

In most other cases, companies settled class action cases through consent decrees, avoiding the possibility of a damaging legal trial and the attendant publicity. These decrees usually contained important concessions that helped to improve the working conditions of black workers. Black workers themselves usually saw the decrees as a sign that the company had caved in because the evidence against them was so compelling.[128]

In the vast majority of the textile cases, the plaintiffs were represented by the black attorneys Julius Chambers and James E. Ferguson II. Their Charlotte law firm was at the forefront of a drive to represent black workers and make Title VII of the Civil Rights Act a reality. James Ferguson remembered that when he started practicing with the firm in the 1960s, the South had a "labor apartheid" which he was determined to change: "We as a law firm set about to implement Title VII to provide new opportunities, greater opportunities for African-Americans than they had had before, and to make the promise of the act real."[129]

Julius Chambers had grown up in the town of Mount Gilead, east of Charlotte, and was a 1962 graduate of the University of North Carolina Law School. He first established his civil rights law practice in 1964 after working for a year on the legal staff of the NAACP Legal Defense Fund in New York City. From the beginning, Chambers worked in close cooperation with the Legal Defense Fund's New York lawyers in handling a huge volume of civil rights cases. During his first year in Charlotte, Chambers filed thirty-four school desegregation lawsuits, ten public accommodations lawsuits, ten suits challenging discrimination by public hospitals, and several others to save the jobs of black teachers faced with dismissal. A few years later, Chambers was joined by Adam Stein, a

Despite black entry into production jobs, most black men, in particular, continued to be assigned to traditional areas such as the card room.

white attorney, and their law firm of Chambers and Stein marked the first time in North Carolina's history that a black and a white lawyer had joined forces. Chambers was best known for handling the *Swann v. Charlotte-Mecklenburg Board of Education* case, which was concerned with the desegregation of Charlotte's public schools. In 1967, Chambers and Stein were joined by James Ferguson, a graduate of North Carolina Central University who had grown up in Asheville, North Carolina. By the early 1970s, Chambers had established himself as the preeminent civil rights lawyer in the South.[130]

The Southern Textile Industry in 1965

Surveys of racial employment patterns prevailing in the textile industry around the time that the Civil Rights Act took effect on July 2, 1965 illustrate

Table 1. Number of Shift Foremen, Total and Black, at Dan River Mills, 1965–1973

Date	Total Number of Shift Foremen	Number of Black Shift Foremen	Percent of Black Shift Foremen
Oct. 3, 1965	190	0	0
Jan. 19, 1967	196	1	0.51
Nov. 1969	210	4	1.90
Dec. 31, 1971	181	7	3.87
July 2, 1972	190	10	5.26
Nov. 16, 1973	230	15	6.50

Source: Plaintiffs' Proposed Findings of Fact and Conclusions of Law, September 16, 1974, *Adams v. Dan River Mills*, p. 11.

why so many lawsuits were brought against textile companies. Early data produced by the EEOC show that African Americans were grossly underrepresented in the industry and were restricted to the lowest-paying, least desirable jobs.

In 1966, for example, the EEOC highlighted the major problems in the industry's treatment of black workers: blacks on the whole were under-utilized and black women were "significantly under-utilized"; blacks were not being hired for white-collar jobs; and African Americans were concentrated in the lowest occupational categories. The general employment pattern that prevailed in the textile industry in the 1960s was well summarized by a TEAM report of September 1968: "Negroes get the lowest paying jobs and the most under represented is the Negro female."[131]

The exclusion of African Americans from high-paying jobs was particularly striking. Composite data of forty-six companies compiled by Richard Rowan in 1966 showed that only 0.7 percent of all white-collar jobs were held by African Americans.[132] In the same year, EEOC data from Burlington Industries, J. P. Stevens, and Dan River Mills provided a graphic illustration of why blacks complained about being restricted to low-paying jobs. The three companies were industry leaders, employing over 133,000 people, 25 percent of total textile employment. Altogether, blacks held 11.7 percent of all jobs at the three companies but only 16 of the 8,437 jobs as officials and managers (0.2 percent). This meant that one of every sixteen whites worked as an official or manager compared to one out of every thousand blacks. Conversely, African Americans held 35.9 percent of jobs as laborers and 36 percent of jobs as service workers—the lowest rungs of the occupational ladder. In 1969, EEOC chairman Clifford L. Alexander called this data "appalling" and asked, "What credibility does this lend to the label of 'Equal Opportunity Employer' that each of the companies probably displays in its classified ads?"[133]

Across the South, blacks were almost completely excluded from supervisory positions. In the 1960s and 1970s, blacks made very few gains into supervisory jobs, and the battle for these positions was a central issue of many lawsuits. At the time of the Civil Rights Act, all supervisors were white; by 1980, a tiny minority were black. Table 1, from the Dan River Mills case, illustrates how slowly blacks made progress into supervisory jobs.

EEOC data from the mid-1960s revealed stark patterns of discrimination, highlighting the industry's legacy of racial discrimination. The key question during this period was how an industry with such an extensive history of excluding blacks from all but the most menial jobs would react to federal legislation calling for a rapid end to historic employment patterns. In the context of the textile industry, indeed, the Civil Rights Act was a revolutionary piece of legislation, abolishing at a stroke the discrimination that had locked blacks out of the New South's biggest industry since the Civil War, and paving the way for an unprecedented degree of integration. Perhaps most important of all, with the passage of the act the pressure was put on textile companies. No longer could they freely decide to exclude blacks from production jobs. The act gave African Americans who were unjustly excluded from the industry a recourse under the law, and they used it. Within five years of the act's passage, a rash of major lawsuits had been brought against many of the South's largest textile companies. The companies were called on to explain and analyze their racial hiring records in a way that they had never had to do before.

The Government Brought About the Real Change

Causes of the Racial Integration of the
Southern Textile Industry, 1964–1980

two

Since the 1960s, several historians and economists have claimed that a shortage of labor was largely responsible for the racial integration of the southern textile industry. Richard Rowan's 1970 account, based primarily on industry sources, argues that "unlike the situation in other industries, such as paper, Negroes would have been hired in textile mills without government pressure in the 1960's. The labor market brought the major change."[1] Other studies have also concentrated on the labor shortage, meaning that the role of the federal government in causing the change has received very little attention. The detailed evidence provided by the lawsuits and other sources, however, indicates that the federal government in fact played a central part in the racial integration of the textile industry, a role that has not been recognized in the existing literature.[2]

The 1960s was a decade of considerable racial change in American society, and these changes were reflected in the advances made by African Americans in a wide variety of American industries. The racial integration of the southern textile industry reflected the rapid collapse of Jim Crow in the years between 1960 and 1972. At the same time that African Americans opened up the textile industry, segregation was collapsing across the South.[3] It is clear that the federal government played a crucial role in the integration of southern industry as a whole. In the tobacco industry, for example, government action was instrumental in breaking down segregation.[4] In the paper industry, federal intervention was responsible for pushing companies to modify discriminatory seniority systems. As Herbert Northrup's 1970 study concluded, "Government pressure has been THE prime motivating force in altering the practices of the southern mills and in moving them toward a more equalitarian stance."[5]

Nationwide, however, the pace of integration was often more rapid in industries where management was pressured simultaneously by government intervention and by the rising demand for labor generated by the booming economy of the mid- and late 1960s.[6] It is this mixture of government pressure and acute labor shortage that explains why African Americans made employment gains in the southern textile industry at a faster pace than in any other American industry.

In order to appreciate the way that government pressure and the labor market interacted with one another, it is necessary to understand the context in which integration occurred. Between 1961 and 1965, the federal government set the stage for opening up the textile industry through executive orders and the 1964 Civil Rights Act. At the start of the 1960s, the economy was sluggish and textiles suffered as a result. Indeed, the textile industry had been suffering from a lingering depression since 1955. Southern textile manufacturers needed business and were vulnerable to government pressures. In the mid-1960s, however, the economy began to boom and the labor market tightened. Nontextile firms began to move into the Piedmont, luring white textile workers away by offering more attractive pay and working conditions. White workers had seen major improvements in their income since World War II. Car ownership was common, and many white textile workers were willing to commute long distances to attractive jobs. When the industry experienced a severe labor shortage, textile companies found that the federal legislation had cleared the way for them to meet this shortage by hiring blacks, a ready labor source that they had been reluctant to hire before, partly because of social pressure and opposition from their white workers. The Civil Rights Act was used by executives as a way of overcoming white opposition to integration, since the government could be blamed for black hiring. In this way, the federal government played a key role in the racial integration of the southern textile industry.[7]

Most accounts of integration in the contemporary trade press described how the textile industry had integrated because of a combination of federal pressure and a labor shortage. In December 1965, the *Daily News Record* investigated why some mills were starting to hire blacks into production positions and concluded that two pressures had caused the change: "Along came twin pressures . . . economic demand stemming from a growing labor shortage plus Government demand for fair employment practices. The mill passed the word, most discreetly, that it would accept applications from 'qualified' Negroes for training."[8] Similarly, a 1966 TWUA study of integration concluded, "Our industry which resisted integration is now being pushed by law and a tight labor market into token integration."[9]

Many executives felt that the two factors operated together. According to Robert B. Lincks, who was director of personnel development at Burlington Industries between 1959 and 1990, "Those two things went along at the same time—as more industry moved South and more jobs were created, generally paying higher than textiles and furniture, a labor shortage was created, and at the same time you had this whole movement [of government regulation]. . . . So you can see that those things went hand in hand, government regulation and job shortage."[10]

The fact that federal laws had changed the racial climate by the mid-1960s encouraged many textile executives to meet the labor shortage facing the industry by hiring blacks. Some executives admitted that the government's efforts had made black employment more acceptable. In March 1969, for example, Russell Mills in Alexander City, Alabama, claimed that the company's hiring of blacks had been accelerated by a "tight labor market situation" but added that government regulations had also played a major role: "One important reason for Negroes now being used in the Company was that since the Civil Rights Act and other government pressures stemming from 1960 the white southerner has begun to recognize the Negro as a human being."[11]

The Importance of Federal Initiatives

Although the Civil Rights Act of 1964 was the most important single cause of racial integration in the textile industry, other federal initiatives also played a role, including efforts to enforce nondiscrimination among federal contractors. Federal regulations were important both in pressuring companies to hire blacks and because they could be used by executives as a way of bypassing white workers' potential opposition to integration.

In the early 1960s, federal regulations played a major role in pushing the southern textile industry to integrate. Executives active in the integration of the industry unanimously stressed the importance of the regulations in securing black entry. Several federal actions spurred integration of the textile industry. According to one analysis of integration in the *New York Times* in 1969, President John F. Kennedy's Executive Order 10925 (1961), which strengthened the requirement that government contractors hire and promote without regard to race, marked the beginning of integration in the industry: "Industry officials refer repeatedly to that order as the beginning of noticeable movement against discrimination." In the early 1960s, in particular, poor market conditions in textiles made the industry willing to integrate rather than lose vital government business.[12]

An analysis of industry compliance conducted by the TWUA in January 1962 found that many southern companies had begun to integrate following the order. The union found that the order "has resulted in a movement by several of the large textile chains to increase employment of Negroes" as a way of avoiding "charges of failure to fulfill their obligations as government contractors." Burlington Industries, in particular, was found to have increased its hiring of African Americans "appreciably" because of the order.[13]

The AFSC's Merit Employment Program also noted that the passage of Executive Order 10925 and the establishment of the President's Committee on Equal Employment Opportunity had caused some improvements in the numbers of African Americans hired in the textile industry. In one 1963 report, it described the committee as a "positive factor" and claimed that "the forthright and positive approach of the President's Committee on Equal Employment Opportunity has had its effect in many southern communities." It cited one large textile firm in Greensboro, North Carolina, that had received several multimillion-dollar contracts in 1962 but "cannot get another contract until they eliminate some of their discriminatory employment practices."[14]

The most important federal initiative, however, was the Civil Rights Act of 1964, which became effective on July 2, 1965. Its significance can be seen by the fact that in many companies the first black workers were not hired until the act was passed. As the detailed study of the South Carolina textile industry by economists James J. Heckman, Brook Payner, and Richard J. Butler has shown, the passage of the Civil Rights Act led to a "breakthrough" in black employment across a variety of labor markets. After remaining stable between 1910 and 1964, black employment suddenly surged in 1964–65.[15]

The passage of the Civil Rights Act clearly pushed many companies to start integrating. Indeed, the lawsuits and other records offer repeated examples of companies who hired their first black worker in 1964 or 1965, often deliberately to avoid charges of discrimination. This was especially true regarding the hiring of black women. At one major plant of the large West Point Pepperell Company, it was reported that "the first Negro women were hired in July, 1965, even though there had been no complaint of discrimination."[16] Similarly, at Southerland Mills in Mebane, North Carolina, the first four black female workers were hired shortly after Title VII went into effect.[17] Across the South, the Civil Rights Act led to black women being hired in large numbers for the first time. Companies themselves referred to 1965 as the date when black employment took off. In *Lewis v. Bloomsburg Mills*, the company stated in its defense to the case that "it was only subsequent to 1965 that black females were a significant factor in the textile workforce in South Carolina." Bloomsburg

Mills produced data showing that the percentage of black women employed in textiles in South Carolina increased from only 0.7 percent in 1965 to 9.1 percent in 1972.[18]

Other sources indicate that the first crucial steps toward the hiring of blacks into nontraditional positions often occurred shortly before the Civil Rights Act became effective. The AFSC reported in 1964 that many companies were starting to hire blacks before the effective date of the act: "The law already is causing some corporations to hire Negroes or upgrade them in jobs in anticipation of 1965."[19] In *Sherrill v. J. P. Stevens*, it was established that at the Stevens plant in Stanley, North Carolina, the first placements of blacks into all-white production jobs occurred in June 1965.[20]

Executives who worked in the industry throughout the period of racial integration believed that the Civil Rights Act had played a central role. George C. Waldrep Jr., a personnel executive with Burlington Industries during the 1960s and 1970s, felt that "the 1964 Civil Rights Act really was the driving force behind the integration of the plants." Waldrep thought that the act was crucial in initiating integration in the textile industry.[21] Many executives described how the passage of the Civil Rights Act had caused them to meet with all of their supervisors and make it clear that the numbers of blacks hired must be increased. Executives often remembered the Civil Rights Act as legislation that forced them to think about changing their hiring practices. One superintendent reported that when the act passed, all managers "had a meeting and it was told to all supervisors that we had to employ the colored race." To many managers, the Civil Rights Act meant that they had to "hire the colored" or "hire the black."[22]

Many other sources confirm the importance of the Civil Rights Act in the integration of the industry. A wide-ranging questionnaire sent out in December 1966 by the TWUA to its southern locals illustrates that many workers and union officials felt that the hiring and upgrading of African Americans began in 1965.[23] In many cases the first blacks were hired soon after the act became effective in order to avoid charges. From Roxbury Southern Mills in Chattanooga, Tennessee, for example, the union reported that "management has been very hesitant toward hiring Negroes." In October 1965, however, the company had been "frightened by a civil rights probe into their hiring practices" and had started to hire its first African Americans.[24] At another company the union representative reported that the first black production workers had been "hired after law required it."[25] Union organizers also remembered 1965 as a watershed year in black employment, claiming that seniority lists they obtained when they were trying to organize a plant showed clearly that black employment started to increase dramatically once the act became effective.[26]

A research report on the textile industry prepared by the EEOC in December

1966 confirmed that the Civil Rights Act had caused a sharp increase in black employment in 1964–65. A comparison of 136 textile companies in the Carolinas between 1964 and 1965 indicated "significant increases in Negro employment." In North Carolina, employment increased by 54.8 percent for black men and 312 percent for black women. Indicating how the industry was changing, black employment constituted 62 percent of the total increase in employment between the two years. In South Carolina, black employment in 1965 increased 58.6 percent over the 1964 total.[27]

Studies made by team into the racial hiring practices of southern textile companies also found that there had been a clear shift in the hiring of blacks when the Civil Rights Act went into effect. Between 1926 and 1965, for example, data from the South Carolina Department of Labor showed that the percentage of blacks in the textile industry in South Carolina remained constant. In 1925, 6 percent of male workers in South Carolina's textile industry were black. In 1965, at the time the Civil Rights Act took effect, the figure was still 5.5 percent. By 1966, however, it had jumped to 8.1 percent. The figures for African American women showed a similar sudden increase. Indeed, team reported, "It is interesting to note the increase that took place between 1965 and 1966 after Title VII of the Civil Rights Act went into effect."[28]

The records of the lawsuits repeatedly show that there was a large jump in black employment when the Civil Rights Act was passed. There were similar jumps when eeoc charges were filed against companies who then realized that they would probably have to prove in a federal court that they did not discriminate. These sharp jumps in black employment are another powerful argument against accepting the companies' claims that the hiring of African Americans increased gradually purely in response to the labor market. This labor supply argument was used extensively by Bloomsburg Mills in *Lewis v. Bloomsburg Mills*, and also in *Sledge v. J. P. Stevens*.

In *Lewis v. Bloomsburg Mills*, the court rejected the company's claim that blacks were hired gradually as their position in the labor market grew stronger. Rather, the court concluded that "the increases in the hiring of blacks were not gradual and spaced over a long period of time, but were both sharp and sudden." The first black woman was hired by the company three months after the effective date of Title VII, even though the personnel manager testified that the company had always had black female applicants. After hiring the first black woman, the company then opened up different production categories to black women in a sudden fashion, as groups of black women were hired simultaneously into certain positions.[29]

Many companies themselves admitted that the Civil Rights Act and other federal pressure was crucial in allowing them to break with established employment patterns and increase their hiring of African Americans. After visiting the Uniroyal Company in Winnsboro, South Carolina, in 1969, one investigator reported that the company had told him, "The federal government's effort has caused Negroes to be employed. 'Without it very little would have been done.'"[30] Many companies admitted that the government had pushed them to hire more blacks, even though they often deeply resented this federal interference. Riegel Textile Corporation, for example, conceded in 1969 that "government activity has aided Negro employment" but added, "Some of the investigators are too much."[31] Similarly, the large Bibb Mills felt that "government action has been influential" but noted "government seems to select the firm that is doing something as a target."[32] Some companies were more positive about government pressure. At Fulton Cotton Mills in Atlanta, the company felt that "government pressure has been effective and needed."[33]

In other cases, mill owners admitted that the federal government had played an important role in pushing them toward integration. American Textile Manufacturers' Institute (ATMI) director Sadler Love conceded in 1970 that the Civil Rights Act and the leverage of federal contracts had "continually prodded textile companies to accelerate their minority hiring."[34] In *Adams v. Dan River Mills*, the company even admitted during the trial that pressure from the federal government had pushed them to hire more African Americans. The company claimed that it was not just the Civil Rights Act that had influenced them but the fear of losing federal contracts under Executive Order 11246. Robert Gardiner, Dan River's director of industrial relations, acknowledged at the trial that Dan River had entered into an affirmative action agreement with the federal government in 1969 to avoid losing government contracts.[35] Similarly, it was established in *Sledge v. J. P. Stevens* that Stevens, one of the companies criticized in 1969 for continuing to receive government contracts after only giving oral assurances to combat discrimination, had opened up weaving jobs to black women in direct response to federal pressure.[36]

After the Civil Rights Act had been passed, other federal efforts helped to push the pace of integration in the textile industry. The textile employment forum held by the EEOC in January 1967 also helped to increase the hiring of African Americans in the industry. EEOC officials claimed that the forum led to a cooperative effort between federal agencies and the textile industry in the Carolinas to open up new job opportunities for African Americans. The EEOC reported that during June and July of 1967, for example, "voluntary affirmative action" programs among ten textile mills in South Carolina provided 246 new jobs for blacks. These 246 jobs constituted 41 percent of all new hiring in South Carolina during the June–July period. This compared with an 11 percent hiring ratio for blacks in an average two-month period. Other cooperative efforts between the EEOC and textile companies also increased black hiring. In December 1967, John Cauthen, the executive vice president of the South Carolina

Textile Manufacturers' Association, reported that in South Carolina some 4,000 blacks had been hired out of a total of 6,000 persons since the forum.[37]

In addition to pressuring executives to hire blacks, federal regulations were also crucial in providing mill owners with the justification they needed to integrate. Across the South, mill executives acknowledged that the Civil Rights Act and Executive Order 10925 helped them to integrate because they could blame the law for integration. The law gave them a vital prop because it meant that companies who integrated could claim that they may not have liked hiring blacks, but they had to follow the law. Many companies used this argument as a way of overcoming opposition from their white workers. As the *Winston-Salem Journal* reported in 1968, "If anyone complains the management can blame the government."[38] In a lengthy report exploring integration, the trade paper *Textile Industries* interviewed many mill men who felt that the Civil Rights Act had been essential because it had given companies the confidence to integrate that they had lacked before. As one of them put it when asked what had brought about the change in the hiring of African Americans, "I think it is legislation. Due to the fear of public opinion, many people, even though they are determined in their efforts to further the cause of minority employment, must have a reed to lean on. This has been provided under the law, as they can now justify their actions as observing the law, rather than as a result of following their personal convictions."[39]

The prominent role played by executive orders and federal legislation actually worked to the companies' advantage, facilitating integration because the government could be blamed. According to Robert Lincks, who was head of personnel at Burlington Industries throughout the 1960s and 1970s, "The government gave us a nice way to facilitate it, and if anybody wanted to complain about it—white people who would say, 'Hey, why are you hiring all these black people?'—you'd say, 'Because the government forces us to do this.' You could place the blame on the government." Lincks felt that government regulations were crucial in allowing the company to hire blacks without being criticized by white workers.[40]

The company records of Dan River Mills show that southern textile companies cooperated closely with one another when they introduced African Americans into the workforce, exchanging a great deal of information and advice about the safest methods of integrating their plants. Most large companies adopted a strategy of explaining integration as a federal law that had to be obeyed. The two companies that Dan River corresponded with the most were Burlington and J. P. Stevens, the two largest southern textile companies throughout the 1960s and 1970s. The first flurry of correspondence occurred in reaction to Executive Order 10925, as companies began to ponder how to comply with the order and minimize potential disruption in their plants. In April 1962,

William C. Little of J. P. Stevens wrote Malcolm Cross of Dan River, sending him a lengthy "Suggested Statement to Employees" that Stevens had used successfully to explain the order to their employees and hire the first African Americans into production positions. This statement became the basis for the approach that other southern textile companies took to integration. Its main emphasis was on the lack of choice that companies had in resisting integration. Stevens made clear that equal employment opportunity was federal law and the company could not resist it because it desperately needed government business. Workers were told that if the company did not have government business, "we would probably have to close down some plants or at least cut back to three or four days' work." Thus, the possibility of resistance was reduced by showing that workers' jobs were at stake if equal employment opportunity was not implemented.[41]

The statement by J. P. Stevens also stressed the common ground between the company and its employees. Neither agreed with integration, but neither had any choice. As the statement explained, "I realize that this will involve a difficult readjustment for many of us but in order to meet the requirements of this Executive Order, we must have the full co-operation of each and every one of you." The statement also included a question and answer section so that supervisors would be ready to deal with "likely questions" from the shop floor. The statement and the question and answer section were sent to all of the company's supervisors and to a number of other southern textile companies.[42]

Most other southern textile companies stressed similar points when they began to integrate. In smaller companies, plant managers or mill owners communicated directly with their workers rather than through supervisors, but the message was the same. As one owner of a small mill explained, "I called my workers together and told them, 'Look, we need to hire some Negroes in production. If we don't we might have to close. And the federal government is going to make us hire them anyway. I need your help to make it work out.'"[43] Dan River Mills itself took a similar approach when it decided to integrate, emphasizing the importance of government business.[44] In many cases, the heavy emphasis that management placed on the necessity of obeying the law was clearly exaggerated. At Burlington, for example, government business was not vital, constituting only 3 percent of the company's total business.[45]

A detailed analysis of textile integration in the trade journal *Textile Industries* showed that by the late 1960s, many executives saw the Civil Rights Act as crucial because it had allowed them to overcome the opposition of their white workers to hiring blacks on production jobs. Executives' perception of worker opposition, as the AFSC records of plant visits clearly showed, had been the main reason many companies had been reluctant to integrate before 1964. One executive, for example, called the Civil Rights Act "a blessing in disguise for us," because "the Southern textile employee has generally proved to be one of the most difficult groups to accept the changing social mores of our times. This has had a hindering effect on efforts . . . [to] implement changes in hiring practices, and such was the case with our company." By freeing executives from their reliance on a restricted pool of white labor, the Civil Rights Act also allowed companies to lower their wage costs and, in some cases, to use the introduction of blacks as a way of increasing workloads.[46]

Besides providing positive evidence that the federal government played an important role in integrating the textile industry, written records also show that some companies did not in fact face a labor shortage that forced them to hire African Americans. Many of the lawsuits reveal that as late as the 1970s companies often operated in towns where they had little competition for labor. In many cases, the mill still constituted the only source of manufacturing employment, with workers commuting by car from the surrounding rural area. Often, management officials were blissfully unaware of any labor shortage because they were able to operate successfully by hiring from the same white families that had worked in the mill for generations. This was especially true in the *Lea v. Cone Mills* case, which was brought by a group of black women who had tried unsuccessfully to secure jobs at a Cone plant in the small town of Hillsborough, North Carolina. The plant had never hired a black woman and actually had a policy of hiring relatives of existing employees. Of all the cases that attorney Julius Chambers brought in the textile industry, this one stuck in his mind for that reason: "Cone Mills was one [case] that stands out largely because that was one of the earliest cases that went to court and had some of the most interesting evidence. . . . During that hearing we found out that that particular industry hired primarily brothers and sisters."[47]

Testimony from company officials confirmed that the mill, the only manufacturing plant in the area, was not short of labor. Personnel manager Otto King testified in 1968, at the height of the industry's labor shortage, that "our experience at Hillsborough has been that the Eno plant is practically the only manufacturing plant there, and we have always been blessed with more help than we could use." The company admitted that "we have never had to take any steps to recruit. Our recruitment consisted of receiving applications." Rather than turning to blacks because of a labor shortage, the company continued its policy of hiring the relatives of its existing employees, who were overwhelmingly white: "Quite often we have a husband and wife or father and son, and so forth. . . . I would look for someone who had a relative working for us at the present time, which we think is one of the best references that we can get on a person." This policy effectively froze blacks out of the plant and was found to be discriminatory by the court.[48]

There is no mention of a labor shortage in the records of some of the major textile firms. The detailed statistics compiled in *Sledge v. J. P. Stevens* indicate that the company consistently had far greater numbers of people seeking jobs at its Roanoke Rapids plants than the number of positions available. At the height of the industry's expansion in 1973, for example, the company received 2,939 applications for only 420 jobs at its large Rosemary Griege plant. The same pattern was evident at other Stevens plants throughout the 1970s.[49]

It is clear that mills located in larger population centers did have to compete for labor in the late 1960s and experienced a genuine shortage that pushed them to hire blacks. Nevertheless, across the South, many mills were located in small towns where they dominated the local economy and were able to secure all the labor they needed from the white community. At the textile forum in 1967, Vivian W. Henderson, the economist and president of Clark College, complained that the textile industry was characterized by all-white mills located in rural nonfarm areas. He claimed that "all-white plants are the rule rather than the exception in East Tennessee, Southwest Virginia, North and South Carolina, Georgia, Alabama, and Mississippi."[50]

Some of the most compelling evidence supporting the role played by the federal government in integrating the textile industry is provided by textile workers themselves. Both black and white workers felt that the textile industry would never have integrated without pressure from the federal government. All of the workers interviewed, both black and white, shared this feeling.

The overwhelming majority of African American workers interviewed in this study were unaware of any labor shortage when they were hired, even though most were hired in the late 1960s. Rather, these workers felt that companies only started to hire African Americans because they were forced to by the federal government. The idea that textile companies would have automatically turned to blacks because of a shortage of labor seemed little short of ridiculous to them. Corine Lytle Cannon, who was one of the first African Americans to be hired at Cannon Mills in Kannapolis, North Carolina, was as forthright about this point as many other black pioneers: "That was the whole thing. It would never have been if it had not been for the Civil Rights Act. It would still be just like it were."[51] Similarly, Gladys Trawick, a pioneer black textile worker in Andalusia, Alabama, remembered that integration was not even considered by the local textile company until the Civil Rights Act: "They wouldn't even talk about it until the law was passed."[52] Ollie Seals, a black textile worker from Columbus, Georgia, thought that "the government brought about the real change."[53]

These feelings were echoed across the South. Thomas Pharr, a black worker at Rock Hill Printing and Finishing Company, felt that blacks were hired "primarily because of federal law, the Civil Rights Act . . . and the federal government dictated that this was to take place."[54] Alton Collins, a black worker at

Leshner Manufacturing Company in Hawkinsville, Georgia, expressed the feelings of many black workers that even with federal legislation, the companies discriminated against African Americans. Thus, without such legislation, Collins felt, little would have changed: "It's changed a lot, that is, today from back then what it was, but you know, if they didn't have a law I don't think it would have changed. . . . Especially down here in the South, if they didn't have a law to change the way they did, it would have been the same."[55]

Union representatives who were active in the South shared this opinion that integration was caused by the Civil Rights Act. Clyde Bush, who worked as a southern organizer for the TWUA in the 1960s and 1970s, expressed the typical view: "No, if it hadn't been for the Civil Rights laws, today in my opinion you'd be sitting here, there wouldn't be black workers working in higher-paying jobs. . . . So if you'd have left it up to the textile companies in the South, no, they'd have never done it."[56] Other union leaders differed slightly from this view, feeling that change might have come eventually, but that the Civil Rights Act greatly increased the speed of the change. As Sammy Glover, a union representative in Andalusia, Alabama, put it, "I don't think it would have happened at the pace that it did. I think it would have happened a lot slower because there would have been pressure from the white worker not to do what the law compelled them to do, so I think they would have held out to the end. . . . A lot of southern companies, especially private, we have a lot of private-owned companies where they are owned by families and individuals, and I think they would have been very, very slow to come around to hiring Afro-American workers without some pressure."[57]

It is especially interesting that white workers who were employed in the industry in the 1960s and 1970s shared this feeling that companies were being forced to integrate by the federal government, because black and white workers often disagreed about many other aspects of the integration, especially the amount of discrimination remaining in the mills. White workers who witnessed the racial integration of their plants felt that the mill companies were acting to comply with the law rather than being forced to integrate because of a labor shortage. Fletcher Beck worked at Rock Hill Printing and Finishing Company from 1948 until 1993. Although the company claimed that a labor shortage was pushing it to hire more blacks, Beck, a small, thoughtful white man, disagreed: "My feeling was the reason they were changing the hiring practices and hiring the blacks was that they were complying with the law. That's basically the way I saw it. I don't recall a whole lot of opportunities opening up in this area that would cause them to hire black. I think in this area there has always been a plentiful supply of white workers. My feeling was that they were just complying with the law."[58]

White workers generally felt that the federal government was forcing textile mills to integrate against their will and claimed that if companies had not integrated, they would have been forced to. Many white workers believed that because companies were forced to hire blacks, they had to treat black workers better because they feared the federal government. According to Mae Dawson, a retired white textile worker in Tarboro, North Carolina, "If the government hadn't have made them, they would never have done it. And of course they had to pander to blacks, because the government was saying employ so many."[59]

The Impact of the Civil Rights Act on Southern Textile Workers

Regardless of the reasons for integration, federal initiatives still caused lasting changes in the lives of southern textile workers. The Civil Rights Act, in particular, had a huge impact on the everyday working lives of African American workers. The significance of these changes, and the way that the federal government transformed the lives of thousands of African American textile workers, cannot be overlooked.

In *Ellison v. Rock Hill Printing and Finishing Company*, federal law superseded a state law that required rigid segregation within textile mills in the state of South Carolina. As a result, a whole range of everyday facilities in the mill were immediately integrated. These included not just toilet facilities and water fountains but also showers, changing rooms, and a variety of others. For example, the passage of the Civil Rights Act meant an end to separate time clocks and separate entrances. For the first time, black and white workers entered the plant together and clocked in together. These were major changes in workers' lives, especially as the workplace was the area where blacks and whites were in contact probably more than anywhere else. Oscar Gill, who was one of the lead plaintiffs in the *Ellison* case, summed up how important these changes were to black workers who had endured years of segregated facilities: "That Civil Rights Bill was passed, my supervisor told me we had the privilege to come inside. . . . I worked outside. . . . I was hired to work outside. . . . We wasn't allowed to drink from the same water fountain till the Civil Rights Bill was passed, wasn't even able to use the same toilet facilities till the Civil Rights Bill went through. . . . They had black way down on the outside where you go through a tunnel, a black toilet down there and over in the shipping department. . . . They changed it all once they passed the Civil Rights. They got black supervisors now throughout the plant. . . . It was a great change." Like many black workers, Gill made friends with white workers after integration: "We sat down and ate together . . . after the bill. We sat down and we ate together every day in the week that I went to work. . . . I'd sit down with my white brothers and we'd eat together and nobody said nothing. They all seemed to like me, and I liked them."[60]

Workers' perception that integration was caused by the Civil Rights Act is significant because it shows that the law had a major impact upon working people throughout the South. To these workers, it was the federal government that was responsible for giving them a job. It was because most companies had done so little to employ blacks until the government intervened that African American textile workers often felt that companies would have never have changed without being "forced" to. At Rock Hill Printing and Finishing, for example, black worker Johnnie Archie felt that only the federal government could bring about a change in the company's behavior: "One thing about the southern white man, if the stick was big enough he obeyed it, but if the stick was small he'd try to take it and bend it. What I'm trying to say there, they would not have, I don't think, obeyed a state government like they did the federal government because they knew the governor and the people in the state legislature. They feared the federal government, no doubt about it. . . . Had it been left for them to do it their way it would have taken years, with their token approach." Like other African Americans who had witnessed how the federal government had brought major improvements in their working conditions, Archie was concerned about the current debate over affirmative action and the argument that the federal government's influence should be restricted: "What the public is crying about now is government interference. This comes from white people, not black people, in this country. 'We want to get the government out of our business.' Well, if it hadn't have been for the federal government we would not have had civil rights laws passed. If it had not been for the federal government we would probably still have had slavery in this country."[61]

Black workers also credited the Civil Rights Act with bringing about more respect in the workplace and giving them more confidence and self-esteem on the shop floor. As one worker remembered, after the Civil Rights Act blacks were able to call their supervisors by their first names, "just like the whites always have."[62] It is clear that the act had a far-reaching effect on the lives of black textile workers across the South. Many felt that it was not until the law was passed that companies started to treat black workers with any respect or make any effort to place them in better-paying jobs. One black worker in Kannapolis, North Carolina, thought that things improved at Cannon Mills after the passage of the act because a new standard had been set for companies to obey: "The U.S. government drawed the line with what they had to do, and they didn't want to defy the government."[63]

The Civil Rights Act also gave African American workers an opportunity to challenge the discriminatory practices they had witnessed and endured for many years. It provided the machinery for workers and community leaders to set in motion litigation that would help to reduce discrimination in the workplace. Workers often described how they saw the passage of the law as their chance to finally challenge discrimination. Johnnie Archie, for example, had started working at Rock Hill Printing and Finishing Company in 1953 and was one of the original plaintiffs in *Ellison v. Rock Hill Printing and Finishing Company*. Archie remembered that the original plaintiffs had brought the suit because they saw the opportunity that the Civil Rights Act provided: "Discrimination was accepted because this was the law of the land. It was accepted because there was nothing else we could do, and after the Civil Rights law was passed . . . then we saw a chance to make our move. We asked the company and our supervisors for the jobs that had been closed to us. . . . The company you might say stonewalled . . . so this was where some of us, led by Rev. Ellison, made our move. We requested them that they open up these jobs, they refused, then we contacted what is called the EEOC, and we went from there in '66. It took until 1972 until we actually got into litigation."[64]

In many other communities as well, black workers and community leaders used the new opportunity provided by the Civil Rights Act to bring lawsuits against textile companies. In *Galloway v. Fieldcrest Mills*, a group of black workers initiated the case by writing a detailed letter to the EEOC. They described the discrimination they faced in the plant, especially the inability to secure promotions out of an all-black department. The passage of the Civil Rights Act meant that workers felt that the time had come for discrimination to end: "The Negroes in our department were not put in this world just to do the hard, common work. The Civil Rights Act gives us certain privileges and we would like to exercise these rights now."[65]

At the J. P. Stevens plants in Roanoke Rapids, North Carolina, *Sledge v. J. P. Stevens* was brought to litigation partly through the efforts of a local civil rights leader named Joe P. Moody. He was responsible for bringing the original plaintiffs together and convincing them to participate in a lawsuit. Moody, whose wife was one of the original plaintiffs in the case, remembered that the main reason many workers were willing to participate in the case was the moral and legal support that the Civil Rights Act gave them. Moody remembered that before the act, "we had no leg to stand on, you know, you didn't have a leg to stand on. It was difficult to do anything before the Civil Rights Bill was passed, wasn't anything to do, you were scared to talk. . . . During that time you couldn't even sit in the back of a car with a white lady, you had cops all over you."[66] The importance of the act was also stressed by attorneys who handled the textile cases. T. T. Clayton, an African American attorney who was cocounsel in *Sledge v. J. P. Stevens*, recalled that the act was crucial because "we could have gotten into court, but we couldn't have got any results without the Title VII of the Civil Rights Act. See, the rules of discovery, the burden of proof, that kind of thing, makes a great deal of difference in determining whether, what you have to overcome."[67]

The lawsuits offer repeated examples of workers who used their awareness of the Civil Rights Act to challenge company policy. It is clear that the act gave African American workers more confidence in the workplace and a new standard against which to measure companies' performance. At Dan River Mills in Greenville, South Carolina, two black workers who were the only blacks in their department asked their supervisor in 1970 why so few black workers were being hired. When the supervisor replied that they were not required to hire blacks, one of the workers, Bertha Louise Farrow, cited the Civil Rights Act: "We knew that the Rights had passed, so we told him that it was supposed to be equal. . . . [W]e told him that the Civil Rights Act had passed." To Farrow, the act meant that the company should "hire equal to the white" because "it's supposed to be equal."[68]

The Importance of Title VII Litigation

Although the Civil Rights Act and other federal initiatives helped to cause integration in textiles, the powers of the EEOC to enforce the act were very limited. The early EEOC was hindered by understaffing and a huge backlog of cases. The chairman of the EEOC himself said of the commission's attempts to eliminate discrimination in employment, "We're out to kill an elephant with a fly gun." After twenty-one months of operation, the commission had received more than 15,000 complaints of discrimination but had successfully resolved only 330.[69] It was still possible for many companies to follow a path of resistance or of token compliance. The Civil Rights Act was crucial, however, because it made possible class action lawsuits against employers, establishing that if companies failed to settle EEOC complaints voluntarily, plaintiffs had the right to sue. These lawsuits were successful in bringing about real change in racial employment patterns in the textile industry, especially as they attacked wide patterns of discrimination rather than individual complaints.

The records of the lawsuits provide many examples of companies increasing their hiring of African Americans shortly after the filing of EEOC charges or when litigation had begun.[70] In *Ellison v. Rock Hill Printing and Finishing Company*, for example, lead plaintiff Leroy Ellison described how "since this case was filed we have a job that has been awarded a black that other times men have bid on and they were refused."[71] In *Lea v. Cone Mills*, the main issue was the fact that Cone's plant in Hillsborough, North Carolina, had never hired a black woman even though 30–35 percent of the workforce was female. However, the first black women were hired shortly after written charges of discrimination were filed with the EEOC. In 1971, indeed, the United States Court of Appeals found that the *Lea* case had "opened the way for employment of Negro women in the Cone Mills plant."[72]

In *Lewis v. J. P. Stevens*, a case brought in 1972 against the Stevens plant in Abbeville, South Carolina, group data showed how the company had rapidly increased its hiring of African Americans since the filing of the case. In the job of utility man, which had always been overwhelmingly white, the percentage of blacks assigned to the position doubled from 10.3 percent before the filing of the complaint to 20.5 percent immediately after the filing of the lawsuit on March 16, 1972. The proportion of African Americans assigned to the job of doffer increased from 3.8 percent to 28.6 percent, while the number of black spinners jumped from 9.6 percent to 24.5 percent. Some positions were opened up for the first time after the filing of the suit. The percentage of African Americans assigned to the job of warper and creel tender, for example, rose from 0 percent to 16.7 percent. The overall hiring rates of black and white women also increased dramatically. In 1971, for example, 10 percent of female hires were black, but with the lawsuit, this increased rapidly to 29.9 percent in 1972.[73] Data produced in *Sledge v. J. P. Stevens* also showed that the proportion of blacks hired increased dramatically immediately after the trial.[74]

Most cases were settled by consent decrees, usually initiated by companies to avoid the type of lengthy and damaging litigation that J. P. Stevens went through. Although they usually contained no formal admission of discrimination, these consent decrees often led to widespread discriminatory practices being outlawed. In the consent decree entered in *United States v. Southern Weaving*, for example, it was laid down that the company could not use the fact that an applicant had a relative or friend working at the plant as the basis for a preference. This was significant because the practice of favoring applicants recommended by workers had prevented African Americans from being hired in several plants. It had been a major issue in *Lea v. Cone Mills* and was also reported as a problem by TEAM aides in South Carolina.[75]

Many of the textile lawsuits provided landmark decisions that became the basis for other successful Title VII litigation. The textile case of *Hall v. Werthan Bag*, for example, provided the first reported class action decision under Title VII, and this decision established the basis for Title VII class action suits, allowing individual workers to bring cases on behalf of all black workers in their plant. In a famous passage, the court ruled that "racial discrimination is by definition class discrimination. If it exists it applies throughout the class. . . . [A]lthough the actual effects of a discriminatory policy may thus vary throughout the class, the existence of the discriminatory policy threatens the entire class." This decision was used as the basis for other class action cases brought in the textile industry, including *Adams v. Dan River Mills*.[76]

Lea v. Cone Mills was another early case that played a key role in Title VII case law. Brought by a group of black women, it was the first case ever in which applicants for employment were the principal plaintiffs, rather than workers in the plant. The court ruled that applicants could be proper plaintiffs under Title VII. It also established that "community reputation" explained the absence of applications at the plant from black women before 1965, rather than lack of interest, as the company tried to argue. Black women had been discouraged from applying because it was well known in the community that the plant would not hire them. Civil rights attorneys claimed that this ruling was "extremely important" in subsequent textile cases involving black women applicants, especially *Lewis v. Bloomsburg Mills* and *Lewis v. J. P. Stevens*.[77]

A clear example of a lawsuit forcing a company to end discriminatory practices it would never have stopped voluntarily occurred in *Ellison v. Rock Hill Printing and Finishing Company*. The main issue in the case was a discriminatory seniority system which helped to lock blacks into low-paying nonproduction departments. Seniority was applied by department, so that if black workers transferred into a higher-paying department in the plant they lost their department seniority. Similar seniority systems were used by many big American corporations, and their application was a key issue in the 1960s and 1970s. The NAACP, led by their labor secretary Herbert Hill, repeatedly attacked the use of departmental seniority in many U.S. companies, leading to major cases involving corporations such as P. Lorillard and U.S. Steel.[78]

In *Ellison*, the seniority system was changed by a consent decree allowing the plaintiffs in the case to transfer to white production departments without losing their departmental seniority. It is clear that the company was not willing to change the seniority system voluntarily. Company officials used a variety of defenses to justify their position. The main argument was that plant efficiency would suffer because inexperienced black workers could "bump" experienced white workers out of a job. This, the company argued, would cost them money and would lead to unrest among white workers.[79]

Black workers at Rock Hill Printing and Finishing Company felt that the *Ellison* case produced many beneficial results. Chris Brown, one of the original plaintiffs in the case, felt that the decree increased the pace of integration in other textile companies who were watching the case: "That lawsuit really helped the South because a lot of them was watching that thing. . . . It really helped." Thomas Pharr, who started working at the mill in 1966, felt that the consent decree "definitely produced positive results. . . . The consent decree, as a result of that taking place, that changed history you could say, made history, and it helped the people, helped everybody." Jake Boger, another plaintiff in the case, remembered that the case opened up many new job opportunities: "You had just a labor job up until this suit got in the way. We were awarded some jobs then, after that, but before then you just actually did what somebody else told you to do."[80]

Several of the major lawsuits were brought against textile unions as well as companies, and it is clear that unions too were forced by litigation to eliminate discriminatory practices. In *Ellison v. Rock Hill Printing and Finishing Company*, a case brought against both the local union and the company, lead plaintiff Leroy Ellison testified in 1972 that before he had filed the lawsuit in 1972, black workers at his plant had received little representation by the local union: "We have grievances stacked up down at the Union Hall that weren't even heard and we were getting no representation. . . . [A]fter we filed the complaint . . . with the EEOC then the Textile Workers Union began trying to represent the blacks."[81]

The consent decree that settled the *Sledge v. J. P. Stevens* case also contained several provisions that the company had bitterly opposed throughout the case, including racial quotas on many production and clerical jobs. The decree abolished the system of departmental seniority that the company had refused to change, instituting plant seniority instead. Plaintiffs in the case remembered that the decree was responsible for big changes in the plant.[82] Plaintiff Sammy Alston, who worked for Stevens between 1966 and 1990, felt that the lawsuit was crucial: "No, nothing wouldn't have changed if we hadn't filed. J. P. Stevens, he was really, he was a lawbreaker. He was a hard man to deal with, that company were, I'm telling you."[83]

Other cases brought concrete material benefits to thousands of black textile workers. The major class action suit of *Hicks v. Cannon Mills*, brought in 1970, was settled in 1982 by consent decree. Under the terms of the settlement, Cannon paid out $1.65 million to 3,700 black workers. This settlement was one of the largest of its type in the South, and Cannon workers were reported to be "happy" with it. In interviews conducted eleven years after the settlement, they also credited it with reducing discrimination in the mills.[84] In many cases, the lawsuits pushed companies to eliminate the vestiges of segregation in the mill. In *Adams v. Dan River Mills*, for example, black workers testified at the trial in 1973 that the company had only integrated bathrooms in the mill following the filing of the suit in 1969.[85]

The attorneys who represented the plaintiffs in most of the textile cases felt that the Title VII litigation was of great importance in forcing companies to hire blacks in greater numbers and in a greater variety of jobs. James Ferguson felt that the textile lawsuits "had a tremendous impact on the employment practices of those companies. . . . Without those lawsuits, there would have been no meaningful change. It was clear at the time that the American workforce, and particularly the southern workforce, was completely segregated. . . . So I think that it did not make just a difference, I mean it made all the difference to bring those lawsuits." Ferguson felt that apart from the specific benefits particular cases brought to their participants, the cases were also important because they allowed black workers across the South to feel "empowered" by the example of those who had brought the litigation: "It gave people courage and encouragement to apply for positions, and to seek positions and promotions, jobs that they had never sought before. So it had sort of a cascading effect in that sense." Ferguson's colleague Julius Chambers also felt that the lawsuits were "extremely important" because they helped to overcome job segregation that companies were unwilling to end voluntarily.[86]

Throughout the South, black workers and union officials believed that companies were forced by litigation to improve their racial practices. Many stressed that textile companies feared potential litigation and implemented changes because they saw what would happen if they did not.[87] Sydney Young, a black worker and union representative who had worked in various locations around the South, felt that textile companies were concerned about their "corporate image" and were anxious to avoid "the negative publicity that would come from those kind of suits. That put pressure on the companies more than any fines they would have to pay."[88] James Johnson, a black worker from Oneita Knitting Mills in Andrews, South Carolina, who went on to become the president of the AFL-CIO in South Carolina, felt that the lawsuits "helped somewhat to improve the conditions, but more so I believe that it put the companies on notice that the government was not going to tolerate this type of discrimination."[89]

"When They Put All of the Coloreds On, They Speeded Them Up"

The overwhelming emphasis that African American textile workers placed on the law indicates how oral history can illuminate the written record, which tends to emphasize the role of the labor market as much as the law. Moreover, black textile workers also felt that the industry's hiring of African Americans was caused by a factor that does not feature strongly in the written record— the ability of blacks to work hard. African American workers believed that although companies had to be pushed into hiring the first black workers, once they found out that blacks were good workers, they actually sought African American workers to fill hard jobs because they knew that they could perform them better than whites. In this sense, integration took on its own momentum once companies learned that blacks were good workers.

Across the South, indeed, black pioneers recalled the way that workloads were increased as production jobs were awarded to African Americans. In 1966, Sammy Alston was one of the first blacks to be hired into a production job in the card room at J. P. Stevens's Rosemary plant in Roanoke Rapids. A thoughtful, perceptive man, Alston was convinced that J. P. Stevens turned to blacks "because he could get more quality out of the black than he could out of the white, just as simple as that. . . . The reason why the black people got those jobs, those production jobs, the white people could not run the machines, period."[90] Similarly, Reverna Crittenden, who was hired at a mill in Columbus, Georgia, felt that the company hired more and more African Americans because "they carried the workload better than the whites."[91]

In many instances, companies increased the workloads on particular jobs as African Americans were hired into that job, thus making it less desirable and converting the job into a "black" job. At the same time, white workers who had been working in the old job moved into to other, higher-paying jobs, thus ensuring that they continued to earn more and work less. This pattern of "integration" was vividly described by workers in *Hall v. Werthan Bag*, the class action lawsuit brought in 1966 against the Werthan Bag Corporation based in Nashville, Tennessee. Lead plaintiff Ray Tate, who had been one of the first black workers hired in the picking machine department in 1964, described in his deposition how the workload was increased as a group of blacks were placed on the job: "They had all of the old picking machines on No. 8 gears. Then when they put all of the coloreds on, they speeded them up. . . . They were speeded up after I took it, in about 1964. . . . That was when all of the colored people had them then." At the same time that the blacks were hired onto the picking machines, most of the whites were moved to other jobs. As a result, Tate felt that "we turn out more work now than they ever turned out the way they were running it." The company had integrated the picking department by upgrading black laborers from a lower department to replace white workers who were moved up to "higher and better job classifications." Thus, the average pay of blacks in the picking department was between $1.44 per hour to $1.63 per hour, whereas for whites it was $1.97 to $2.04 per hour.[92]

The *Hall* case was typical of the way that many companies carried out integration in a discriminatory fashion. TEAM reports from South Carolina frequently described how companies used the hiring of blacks as a means of increasing workloads and introducing new forms of discrimination. In August 1968, a TEAM aide reported that one of the main problems in Cherokee County was that when blacks were hired, "they have work added on them." The aide from Anderson County also explained that "another problem is that of the companies raising production requirements."[93] Blacks were only being hired on low-paid jobs, and when they were hired, "production is raised as blacks replace whites."[94]

This complaint meant that many black workers involved in the integration of the textile industry did not share the sense of improvement that historians have identified with the black influx into textiles. Willie Long, who was hired at the Eagle and Phenix Mill in Columbus, Georgia, in 1972, for example, remembered that as blacks came into higher-paying production jobs in the 1970s, "then I could really see the workload change on those jobs though, when the blacks went on I could see the workload change. There was more demand for production, production went up, you had to work harder on your job." Consequently, workers like Long felt that the textile companies took advantage of the black workers' desire for better-paying production positions by exploiting them when they were finally promoted into those jobs.[95]

Many union representatives had been active in the South since the 1960s and had closely observed why companies turned to hiring blacks. Sydney Young, an African American who was first employed as a textile worker in 1968, later worked for the Amalgamated Clothing and Textile Workers' Union (ACTWU) across the South as an organizer and business agent. Young felt that companies had been pushed into hiring African Americans by the federal government. But he shared the view that once they had made the move, companies continued to hire blacks because they could handle a higher workload: "I think back in the '60s when I started working, companies were hiring blacks not because there was a shortage of labor but primarily because the government required them to hit certain quotas. But I think over time companies were getting to hire blacks because they found out that they could get the work done. But I think had the government not gotten involved initially the pattern wouldn't have changed."[96]

In recent years, one of the central debates of civil rights historiography has concerned the issue of whether the federal government was the movement's ally.[97] This analysis shows that federal legislation, especially the Civil Rights Act of 1964, played a key role in providing greater economic opportunities and personal freedom for thousands of African Americans at the grass-roots level. While many federal officials may have held an ambivalent attitude to civil rights, the impact of the legislation that was passed was far-reaching and significant. It was the opportunity that Title VII of the Civil Rights Act provided for class-action litigation that was especially significant, as the lawsuits pushed the companies involved to improve their records and made others act to avoid litigation.

The Civil Rights Act played a crucial role in the racial integration of the textile industry, producing a new sense of confidence among African American workers across the Piedmont. Because of the act, many African Americans were encouraged to challenge discrimination for the first time, bringing lawsuits under Title VII of the act. This conclusion is especially significant because existing civil rights historiography has tended to concentrate far more upon the classic protests of the 1955–65 era rather than on the long-term impact of civil rights legislation.[98] When historians have ventured outside of this framework, the tendency has been to go back in time, searching for the origins of the civil rights protests, rather than to look at the broader impact of civil rights legislation on southern society. This study shows that the civil rights movement did not end with the legislative achievements of 1964–65. Rather, this legislation stimulated new protest and organization in an area of the South—the industrial Piedmont—that had not participated in the major protests between 1955 and 1964.[99]

This activism challenges existing notions about the timing of civil rights protest. Introduced in direct response to the Birmingham demonstrations, the 1964 Civil Rights Act is usually seen as the consequence of civil rights protest rather than the cause. The act's passage is often viewed as the ultimate success of nonviolent protest in pushing the federal government into action. After 1965, the year the act became effective, the civil rights movement was widely viewed as in decline. Indeed, C. Vann Woodward's 1966 essay, "What Happened to the Civil Rights Movement," already spoke of the era of protest in the past tense. Moreover, subsequent historians have largely come to the same conclusion that the era of protest ended in 1965.[100] In the textile industry, however, black workers mobilized after 1965 to make the mandate of the Civil Rights Act a reality, and they brought important class action lawsuits throughout the late 1960s and 1970s, a period not previously seen as one of significant civil rights activity.

For Quite Obvious Reasons, We Do Not Want to Fill These Mills Up with Negroes

The Attitudes of Textile Executives to Black Employment

three

In the last twenty years, historians have produced an impressive body of scholarship on the South's textile workers. A wide range of studies have concentrated on exploring the worker culture of southern textile communities and the reasons why unions never gained a foothold in the industry.[1] Despite this interest, no comparable body of literature has emerged about textile management. Historians have usually cited the lack of sources as the reason for the absence of literature about executives in the South's largest industry.[2]

One area that has been particularly neglected is the attitudes of textile managers to black employment. The integration of the industry did not mean that executives automatically welcomed black employment, as some recent accounts claim. The black influx into the industry has caused some historians to suggest that textile executives adjusted easily to federal civil rights laws. Mary Frederickson, for example, writes that "the relative ease with which Southern employers, generally a group intransigent in the face of federal mandates, responded to the regulations of the Equal Employment Opportunity Commission (EEOC) and the Office of Federal Contract Compliance reflected the industry's need for new workers and a growing reliance on black labor. Although a few supervisors had to be replaced, by 1969, the transition was over and management in most Southern textile communities feverishly sought to hire black workers."[3]

Although African Americans were hired in increasing numbers in the 1960s and 1970s, even printed sources such as the trade press indicate that textile executives had many intrinsic fears and reservations about the influx of black workers. Employers may have been hiring blacks, but they continually worried about control and expressed concern about the increasing numbers of blacks entering the industry. Textile executives also reacted badly to federal initiatives in equal employment, deeply resenting any moves by federal agencies to interfere with what they regarded as management prerogatives. As the federal government began to push for affirmative action for minorities rather than merely nondiscrimination, the resistance and anger of textile executives deepened, mirroring the stiffening of white resistance to affirmative action that took place across the country.[4] Only the records of the lawsuits, complemented by letters that textile executives wrote their political representatives, really provide an insight into managers' thoughts and fears. These records show that for many executives, the transition to black employment was certainly not over by 1969.

The lawsuits are a particularly valuable source because they forced company representatives to testify and answer awkward questions that the industry was reluctant to discuss in public. Indeed, the only public pronouncements made by the textile industry were positive press releases by employer associations, which tended to emphasize the successful entry of blacks into textiles. The lawsuits, however, required executives and supervisors to answer much more complex and specific questions about why blacks were locked into certain positions and why they had made particular complaints of discrimination in the workplace. As such, they reveal a great deal about the attitude of the textile industry toward civil rights.

The difference between the public pronouncements of the industry and the views revealed in court is well illustrated by the attitudes of lower-level management to promoting blacks. In public, the industry often claimed that it made clear to all its supervisors that they were expected to comply with the Civil Rights Act, and that those who disagreed with the law were forced to leave. The lawsuits show, however, that many, if not most, supervisors viewed black workers with condescension, and that these attitudes were often shared or tolerated by higher management. The lawsuits, together with the trade press, also show that textile executives deeply resented federal efforts to "impose" civil rights upon them, and that they held a number of fears and prejudices about black employment.[5]

The "They're Happy Where They Are" Defense

One of the most common arguments made by companies was that their black workers did not want to advance and were happy working in low-level jobs. In

Adams v. Dan River Mills, Wyllie Smyka, the superintendent of No. 1 Dye-house, was asked at the trial in 1973 to explain why all of the workers in the drug room, which was a nonproduction part of the dyehouse where workers handled chemicals, were black. He answered that blacks worked in the drug room "by choice": "They prefer to work in the drugroom because they have less responsibility and more free time." Smyka made these assertions despite admitting that the drug room was a "much more dirtier" job than machine operator and involved exposure to chemicals. Smyka, like other supervisors, tended to associate black departments with long-serving employees who were dependable but not promotable.[6]

Similar attitudes about African American workers were expressed by other supervisors. The department overseer of the No. 1 dyehouse, Norman Hall, claimed that the black workers in the drug room, who had been responsible for banding together and bringing the original *Adams* lawsuit, were neverthe-less not assertive enough to be promoted. Hall testified that James Shavers, the sole African American to work as a machine operator in No. 1 Dye throughout the 1960s, was not considered for promotion to supervisor because "Mr. Shavers seems to have, as a number of people have, found the level he would like to obtain." Hall thought this "because Mr. Shavers is a very congenial, happy person who seems to enjoy what he is doing."[7] Another supervisor, Fred S. Evans, claimed that to be promoted, blacks needed to have "shown some interest," but the drug room workers never gave him "any indication" that they were not satisfied with their jobs.[8]

These attitudes were not restricted simply to supervisors. Indeed, many of the same arguments were also used by Dan River's personnel manager, Robert Gardiner. The attitudes of supervisors were crucial because the company relied upon information from them when it drew up its affirmative action program. It was supervisors who told Gardiner that there were no "promotable minority employees" in their departments, as Dan River's affirmative action plan fre-quently put it. The plan defended the company's record on black promotion by asserting that "many minorities are content to remain on their present jobs."[9] Dan River's lawyers also utilized the argument that black workers were not interested in promotion as a central part of their defense in the *Adams* case.[10]

Management made similar claims in several other cases. In *Lewis v. J. P. Stevens*, the overseer in the maintenance department, Robert Cann, argued that blacks were not interested in promotions to his department: "None of them have been interested in shop work."[11] At Rock Hill Printing and Finishing Company, officials repeatedly argued that blacks were on the lowest-paying jobs by choice. Many managers had no real explanation for the existence of segregated departments but assumed that it reflected the workers' choice. They had clearly given little thought to the existence of job segregation but had just accepted it as the status quo.[12] In other mills, management was so isolated from the forces of racism facing black workers that many felt that any jobs from which blacks were excluded must be by their own choice, claiming that "the colored" were not interested in higher-paying textile jobs.[13]

TEAM records also show that the claim that blacks did not want to advance was one of the most frequent company defenses. From Cherokee County, South Carolina, for example, TEAM aide Juanita Harrison reported from a visit to the personnel manager of Hamrick and Musgrove Mills: "The information I received from Mr. Fulton was about the same as that of the rest of the personnel managers. Fulton said blacks did not seek advancement."[14]

In many cases, supervisors and other management officials bolstered their claim that blacks did not desire promotion by describing their closeness to the black workers they supervised. Many detailed their friendships with particular blacks as proof that *all* blacks were happy. Thus, in *Sherrill v. J. P. Stevens*, plant manager C. A. Rhyne cited his friendship with two brothers who had been offered higher-paying jobs but had refused. These black workers were clearly "Uncle Toms," and they even testified for the company in the case. Many managers described their closeness to their black friends with a fondness tinged with paternalism. Rhyne, for example, described how "there's not many days when I am there at Stanley that I don't talk to several black friends of mine real close."[15] Similarly, shift overseer Jack Human claimed that he had an open relationship with the blacks who worked for him, and that they never expressed any desire for promotion: "I talked to them on the job. We talk about the black situation and everything else. I'm pretty open with my black people. I don't hide nothing from them."[16]

The closeness that supervisors had to such workers helped to convince management that militant black workers who demanded promotions were unrepresentative and should not be encouraged. Thus, in *Sherrill*, Rhyne described how black workers he was close to had told him that the main plaintiff, A. C. Sherrill, "doesn't represent them."[17] Indeed, companies frequently tried to portray the black workers who had initiated lawsuits as agitators or troublemakers who did not fit in and were not representative of race relations in the plant as a whole. In *Sherrill*, overseer Jack Human claimed that Sherrill had fitted in until "he started talking about black Afro history and all that stuff. I don't know anything about that. I don't know about American history, let alone Afro. That was the situation there."[18] In *Adams v. Dan River Mills*, manager Donald Aichner claimed that lead plaintiff Julious Adams was a troublemaker who "had a chip on his shoulder."[19]

Many companies also argued that the traditional exclusion of blacks from the industry reflected the fact that blacks were not interested in *any* textile jobs. Instead of placing any blame on the industry, company officials argued that it was African Americans themselves who had little interest in taking textile jobs. One plant manager, for example, claimed that his company had always been open to black employment, but that "for years we couldn't get colored people to put in any applications." The manager believed that integration had started because blacks had a different attitude: "We didn't necessarily have a change. The blacks had the change."[20]

This argument often held that African Americans had traditionally had little interest in competing with whites for textile jobs and were "happy" to work on the land rather than in industry. In *Sledge v. J. P. Stevens*, James B. Miller, the company's personnel director, stated: "I think that in past years that blacks have not sought the jobs particularly in the textile mills, they've not come after the jobs, that they have not been applying to us, whereas whites were."[21] Later in the trial, Edwin Akers, a high-ranking company official who had been active in textile management since 1935, made a similar argument when he asserted that before the 1960s, blacks "did not come in large numbers seeking employment and competing with the whites for these jobs." Blacks did not want textile jobs because they were occupied in the agricultural sector.[22] Thus, as Akers put it, "the whites got an earlier start" because "the Negro did not come in and compete for these jobs."[23]

The company's attorney Whiteford Blakeney summarized Stevens's defense in the *Sledge* trial with this argument. Continuing Akers's analogy, Blakeney described the position of white and black workers at J. P. Stevens as a race uphill to the better, high-paying jobs: "White people got started on the track first. . . . [W]hites came in volume; they wanted the jobs." Blacks did not take part in the race, not because they were not allowed to, but because they knew they could not win: "The Negroes didn't compete because they knew they couldn't win in the competition for the jobs. For reasons of qualification. I repeat, the company wasn't saying to the Negro, 'It's no use for you to try, you can't have it.' They weren't saying that to him. But the Negro said to himself, 'I can't win the job and I know I can't. I know that those white people are there, scores and hundreds, seeking the jobs, and if I go there, I'm not going to win out in that competition. They are more qualified than I to do it and I know it.'"[24]

The "They're Not Qualified" Defense

Another argument that companies used to explain the concentration of African Americans in the lowest-paying jobs was that blacks were not as well qualified as whites and hence could not fill the higher positions. Companies repeatedly argued that whites had superior training, education, and work experience to blacks. In *Lewis v. J. P. Stevens*, company representatives stuck doggedly to this line of reasoning throughout an extensive trial. When asked what was responsible for clear racial disparities in job assignments among male workers, Boyce E. Crocker, the company's group training director, replied, "I would say probably experience."[25] In 1975, overseer Robert L. Cann testified that a black worker had never reached the level of machinist or electrician in the maintenance department "because we've never had one qualified to promote." The highest ranking African American in the department had not been promoted because "he wasn't ready for it." In an argument also heard elsewhere, Cann claimed that most blacks did not stick to the job long enough to get promotions.[26] As in many other cases, the company used the qualifications argument to dismiss the plaintiffs' data showing pay and hiring disparities: "Upon analysis, it would seem that disregard of job qualifications is a central fallacy at the bottom of both of the plaintiffs' statistical approaches."[27]

The qualifications argument was a natural extension of the claim that blacks had traditionally shown little interest in competing for textile jobs. Thus, in *Sledge v. J. P. Stevens*, the company argued that because whites had sought textile jobs, they now had the qualifications that blacks lacked. Whites had taken textile jobs and had built up a reservoir of experience, whereas blacks had preferred to stay on the land and therefore did not develop the qualifications for these jobs. Companies felt that they did not discriminate by hiring whites; they had simply hired the more qualified applicants. Companies also argued that as white workers began to leave the textile industry in the 1960s when other higher-paying industries moved into the South, more blacks were hired because of a shortage of qualified workers. The lawsuits were therefore unnecessary because new opportunities were opening up for blacks through the operation of the labor market. As Blakeney concluded in the 1972 trial, "Now, today, the whites have quit coming there to get into that race, as they once did. They don't come in the volume they did. Why? They've gone on to higher paying industries. . . . The Negro is better able to compete today and he realizes that and he comes in greater and greater volume. And we hire him in greater and greater volume." Companies emphasized statistics showing the rapid increase in black entry into the workforce to prove Blakeney's claim about more opportunities for African Americans.[28]

Companies laid great stress on the fact that African American workers, because of their exclusion from the industry before the 1960s, had not had the chance to gain previous textile experience. Many companies argued that such experience was vital. In *Adams v. Dan River Mills*, for example, the company argued that racial disparities in hiring rates were "quickly erased when viewed in light of the statistical data relating to the experience, or lack thereof, of those individuals hired." The company produced its own statistics showing that between January 1, 1969, and May 31, 1971, 67.4 percent of whites hired had previous textile experience, compared to 50.8 percent of blacks. The plaintiffs asserted that this reliance on previous experience was not an objective hiring criterion, but the company claimed that "there is nothing vague or subjective about relying upon previous experience." Dan River repeatedly argued that whites occupied higher-paying jobs than blacks because they had better qualifications: "Those white male employees who gain the highest paying jobs do so for the very logical reason that they have prior experience in a particular job."[29]

As part of their defense that blacks were not as well qualified as whites for textile jobs, companies tried to argue that blacks had failed to compete for those jobs purely out of choice. In developing this argument, however, companies often showed how subtle forms of discrimination had operated in many textile communities to ensure that whites were better qualified. Indeed, the lawsuits offered a revealing look at the forces that kept blacks locked out of the textile industry until the 1960s. In a number of cases, for example, it was established that white high schools ran textile training classes as part of their curriculum, often using equipment given by the local textile company. Black high schools never offered such training. In *Sledge v. J. P. Stevens*, the role that the school system played in perpetuating black exclusion from textiles was explored in the testimony of long-serving company official Edwin Akers. Akers claimed that whites were better qualified for textile jobs because the local white high school had a "textile department" operated by a former dean of the textile school at North Carolina State University. As a result, Akers explained, "many of our employees who are white got their training in the schools and this kind of background which gave them greater skills for the technical operations of our plant; the textile department in our high school had a course in textile design, it had looms and other machines in the high school so that people could learn to operate these machines while still in high school. . . . Many of our employees grew up in Roanoke Rapids, went to these schools and therefore had a better opportunity to perform well on these jobs." Federal judge Franklin T. Dupree Jr., finding the information "interesting," questioned Akers further about the schools, bringing a frank admission from Akers that the company had contributed to the inequality of the segregated school system in Roanoke Rapids:

Dupree: Were any of these educational facilities available to blacks?
Akers: No, sir.
Dupree: What about the black schools, did they have comparable facilities?
Akers: No, they did not have comparable facilities.
Dupree: You say then they were not only separate but unequal?
Akers: Yes, they were.[30]

Under further questioning from Dupree, Akers added that the company had provided the textile equipment to the white high school free of charge. He claimed that no equipment had been given to the black high school because they had not asked for it, although it was unclear whether the white high school had asked for it either.[31] As late as 1962, J. P. Stevens also gave organized plant tours to local white high school students but not to blacks.[32]

The qualifications argument was often used as a way of justifying the lack of African Americans in supervisory and white-collar jobs. To defend their failure to promote African Americans into white-collar and clerical jobs, textile companies usually argued that there were no blacks qualified for these positions. In *Adams v. Dan River Mills*, personnel manager Robert Gardiner claimed that the company had no black departmental overseers because "it takes a lot of know-how to be over a department in these plants, because all of them are very large, and it is a very complicated situation."[33] Executives often argued that even African Americans with the relevant qualifications were not as well qualified as whites, and many supervisors claimed that blacks lacked the educational qualifications to hold higher-paying jobs in the textile industry.[34]

Textile companies also used the qualifications argument as a way of defending themselves against racial quotas. Thus, in *Sledge v. J. P. Stevens*, the company's attorney Whiteford Blakeney rejected the suggestion that blacks should be hired in proportion to how many applied on the grounds that this ignored the qualifications of applicants: "To direct that you hire people on the basis that they apply rigidly without reference to whether you regard them as in any way qualified, that you can use the qualifications standard for the whites but you can't for the blacks, you have got to hire them on the basis if they are there physically present. That's wrong because it ignores qualification." Seeking to defend the company from the persuasive argument that most textile jobs could be learned by the inexperienced, Blakeney asserted that companies must be allowed to choose on the basis of qualifications: "But, Your Honor, people knock on the door who may be in no way qualified for hiring. The lame . . . and the blind can knock on the door. People who haven't got qualifications to do anything can apply. . . . Qualifications, even meager, even rudimentary qualifications are entitled to be considered. . . . Qualifications is what should guide us, and therefore, what should guide courts too. Some of the courts get away from it. Many put quotas on it. . . . This court doesn't have to do that. We ask you not to."[35]

This stress on qualifications carried with it the assumption that blacks did not make as good textile workers as whites, a belief that was held across the textile industry by white managers and workers. Thus, Blakeney added that the company was already moving blacks into jobs "without much regard to whether they qualify, that's without a sufficient regard. In other words, if the company operated, as they tell me, strictly on efficiency, they wouldn't be moving the blacks as fast as they are now moving them because—That's not true of all of them, of course." Blakeney said that he was told by Stevens's supervisors that "the efficiency of the company's operation is suffering" because of their determined efforts to hire and promote blacks.[36]

The qualifications argument was frequently used in the *Sledge* case to defend the company's right to hire and promote based solely upon its own judgment. The plaintiffs argued, and the court found, that Stevens's reliance solely on the subjective judgment of its supervisors with regard to hiring and promotion was discriminatory. Blakeney, however, argued that the company must retain its "right to manage." Not for the first time, he described any application of objective rules as stifling management enterprise: "Casey Stengel never won all those pennants putting people up to bat on seniority. He put them up to bat on qualifications. To say that anything—that you can run any human enterprise on something that works mechanically, woodenly, on a prescribed happening such as seniority . . . it can't be that way, Your Honor. It never can be. The human mind has got to be into the picture somehow, and to some extent. Otherwise you would abolish management. You wouldn't have anybody to run the enterprise."[37]

"We Didn't Hire Any Niggers"

The racial attitudes revealed by textile management in the lawsuits pose important questions about how mill owners viewed the issue of civil rights. Because textiles was the largest southern industry and textile managers comprised a significant part of the South's white power structure, their reactions to the civil rights movement are particularly significant.

While many supervisors expressed views during the lawsuits that were tinged with racism, in some cases company officials used openly racist language during legal proceedings. In *Ellison v. Rock Hill Printing and Finishing Company*, Jerry McKinsey, who was the divisional superintendent of the printing department, testified in 1972 that blacks began to be hired in the printing department in nontraditional jobs after the passage of the Civil Rights Act:

Q: Prior to that was there a policy of not hiring blacks in the Print Department in jobs other than color box washers and janitors?
A: That's right. We didn't hire any niggers.
Q: Didn't hire any what?
A: Any black men.
Q: Prior to 1964 or '65?
A: Yes.[38]

In *Hall v. Werthan Bag*, a class action lawsuit involving a textile company based in Nashville, Tennessee, the plaintiffs' African American attorney stormed out of a deposition hearing after the company's attorney had repeatedly used the pronunciation "nigra" in his questions to the plaintiff. The offended attorney, Avon N. Williams, claimed that he did not "intend to stay here and submit to insults." He later explained that "use of the word 'nigra' in this area is commonly intended and is taken as a slurring and insulting corruption of the word 'Negro.'" The company's attorney "did not so much wish to discover evidence as he did to insist upon his 'prerogative' as a white man to refer to Negroes in the presence of Negroes in any way he pleased."[39]

Other written records provide many more examples of textile managers using racist language. Mordecai Johnson described one company in Union County, South Carolina, which employed very few blacks. Writing in August 1968, Johnson reported that the company's personnel manager "has a practice of hiring a few Negroes and then saying, 'tell the Niggers there are no more jobs, no more Niggers are being hired today.' This company hires many whites."[40]

The opposition of many textile executives to civil rights was vividly illustrated in letters written to their political representatives. The papers of political leaders show that scores of textile manufacturers expressed their opposition to the Civil Rights Bill and other civil rights initiatives. North Carolina senator Samuel Ervin, for example, received over thirty letters from textile executives between June 27, 1963, and July 8, 1964, the period when the Civil Rights Bill was being debated. All of these urged Ervin to oppose the bill, which he did. In a typical letter, one executive from Neisler Mills in Kings Mountain, North Carolina, wrote, "I would like to express my opposition to the Civil Rights Bill. Under the guise of protecting the civil rights of the Negro citizen, the bill will, in my opinion, destroy the civil rights of all the citizens of the United States."[41] Typical of the strong backing that textile executives gave Ervin, one manufacturer wrote, "I admire you greatly and support you 100% in your opposition to the Civil Rights Bill."[42]

The companies that wrote letters of support to Ervin included major textile corporations such as J. P. Stevens, Burlington Industries, Cone Mills, and Cannon Mills. One "employment supervisor" from J. P. Stevens wrote, "I personally appreciate your stand on the Civil Rights Bill and your method of opposing same."[43] It was, indeed, common for mill executives to praise Ervin's stand against the federal government and the Kennedy brothers, who were described in particularly negative terms. C. Almon McIver of a textile company in Burlington, North Carolina, wrote with praise: "It is high time that the Kennedy boys sat back and listened to a MAN speak."[44] Another executive added, "You are doing a fine job of showing Robert Kennedy up. Lots of people over the State tell me how thankful they are that you are fighting our battle against the Kennedys."[45]

The most common argument used by executives was that the federal government had no right to tell them how to run their business. As one manufacturer asserted, "I dont care whether a negro is eating in the same dining area where I am or not. Also, I feel strongly that he has a right to vote, if he has any intelligence at all. On the other hand I certainly dont think that our country should follow the dictator plan of having the state tell people where they will work and wont work."[46] Many claimed that the bill, especially Title VII, usurped states' rights. One manufacturer, for example, called the bill the "Federal Dictatorial Bill."[47]

Similar letters were written to political representatives in South Carolina. Textile manufacturers there also used the states' rights argument in opposing the Civil Rights Bill, mixed with a strong dislike of federal interference. J. J. Norton Jr., of Pacolet Mills, wrote in March 1964, "This Bill with its unparalleled and punitive powers would eliminate in its entirety the basic concept of State rights."[48] Another manufacturer claimed that the Civil Rights Bill was "leading this bountiful nation down the road to socialism where the government owns and operates all businesses and determines every person's life and bondage."[49]

Most textile executives also fervently opposed any efforts to increase the powers of the EEOC, especially when a 1967 bill proposed giving the EEOC judicial powers similar to those held by the National Labor Relations Board (NLRB). A manager from West Point Pepperell urged South Carolina congressman William Jennings Bryan Dorn to oppose a "restrictive" bill that would have increased the powers of the EEOC.[50] Many textile companies argued that they were making progress in minority employment, so there was no need for further pressure by the federal government.[51] Companies claimed that the industry was making "great progress," but that this progress could not "be forced or rushed to a great degree." A typical view, as expressed by one textile manufacturer, was that "voluntary efforts on the part of business will accomplish more significant results than increased federal controls."[52]

Many companies opposed federal involvement both as a principle and because they feared its practical implications. On principle, management invoked their "right to manage" and claimed that if the federal government infringed on this right, it would have the practical effect of mills losing their efficiency and profitability. As one director of industrial relations put it, strengthening the EEOC "could in my opinion open a whole new field of harassment and possible interference with basic management rights and the efficient operation of our plants." The large Deering-Milliken Company opposed the strengthening of the EEOC because "it would create another government agency that would rob management of its right to manage."[53] Other executives argued that further government intervention would interfere with "the efficient operation of our plants."[54]

Companies expressed these fears about efficiency partly because they felt that the EEOC was a biased, liberal agency on a "mission" to interfere and tell them how to run their businesses. John G. Wellman, the president of a large South Carolina textile company, wrote to Dorn in 1970 that he was opposed to the EEOC because it wanted to tell employers who they had to hire and promote. EEOC investigations were a "grotesque ceremony" aimed at carrying out the commission's "affirmative program." A manager of a J. P. Stevens plant claimed that they were trying to comply with the Civil Rights Act "as far as is practical," but they did not want to be judged by the EEOC—"a dictatorial group"—if there was a "minor infraction."[55]

Business fears of the EEOC and of federal "harassment" were expressed well by a lengthy correspondence from executives of the Graniteville Company. The vice president of the company claimed that the EEOC was "politically conceived and motivated" and sat in "biased judgment" over textile companies. No matter how hard they tried, they argued, it was impossible to please such a body. Typical of the apocalyptic tone of many letters, Graniteville executives claimed that granting the EEOC extra powers would mean that "American industry will sink even further into the quagmire which promises to bring disaster to American free enterprise and thereby to the economic stability of our nation." If the EEOC was given greater powers, "American industry will be faced with a pugnacious agency riding piggy-back with Title VII of the Civil Rights Act which has been so liberally interpreted as to make it ridiculous."[56]

Letters written by textile executives to political leaders reveal a common mentality in the southern textile industry. It is striking how little divergence there was in the letters. The vast majority of companies expressed the same opinions, used the same arguments, and wrote their letters at the same time. The letters suggest that the industry acted in a unified manner on racial questions, just as it had traditionally done in setting wage patterns and in fighting to maintain high tariffs on textile products. Textile firms also rallied around when one of their own was attacked. The unionization campaign against J. P. Stevens conducted throughout the 1960s and 1970s, for example, drew widespread industry criticism of the union and support for the company's position. Dorn himself was a regular correspondent with J. P. Stevens's president, Robert Stevens, and he called the union campaign "this diabolical and sinister scheme of the AFL-CIO to destroy the great image of your company and your dedicated employees." The president of Mayfair Mills, a South Carolina textile company, summed up the mood of many other manufacturers when he wrote, "There is no more devoted American citizen than Robert T. Stevens, and he deserves all of our support."[57]

It is clear that textile executives cooperated closely over the issue of integration. The *Charlotte Observer* reported that shortly before the passage of the Civil Rights Act, a "confidential strategy paper" was circulated among South Carolina textile executives advising them of the best ways of handling the integration of their plants. The report, prepared by the South Carolina State Committee for Technical Education, played a key role in helping manufacturers to overcome their fears about integration. It pointed out, for example, that companies could use the entry of blacks to get more production by encouraging competition between the races on the production line: "One does not want to be outdone by the other, for the Negro wants to prove himself and the white does not want to be outperformed." The use of paper cups, which was later reported in a number of plants, originated in the report as a means of avoiding confrontation over the integration of facilities. The report also revealed much about management fears of black militancy and government pressure when it suggested that blacks hired should be spread out across the mill because "this decreases the demands of the Negroes, decreases the risk of unionization, and more adequately satisfies government inspectors."[58]

In a 1970 article exploring the racial integration of the textile industry, *Newsweek* also stressed the role that the report had played in overcoming executives' fears about black employment. Indeed, the report's main conclusion, made with an air of scientific discovery, was that blacks could make good production workers: "It has been found that the Negro is capable of producing both qualitatively and quantitatively as well as any white worker."[59]

The company records of Dan River Mills also show that southern textile companies cooperated closely with one another when they introduced African Americans into the workforce, exchanging a great deal of information and advice about the safest methods of integrating their plants. This pattern of collusion is especially revealing because the textile industry was an intensely competitive industry. Such cooperation occurred, moreover, between companies that were unionized, such as Dan River, and those that were stridently anti-union, such as J. P. Stevens and Burlington Industries. Thus, the Dan River records provide a valuable insight both into management strategy during integration and also into the amount of white resistance that the introduction of black workers caused.

Companies shared information on compliance reviews, on how they dealt with federal regulations, and on the status of integration in each other's plants. It was common for companies facing compliance reviews to contact Dan River to ask if executives there were familiar with the Defense Supply Agency (DSA) representative who would be visiting them. An official of Pacific Mills, for example, wrote Dan River in 1961 wanting to "find out more about this inspector at Dan River, including his name, what kind of person he is, and anything else you can tell me about him. Thanks for calling me today." Companies also carefully monitored the reaction of their white employees to integration and circulated this information. As Frank Talbott told Malcolm Cross concerning one such communication from Fieldcrest Mills, "It is always helpful to know what other people are doing. This is for your confidential file if you want to keep it."[60]

"The Carolinas' Textile Industry Is to Be Singled Out as a Whipping Boy"

The letters written by textile executives to political representatives reflected the fact that mill owners disliked federal initiatives into equal employment. The textile trade press, in particular, adopted an uncompromising stance of opposition toward the federal government's civil rights initiatives throughout the 1960s. Indeed, it is possible to observe attitudes of resistance and hostility to the federal government through the 1960s and beyond. This attitude can be identified from the industry's reaction to President Kennedy's nondiscrimination Executive Order 10925 in 1961, through the Civil Rights Act of 1964, the EEOC textile forum of 1967, and the legal cases of the mid-1960s on.

When President Kennedy's 1961 order was passed, for example, one trade paper, *America's Textile Reporter*, reported that the industry was very concerned about being required to comply with the order. The paper reflected the mistrust and suspicion with which mill owners generally viewed the federal government. Some owners even questioned whether the order was "President Kennedy's way of inducing sections of the textile industry to return to his home state of Massachusetts." Others felt that Secretary of Labor Arthur Goldberg, a former union attorney, was behind the order "as an effort to put a new group of workers in Southern textile mills who might be more receptive to the blandishments of union organizers than the tough-minded people who now work there."[61]

The 1961 executive order prohibiting racial discrimination among government contractors marked the beginning of resistance by many mills to federal equal employment initiatives. Some mills refused to bid on government contracts following the order because they did not want to comply with the nondiscrimination provisions.[62] Reaffirming their argument that nondiscrimination was impossible because of southern cultural mores, *America's Textile Reporter* claimed that the only way to ensure a continued supply of textiles for government orders was to order from Japan or "send troops into Southern mills to prevent race riots." In the trade press, mill management continually asserted that integration was impossible because of the opposition of white workers: "Mill management might be willing to go along with the new regulations but putting Negroes to work in spinning and weaving jobs could result in many white workers walking off their jobs."[63]

Despite the passage of the Civil Rights Act in 1964, some companies simply refused to integrate. The 1967 textile forum established that all-white plants remained quite common throughout the 1960s.[64] A TWUA report from Crown Cotton Mills in Dalton, Georgia, described how there were still "no Negroes employed" in December 1966. The report described the attitude of the management as "silence. 'They would prefer not to discuss the subject.'"[65] Even when integration did occur, it did not happen uniformly. Thus, many reports described the attitude of management as "dubious" or "reluctant."[66] A TWUA report from 1964 found that while some companies had started to integrate, others, especially those in Alabama, had made "no change."[67]

It is clear that in many cases, top-level management intensely disliked making the first moves toward integration, as the Civil Rights Act required. At the large Cannon Mills in Kannapolis, North Carolina, the company employed almost no black workers until the 1960s, and they were hired only "to heave cotton on the loading dock and do unskilled maintenance." Cromwell Russell was one of the first blacks to work inside the plant when he was transferred from his job on the loading deck. The *New York Times* reported that "'Old Man Cannon,' meaning Charles Cannon, the last family member to run the company, used to always chat with him on the loading deck. But, Mr. Russell said, the boss never spoke to him again after he moved inside."[68]

It was the fact that some mills made no efforts to comply with the Civil Rights Act that made many of the lawsuits necessary. Attorney James Ferguson, for example, remembered: "Now once the act was passed, nothing much happened. It was only the filing of lawsuits to implement the change, as we call it Title VII, to implement Title VII, that made the difference there." Most textile companies "instead of looking for ways to comply were looking for ways to avoid compliance or to do only minimum compliance."[69]

The industry's hostility to federal interference was further illustrated by its reaction to the EEOC textile forum that took place in Charlotte, North Carolina, in January 1967. Although invited to participate, industry executives boycotted the meeting and sat in the public gallery taking notes. The industry argued that the forum would only serve to damage its reputation because civil rights and union leaders were being allowed to take part and "put the textile industry on the block as a discriminating industry." The ATMI stated that "such 'town hall' sessions can encourage unfounded and irresponsible accusations which might do serious damage to the harmonious relationships which now exist in the industry." When civil rights leaders did criticize the industry, the trade press referred to the forum as "the Charlotte slugfest."[70]

When the EEOC announced plans after the forum to make textiles its first target "to win better jobs for Negroes," the industry claimed that it was being victimized for failing to participate in the forum. The industry felt that the federal government was forcing it into unrealistic progress and was trying to "disrupt the harmony of orderly compliance that has been the rule . . . in the Textile South since the Civil Rights Act was passed." The EEOC's idea of compliance reminded the industry of "old Russian Secret Police actions and even the German Gestapo."[71]

Textile companies disliked federal interference partly because they felt that the government was forcing them to hire unqualified blacks. Stressing again that blacks had inferior qualifications, the *Southern Textile News* reported in 1966 that the current labor shortage had forced the industry to employ more blacks, but that many had been rejected "because these workers simply couldn't do the job." The industry claimed that blacks could not be upgraded into white-collar jobs, as the federal government wished, because they were not even qualified for many blue-collar positions: "If a person can't pass the intelligence tests to qualify as a sweeper—how can you make a spinner, knitter or weaver out of him? That's what it amounts to. And all the commissions in the Washington bureaucracy can't change it. The textile business isn't like the bureaucrat business. To hold a job making yarn or cloth, you've got to be able to do the work. There's no skating by on someone else's abilities."[72]

The firm belief that they were not discriminating led companies to feel that the federal government was picking on them when it tried to enforce compliance. The case of *United States v. Southern Weaving*, for example, which was brought against the company by the EEOC, reflected typical company arguments about being unfairly treated by federal officials who had unrealistic goals of racial progress. The company argued that "Southern Weaving has been picked out as an example" and claimed that because it had hired one African American woman since the filing of the suit, the whole case was "much to do about nothing."[73] Similarly, in *Graniteville Company v. EEOC*, the company argued that the EEOC was pursuing unspecified charges, launching a "carte blanc fishing expedition against an employer." They claimed that the charge "was prepared with a shotgun launching a fishing expedition by an agent of the EEOC."[74]

In April 1967, James P. Wilson and Horace Hill, two leading executives of Leaksville Woolen Mills in Leaksville, North Carolina, sent a telegram to Senator Ervin to protest the EEOC's emphasis on the textile industry. Expressing the views of many other executives, they claimed that "the Carolinas' textile industry is to be singled out as a whipping boy for investigation and persecution by the commission." The executives argued that it was wrong for the EEOC to concentrate attention on the textile industry, because the industry had made "sincere and effective efforts" to comply with the Civil Rights Act. Ervin sympathized with the men's fears, claiming that he was "strongly opposed" to Title VII of the Civil Rights Act because it placed business under "the subjective regimentation of the Federal bureaucracy."[75]

Company alienation from federal investigations, however, was best expressed by the management of Southerland Dyeing and Finishing Mills in Mebane, North Carolina. In 1966, the EEOC upheld complaints of racial discrimination at the mill. The federal agency found that African American workers made less money than their white counterparts, with blacks restricted to the lower-paying jobs.[76] However, the company's president, Frank Southerland, claimed that the entire investigation was "nothing but a farce, to say the least."[77] He added, "It is my understanding that the Fair Employment Act was for the purpose of advancement of the negro race. I do not think that this can be accomplished through harassment of employers, by unfair investigation of this type." Southerland sent all the details of the EEOC investigation to Senator Ervin with a covering note that simply read, "This is the junk that we have to put up with."[78] Ervin sympathized with the company's position, writing, "I deeply regret the difficult burden that is placed on fine productive enterprises, such as yours, by Title VII of the 1964 Civil Rights Act."[79]

Many textile executives felt that the industry was put under undue pressure by federal officials who failed to understand that the industry's ability to integrate was itself restricted by the opposition of white textile workers to black advancement. Across the South, executives complained that they were pulled in different directions by pressure from both the federal government, on the one hand, and their own white workers who resisted black advancement, on the other. As one mill owner asked about black employment in 1965 responded, "I've got the Ku Klux Klan on one side and the Federal Government on the other. For God's sake don't start a squeeze."[80]

Executives' Fears of Black Employment

While the written record establishes that textile management was strongly opposed to federal efforts to enforce civil rights, it is important to look more closely at the reasons for this opposition and to examine why textile executives feared a large-scale increase in black employment.

Textile managers had a number of deep-seated fears about black employment. One of their biggest concerns was the creation of a majority black workforce, and they feared that the government, by pressing for hiring the percentage of blacks in the community, would force this to happen. Companies worried that implementing equal employment opportunity would result in a black takeover of the industry, causing white workers, whom they regarded as their best employees, to leave the industry in droves. An investigator who met with Louis Hipp, the personnel director of Burlington Industries in 1967, reported that "Mr. Hipp voiced grave concern over what he calls the 'chock full-o-nuts' phenomenon. If the government expects companies to hire Negroes on a ratio similar to the ratio living in the community, there would probably be a point, he said, at which white women especially would no longer work in the plants. The white men would leave at or near this same point." Companies regarded 25 percent as the "breaking point" in this regard, and a desire to stay well below this level had "caused some serious questioning of how fast companies are willing to move."[81]

Many textile executives described racial integration as a process that was happening too fast, pushed along by the pressures of the labor market and the federal government. They felt out of control, unable to stem the influx of blacks as they wished. They feared that they would be unable to stop their nightmare of a predominantly black workforce from coming true. In 1969, a manager at Burlington Industries told one investigator about "the unfortunate circumstances that may result in having an all Negro labor force even though it cannot be avoided, even if the industry wanted to do so. Most employers with whom I have talked have indicated that the labor market is simply Negro women today and even if they wanted to do something about not hiring Negroes they wouldn't be able to do so."[82]

Other companies repeatedly expressed the same fears as Burlington. Indeed, Robert W. Armstrong, the director of public relations for the ATMI, admitted in 1970 that, across the industry, "there is still some fear that the industry will eventually become virtually all Negro, especially in the production job categories." Mill owners worried that this would lead to "employee and community resentment."[83] At Fieldcrest Mills in 1969, the company anticipated problems in the future "as plants become more heavily Negro."[84]

The company records of Dan River Mills indicate that keeping the percentage of black workers down was a major concern of the company. The top management of the company wanted to restrict the large-scale employment of blacks because they did not want the company to become dominated by African Americans, to achieve a reputation as a place where large numbers of blacks worked. As Robert Gardiner wrote in March 1969, "We are still not hiring or are rejecting Negroes because we do not wish the percentage to get too high. I frankly do not see any answer to this problem because, for quite obvious reasons, we do not want to fill these mills up with Negroes." This desire to keep the percentage down meant that, inevitably, capable blacks were turned down from departments where the company thought that enough visible progress was being made, or where they felt the DSA and other government agencies would not exert pressure. Thus, in February 1968, one black female applicant, who was described as "intelligent, 5 feet 4 inches tall with nice appearance and good work attitude," was turned down for the job of winder tender by being told "We have been instructed not to hire anymore colored employees at this time." According to the department head, however, his department "did not really turn this girl down for her color but were just trying to keep the percentage of colored as low as possible without creating an imbalance in this division."[85]

A related fear of textile management was that the increased hiring of African Americans would alienate white workers, who would leave the industry if they saw black workers entering higher-paying jobs. Companies feared that this would damage the efficiency of their plants because the black workforce had less textile experience than the white. In *Sledge v. J. P. Stevens*, for example, the company's attorney Whiteford Blakeney claimed that the adoption of job quotas "will indeed alienate the white people in the plant. . . . Whites have waited, served, worked, they have asked. . . . If they see blacks leaping over them or gaining advantage and promotions which they never have had . . . if they see much of that, if Your Honor doesn't believe that will harm the operation of a plant, then Your Honor doesn't know the practicalities of a plant. It is true it will harm it and harm it greatly."[86] Blakeney added that the vital questions were "efficiency, morale of employees, reactions of employees." He argued on these grounds that it was impossible for the company to give African Americans the same hiring opportunities as whites: "If we went to hire at the rate of the blacks knocking on the door, we wouldn't have white employees long."[87]

Another fear of textile companies was that increasing the representation of African American workers would lead to more unionization. Given that the industry was only around 10 percent unionized in the 1960s, this was a serious concern of most companies. Burlington executive Robert Lincks remembered that in the 1960s, "probably one of the greatest fears of textile management was that the more blacks you have in your workforce, the higher the danger of unionization, and as you know the industry is traditionally nonunion, and let's say staunchly so. And everybody was saying, 'You know if you bring these blacks in, they'll vote for the union.'"[88] As Clarence E. Elsas of Fulton Cotton Mills in Atlanta told the AFSC in 1962, he was reluctant to hire too many blacks because he wanted a nonunion mill: "The shop is non-union and he hopes it will continue so. The introduction of Negroes at higher occupational levels, he fears, would be an open invitation to labor agitation."[89]

Many mills visited by researcher Richard Rowan in 1969 expressed the concern that hiring more blacks would increase the prospects of unionization. At the large Bibb Mills in 1969, for example, management reported the common belief that "Negroes are more prone to join unions."[90] Similarly, another textile executive declared in the same year that "they have been advised by their labor lawyers that the more Negroes that are hired the greater the potential for unionization."[91]

Textile Companies' Concepts of Affirmative Action and Civil Rights Compliance

Not surprisingly, textile manufacturers' concerns about black employment were reflected in the hostile attitudes that their companies exhibited toward affirmative action and civil rights compliance. Many textile companies made little effort to implement affirmative action plans and held a very limited definition of what constituted affirmative action. Numerous lawsuits revealed that such plans were merely window dressing. In *Lewis v. J. P. Stevens*, for example, it was established that company officials responsible for administering the plan had done very little to implement it because they held the typical attitude that they did not discriminate, and hence there was no need for any action. Thus, Richard R. Rice, the personnel manager and equal employment opportunity coordinator under the plan, claimed that he had not identified any "problem" areas for affirmative action, as the plan specified, because there were none. He testified that he had never noticed any major discrepancy between black and white applicant/hire ratios, even though white women were approximately four times as likely to be hired as black women. When confronted with these statistics, Rice argued that they did not mean anything, reasserting the company's "qualifications" argument: "These are numbers, statistics. They are numbers, and it doesn't treat each person as an individual as far as experience and qualifications for jobs."[92]

Dan River Mills and J. P. Stevens developed affirmative action plans in 1969 only because they were threatened with losing government contracts, and it is clear that these companies made little real effort to implement affirmative action. One ACTWU attorney who analyzed Stevens's plan and data, for example, wrote that "I have studied the Affirmative Action Programs filed by the Company for these plants and am of the opinion that they merely give lip service to a policy of Equal Employment Opportunity." Indeed, Stevens was found guilty of practicing widespread discrimination in *Sledge* and *Sherrill* while its affirmative action plan was in place.[93] In *Adams v. Dan River Mills*, it was also made clear in the 1974 trial that the company had "substantially failed to meet its goals under the Affirmative Action Plan" of 1969. In the first six months of the operation of the plan, Dan River failed to attain even 10 percent of the goals stated for the first year. Many of the people in key positions to meet targets were never made aware they existed.[94]

In *Sherrill v. J. P. Stevens*, the testimony of black workers and of supervisors indicated that the company had not successfully communicated the need for affirmative action in its plants. In 1973, indeed, many black workers were unaware that the company even had an affirmative action plan, although the company claimed that it had informed all black workers of its policy.[95] Some of the supervisors and superintendents in *Sherrill* also admitted that they had never read the company's affirmative action plan or talked about it with the black workers they supervised.[96] Many supervisors saw no need for affirmative action because they believed the company was already making a lot of progress in race relations. Riley Skidmore, for example, thought the company's record on the treatment of blacks was "good" because "we have blacks."[97]

Many managers held the perception that race relations were improving because they saw blacks entering an industry that had previously been lily white. They concentrated on the increasing representation of blacks in the total workforce, overlooking the issue of which jobs blacks were distributed in. For plaintiffs, this was the key issue, because African Americans tended to be concentrated in the worst jobs. Across the South, civil rights workers complained that companies saw no need for black upgrading. TEAM's Mordecai Johnson, for example, reported in 1968 that companies were giving blacks "the bad jobs," and that "the breakthrough must be in Negro upgrading."[98] John C. Cauthen, the vice president of the South Carolina Textile Manufacturers' Association, however, wrote Johnson emphasizing the overall increase in black employment, adding, "We are quite proud of the very large increases in Negro employment in the industry."[99]

The wide difference between the plaintiffs' and the companies' concepts of civil rights compliance was often reflected in arguments over the use of statistics. The plaintiffs' attorneys attempted to use pay disparity statistics as their main method of proving discrimination, an approach that companies consistently refuted the validity of. In *Sledge v. J. P. Stevens*, hundreds of pages of legal arguments were devoted to disputes about the validity of statistics. Attorney Whiteford Blakeney claimed that Stevens could explain individual cases of pay disparities, but the use of classwide statistics put the company in a very difficult position: "What is the reason that blacks are not up here [in high-paying jobs]? In individual cases each time we can prove why and prove to the Court's satisfaction. . . . And yet, when we are confronted with thousands of statistics and nobody comes forward and says, 'Take the case of Mary Jones' . . . where nobody is saying that, they are just saying look at the statistics, then we are in a pretty helpless position. . . . And so we come to, being under the gun, as to what should be done to us."[100]

In *Sledge*, the plaintiffs' emphasis on statistical evidence was in marked contrast to the defendant's emphasis on qualitative evidence. Indeed, in general, most companies made very little use of statistics in their defenses, preferring instead to rely on legal and rhetorical arguments. Blakeney expressed a typical attitude to statistics when he asserted in 1976 "that statistics in and of themselves don't prove anything . . . in this case beyond the fact that here are people white or black making certain rates. . . . They don't speak to the issue, it is because of race that they are here and they are here. Statistics don't speak to that. It merely shows there is A and here is B."[101]

Other companies showed similar attitudes in the lawsuits. They rejected the significance of data showing racial disparities, claiming that these were just "numbers." No action was taken to correct the statistical disparities because companies did not recognize that they existed. In *Adams v. Dan River Mills*, the company's personnel manager, Robert Gardiner, when confronted by direct evidence of racial disparities in hiring rates, testified that he had done "nothing" to tackle the disparities because "you cannot look at a number and play a numbers game." Gardiner held the view that absolutely no discrimination was taking place. No action was necessary "because I know we are not rejecting people on the basis of race, period." When confronted by statistics showing racial disparities in pay compiled from over 8,000 workers, Gardiner claimed that individual differences, rather than racial discrimination, was responsible. He again rejected the validity of statistics: "You can't take a whole group of people and say, 'why should they be making less than this group of people.' You would have to take each individual and say, 'why are you making less than this person.' "[102]

Gardiner's testimony was also typical in showing that the company did not see the need for any formal system of affirmative action to promote blacks. There was no "written system" to allow blacks to be promoted, but supervisors had been "encouraged" to recommend blacks for promotion. Gardiner added that "the line management runs these plants," but he claimed that the company did not need "a system . . . whereby we could, through some kind of magic, determine that somebody is discriminating" because "these supervisors are not discriminating." The company records of Dan River Mills, however, vividly highlight how great the gap was between the public and private record, showing that in reality supervisors discriminated a great deal against black workers.[103]

Across the South, many companies simply refused to believe that statistics indicating clear racial disparities in hiring and pay were proof of discrimination, and they reacted with anger and disbelief when federal agencies helped institute legal action against them. These companies had a very narrow definition of compliance with the Civil Rights Act and seemed to genuinely believe that they were in accordance with it even when the evidence against them was so compelling.[104]

Many textile companies also clearly regarded the employment of African Americans as little more than a ritual that had to be gone through in order to keep the federal government off their backs. Some were remarkably candid about the fact that they exaggerated their employment of African Americans in order to keep the EEOC at bay. The large West Point Pepperell Company, for example, told one visitor in 1969, "The company follows the EEOC guidelines but 'does not mind stretching things a bit to make the report look good.'"[105] Daisy Johnson, a placement director at South Carolina State College, claimed in 1969 that very few textile companies were making a "sincere effort" to hire one of the college's graduates. Most, she noted, were more concerned with contacting black colleges so that they could "write a pretty report for the Equal Employment Opportunity Commission."[106]

Other cases provided similar examples of efforts to appear integrated. At Dan River Mills, one black worker, Birdie Ruth Harris, even described how the company had moved her into a high-paying inspector's job when her plant was toured by government officials. Once the government officials had left, however, her supervisor told her immediately that she was "needed" back in her regular job as a creeler, which was a much lower paying position. Harris never returned to the inspector's job again.[107] In *Sherrill v. J. P. Stevens*, black workers from the company's warehouse described how the company had started to hire white students on a temporary basis in an effort to integrate the warehouse, an area which had always been all-black. The testimony of established black warehouse workers showed that they did not respect the ability of the white workers and saw them merely as an attempt to give the appearance of an integrated department. Ray Lewis McDowell, for example, described how the company only hired high school students rather than white men in the warehouse: "Little white school boys—they don't have no white men in the warehouse." These white students were not given heavy jobs to do, as blacks were expected to perform this work while the whites drew the same salary. McDowell described the white workers as "children. . . . About 16. They come in when they get out of school. They come and go every day." When asked what the whites did in the warehouse, McDowell replied, "Nothing mostly. They try but they can't."[108] Another warehouse worker, Robert Costner, who had been at the plant since 1949, testified that it was only in the 1960s that whites began to be assigned to the warehouse.[109]

The records of Dan River Mills show that the company was more concerned with showing it had made an effort to integrate black departments than with actually integrating them. Facing the problem of white workers who refused assignments in black departments, an internal company memo written in 1972 was particularly revealing on this point: "You should keep on record by name and date of all white applicants who refuse to accept employment on all-black jobs so that we can at least *prove* [original emphasis] that we make an affirmative effort to integrate such jobs." Once again, the company went through the motions to satisfy the federal government, reasoning that the appearance of making an effort, rather than actually producing results, would be enough to stay in compliance.[110]

Reverse Discrimination and Quotas

At the heart of textile executives' opposition to affirmative action was their belief that it constituted "reverse discrimination." Many textile companies viewed affirmative action as discrimination against whites. They claimed that the type of compliance with the Civil Rights Act envisaged by the federal government and by plaintiffs' attorneys discriminated against their white employees, and they were unwilling to tolerate this. Any suggestion that companies should follow a hiring quota drew a strong reaction. In *United States v. Southern Weaving*, for example, the company argued that the federal government was trying to force them to discriminate against their white workers: "Frankly I think when the Government frequently talks to you, they're not talking about anti-discrimination; they're talking about affirmative discrimination in favor."[111]

In letters written to their political representatives, many textile executives claimed that the Civil Rights Act and the EEOC gave special privileges to African Americans at the expense of whites. One manufacturer, for example, wrote in 1963 that passage of the Civil Rights Bill "will deprive the majority of our population of their rightful constitutional protection while giving 'Super Rights' to certain minority groups that are fomenting discord and disruption of local law and order and trying to intimidate the Congress of the United States." No minority group should rule the majority by gaining "Preferred Treatment."[112] Some companies claimed that upholding civil rights was very difficult because their own workers believed that the company was engaging in reverse discrimination. Strengthening the EEOC would therefore "act as a catalyst to the already existing cries of 'reverse discrimination.'"[113]

With the riots of the late 1960s and the rise of black power, companies used the reverse discrimination defense even more, claiming that civil rights leaders wanted special privileges. D. B. Barlow wrote Senator Strom Thurmond of South Carolina from Standard-Coosa-Thatcher Company in Chattanooga, Tennessee, asking "why something cannot be done to muzzle such characters as Rat Brown and Stokely Carmichael in their campaign of insighting to riot over the country. . . . We hear so much about the rights of the minority groups. How about the rights of the inarticulate majorities."[114]

At Dan River Mills, company records show that the relationship between the company and the federal government was one of continual conflict based on real differences over the meaning of equal employment opportunity. The main issue that consistently divided the two parties was that of reverse discrimination. The company complained that the DSA wanted them to advance blacks "without regard to qualifications." In 1968, company notes from a meeting with representatives from the Department of Defense indicate strong differences over this issue. On another occasion, the company noted that "we can discriminate to our heart's content as long as we only discriminate against the white race. It becomes quite evident that if we follow a policy giving preference to the Negroes and discriminating against whites, we will have scored a number of points with the government." Dan River adamantly refused to "adopt a program which will give our white employees the feeling that we are discriminating against them." Thus, in May 1968, Dan River rejected the DSA's calls for "specific goals" because this would entail "preferential treatment of non-whites through the use of a quota system, contrary to the Civil Rights Act." The DSA suggested on a number of occasions that one of the ways for Dan River to increase black employment was to make contacts with the NAACP and begin positive recruitment of black employees. It was clear, however, that the DSA and Dan River regarded the NAACP very differently: "We have in the past and intend to use only normal sources of recruitment and therefore do not envision going to the NAACP and other such unusual and abnormal recruitment sources. For example, we do not go to the KKK to recruit white people." Robert Gardiner, meanwhile, concluded that his comments about the Defense Department's proposals were "unprintable."[115]

In *Sledge v. J. P. Stevens*, the reverse discrimination argument became central to the company's defense after Stevens was found guilty of racial discrimination in 1975. Stevens rejected any idea of quotas to achieve class relief, claiming that they constituted racial discrimination. In a hearing to discuss the proposed consent decree in February 1976, attorney Whiteford Blakeney declared: "Quotas, Your Honor, racial quotas should be named what they are. They are discriminations on the basis of race; pure and simple, that is what they are." Blakeney added that the plaintiffs' "method of eliminating discrimination is to create discrimination."[116] Stevens's attorneys claimed that the plaintiffs wanted to impose a "total regime of pro-black and anti-white discrimination," adding that quotas would cause white workers "to be shoved around unmercifully," which would destroy morale and thereby make the mills less efficient.[117]

Patterns of Resistance

Although companies frequently expressed the same arguments to defend their racial hiring practices, the attitudes of textile companies sometimes differed on race. Patterns are hard to identify, however. Civil rights attorneys, for example, claimed that they could not identify any real differences between textile companies because they all had such poor records. As James Ferguson recalled, "There were no significant differences between them; it was all resistance from start to finish."[118] It is particularly difficult to identify patterns in the written record. When a company can be found that is more positive than most, another company can also be found with similar ownership characteristics but a very negative attitude, thereby frustrating any generalization.

One clear pattern that does emerge is that union plants were no better on race than nonunion plants, and they may have been slightly worse. A TEAM study in South Carolina, for example, found that "a check of union plants indicates that the racial mix is no better."[119] Paul Swaity, the southern director of the TWUA, admitted to the EEOC textile forum in January 1967 that the racial hiring patterns and practices of union and nonunion plants were "not significantly different."[120] In addition, some large southern companies that were very anti-union had a reasonably good record on black employment. One of the best examples of this was the large Georgia-based Bibb chain, a company that had always fiercely resisted unionization. Indeed, during the Operation Dixie campaign of 1945–46 the company had even used the Ku Klux Klan to help defeat the union's drive.[121] By the late 1960s, however, the company was one of the region's leaders in employing African Americans. One of Bibb's plants was 65 percent black, and the company's affirmative action plan was drafted by an African American.[122] The company's large No. 2 mill in Macon, Georgia, was more than 50 percent black by 1969.[123] In May 1969, the company's internal magazine, *The Bibb Recorder*, published several pictures of an integrated golf tournament that had been won by a black employee, Henry Hutchinson. Pictures of Hutchinson shaking hands with the white workers he had defeated appeared on the front page of the *Recorder*. While the pictures looked rather stiff and staged, the prominence of black achievement in the *Recorder* contrasted to many other company magazines that continued to feature only white workers in the late 1960s.[124]

Similarly, the large Russell Mills, based in Alexander City, Alabama, was another company that had always vehemently resisted unionization. In 1968, however, an EEOC review found that the company was in compliance with the Civil Rights Act and was implementing many steps that unionized companies balked at. It had instigated an affirmative action program that included extensive contacts with "minority group leaders," something that unionized Dan River Mills repeatedly refused to do.[125]

It is also possible to detect some patterns from the records of the Merit Employment Program conducted in the 1950s and 1960s by the AFSC. As the program operated out of High Point, North Carolina, it spent a great deal of time conducting visits with Cone Mills and Burlington Mills, two major textile corporations that were based in nearby Greensboro. Cone Mills was the largest single employer in Greensboro, with twelve mills located in and around the city. These mills together employed around 14,000 workers in 1968. Burlington's operations were scattered across several countries, and in 1968 it was the largest textile company in America, with more than 83,000 employees. Burlington's corporate headquarters, however, were located in Greensboro. AFSC representatives found that the two companies had very different attitudes toward discussing merit employment. While Cone Mills executives were consistently genial, helpful, and open to ideas, those from Burlington were much more evasive and reluctant to consider change.[126]

An indication of these differences came in the first plant visits that AFSC representatives made to the two companies in 1953 and 1954. At the first visit to Cone Mills, Herman Cone, the company's president, declared that he was in "hearty accord" with the AFSC's goals and added that "*all* men should have the opportunity to use their abilities, should have opportunity of advancement, should not be discriminated against because of race." At the end of the interview, Cone brought up the topic of Cone Hospital, a company-financed facility in Greensboro which was in the process of being built. He suggested that the AFSC help him to ensure that the hospital had "*total integration* so far as staff and workers are concerned."[127] AFSC agents were very encouraged by Cone's attitude and followed his suggestion with a series of visits to Joseph S. Lichty, the director of Cone Memorial Hospital. Lichty was also open to AFSC help and explained that he had tried to integrate the hospital as far as possible. The hospital, for example, had an integrated cafeteria and only one entrance. An AFSC representative went as far as to describe Cone hospital as "a real symbol in Greensboro and in this area, a totally integrated institution."[128] Further visits to Cone plants confirmed that the company was hiring more blacks in nontraditional jobs than the AFSC had previously encountered. Indeed, union representatives told the AFSC that Cone employed more blacks in nontraditional jobs than any other company in the South.[129]

In contrast, AFSC representatives found it very difficult to secure an interview with J. Spencer Love, the founder and chairman of Burlington Mills. AFSC staff members Tartt Bell and Ralph Rose tried for two years to get an interview with Love, while a third agent tried for a year. Finally, Bell succeeded by calling Love at home in the evening. The interview was not a great success. Love explained that because he had been born and raised in New England, he had "never understood the Southerners' prejudice. However, after coming to the South at the age of 22 to go into business, I conformed to the South's pattern." He claimed that he had "given no thought to the matter" of hiring blacks but added that "segregated textile plants have demonstrated that Japanese are more skillful than white Americans and Negroes less skillful than they as textile workers." Love ended the interview by promising to bring up the subject of merit employment with his associates, and he suggested that he might make a donation "sometime" to the AFSC.[130]

The AFSC staffers continued to try to influence Love by contacting one of his close personal friends, Dr. George D. Heaton. Heaton was the long-serving chaplain of the Southern Industrial Relations Conference, a yearly conference attended by industrialists from across North Carolina. Heaton also worked as a paid consultant to management on industrial relations issues. Heaton promised that he could "pave the way" for the AFSC to get "real results" from Love, but further meetings with the Burlington chairman apparently never took place. Heaton did, however, criticize Love's opinion that whites were more skillful textile workers than blacks: "As for Spencer's claim to you that experience had established that Negros are less skillful than whites, I think he is in error." Heaton pointed to evidence that blacks made as good textile workers as whites.[131]

AFSC representatives rarely expressed any frustration with companies' unwillingness to change, and generally their reports gave most executives the benefit of the doubt when they said they would try to improve. After another visit to Burlington in 1955, however, AFSC representatives began to doubt that company's commitment to change and expressed frustration with Love's unwillingness to declare any policy of equal employment. AFSC representative Mayes Behrman told Burlington officials in 1955 that they would make "very little progress until top management declared a very definite policy for the organization as a whole." Burlington repeatedly refused to implement such a policy, however. Thelma Babbitt of the AFSC became frustrated by the company's unwillingness to move: "Until Spencer Love makes some kind of policy decision and announces it at least to the top echelon of management, no plan for integration will get far. . . . Why couldn't Mr. Love make a policy decision at least for the home office? I can't believe he doesn't have this much responsibility or power." Babbitt also doubted the company's claim that it was considering a move toward equal employment, asserting that Love was simply concerned about holding on to "sizeable government contracts."[132]

The AFSC also reported that Burlington employed very few African Americans and restricted them to fewer positions than at Cone Mills. Whereas in 1953 Cone Mills had "full integration" in two departments and was described as "a very excellent situation," in 1955 Burlington was said to have "few Negroes" in its plants and none in its offices. The few blacks that were employed were in "traditional jobs."[133]

The failure of major companies such as Burlington Mills to take the lead in changing racial employment practices was clearly very influential for the industry as a whole. These companies generally set wage patterns in the textile industry, and a strong example on equal employment would have cracked resistance elsewhere. AFSC representatives concentrated on companies such as Burlington because they believed that these companies could change the practices of the entire industry. In July 1955, for example, an AFSC report concluded: "We hope to have something constructive, concrete from Burlington Mills, before returning to Hickory, and are of the opinion that a move by Bur-Mil, will have strong influence on any textile mills with whom we later talk." The AFSC felt that "if and when Bur-Mil moves, the most impressive and influential textile company in America will have moved."[134]

Although there were clear differences in the attitudes of textile companies to merit employment, the AFSC visits also revealed striking similarities as well. Although Cone had made more departures from traditional employment patterns than other companies, it shared the prevalent belief that real integration was impossible because of opposition from white workers. Herman Cone, for example, told the AFSC in 1953 that "I believe thoroughly in merit employment, but I do not know any place that really practices it—even among the white race." Like other textile executives, Cone linked textile workers' racism with their low educational level: "Mr. Cone indicated that most of the work in the textile industry is not even semi-skilled let alone skilled, and that for that reason their employees were certainly of an educational level which made them carry prejudice very easily. . . . [T]heir economic status had been so close to that of the Negro for so long, they have a deep-seated prejudice against him."[135]

Spencer Love and Burlington Mills used the same arguments. In 1955, an AFSC report referred to a recent meeting with Love at which he had claimed he was unsure that white workers would accept blacks in nontraditional positions: "I do not know but what all my employees would walk out." The AFSC revisited Burlington to try to overcome Love's objection by pointing to the example of Western Electric, which had successfully integrated in North Carolina. The response of Burlington's personnel manager, however, was similar to that of Herman Cone: "Don't you find that low income bracket employees are more violently opposed than those at executive level?" A lengthy discussion ensued, with the AFSC agent trying to convince Burlington executives that this was not the case. In 1956, however, Burlington was still reported to have made no move toward merit employment because of "fear of stirring something up."[136]

The AFSC also concentrated particular attention on the J. P. Stevens Company, another major textile corporation based largely in North Carolina. The AFSC made little progress with J. P. Stevens. The company shared many of the same fears as Burlington and Cone, arguing that the racism of white textile workers made integration impossible. In a 1955 visit, for example, the company raised fears about the "reaction of present employees" and whether black pioneers could become "acceptable members of the work group." The real problem at Stevens, as at Burlington, was the reluctance of the company's national office to adopt any policy of nondiscrimination. Thus, although the AFSC found that local managers were usually willing to discuss black employment, very little was actually achieved because of the refusal of "the top Stevens man to declare a policy of EOM [Employment on Merit]."[137]

Other visitors who approached Burlington Industries also found that the company had a very defensive attitude to inquiries about racial integration. Richard Rowan found the company to be particularly unhelpful while he was carrying out his Wharton School study of racial employment in the textile industry in the late 1960s. Unlike many other companies, Burlington was unwilling to supply data for Rowan's study, although he did finally manage to carry out a plant visit in July 1969. The interview with executive Edward Crothers did not go well. As Rowan wrote, "Mr. Crothers began the interview in a very defensive manner, and I saw quickly that we would not get very much cooperation. . . . Mr. Crothers said that they had rather spend their time on 'constructive' things than to be talking to newspaper people and others such as I about what they were doing. He is the kind of person that I expected to find generally in the industry, and have been pleasantly surprised to find his exception." Rowan concluded his report by providing his own explanation of Burlington's unhelpful attitude, claiming that the company "regards itself as so large that it really doesn't care what other companies in the industry are doing. It is not difficult to understand why Burlington gets itself into a bad shape with the government as you sit and listen to the comments of a man like Crothers. He was trained at Cornell, having lived most of his life in Philadelphia, and he appears to have learned very little or nothing about the southern Negroes." Rowan felt that Burlington's official company position was "to do as little as possible and not get caught by the government."[138]

This account is one of the first to examine in detail the beliefs of textile executives. It has found that, rather than being enthusiastic about black employment, as existing studies have suggested, textile executives in fact opposed many civil rights initiatives and feared the increasing number of black workers in the industry. They clashed repeatedly with the federal government, which wanted the industry to carry out more affirmative action. At Dan River Mills, an internal company report that provided an overview of Dan River's dealings with the EEOC and the DSA in the 1960s showed that Dan River resented the federal government's efforts to ensure that the company developed an affirmative action program. It was entitled "The Development of an Affirmative Action Program—Harassment by Federal Agencies."[139] Textile executives' resistance to affirmative action, especially to "hard" remedies such as preferential treatment and racial quotas, mirrored the attitudes of white Americans across the country.[140]

It is clear that even though the number of African Americans hired into the textile industry increased significantly in the 1960s and 1970s, most textile executives resisted fundamental change in their racial attitudes. Many executives did not see the need for any type of affirmative action, and they continued to hold a number of deep-seated fears about black employment. The main impression that emerges from the written record is that the racial changes that took place in the industry in these years happened despite textile executives rather than because of them. The labor market and the federal government, together with a considerable degree of pressure from African Americans themselves, pushed the pace of change. Textile companies, however, never really embraced black employment, at least not to the extent that the federal government wished. Blacks came to the companies, rather than vice versa. At Dan River, one of the recurrent themes of the compliance reviews carried out by federal agencies was that the company should undertake affirmative recruitment in the black community. Federal officials argued that such efforts were vital to overcome the company's "credibility gap" in the black community and to encourage black applicants for jobs that Dan River claimed no blacks applied for. Like many other textile companies, however, Dan River consistently rejected the idea that it should positively recruit blacks. The company interpreted the Civil Rights Act to mean that it should not discriminate against black applicants, but it saw no need to seek black applicants. In a passage that epitomized the passive concept of equal employment opportunity that many textile companies held, Dan River claimed: "Title VII does not require an employer to go out into the streets looking for black applicants. It only requires that the employer not discriminate against those individuals who express an interest in employment by taking the time to apply at its employment office."[141]

I Felt Myself as a Pioneer

The Experiences of the First

Black Production Workers

four

The hiring of the first African American workers into production positions was a momentous change for the southern textile industry in the 1960s, representing a clear break from employment practices that had been followed since the late nineteenth century. The experiences of the first black production workers were crucial to the success of integration as a whole, and companies realized this. Most pioneers were carefully selected in order to minimize the possible disruption caused by integration. They were often specifically chosen as test cases or guinea pigs responsible for determining the wider fate of integration in their plants. It is important to look at the individual experiences of these pioneers in closer detail because they provide answers to significant questions that can easily be overlooked by concentrating only on broad patterns of employment change in the industry. How were they selected? What kind of reaction did they face from white workers? Did they feel that the company treated them the same as white workers?[1]

The experiences of the black pioneers are especially valuable for determining how much resistance blacks met from white workers and supervisors upon their entry into the mills. Accounts written at the time of the integration tended to be generally positive, especially in the coverage that the process received in the national and southern press. In public accounts of textile integration, management universally reported that there had been no problems encountered between black and white workers, and mills were reported to have become "colorblind" places of employment. A manager of Erwin Mills, a division of Burlington Industries, declared in 1969 that "I think the greatest surprise some of our managers had at first was the acceptance by whites of the Negroes." Reports by journalists also gave optimistic accounts of the amount of acceptance between black and white workers. Several articles printed pictures of black and white mill workers happily socializing together. One journalist who visited Roanoke Rapids, North Carolina, in the 1970s read much into an interracial baseball game among textile workers: "The white mill women scream and cheer as loudly for black players as for whites, and the sight of a middle-aged white man, a weaver playing first base, raising his clenched fist in exultation over a double play—the old Black Power salute—may indicate black and white mill hands no longer will turn on each other."[2]

Some academic accounts have also stressed the immediate acceptance of blacks by their white coworkers and by supervisors. Richard Rowan's 1970 study, for example, claimed that "one of the revealing aspects of this study was the appearance of cordial relations between Negroes and whites. . . . It was a usual situation to find blacks and whites talking, eating, and joking together during their lunch or break periods."[3] Other studies have given a more balanced assessment, suggesting both black advancement and lingering white resentment.[4]

Existing accounts, however, have not really concentrated on the experiences of the first black workers in detail. Very little is known about how companies chose their first black workers and how these workers were treated when they went into the mills.[5] The records of the lawsuits provide an opportunity to explore the process of integration in closer detail; indeed, they often specifically probed the question of why and how companies first hired African Americans into production positions. Supplemented with other written accounts that closely monitored the process of integration, along with a broad range of personal interviews conducted with the first black production workers, these records provide invaluable personal insights into the experiences of the pioneers.

Both written and oral records indicate that there was in fact considerable white resistance to the hiring of blacks, especially in higher-paying jobs. This resistance meant that companies generally took a cautious approach when they integrated their workforce. To minimize resistance, executives required blacks who were hired to be well-known, well-liked, overqualified, and light-skinned. The need for blacks to meet these strict criteria increased depending on how high-paying and "white" the position to be filled was.

White Resistance to Integration

A variety of written and oral sources repeatedly document resistance by both white workers and lower management to the introduction of blacks in the textile industry, especially into higher-paying positions. In some cases, it was fear of direct economic competition that motivated white resistance. In others, it was a desire to remain socially separate from blacks. African American union representative Sammy Glover, who had worked as an organizer and staff representative in textiles for thirty years, felt that both economic and social fears were responsible for the white resistance that he had witnessed in many plants across the South: "I think that there was this fear of competition, that the black worker would take their job from them, and then there was this attitude that they were . . . superior to the black worker, and they just, they didn't want to work with them. They didn't want to share a restroom facility with them, they didn't want to share a water-fountain with them, they didn't want to share their jobs with them. . . . I think it was a fear of competition and just a superiority complex."[6]

Social Integration

One area where resistance was especially notable was in the integration of social facilities in the mills. Refuting optimistic accounts of workers gladly sharing facilities, many of the first black workers had vivid memories of white workers who bitterly resented the integration of bathrooms and water fountains. Former J. P. Stevens worker Sammy Alston, for example, recalled that many whites refused to share facilities with African Americans after they were integrated: "When they had the segregation, you know, they had a black water fountain and a white one, and a bathroom for the black and a bathroom for the white. I know some of the white people, when they took one of them water fountains out, I know a lot of them white people they would go all day long without drinking a drop of water. Then they started bringing a little cooler of water to work. . . . They would go in the bathroom, if a black person was in the bathroom, they would turn around and come out, I'm telling you. And I've been in them stalls . . . you go in the bathroom and they've got them stalls, you'd be sat out behind them and [you'd hear] the white people, what kind of names they called the black."[7] Similarly, at Columbus Towel Mill in Columbus, Georgia, black worker Jacob Little recalled that when the water fountains and bathrooms were integrated, there was a widespread boycott of the facilities by whites: "I remember when they first started, first integrating it right after I got there . . . the white people they quit drinking water out of the water fountain, they quit changing clothes in the bathrooms because we were changing clothes with them. For a long time that when on. . . . A lot of them quit using the facilities, you know."[8]

The *Adams v. Dan River Mills* case also revealed that many white workers were reluctant to use integrated facilities after 1964. The former superintendent of the finishing division, Donald R. Aichner, testified about an incident that occurred when lead plaintiff Julious Adams was the first black promoted to a production position in his department. Aichner reported that white workers complained to him when Adams started to use the water fountain in the department: "You have to realize that a lot of people there weren't ready for some of the things that happened." Aichner recalled one white worker who was "just furious. And his comment to me was, 'I guess I will have to work for him, and I don't really mind working with black people, but I don't have to eat with them and I'm not going to.'"[9]

Other sources show that many white workers resisted any social contact with blacks in the plant. The integration of social facilities within the plants proved to be problematic in many cases. At the West Point Pepperell plants in the Chattahoochee Valley area of Georgia and Alabama, the company reported that their "greatest difficulties have been in integrating restrooms."[10] "Restrooms" were also reported to be a problem area at Fulton Cotton Mills in Atlanta in 1969.[11] At one DuPont plant in the South, it was reported that when facilities were integrated, "white employees refused to use the cafeteria facilities for lunch breaks."[12] At a J. P. Stevens plant in Dublin, Georgia, a compliance review revealed that management acquiesced to the fears of white workers by providing paper seats and cups in the washrooms. This move reflected the tension prevailing between whites and blacks in the plant. As one report noted, "In this area, white workers remain clannish and, to some extent, exclude the Negro."[13]

Many textile companies pandered to white workers' fears by allowing facilities to remain segregated long after the Civil Rights Act. Across the South, companies took down "white" and "colored" signs but allowed separate facilities to remain, ensuring that workers continued to use them out of custom and fear. In *Graniteville Company v. EEOC*, black worker Edward Price wrote to the EEOC that as late as 1968, "even the dining concessions stands and the lockers and toilet facilities are allowed to be segregated on the basis of race, as are the jobs and the advancement opportunities." As Price's complaint explained, the persistence of segregated facilities was often an extension of the segregation that continued in all areas of the workplace, especially in job assignments. What was especially alarming was just how long separate facilities persisted after the passage of the Civil Rights Act. In *Seibles v. Cone Mills*, for example, the court found that the company "maintained segregated locker, toilet and shower facilities until 1973." In *Adams v. Dan River Mills*, black worker Leroy Johnson testified that although "white" and "colored" signs had been removed, the restrooms in his department were still partitioned in 1973, meaning that blacks and whites continued to use separate bathrooms. Another Dan River worker, Henry Wilson, described in 1970 that in his department, "they taken the sign down. Still we go in like it was at first. Colored go on their side. White go the other side." Separate facilities were reported in a variety of other companies well after 1964.[14]

In some of the major class action cases, segregated facilities formed part of the complaint. In *Adams v. Dan River Mills*, filed in 1969, one of the central complaints was "the maintenance of restroom and other facilities segregated as to race."[15] In *Georgia Hall v. George P. Shultz*, a case brought against the federal government because of its alleged failure to enforce nondiscrimination at Burlington Industries, J. P. Stevens, and Dan River Mills, a group of black plaintiffs complained in 1969 about the "maintenance of segregated locker and restroom and other facilities."[16]

Companies' reluctance to integrate facilities often pushed black workers to try to integrate the facilities themselves. At the Eagle and Phenix Mill in Columbus, Georgia, African American worker Willie Long remembered that bathrooms were still segregated when he started working at the mill in 1972. As in most cases of segregation after the Civil Rights Act, the company had taken down the "white" and "colored" signs but workers continued to use separate facilities by custom. Long, a tall, amiable man who still worked at the mill in 1996, remembered that he and a friend were the first to use the "white" bathroom: "In '72 right, everybody was understood it that you don't go to that bathroom downstairs. We had our bathroom upstairs and went to it. So then I had a friend of mine named Freddie Holland . . . he just started going to the bathroom downstairs. He could see the eyes, you know, the way they looked at him, but then gradually we started going to them, and then the company never said anything though, so that's how we really got integrated. The bathrooms got integrated while I was there."[17]

In several cases the integration of company housing also led to resistance from white textile workers. At Cannon Mills in Kannapolis, North Carolina, housing was a major issue in integration because the company was one of the few textile companies that still owned large numbers of houses. The Cannon houses were still strictly segregated as late as 1969, and a Kannapolis resident interviewed by the *Wall Street Journal* claimed that forcing integration of housing would lead to a "race riot."[18]

Although contemporary accounts often commented on the excellent social relationships between white and black workers outside the plant, African American workers interviewed in this study usually felt that even if relations between the two groups were good in the plant, this never extended outside the plant. Many felt that white workers whom they spoke to at work ignored them if they met them outside the plant, and they claimed that this occurred because whites feared that they might lose face in their community if they were seen socializing with blacks. As African American worker Joe Gaines explained, "Once they leave the plant its like, once they walk out the door, they take off their worker's hat, and you see them in the community and they don't know you. But once you get back into the plant they would talk to you. It's like they didn't want the community to know they had been socialized with you inside of the mills."[19] Some black workers were clearly hurt by the refusal of their white coworkers to acknowledge them in the community. James McGhee, who worked at a textile plant in Andalusia, Alabama, remembered that "some of them would go along with you on the job, but when you got off your job, they wouldn't speak to you. I worked with them side by side; when I get off the job, they didn't know me."[20]

Economic Integration

White resistance to social integration coexisted with fears about economic competition. Many black workers who were hired into the industry in the 1960s and 1970s have vivid memories of white resistance to blacks being hired into production jobs. In Tarboro, North Carolina, supervisor Spencer Etheridge remembered that white workers resisted the introduction of blacks and were still going through a process of adjusting to their entry: "They very much resented blacks coming in and taking jobs, and whites had the perception that blacks were inferior as far as morals and intelligence, and a lot of whites, probably the majority of whites today that are in textiles, do not feel that blacks are equal to whites."[21]

This resistance was greatest when blacks were placed in better-paying production positions, jobs which had previously been considered "white." James Johnson, an African American who worked in a textile mill in Andrews, South Carolina, before becoming active in the labor movement, remembered that he observed a lot of hostility when blacks moved into better jobs: "The better jobs really didn't come along until the very late seventies. . . . But there was some resentment, there was a great deal of resentment on behalf of whites when this began to develop. . . . They didn't accept it at all, really; they were very bitter. They made racial slurs toward the black workers, things of that nature."[22]

Many black workers who were hired into production jobs in the 1960s and 1970s remembered that white workers refused to train them for higher-paying jobs or to cooperate with them in the workplace. Willie Long, who was hired at the Eagle and Phenix Mill in Columbus, Georgia, in 1972, remembered that blacks were only being hired into low-paying jobs at the time, and white workers were reluctant to help them learn the better-paying jobs. This was especially true of the job of roving tender, which was one of the highest-paying jobs and was overwhelmingly white: "The roving tenders, which was mostly white, they really didn't want to show you anything about the job. . . . They didn't want you around them." Long felt that the supervisors and the white workers "just wanted to make sure that the blacks stayed on the lower wage jobs. They didn't really want them moving up on the higher paying jobs."[23] Earl Moore, who also worked in Columbus, recalled that when he was hired by Fieldcrest Mills in the late 1970s, white loom fixers tried to scare or intimidate blacks who signed up for training to become loom fixers, which was the highest-paying production job in textiles and had always been held by whites.[24] The promotion of blacks into "white" jobs led to more opposition than the hiring of blacks from outside to fill entry level jobs. As one executive of Burlington Industries remembered, "The advancement issue caused more issues in a lot of places than the actual integration of the workforce."[25]

There was also considerable resistance from white workers when blacks were promoted into any position of authority within the mills. Some black workers remembered whites quitting in large numbers when the first blacks were promoted into supervisory positions. Clinton Davis, a large African American man who started working for Muscogee Mills in Columbus, Georgia, in 1966, recalled that there was a significant exodus of whites from the plant when blacks began to be placed in supervisory jobs: "A lot of them actually quit because, you know, they said we're not working under blacks."[26] White workers themselves admitted that it took a long time before most whites accepted that blacks could hold responsible jobs. Elboyd Deal, a white worker for Cannon Mills between 1961 and 1991, felt that "we were slow to really accept that black people could work their way up to supervision and stuff like that, and I know a lot of people that resented a black man being over them."[27]

In many cases, white workers who were willing to tolerate blacks in low-paying positions were pushed into collective resistance when companies hired them into supervisory positions. Joe Gaines, an African American man who had been a textile worker in Sylvester, Georgia, before becoming active as a union organizer for ACTWU, explained that he had seen white workers organize themselves in protest against black promotions on many different occasions: "I have seen some more or less concerted activity . . . on behalf of whites when they felt like a black was getting into a position that meant he or she had authority to tell them what to do. They would sort of form their little sit-in group. They would make sure they would go to the top man, to the supervisor or manager, and just lay it on the line: 'It's okay to have this guy in a position but don't put him in a position where he's going to start telling us how to do our jobs and things like that.' . . . That happened on many occasions."[28]

Managers themselves continually argued that they could not promote blacks into higher-paying or management positions because of resistance from white workers. In a discussion of the subject in a trade paper, the *Daily News Record*, in 1968, for example, one mill owner claimed that "like it or not, our mill employees grew up before civil rights legislation was enacted. Their thinking is geared to another era. . . . [B]efore the Negro can gain management status . . . non-Negro workers have to accept the fact that he is worthy of the management slot."[29] Management also cited examples of resistance to justify this view.[30] At Russell Mills, a major textile company based in Alexander City, Alabama, management described in 1969 how "the greatest difficulties in the plant in regard to Negroes is in moving a man into a supervisory job. . . . They know that if the wrong type of Negro is selected to supervise whites, it would cause a great deal of trouble at the outset."[31]

Although whites reacted strongly when blacks were promoted into higher-paying positions, other pioneers remembered whites who quit when blacks were hired in large numbers in regular production jobs. At J. P. Stevens's plants in Roanoke Rapids, veteran black worker Sammy Alston recalled that "a lot of them [whites] quit" when blacks began to be hired in larger numbers in the late 1960s.[32] Burlington executive George Waldrep, who was a plant manager in the 1960s, remembered that in most Burlington plants there was "a hardcore" of white workers who refused to work with blacks: "You had people walk off their job, you had people quit, you had people who made statements that they would not work with blacks. That happened, and they had those choices."[33]

Written records also show that on several occasions white workers engaged in organized walkouts when integration occurred. One such incident happened at a Celanese plant in Rome, Georgia. A Celanese vice president reported in 1969 that there had been "a wildcat strike at the Rome, Georgia plant when they attempted to integrate certain departments." Firm company action brought an end to this strike.[34] Similarly, white workers at another Burlington plant, some of whom were members of the Klan, engaged in a walkout when the company tried to hire black workers in the mid-1960s. The strike was broken when plant manager George Waldrep fired the ringleaders, causing the other workers to troop back into the mill. Waldrep remembered that overall it took "five to ten years" before the company was able to quell all protests and clean out racist supervisors.[35]

Waldrep claimed that Burlington minimized resistance by stressing federal law and also by utilizing strict disciplinary powers. As he recalled, "The standard comment was, if you came to me, Tim, and said, 'I'm not going to work with blacks,' I'd say as management, 'Well, the law is this, and we're going to abide by the law. If you can't do that, then you need to quit and go and find you another job to save me the trouble of terminating you.'" On occasions when there was organized resistance, such as occurred among one group of whites who objected to the employment of blacks in their department, the ringleaders were fired "on the spot," thereby killing the protest. Burlington's proven ability to crush labor protest seemed to help it in overcoming the resistance of white workers, and the method used—selective firings of activists—was the same in both cases.[36]

Many of those who were fired or who left textiles when integration occurred left industry altogether, as most other industries in the South were also integrating at this time. They went back to farming or set up their own small businesses, where, according to Waldrep, "they didn't have all these government rules and regulations to contend with." In this sense, the federal government again played a central role in the integration of textiles because it prevented workers from escaping contact with African Americans in any industry. White textile workers who opposed integration thus had limited options.[37]

There were many incidents of sabotage and harassment when integration occurred. At Pacific Mills in Columbia, South Carolina, for example, it was reported that "one colored man's coat was torn up" when the first black workers were hired in the plant in 1962.[38] At Dan River Mills, black worker James Montgomery complained in 1970 that the dressing room in his department had a partition, with the whites using the dressing room on the right. When some black workers used the "white" shower room, "the next day somebody had broken glass up all in the bottom of the shower."[39]

The opposition of many white workers to workplace integration reflected their more general opposition to integration as a whole. At Brenton Textiles in Statesville, North Carolina, workers even drew up a petition expressing their opposition to the proposed Civil Rights Act of 1964. The petition was signed by 192 workers and then mailed to North Carolina senator Samuel Ervin, an outspoken opponent of civil rights legislation.[40] Civil rights attorney Julius Chambers remembered that there was violent reaction from many textile workers in all the communities where he tried his lawsuits: "Because of the education level, we had some of the most militant people in the textile industry. That's where we had a lot of Klan activity. . . . You had tension, you had a lot of violent reaction, because again you had a number of Klan sympathizers at least in the industry . . . and they fought tooth and nail to preserve segregation."[41]

The records of textile unions also show that white textile workers were strongly opposed to civil rights and integration. In 1962, for example, Johnnie E. Brown, a southern representative of the United Textile Workers of America (UTWA), described how in certain areas textile workers had become very alienated by civil rights demonstrations: "Locals 163 and 201 are in the heart of an area where K.K.K and White Citizen Council organizations flourish. The situation is tense because of sit-in demonstrations in Talladega, Albany, Atlanta, etc." In the union's South Carolina locals, Brown reported that white leadership prevented blacks from attending union meetings.[42]

The resistance of white workers meant that companies found it very difficult to integrate all-black departments in the 1960s. Pressured by federal agencies, some companies tried to integrate their plants by hiring whites into all-
black departments as well as by promoting blacks into white areas. Records
show, however, that companies had trouble finding whites who were willing to
work in black departments. At J. P. Stevens's plant in Stanley, North Carolina,
the only whites who accepted jobs in the all-black warehouse were high school
students looking for temporary summer work. An Hispanic and a Vietnamese
worker were also hired in an effort to integrate the warehouse. The only white
adult worker in the warehouse was described by a company official as "semi-
handicapped."[43] Dan River Mills also realized that progress could not be made
unless whites were hired into traditionally black jobs. The company was completely unsuccessful in trying to hire whites for these jobs, illustrating the
rigidity of notions of what constituted "black work." Indeed, it is clear that
integrating "black" jobs was equally as problematic as hiring black pioneers.
Dan River's personnel manager, Robert Gardiner, described how "we have
employed whites for those departments, they have gone to those departments
and refused to take the job." When pushed by the plaintiffs' attorney, Gardiner
added that whites would not take these jobs because "they don't want to work
in a predominantly black area."[44] Dan River came under consistent pressure
from the Defense Supply Agency because of its repeated failure to integrate all-
black jobs.[45]

White Resistance: The Legal Evidence

A large number of lawsuits indicate that the resistance described by black
workers characterized the textile industry's integration across the South. The
opposition that African Americans faced when they tried to penetrate "white"
jobs is especially clear from a wide variety of lawsuits. Indeed, the harassment
of blacks who tried to break into higher-paying "white" jobs was one of the
most common causes of legal action. The records reveal that this harassment
was often encouraged by supervisors, contradicting the assertions of management that they stamped out any resistance from white workers.

There was particular resistance to blacks entering the job of weaver, a well-
paid production position that was usually seen as a stepping-stone to becoming a fixer, the highest-paid position outside of management. In *Foster v. Fieldcrest Mills*, for example, plaintiff Robert Foster described how he was the first
and only black weaver in his department at a plant in Eden, North Carolina.
Foster was repeatedly urged by his white supervisor to do doffing work instead
of weaving. Doffing was a harder job than weaving and was done entirely by
blacks in the plant. In a detailed letter to the EEOC written in 1975, Foster

described how "the supervisors, forman and fixers were determined to prevent me from earning top pay as a qualified weaver. Because of their ingrained prejudices they acted as if I should accept the lower-paying, physically exhausting job of cloth doffer." As in other cases, when Foster refused to be downgraded, his supervisors and some coworkers started to harass him and tried to ensure that he failed in his quest to be the first black weaver. They interrupted his training on the weave machines and tampered with his machinery so that he got poor production figures. Foster was even offered a pay raise if he accepted the job of doffer. Like other pioneers, he was fired for failing to meet production goals when he refused to take this offer.[46]

Another clear example of white resistance to blacks entering weaving jobs occurred in *Lindsay v. Cone Mills*, a case involving a black woman who had been one of the first blacks to become a weaver at a Cone Mills plant in Gibsonville, North Carolina. Geraldine Lindsay had gotten the job in 1973 through the plant's union contract, which allowed her to use her lengthy plant seniority to her advantage. It was apparent from the beginning that the white fixer and supervisor that Lindsay worked with were not happy about the promotion. As Lindsay explained in a letter to the EEOC in 1974, "I got the weaving job but the boss over the weaving department and the fixer did not want me to have the job." Lindsay found it very difficult to perform her job because she relied on cooperation from white coworkers in order to be successful. It was in fact common during textile integration for whites to refuse to help blacks who were new to the job. In Lindsay's case, she depended on her fixer to keep her looms running: "The problem is that my 'fixer' will not fix my looms. I went to my supervisor about this constantly, it did no good. I had some looms to stand as much as three and four hours at a time." Neither the supervisor or the plant manager would do anything to help Lindsay, and she was fired for failing to make production.[47]

Many other pioneer black workers wrote letters to the EEOC in which they complained of harassment when they entered "white" production jobs. In *Lewis v. Bloomsburg Mills*, a lengthy letter written in the early 1970s by a black worker described in detail the type of harassment that the first African Americans often faced, and the way that supervisors often supported the position of white workers when incidents occurred. Joann W. Calhoun, a worker at Bloomsburg Mills in Abbeville County, South Carolina, described how she was hired into a production job where she had to work with "old white ladies" who harassed her. One night one of the women "threw a Bobbin and tried to hit me and she called me a damn nigger. so I told my supervisor so he told me if I couldnt get alone with people he would fire me." Following this incident, Calhoun was transferred to a less desirable, heavy job and then fired when the job caused her stomach pains.[48]

These complaints mirrored those filed by groups of black workers across the South. Harassment of black workers who were hired into production positions was a central complaint in *Harris v. Golden Belt Manufacturing Company*, a suit brought against a small mill located in Durham, North Carolina, in 1976. The official complaint in the case charged that "throughout his employment by Golden Belt, plaintiff and other black employees were subjected to harassment by white workers and supervisors. This harassment included but was not limited to unfounded complaints about their job performance and work breaks. On at least one occasion, plaintiff's foreman called him 'boy.'"[49] Similarly, the testimony of several workers in the *Adams v. Dan River Mills* case showed that there was considerable resistance from white workers and supervisors toward black workers moving into production jobs at Dan River Mills. Russell Dodson testified that in the No. 1 dyehouse, blacks were repeatedly threatened when they were placed in the all-white job of machine operator in 1966 and 1967: "They would be threatened to be fired if they didn't get off that job and take another job. . . . At the time the supervisor who told them was a man by the name of Sid Jones."[50] Other black workers testified that black workers across the plant were put under greater pressure than whites when they were placed in nontraditional jobs: "More pressure is applied to a Negro even when he gets transferred to a higher paid job."[51]

African Americans also faced resistance when they tried to become supervisors or salaried workers, jobs that remained overwhelmingly white throughout the 1960s and 1970s. This was well illustrated by the experiences of Jerdean A. Mark, who was the first black office worker to be hired at a plant of Burlington Industries in Gibsonville, North Carolina. Mark was hired into the office in July 1969, shortly after Burlington had been subjected to considerable pressure from the media and the federal government when it was awarded federal contracts despite being criticized for discriminatory employment practices. Although it is not certain that this episode was responsible for Mark's being hired, the company's attitude suggested that they were less than enthusiastic about promoting blacks into salaried positions but were merely responding to federal pressure. Thus, when Mark was offered the job she was told by the personnel manager that the company "was required to hire a Black office worker." Like many pioneers, Mark was promoted from within, after having worked in a production position with the company. Despite being told that this promotion would lead to a pay increase, Mark explained in her letter to the EEOC that the company held her pay at $1.91 an hour because she was "still in training." The company continually refused to raise Mark's pay, while giving her a "work-load and job assignments [which] were far greater than that of comparable white co-workers." The case, which was taken up by the EEOC after its investigation confirmed Mark's claims, was eventually settled by a consent decree in 1974.[52]

White resistance to blacks entering higher-paying jobs was a central issue of *Sherrill v. J. P. Stevens*, brought in 1973 by a group of black workers at a J. P. Stevens plant in Stanley, North Carolina. The *Sherrill* case showed conclusively that textile companies wanted to strictly control and limit integration. They wanted to decide who was to be a pioneer, and any attempts by black workers to force the pace of change were fiercely resisted, both by workers and management.[53]

In *Sherrill*, the main issue was the harassment of A. C. Sherrill, who became the first black worker in the plant to work in a production position when he was hired as a doffer in the spinning department in February 1968. Sherrill was the only black doffer in his plant and was more highly paid than any other black worker. Although Sherrill was told by his supervisor that he was a "great doffer" and had the highest production on his shift, he ran into problems when he repeatedly asked about a promotion in 1969–70. At first the company tried to discourage Sherrill, telling him that he had "a good job" and that they "would look into it." When Sherrill persisted in requesting a section foreman's job, the head supervisor told him that "the mill wasn't open for blacks in that area now. He didn't think it was time for blacks to be moving into a position like that."[54]

Company officials repeatedly cited the opposition of white workers as the reason for refusing to promote Sherrill. Plant superintendent Riley Skidmore, for example, told Sherrill that "out of the percentage of people there, he said the percentage was white and that out of that percentage some of them didn't like him and he said how would it look if they put me out there in a section man's job, so he felt it wasn't the time." Similarly, a black worker also testified that some of the white workers would have worked against Sherrill if he had been given the promotion.[55]

Although opposition from white workers was often used as an excuse by companies, in *Sherrill* it is clear that such opposition was genuine. Sherrill was subjected to continual harassment from white workers. In August 1971, white workers placed trash in Sherrill's car.[56] On several occasions he was "threatened with bodily harm." Sherrill described one incident where a white worker "walked up to me with a knife in his hand and asked me had I seen nigger blood before." White workers told Sherrill that if he were given the section man's job all the whites would leave. Sherrill recalled a conversation with a group of white workers led by a Billy Steele: "Billy Steele. He said—'If they give you a section job everybody in this place will quit.' I said—'Billy, they could have black people to do the job. You ought not to feel that way.' He said—'I'm telling you everybody will quit.'" White workers told Sherrill that "Stanley would never have a black section man in there" and that "the NAACP can't help you a bit."[57]

Management responded to Sherrill's promotion requests by calling him in for discussions, which frequently became heated. After a session with management on December 10, 1971, Sherrill described how he became "terrified" because he was the only black in a meeting of white supervisors, some of whom were in "a rage." Following this meeting, Sherrill left the company, although Stevens disputed that he had been forced to resign.[58]

Sherrill's demands for promotion, and the opposition it generated, must be viewed in the context of race relations in the surrounding area. Like many Piedmont textile communities, Stanley was a small town lacking a history of black activism. Sherrill himself described Stanley as a town where "the black people stay to themselves and the white people stay to themselves." The condition of blacks was "mostly low income," and the town lacked any black businesses or elected officials. Any challenge to the racial status quo was fiercely and widely resisted. Sherrill described how harassment continued even when he changed jobs and started working for another textile company in Gaston County: "Some fellow employees from Stanley that had heard about J. P. Stevens came to work . . . and they was riding me with this constantly, and, in other words, they was blackballing me." Sherrill lost his job after these white workers sabotaged his machinery. Sherrill also described how the company refused to hire any members of his family or those whom he recommended.[59]

Sherrill's experiences were typical of many other African Americans who tried to be the first to enter "white" jobs. Indeed, at another J. P. Stevens mill in Clover, South Carolina, black worker Dell Carter had almost identical experiences when he tried to become a supervisor, including having his car vandalized.[60] It was a sign of the strength of white resistance that most African American workers felt they were only able to get promoted into higher-paying jobs through court decrees that mandated black promotions or through the seniority provisions of union contracts. Seniority was very important because it allowed blacks to be promoted fairly, avoiding the favoritism that supervisors had previously used to promote their friends and relatives. Court decrees were also important because they forced companies to make efforts to upgrade black workers.[61] Many African American workers and union officials felt that court decrees and the fear of lawsuits played a key role in pushing companies to hire blacks into better jobs.[62]

By forcing the companies to place blacks into better-paying jobs, however, lawsuits could cause a great deal of resentment from white workers. A good example of the hostility that could be generated by a lawsuit occurred at Rock Hill Printing and Finishing Company in Rock Hill, South Carolina. The company was sued in the major class action case of *Ellison v. Rock Hill Printing and Finishing Company*, and it is clear that the suit caused considerable racial tension in the plant, especially when a consent decree allowed experienced African American workers to transfer between departments without losing their seniority. Fletcher Beck, a white worker who remembered the lawsuit vividly, explained that there was already a great deal of racial tension when blacks transferred into production jobs in the 1970s: "They come on the machines . . . and they wanted us to teach them, and a lot of the white men wouldn't tell them what to do and show them what to do. They resented the fact that they had to put the black guys out on the production jobs. . . . They would cuss about it and say that they were going to take their jobs away from them and give them to the black people, but they didn't say black people, they would use the term 'nigger.'" Many whites felt that the decree was "taking the rights away from the whites and giving it all to them."[63]

Black workers also had vivid memories of the way that racial tension increased in the plant because of the rights given to blacks by the consent decree. Black workers frequently had their cars vandalized in the company parking lot and were intimidated and threatened on the job.[64] The lead plaintiffs in *Ellison* were subjected to extensive harassment and discrimination when they sought to exercise the seniority rights given them by the lawsuit. Lead plaintiff Leroy Ellison remembered that when he transferred into a previously white job under the terms of the consent decree, "the white folk were opposed to me . . . the department head, one of the men that was in charge, he did some things real nasty against me." Ellison described in his deposition how the white workers in the department subjected him to a lengthy campaign of discrimination and harassment, including refusing to speak to him.[65] Ellison was promoted to the job of assistant operator in the screen print department, but a white coworker was determined to discredit him: "He would misprint a lot of cloth just to make it look like I was doing it." Ellison was also threatened outside the plant by a white worker with a gun. Another plaintiff, Johnnie Archie, believed that whites felt threatened by blacks because so many African Americans had very long service with the company. Many whites consequently feared that blacks could take their jobs.[66]

In *Hicks v. Cannon Mills*, black workers were also given transfer rights under a consent decree as a way of overcoming past discrimination. When they sought to exercise these rights in the 1970s, however, there was again a great deal of resistance from white workers. In 1977, for example, the EEOC reported that blacks who had sought to transfer into "white" jobs under the terms of the decree had been "intimidated into not exercising their transfer rights." Very few blacks at Cannon were able to successfully transfer from all-black departments as the consent decree intended.[67]

The fears of white workers were expressed in a lawsuit filed by one worker, Norman Youngblood, in 1979. *Youngblood v. Rock Hill Printing and Finishing Company* was filed in protest against the consent decree in *Ellison*, claiming that it allowed "reverse discrimination" against white workers. The complaint alleged that "the seniority and promotion systems . . . discriminate against whites." Youngblood claimed that he was "pulled from my job by members of the negro race with more seniority than I had; however, I was not afforded the same right in that I was not allowed to pull members of the negro race with less seniority than me."[68]

They Had to Hire Them: Gradual White
Acceptance of Black Employment

Although both written and oral evidence provides plenty of examples of active resistance from whites toward the introduction of blacks into textile mills, it was probably more typical for white workers to complain about black employment but to make no collective protest about it. This type of reluctant acceptance was reported even in areas where white hate organizations existed. Indeed, although Klan influence was pervasive in some of the areas where textile plants were located, in many instances there was no organized resistance by white workers when integration occurred. A detailed report compiled by the TWUA at Cone Mills in Greensboro, North Carolina, described how white workers disliked the introduction of blacks into their departments but offered no organized resistance against it: "The attitudes of white workers in these plants has not been characterized by any active resentment against the employment of Negroes. They do not encourage it. They may complain about 'niggers' and their shiftlessness, low production or bad attendance. They do not seem to mobilize to stop integrated employment." Race relations had been tense during a period when "Klan literature was handed out at the White Oak gates and several Klan meetings were held in areas close to mill neighborhoods." However, "no retreat in employment practices occurred during this period."[69]

The reaction described at Cone Mills was typical of many white workers. Most did not engage in organized protests, but they did grumble about integration and held negative views of blacks, especially with regard to their work performance. Although white workers claimed that they would engage in protests if blacks were hired, in many cases the threat was not carried out. Instead, they complained about the introduction of blacks but did nothing to prevent it. Mildred Edmond, a white textile worker in Burlington, North Carolina, remembered that when the company told white workers that they were going to hire the first black workers in 1962, "some of them said they'd quit. They wasn't working with no nigger." When the first blacks were hired, however, "they didn't quit. . . . [T]hey didn't like it too much but they didn't say too much. They still don't like it. You can hear them very often making remarks after they get out up there."[70]

Many older white workers claimed that blacks were only hired because companies were forced to integrate by the federal government and that as a result, blacks received special treatment in the plant. In a sense, these views seemed to be used to justify inaction, because white workers blamed the government rather than the company for hiring blacks. They felt that protesting would only victimize the company, which was seen to be as unhappy about the change as many white workers were. Many white workers still expressed these views thirty years after black entry into the industry and had vivid memories of integration, indicating the major change it constituted in their working lives. Mary Latham, a white textile worker who had worked at Opelika Manufacturing Company in Opelika, Alabama, for more than thirty-five years, claimed that blacks "really got treated better than we did. I mean, you know, if they didn't like the way they was doing them they could get something done; we couldn't. . . . They knew they had the government on their side because they could holler discrimination and that would be it."[71]

The feeling of white workers that blacks got special treatment when they came into the mills indicates the wide gap between white and black memories of integration. While white workers claimed that blacks had an easy ride, black workers who were hired into textile plants claimed that they were discriminated against and had to work much harder than whites in order to hold their jobs. Sometimes these views were expressed by workers from the same plants, illustrating how segregation extended even to memory. Many African American workers explained that when they were hired into the textile industry, they automatically knew that they would have to work harder than whites. This occurred partly because blacks feared that they would be fired if they did not work very hard. Joe Gaines, who worked in a textile plant in Sylvester, Georgia, before becoming active in the TWUA, explained that "I guess you could say that once you put a black to work back then, they knew they had to do twice the amount of work that the white person did in order to keep their job. The mentality was sort of embedded into them, 'I've got to do twice the amount or I've got to do it twice as fast.' . . . So they had to come in there with that form of mentality that they had to be twice as good in order to survive."[72] It also became a matter of pride for some black workers to stick to a textile job and prove that they could run it successfully.[73]

It was especially common for whites to claim that blacks were lazy and did not make as good textile workers as whites. At a Uniroyal plant in Winnsboro, South Carolina, for example, it was reported that white workers said, "These Niggers will only work 2 or 3 days at a time."[74] White workers and supervisors tended to stereotype black workers with certain traits. At Riegel Textile Corporation in Trion, Georgia, it was reported that blacks could only work in areas "where there is not much diversity, a clear cut job in one place, and where they are confined to a small area."[75] Supervisors also claimed that blacks did not work on Saturdays as willingly as whites because they wanted to use the day "to go into town, drink a few beers, fish, and loaf around."[76]

While many white workers complained about the introduction of black workers, these views were not the only ones put forward. Indeed, white workers expressed a wide range of opinions concerning the integration, and many of these were both contradictory and complex. Ora Lee Smith, for example, a retired textile worker from Tarboro, North Carolina, felt that integration had a positive effect on race relations in the long term: "I think it helped the relationship between the blacks and the whites a lot, and I think it changed the attitudes of the whites a whole lot, because I mean at one time I guess everybody felt like we were supposed to have the better jobs, but if a person's capable of doing a job, let them have it, whoever. That's the way I feel about it now; maybe I didn't years ago. If a person is capable of running a job, he applies for it, is qualified for it, let him do it."[77] Many other white workers reported that they had "no problem" or "got along just fine" when black workers were brought into the mills. On the whole, it was often female workers who reported these more favorable reactions, while male workers gave more negative opinions.[78] Eula Durham, a retired worker from Bynum, North Carolina, felt that the black workers that came into the plant were "a pretty good bunch" and got along "pretty good" with the white workers. Other female workers often felt that blacks were just as good as whites and regarded the integration as good because it had been wrong for blacks to be excluded from the mill. Carrie Yelton, a mill worker in Hickory, North Carolina, for example, said, "I liked them. They were just as sweet as they could be, the ones that works out where we do, and friendly. And they're good workers."[79]

The "Safe Negro" and the "Super Negro": The Pioneers

White resistance to black assertiveness determined the way that textile companies integrated their plants. In many instances, the companies chose well-known black men from within the mill to be pioneers, usually asking them if they wanted to be promoted. Popularity with whites was an important issue, given the possibility of white opposition. Thus, workers who were seen by whites as troublemakers were unlikely to be asked if they wanted to be promoted.[80]

The pioneers who actually got promotions, therefore, were not the assertive black workers who sought to challenge discriminatory barriers, but were always individuals deliberately chosen by textile companies. They were not necessarily deferential and pliable, but they were usually long-term, established workers who were well known in the plant. Many pioneers, in fact, were not hired from outside but were upgraded from within. As Robert Lincks, the head of personnel at Burlington Industries between 1959 and 1990, recalled, "In these big plants, particularly here in the Carolinas, you had a whole lot of blacks in the workforce that you could just move up. It wasn't a question of integrating the workforce, it was a question of integrating jobs. . . . You had good people to pick from, so you were really integrating occupations and not the workforce." In particular, black men who had worked in heavy, nonproduction jobs in the industry for many years were often asked to be the first production workers. Many of these workers were older blacks who had grown up under segregation, and they were usually very grateful to the company for giving them the chance.[81]

A typical example of this type of integration occurred at the Southern Weaving Company, a textile company based in Greenville, South Carolina. The company's first-shift supervisor in the Hudson Narrow Fabric Mill described how the first black production workers had been promoted from positions in the basement.[82] Rather than requesting their promotions, the workers were handpicked by the company and told they were being promoted. The superintendent of the weaving department, Fred Cisson, recalled in his deposition that the first black production workers were specifically selected: "We actually called in some and told them they were to be promoted, when we had their replacement for their present job, we would move them into production jobs."[83] At the J. P. Stevens complex of plants in Roanoke Rapids, North Carolina, the first African American chosen to work in the large cloth room was promoted rather than hired from outside.[84] Similarly, the EEOC reported in 1968 that the large Russell Mills in Alexander City, Alabama, had started integrating by "transferring current Negro male employees into previous all-white departments and jobs."[85] Other compliance reviews showed how companies picked out established black workers who had started in the mill as janitors.[86]

In *Sherrill v. J. P. Stevens*, the blacks chosen as the first production workers also came from laboring jobs within the plant and were clearly less outspoken than those who brought the case against the company. Stevens picked a middle-aged warehouse laborer, Miles Luckey, to be the first black person to work in its No. 2 plant. Luckey defended the company throughout his deposition, claiming that he could have gotten "any other job" that he wanted in the plant. He also admitted that his approach to working at Stevens was a "humble" one, adding that "when you're a little outspoken you can't get with the people like you should." Like many company representatives, he also claimed not to know why blacks had not been promoted into higher-paying positions and claimed ignorance in response to many awkward questions. Luckey also refused requests by the company to accept a foreman's job, which he did not feel qualified for because of his sixth-grade education. Luckey's repeated rejection of supervisory jobs clearly helped the company because they could use it to claim that they did not discriminate.[87]

Similarly, J. P. Stevens asked wastehouse worker Thomas McCorkle to be the first black production worker in his plant in 1964. Shortly after McCorkle was hired in the picker room, the second black hired was his wife, a clear example of how companies attempted to hire "safe" blacks and their relatives. Company officials also pushed a reluctant McCorkle to go on the training course to become a section man (the same job that Sherrill wanted), but when it came to appointing section men, the company appointed whites from other plants.[88] Following Luckey and McCorkle's transfers, Stevens continued the same method of integration by transferring six or seven other blacks from the warehouse into plant production jobs.[89]

In many cases, companies encouraged their white employees to recommend blacks for the first production jobs. The pioneers thus had white approval, which management hoped would overcome potential opposition. This method of integration was used at several plants of the Riegel Corporation in South Carolina. It was reported that integration had been successful there because the only blacks hired had been recommended by white workers, thus ensuring that the whites would want the blacks to do well: "Company made smooth progress because whites recommended blacks to work and a proprietary interest developed." Similarly, the *Daily News Record* noted in 1965 that "one of the most successful" examples of textile integration was "by a mill which called on its white employees to recommend Negroes they knew and thought trainable for textile production."[90]

The *Record* reported that many companies were asking their current employees to recommend black workers because of the labor shortage. Most of the pioneers that the *Record* highlighted had been hired through the recommendation of existing workers or upgraded from nonproduction positions. Joe Wilkins, a trainee in the card room of an unidentified mill, had been hired after being proposed by his wife, who worked as a maid at the mill. A black woman chosen to be the first spinner had worked for many years in a cleaning and sweeping job and had been selected by the company because of her "conscientious attitude."[91]

Both white and black workers often remembered the way companies picked out popular existing workers to be the first black production workers. On some occasions, the workers themselves played a role in encouraging popular blacks to be the first. At Opelika Manufacturing Company in Opelika, Alabama, for example, long-term white worker Billy Buck recalled that the company employed its first black production workers by promoting two male workers already working on the second shift. One of these workers, Daniel Butler, had been working in a nonproduction position but was encouraged by the white workers to learn how to be a loom fixer. Butler became a successful loom fixer and was still in the position over thirty years later. The story of how he became a loom fixer was well known in the plant, and Butler was still popular with the white workers: "Everybody likes old Daniel."[92]

The first African American supervisors were also usually promoted from within. For example, in *Ellison v. Rock Hill Printing and Finishing Company*, John H. Marshall, the company's vice president for public and industrial relations, testified in 1972 that the company had recently promoted "three or four" black workers into supervisory positions. Marshall added that "all of those came through the ranks."[93]

Companies found other advantages in promoting experienced employees to be the first black production workers. In many plants, older black workers had often built up experience in production jobs by performing them while white operators were on a break or were absent through sickness. Thus, many black workers were familiar with a wide variety of production jobs. Textile companies often upgraded blacks into white jobs that they had already performed on a sporadic basis, thereby minimizing training and disruption, especially if white workers were used to seeing an African American in the job. At Dan River Mills, for example, black worker Russell Dodson, who had worked in nonproduction jobs since 1940, explained in 1973 how he had been upgraded to a white production job in the late 1960s: "I was working as a janitor and a white man was doffing beams and whenever he was out I would work his job and as soon as the job came open I had experience on it so they gave it to me."[94]

In textile plants, getting hiring often depended upon having a relative or friend working in the plant who could "put in a good word" to their supervisor when a vacancy occurred. This system was commonplace across the South, and it often functioned as a means of excluding blacks, since supervisors had much stronger contacts with the white community. In several of their campaigns, TEAM reported that being hired depended on having a relative in the plant.[95] Nevertheless, companies also used this practice as a way of hiring the first black workers. TEAM director Mordecai Johnson reported that at one of J. P. Stevens's plants in Greenville, South Carolina, "a Negro was hired as a doffer [a low level job] with a commitment for quick promotion because his uncle had been with the plant for quite some time and was liked by the supervisor. After 2 months, he was given 6 weeks of training to become a weaver and he got one of the first weaver openings thereafter. Of about 500 weavers on his shift, he knows no other Negroes."[96]

For civil rights activists like Johnson, the way that companies hired a few blacks through personal contacts but refused to open up their plants more widely was not integration but tokenism. Companies stayed in control of racial hiring by carefully choosing who they recruited rather than opening their doors to full equal opportunity. Thus, when a company in Anderson County, South Carolina, employed their first black worker, TEAM reported that "he is the son of an oldtimer with the company and is serving as their token Negro." Companies argued, however, that they had to select blacks carefully in order to keep the goodwill of their white workers. As one industry spokesman declared in 1969, "We've got to be careful about how we hire Negroes or we'll lose the confidence of the whites they'll be working next to."[97]

Even when companies took great care to hire their pioneers through families that they knew well, they sometimes ran into opposition from white workers. At one textile firm visited by AFSC representative Noyes Collinson in 1962, the president had recently taken the first steps toward integration by hiring the husband of his wife's maid as an office mail clerk. Illustrating the complex and contradictory nature of racial attitudes, however, the president "was surprised to find that the women on his office staff who probably have Negro maids whom they 'love' resented working with a Negro."[98]

It is obvious, however, that on many occasions the hiring of black pioneers through existing workers was of enormous benefit in helping integration run smoothly. The trade journal *Textile Industries* highlighted an incident at one mill where "a young Negro employee asked a white female employee for a date." The woman complained, leading to what the company described as "a real touchy situation." The company did not want to lose the black worker because he was showing "exceptional promise." The incident had occurred because "the girl had gone out of her way to be nice to him, and to try to make him feel accepted. The Negro simply misinterpreted her intentions." The situation was resolved, however, because "the Negro's father was a trusted and valued employee of long standing. He straightened his son out . . . and we ended up being able to keep both employees."[99]

Aware of the sensitivities of integration, most companies proceeded cautiously. As well as carefully selecting who was to be a pioneer, companies also closely monitored the areas in which blacks were introduced. Many companies were very careful to minimize contact between black men and white women. The TWUA's H. S. Williams reported in 1962 that Pacific Mills in Columbia, South Carolina, had started to integrate but that "on jobs where the workers may rub against women there are no colored people."[100] At Cannon Mills in Kannapolis, North Carolina, the company hired blacks into a separate building outside the main mill before deciding to introduce them slowly into the plant.[101]

One of the aspects of textile integration that affected both male and female workers was that pioneers had to be overqualified compared to their white counterparts. This trend again reflected management concern about white opposition to black promotions. Sarah Herbin, who met with many textile companies to encourage minority employment in her work as head of the Merit Employment Program of the AFSC, told the EEOC textile forum in 1967 that "perhaps the most frustrating experience" in referring prospective employees to textile companies was "requests for the 'super' Negro."[102] Similarly, the *Charlotte Observer* reported in 1968 that personnel directors admitted privately that any black who was promoted into a white-collar job had been "meticulously screened" because if the "first few" were not excellent choices, it would "harm the chances of others." Boyce Medlin of the North Carolina Good Neighbor Council explained that in his experience, managers often promoted "super Negroes" because they knew that if they did not, there would be bad feelings among the white workers, which would reduce morale.[103] Indeed, the qualifications of many pioneers make it clear that companies covered all their bases during selection.[104]

One plant visit Sarah Herbin made to the personnel department of Burlington Industries illustrates the "super Negro" problem. Seeking to encourage the further employment of black office workers, Herbin asked what the company required of their clerical applicants. She was told that Burlington was only interested in "top rate" black applicants. Herbin responded that she had already referred such applicants and they had not been hired. She explained that a local black university was very upset that Burlington had not hired one of their top graduates because she did not pass the company's employment test. Herbin said that the black community wanted to know "if all of the white girls employed are 'top rate.' Aren't there any 'average' girls who work there? Why is it that all of the Negro girls have to be sharp, keen, competent, likeable persons?" Burlington, however, held firm to its policy of seeking "super Negroes." The company responded that "they did have some average girls, but felt that in a new situation it was important for the Negro girls to be above-average."[105]

The "super Negro" problem was identified as one of the greatest obstacles to black progress in the textile industry at the EEOC textile forum in 1967. Vivian W. Henderson, the president of Clark College in Atlanta and chairman of the Task Force on Employment at the White House Conference on Civil Rights, told the forum that companies' desire for well-qualified black workers denied many blacks the opportunity to learn on the job that whites received: "Negroes must be given a better shot at on-the-job training. In too many instances, they are looking for the 'instant Negro.' White women have all of the opportunity in the world to go on the job and make mistakes, have on-the-job training, and qualify for the job. In the case of the Negro, he's got to bring his qualifications with him." Henderson argued that the same opportunities should be given to the "limited qualified Negro" as to the "limited qualified white," so that inexperienced African Americans had a chance to move into the textile industry in greater numbers.[106]

In many cases, the hiring of pioneers through personal contacts and requiring overqualification went together. Realizing that integration was a big change requiring a period of adjustment for workers, textile management aimed to minimize the disruption that might occur by selecting overqualified workers who would also be "safe" because they were hired through contacts. Burlington executive Robert Lincks, for example, remembered that the company deliberately hired "respectable" blacks, who were often vouched for by well-established white contacts. The company, according to Lincks, "may have been guilty of, like baseball, trying to hire Jackie Robinsons when we were bringing our first minority people in. We didn't want anyone that we would have to apologize for. We weren't naive about the risk involved, and when we started to integrate we would systematically seek people that were well recommended, good record in work. . . . Often it was someone's maid that you knew."[107]

In addition to seeking overqualified African Americans and hiring through contacts, companies also took other precautions when they hired the first black production workers. One of the most common was to hire light-skinned African Americans as pioneers. Sarah Herbin of the AFSC wrote that textile companies had inundated her with "shocking requests for 'light-skinned' Negroes," especially when they wanted to make "a show case placement so they can say, 'Oh, we have one!'"[108] African American workers themselves remembered that when companies first started to hire blacks in the 1960s, the chances of getting hired increased relative to the lightness of one's skin color. Jettie Purnell, who worked for J. P. Stevens in Roanoke Rapids, North Carolina, for example, recalled that the company's preference for light-skinned workers made a mockery of their nondiscrimination statements to hire without regard for color: "People can say color doesn't mean anything, that's a lie. Color means something, because I can tell you people that I know that I have sent to the mills, and they was fair-skinned women. They hired them. And I can show you a couple of dark-skinned women, they wouldn't hire them. They didn't blend in. . . . When they first started hiring blacks . . . it was pretty bad to overcome that hurdle." Lucy Sledge, the lead plaintiff in *Sledge v. J. P. Stevens*, remembered that when she started working for the company in 1966, "they weren't hiring any 'ugly blacks.' I hate to say that, but I don't know another way to put it. All I know is there were no 'ugly blacks' in there. You had to be light and nice-looking. Now, I can't call myself beautiful, but I am light-skinned."[109] Stevens workers also claimed that well into the 1970s, having light skin was a big advantage when it came to being promoted.[110]

It is clear that a large gap exists between public and private accounts of the racial integration of the textile industry. In newspaper accounts, mill owners stressed the lack of opposition to integration and the ease with which the industry had introduced blacks. The complaints of black workers in the lawsuits, however, together with the oral history accounts of black pioneers, reveal a hidden history of resistance to integration that was never publicized. Indeed, most black workers who were hired in the first wave of black production workers had powerful memories of white workers who abused them or refused to help them on their jobs. Sammy Alston, who was promoted to a production job at J. P. Stevens's Rosemary plant in 1966, remembered a whole catalogue of incidents that epitomized the integration experience for many pioneers: "You'd be working a production job, the machine would break down. Well, that's when you would have had nothing but white fixers. I have told the fixer, I say, 'Well, how about coming here and fixing this frame for me?' He'd say, 'F this frame' and keep right on walking. The frame would stand for about three or four hours. I'm supposed to get downtime on that; I wouldn't get no downtime, running those frames that was standing. . . . It was rough, I'm telling you. . . . You didn't have no say-so whatsoever."[111]

These experiences of resistance and noncooperation meant that pioneers had to be both well-qualified and determined to succeed. As Nick Builder, a union organizer and business agent who worked in the South throughout the 1960s and 1970s, remembered, textile pioneers were a unique group marked by their exceptional qualifications and determination: "I knew a number of people in different plants who were the first African American fixer or the first African American maintenance worker, and like their equivalent the first woman mechanic or so on, they frequently had to be pretty strong, tough individuals who withstood, you know, quite a bit of, if not outright harassment, certainly ostracism and jokes, or things like no one really giving them any help, like they would other people on the job, and therefore they had to be, you know, much better than average at the job to hold it, and they had to have a certain strength and a certain sort of angry commitment to being a pioneer, you know what I mean, in hostile territory. Those that followed didn't need those same qualities. . . . The pressure or harassment that I'm talking about came frequently from fellow workers, and frequently from management."[112]

Black workers who were hired in the 1960s and 1970s felt that blacks were only used on the worst jobs that whites did not want. Bennett Taylor, who was hired at J. P. Stevens in Roanoke Rapids in October 1965, for example, believed that "blacks then was getting hired, but they was getting hired in a job that that was the only place that they could go. It was a dirty job that a white person didn't want to do."[113] Another Stevens worker, James Boone, hired in May 1971, felt that companies saw blacks as a way of filling undesirable jobs: "We took the jobs that the whites didn't want to do . . . and right now we're still taking the jobs that they don't want to do. . . . If you go and look at most of the nasty jobs and the hard jobs, you have more blacks in those jobs right now. This is in the 1990s."[114] Joe Gaines was hired into a textile plant that made car upholstery in

Sylvester, Georgia, in 1969. He felt that companies knew that most African Americans would take any job in a textile plant because they had always been excluded from the industry and made to work in agricultural jobs that "were considered to be much, much lower than working inside of a mill." Hence, when companies were forced to integrate, they made a conscious decision to restrict blacks to the worst jobs: "If we've got to bring the blacks in, make them do the harder jobs. . . . We'll still keep the better jobs. . . . We'll make sure our people are promoted. . . . And that was the trend throughout the South."[115]

Union representatives who worked in the South also believed that blacks were only hired in a few jobs where the companies had no other source of labor. Clyde Bush, who had been either a textile worker or a union organizer since the 1960s, explained: "You see what they started doing when they started bringing the blacks into the workforce, they started out putting them on the lowest undesirable jobs that there were in the plant here. Like I said earlier, they put them into the card room, they put them into the wastehouses, they had them in the opening rooms—they had them in the most undesirable places there were to work."[116]

The hiring of blacks into low-paying jobs was the most common technique that companies used to minimize resistance from white workers. On some occasions, textile companies also went to great lengths to assure their white workers that blacks were not their economic equals. TEAM reported in 1968 that in the major textile center of Spartanburg, South Carolina, one company had arranged with the city for a bus to transport black workers to their jobs. This bus overcame the transportation problems that prevented many blacks from taking textile jobs. The workers took the bus, however, with the arrangement that they "agree not to stop riding the bus after they make enough money to buy a car." The "white power structure" was concerned about employing blacks discreetly, "so the whites won't find out what they are doing for Negroes."[117] Similarly, black workers who were hired into the industry remembered that they had to be discreet about the economic advance that they were making. Willie Long, who worked at the Eagle and Phenix Mill in Columbus, Georgia, remembered that many blacks had to hide any sign that they were doing well when they were at work because supervisors would then harass them. He remembered one black worker who "had a brand new Cadillac, but he was afraid to bring it down to the mill because the boss could look out there and see him with a new Cadillac and really crack down on him, and up until the time he retired, he was afraid. He always drove an old ragged car down there; he was afraid to drive that car down there. They would make it hard on him, you know. When they figured you was doing well, then they would make it hard on you. They would fire you, any little thing they would fire you."[118]

If resistance was so marked, how did any integration occur? White resistance was most intense when blacks were promoted into higher-paying jobs. Black workers felt that in general, integration proceeded smoothly only because companies hired African Americans into lower-paying positions that few whites wanted to work in. The labor shortage in the industry often meant that whites were leaving these jobs in any case. Although the number of jobs that blacks worked in increased, whites still held the vast majority of the higher-paying positions. Fully aware of the resistance of white workers, and sharing many of their concerns, textile companies integrated their mills in a way that did not threaten whites. One of the themes that emerges throughout this study is that integration of the mills was usually not as large a change as it may appear. In a variety of ways, companies deliberately limited the jobs that they allowed blacks to come into, and many jobs, especially those that were higher-paying or prestigious positions, clearly remained "white" jobs.

The Only Ones That Got a
Promotion Was a White Man

The Discriminatory Treatment of Black
Men in the Textile Industry, 1964–1980

five

In recent years, several historians and economists have noted the entry of blacks into textiles as a positive and significant change. Drawing on overall statistics showing that blacks were able to secure a significant representation in the textile workforce by the mid-1970s, they have pointed out the scale of this change in an industry with a history of excluding African Americans.[1] This emphasis on the entry of African Americans into the workforce, however, has meant that the long-term experiences of black textile workers have been somewhat neglected. Very little is known about the experiences of black textile workers after integration, particularly the degree and type of racial discrimination that they faced in the workforce.

The problem with concentrating on overall industry statistics is that they provide a misleading and incomplete picture of black employment in textiles after 1964. By the mid-1960s, the problem for many African American workers was not only getting hired but upgrading into skilled and white-collar positions. The issue of discrimination was particularly important given the context that integration occurred in. Because most companies had been pushed to integrate by the federal government and a labor shortage, and they still had many deep-seated reservations and fears about black workers, it is clear that discrimination within the mill would be a serious problem.

Indeed, the issue of discriminatory treatment was the central concern of black textile workers in the 1960s and 1970s. Joe Gaines, a black worker hired into a textile plant in Sylvester, Georgia, in 1969, became an organizer for the TWUA in the 1970s. A quiet, self-effacing man, Gaines felt that discrimination was the major problem facing black textile workers. While laws had pushed companies to hire blacks, they could not prevent discrimination once in the mill: "To get into the mills, into the workforce was one thing. To be treated fairly in the workforce, in terms of on-the-job situations, hiring and promotions, and even firing practices, was a whole different ballgame after we got into the mills, so that's an issue that had to be dealt with in some type of way. There was no laws. The law had got us in, but there was no law per se to keep you in."[2] Similarly, Vivian W. Henderson, president of Clark College in Atlanta, told the EEOC textile forum in 1967 that although hiring discrimination was a problem in the industry, there were equally serious problems once inside the mill: "If a Negro somehow manages to get a job in textiles, if he gets through the door, he finds himself in menial tasks and in dead-end situations. . . . These are important problems. Just as important are problems of promotion and work arrangements."[3]

The way that textile executives used statistics demonstrates how overall data could conceal the amount of discrimination that remained in the industry.[4] While industry representatives such as Sadler Love of the ATMI were eager to promote overall statistics showing how African Americans were increasingly being hired, the industry had what the *Charlotte Observer* called "a policy of silence" about how many blacks were in better-paying jobs. In a series of articles exploring the racial integration of the southern textile industry, the *Observer* found that many companies refused to reveal their promotion statistics. The *Observer* concluded that progress in upgrading blacks was minimal. Companies, indeed, "seize upon a single black promotion as a spectacular leap forward. . . . But company spokesmen concede that in terms of absolute numbers, the statistical battle the government forces them to fight, the promotions picture looks weak."[5]

In the 1960s and 1970s, the vast majority of black textile workers were men. Black women had traditionally been excluded from the industry, but black men had always been hired to work in heavy or dirty nonproduction jobs.[6] Even when production jobs were opened up in the 1960s, most black men were hired either into the lowest-paying production jobs or into traditional black nonproduction positions. This remained true even into the late 1970s. Black men who were hired into the industry repeatedly asserted that overall entry statistics concealed these problems. In 1978, Bennett Taylor, a black J. P. Stevens worker, declared in an article about the Stevens campaign that the company's concentration on overall statistics hid the more important issue of discrimination in job assignments: "Stevens has put out a lot of propaganda about how well they treat their black employees. They keep saying that 23% of their workers are members of minority groups. But they refuse to say how many of these workers are in different jobs." In fact, although Stevens had started to hire blacks "on the inside," Taylor asserted that "even then it was only to do the dirtier jobs—opening, picking, carding, the waste house and cleaning up. . . . There are very few in the better jobs. And there certainly aren't any on the J. P. Stevens Board of Directors. I think that tells you what most of those 23% are doing."[7]

The exhaustive records provided by lawsuits, and indeed the existence of the lawsuits themselves, reveal that black workers endured considerable discrimination in textile plants throughout the 1960s and 1970s; that, contrary to common belief, some companies were still reluctant to hire African Americans; and that, when they were hired, black workers were usually placed in the lowest and least desirable positions, with little chance of moving up. Although a labor shortage existed, it did not induce companies to accept blacks and whites as equals in the workplace.

Written evidence indicates that the problems highlighted by black textile workers in the lawsuits were typical of those suffered by African American textile workers elsewhere. In 1967, AFSC field representative Sarah Herbin wrote about her experiences over ten years with the AFSC's Merit Employment Program. Herbin provided broad insights into how black textile workers felt about their treatment in the industry, showing that they felt unfairly treated and trapped in low-paying jobs: "Talking with textile employees, I find that their biggest complaints include: 1) no opportunity for upgrading like their white counterparts; 2) whites get promoted with less seniority; 3) difference in pay, even when they are doing the same jobs; and 4) there is no one to whom they can turn to correct these problems."[8] A report submitted by four economists at North Carolina Agricultural and Technical State University in 1972, using interviews with 233 black textile workers from eight different cities in North and South Carolina as part of an EEOC investigation into the textile industry, also revealed that black workers faced a great deal of discrimination, with the inability to advance again being the main problem.[9]

The companies' discriminatory practices led to a considerable degree of alienation, anger, and disillusionment among black workers. The records of the lawsuits reflect these feelings, especially the letters that African American workers wrote to lawyers or to the EEOC. These letters, like those written by textile workers to President Franklin Roosevelt during the New Deal, provide the reader with a valuable insight into the working conditions in the South's textile mills. Workers' depositions are also a useful source because they offered an opportunity for black workers to talk at length about racial discrimination in textile mills and produced some revealing testimony. Detailed statistics compiled directly from corporate records provide quantitative data to support the workers' claims. As a result, these records make it possible to move beyond the initial integration of the plants and to explore the long-term working experiences of the first generation of African American production workers in the southern textile industry.[10]

"We Feel as Though We Are Being Discriminated Against"

One of the most striking features of the textile lawsuits is that many were initiated by workers who wrote to the EEOC complaining of racial discrimination. In their letters, workers described in vivid detail the problems facing African American textile workers. Their most common areas of complaint were the assignment of blacks to the lowest-paying jobs, the persistence of segregated jobs, the hazardous and dangerous working conditions that African Americans were required to endure, and the racism of white supervisors and their unwillingness to promote black workers. In addition, these letters reveal the collective determination of black workers to end discrimination and improve working conditions.

In February 1971, a group of black men from Fieldcrest Mills in Eden, North Carolina, initiated the major class action lawsuit of *Galloway v. Fieldcrest Mills* by collectively writing two letters to the EEOC district office in Atlanta. At the time the letters were written, Fieldcrest Mills was one of the largest southern textile companies, employing over 11,000 workers in a series of plants around the town of Eden, located in Piedmont North Carolina near the Virginia border. The Fieldcrest letters contained many of the themes of other black workers' letters, particularly the complaints of job segregation and hazardous conditions, as well as the determination of black workers to enforce the rights given to them under the Civil Rights Act of 1964.[11]

Led by two senior male employees, the writers of the first letter described how black workers were still restricted to lower-paying jobs and were refused promotions to better-paying positions. Speaking as a group in a way that was typical of the letters written to the EEOC, they explained: "We the Black employees of the Fieldcrest Mills wish to file a Complaint of Discrimination and Unfair Labor Practice. We are not given Equal Chance to upgrade as Whites. All Work for the Blacks are undesirable and are on a lower pay scale. There are no Whites at all placed on the bottom pay scale. Only Blacks are placed on the bottom pay scale." The Fieldcrest workers explained that despite "integration," notions of "black" and "white" jobs still persisted in their company as in many other southern textile companies: "There are no Whites ever placed in Certain Departments—Only Blacks." Jobs such as bailing cotton and handling coal were "on a low pay scale and strictly for Blacks." The workers were "asking that someone from the Equal and Fair Labor Commission come and interview this matter as proof and evidence of Discrimination and Unfair Labor Practice used upon the Blacks."[12]

A second letter was written by a group of workers in the "Karastan Dyeing Department" who asked for their names to be kept confidential "because we cannot afford to get fired." The main complaint of these workers was that they worked in an all-black department with hazardous working conditions. The black workers felt that if their department was integrated, working conditions would be improved: "We would surely appreciate an integrated department and we feel confident that things would be a lot better if it were." Whites, however, were not placed in the department. The letter explained that "white men are not even sent to interview jobs in our department. None of us knows why, but we think it is because the working conditions are so hard, dangerous and lousy." Indeed, the workers claimed that the company "does not care about its black employees in the dyehouse. We work in a very unhealthy environment." Workers claimed they were exposed to harmful toxic chemicals but that "nothing is being done about it."

The workers blamed a racist white supervisor for these conditions: "Our superintendent has been head of this department for about 25 years. He is always reminding us of how things were in the old days. It seems like he cannot accept the fact that Negroes are equally human as he is. He also, as it seems, thinks we have to be told or showed everything. There have been several occasions where employees have applied for better jobs and our superintendent fixed things in his own sly way so we could not transfer to better ourselves. This is the type of guy we have to deal with. He is all for himself."

Black workers were determined to protest about these conditions, as the writing of the letters indicated. Indeed, the Fieldcrest workers displayed the confidence that the Civil Rights Act had brought to the workplace for many black workers. They declared that "this is 1971 and nobody has to be a fool these days regardless of race, creed or color. The Negroes in our department were not put in this world just to do the hard, common labor. We are getting tired of not qualifying for better jobs because we are black. The Civil Rights Act gives us certain privileges and we would like to exercise these rights now." Significantly, the Fieldcrest workers showed their determination by also sending their letter to the NAACP.[13]

Data produced by the ensuing lawsuit, a class action on behalf of all African American workers at Fieldcrest's large division in Eden, clearly illustrates the job segregation that workers complained of and the large pay disparities that it produced. In 1971, all thirty-seven loom fixers in the large No. 1 blanket mill were white. In the Karastan dyeing department where the lead plaintiffs worked, the workforce was 99 percent black, with heavy jobs filled entirely by

African Americans. On the whole, many job categories were either entirely black or entirely white. These patterns meant that even in the 1970s, whites at Fieldcrest took home about 20 percent more in pay than blacks.[14]

Many other letters were written by black men who complained that they were restricted to the lowest-paying jobs. From the Graniteville Company's division in Augusta, Georgia, for example, two black male workers, Edward Price and James C. Walker, wrote a letter to the EEOC in February 1968 entitled "Alleging Discrimination." This letter was responsible for initiating the major lawsuit of *Graniteville Company v. EEOC*. It is clear that the position of African American workers at Graniteville, one of the South's oldest textile plants, had failed to improve despite the passage of civil rights legislation. The letter described how "out of the approx. 210 negro employees there are only 9 with the same type of high paying jobs as the whites." Blacks complained that white workers were promoted ahead of them without regard for seniority: "The Company Policy on advancement or promotion is based on seniority, but this does not hold true where negroes are involved." Indeed, promotions were denied to capable black workers: "When we find that a job is open, we ask about the job and the way inwitch we may obtain the job, we are then told that we will be notfied later or that they will let us know something later, and we are never notified; later we learn that the job has been filled by a white, this type of thing happen constantly." Whites were "consistently promoted to supervisory and higher positions, by-passing Negro employees with established rights. There are no Negro supervisors, fixers, weavers or any major job in this textile plant." The workers claimed that discrimination existed in every facet of employment, including job assignments, promotions, and treatment by supervisors: "White employees are treated fairly in every instance, We the Negroes are consistently treated differently in every way."[15]

The Graniteville pattern was typical in that production departments were integrated, but blacks were still kept in the most menial positions in these departments. The workers explained that in the card room, for example, "the employees are mixed, but all of the major jobs are held by whites." In other production areas, "the only job the negro get is the low paying ones." At the same time, most African Americans still worked in large nonproduction departments where the work was very hard and dirty. In short, as the letter concluded, there was "no job advancement, security, or promotion for the negroes. . . . [A]fter you have been excepted for employment, you are sent from the office directly to a labor's job witch always consist of hard work, and low pay and in an all negro area of work."[16]

When the EEOC investigated the Graniteville workers' complaints, the data they collected from the company's records supported the allegations of job segregation and the concentration of blacks in low-paying jobs. Just as the

workers had described, for example, the EEOC found that the highest-paid production job, that of weaver, was still an all-white position in June 1968. Supervisors, loom fixers, and a variety of higher-paying production positions were
also all-white. Blacks did work in the weave room, but only within "the all-
Negro classification of 'Cloth Doffer,' or the job, 'Battery Hand.'" These patterns produced considerable pay disparities between white and black workers,
with blacks earning around thirty cents an hour less than whites.[17]

These letters typified many others that were responsible for initiating lawsuits in the textile industry.[18] The promotion of inexperienced, unqualified
whites over black men with long service prompted many black male workers
to write letters or file EEOC charges. One worker from a Burlington Industries
plant in Lexington, North Carolina, wrote to the "Civil Rights Commission"
complaining that only whites were allowed to take weaving jobs, which was
"one of the top jobs in textiles." Blacks with seniority were passed over so frequently that the worker thought this was "a policy in the mill." Like many black
workers, he also complained about racist management. Indeed, his supervisor
had told him "that no Negro had the intelligence to even be a weaver. If this is
his attitude, which all signs indicate it to be, of course no Negro can ever weave
or move forward in this plant. Therefore as far as this plant is concerned you
can tear up the equal opportunity law as long as he is manager." The worker
concluded, "I am willing to work hard and learn to do a better job but if the
road is blocked for advancement by an individual whats the use."[19] A similar
mood of frustration at being passed over for promotion moved a black Fieldcrest Mills worker to file EEOC charges in 1970, soon after he was refused a promotion by his supervisor. Like other workers, Dexter Law used his EEOC charge
form as a chance to describe his frustration: "But just because I am black I am
not suppose to better myself. I think that I am capable of doing this job but he
wont give me a chance to even try."[20]

While many lawsuits largely concerned themselves with one area of discriminatory practice, others made broadly based complaints about a wide
range of grievances. Letters of complaint written by workers in two class
actions against Cannon Mills, in particular, illustrate clearly how racial discrimination in employment could affect many different areas of workers'
lives.[21] The major Cannon case, that of *Hicks v. Cannon Mills*, was initiated by
black worker Donald Ray Hicks, who repeatedly wrote the EEOC complaining
about racial discrimination at the company. The beginning of one letter
summed up the mood of Hicks's letters: "I want you to write *Cannon Mills Co.*
about how they do the *black* workers there. They do them any kind of way."[22]

Other Cannon workers supported Hicks, and the wide variety of complaints
made by Cannon workers were put together into a formal charge of discrimination signed by three lead plaintiffs and mailed to the EEOC. The letter listed

thirteen discriminatory practices and showed how broad-ranging racial inequality could be in textile towns, especially in communities such as Kannapolis, North Carolina, where the company had considerable control over the community. One of the central complaints in the Cannon case was the segregation of workers in company housing. Cannon workers complained that "housing for Negro employees is inferior to the housing for white employees."[23]

This area of dissatisfaction was unique because most southern textile companies had sold their company housing to workers by the 1960s. Cannon Mills, however, still owned more than 2,000 houses as late as 1970. When Kannapolis was built in 1887, African Americans had been confined to a separate mill village that was built specifically for them, and in the 1960s, most black workers still lived there. Houses in the black village were smaller than houses in the white village and were also of inferior construction. Also, the company did not modernize the black houses in the postwar period to the same extent that it did the white houses. A journalist from the *Wall Street Journal* described his impressions of the housing in Kannapolis in 1969: "White families' homes are on spacious lots, while Negro homes are crammed together. The Negroes' homes generally appear smaller and not as well maintained." One of the central complaints in *United States v. Cannon Mills* was that despite these clear differences, blacks paid the same rent as white workers for their inferior homes.[24]

The obviously inferior nature of the black houses, and the location of the black mill village on its own site well away from the white mill village, was a clear reminder to all of the economic and social inferiority of African Americans and showed how deep-seated discrimination often was in textile communities. Indeed, perhaps most telling was the social stigma attached to the black mill village in Kannapolis. The plaintiffs' lawyer, James Ferguson, remembered that when he visited Kannapolis to investigate the workers' complaints, he felt that the town, with its separate mill village, "was built on the notion that blacks and whites were going to be separate and unequal forever. They were going to live separately and unequally, going to work separately and unequally. . . . Any aspect of life was going to be separate and unequal for blacks and whites."[25]

The complaint letter in the *Cannon* case described many other types of discrimination in detail. As in other cases, black workers complained that they worked in the lowest-paying, hardest jobs.[26] Cannon was accused of depressing all workers' wages by segregating jobs, "assigning white employees to 'white jobs' and Negroes to 'Negro jobs' and paying them the lowest wages possible under the circumstances; thus Negro wages are held down by the force of segregation and white wages are held down by the implied threat of cheap Negro labor." Black workers were also said to be discouraged and intimidated from seeking promotions or protesting about the company's discriminatory policies.[27]

The workers' complaint letter also illustrated how "subtle forms of employment discrimination" affected every aspect of their jobs in the mills. They claimed that the company was more vigorous in defending itself against the workmen's compensation claims of black employees injured on the job, while at the same time being more vigorously opposed to unemployment compensation claims filed by African Americans. They also described how "Negro employees are more quickly suspected of theft—and discharged on less evidence." On the whole, blacks were "expected to have higher qualifications for any job, to be more productive, to be more submissive, to be more punctual, and to be absent less often and for more compelling reasons."[28]

While a wide variety of textile lawsuits provide information about the grievances of black textile workers after integration, it is perhaps fitting that the largest and most important lawsuit, that of *Sledge v. J. P. Stevens*, offers some of the most revealing insights. In *Sledge*, the class comprised over 3,000 persons and could have been even larger. Indeed, the case covered the nation's second largest textile company, which employed nearly 50,000 workers in 1968. The *Sledge* case was originally filed in 1970 and applied to the company's main concentration of plants in Roanoke Rapids, North Carolina.[29] All 3,000 plaintiffs in the case were interviewed by African American cocounsel T. T. Clayton, a local lawyer who set up an office at Horne's Motor Inn in Roanoke Rapids where workers could come and see him and fill out a "Back Pay Questionnaire and Claim Form." Many took the opportunity to include detailed letters with the forms explaining how they felt the company had mistreated African Americans. As a result, these documents offer a rich insight into the types of problems facing African Americans who worked for the textile giant in the 1960s and 1970s.[30]

One of the most common areas of complaint was the refusal by Stevens to hire blacks at the same time that whites were being hired in considerable numbers. While this problem was particularly acute for African American women, it affected black men as well, especially in the *Sledge* case.[31] Data produced in the case showed that whites were consistently hired more frequently than blacks between 1967 and 1980. Between 1969 and 1980, the black hire rate was 29.4 percent, compared to a white hire rate of 52.6 percent. Thus, the black hire rate was only 55.9 percent of the white hire rate. (See table 2.) Based on these statistics, the court found Stevens guilty of hiring discrimination in the *Sledge* case.[32]

Several black men wrote detailed letters to accompany their back pay claim forms in which they described their anger and frustration caused by the company's refusal to hire them. Larry Cornelius Dowton, for example, expressed these feelings well in describing his attempts to get employment at Stevens in the 1970s: "The people who got jobs was white and I wonder why. Is my skin

Table 2. Comparison of Black and White Hiring Rates at J. P. Stevens, 1969–1980

Year	White Hire Rate as a Percentage of Total	Black Hire Rate as a Percentage of Total	Black Hire Rate as a Percentage of White Hire Rate
1969	67.3	44.1	65.5
1970	73.7	43.9	59.6
1971	63.3	31.8	50.3
1972	65.6	39.4	60.0
1973	60.4	41.6	68.9
1974	36.4	18.1	49.7
1975	44.9	20.7	46.2
1976	20.6	12.9	62.9
1977	24.9	16.4	65.9
1978	15.0	8.1	54.3
1979	39.4	33.0	83.8
1980	35.5	25.9	73.0
Total	52.6	29.4	55.9

Source: Attachment MM, Plaintiffs' Submission of Additional Documents of Record in Support of Their Motion for Partial Summary Judgement on Issues Not Reasonably Open to Dispute, for the Determination of Certain Preliminary Legal Questions Concerning the Back Pay Claims, *Sledge v. J. P. Stevens*.

the wrong color or is it no place for a black man trying to live and make it in a white man world. . . . You white people might be smart, but a dummy didnt write this, a 'black man did.'" Such frustration often sprang from the suffering that the company's refusal to hire had caused blacks, a real problem in a one-industry town such as Roanoke Rapids. Sometimes the only alternative was to drive long distances in order to find work, most of which was considered inferior to that offered in the mills. As one black worker who had been forced to relocate to Virginia explained, "If the people at J. P. Stevens had done right, I would have had a job there now, and wouldn't have to drive 200 miles to look after my mother every week."[33]

Despite the difficulties involved in getting hired at J. P. Stevens, most African Americans were remarkably persistent in their efforts. In a story typical of many others, one black man described how in the 1970s, "for a long period I applied each morning for a job. During this time I watched and talked with unqualified, illiterate whites that received jobs. All the whites had applied afterwards. Finally the employment official asked me not to come around the office anymore." Another African American described how "he would sit for hours when applying before they would wait on him [but they would take whites immediately]." Some black workers told how they had finally been able to get hired only after being recommended by a white person. Other African Americans who were eventually employed claimed that they had to wait a very long time to be considered. Some, meanwhile, even used the claim form to appeal for a job: "I need a job, help me please." These stories show just how difficult it was for African Americans to get hired at Stevens. Even though black hiring had increased, it still did not match black demand for jobs.[34]

Stevens workers also complained about the type of jobs that were given to those who managed to get hired. One black male worker summed up the feelings of many others when he wrote, "The people at J. P. Stevens gave all whites the best jobs. The blacks had jobs like sweeping floors, whites ran machines and made the most money. They also gave whites more overtime than blacks."[35]

Although many of the comments that plaintiffs wrote on their claim forms described particular types of discrimination in hiring, promotion, or layoff, some used the form simply as an opportunity to make general statements about how they felt about J. P. Stevens. These statements show that there was considerable hostility to the company in the African American community, as many applauded that the lawsuit was finally bringing the company to task for what they viewed as decades of mistreatment against African Americans. Plaintiff David L. Burnette, for example, scrawled on the bottom of his claim form, "I would like to thank some one, because it time for somebody to do something about J. P. Stevens and start helping the Black. Thanks." Another plaintiff wrote that he wanted to participate in the lawsuit because the company had "a nasty attitude" toward African Americans. Many plaintiffs seemed glad to have the opportunity to record how they felt about the company. Some, for example, claimed fearlessly that they were willing to answer questions about the company's discriminatory practices "anytime." Others wanted to expose the company's past treatment of African Americans. One added to his form, "At one time they only hired white."[36]

The letters thus indicate that many black workers felt there was massive discrimination in the textile industry long after the passage of the Civil Rights Act of 1964. Although blacks worked in the industry in increasing numbers, they still felt discriminated against, especially in job assignments and opportunities for promotion. It is important, however, to look at the detailed record provided by trial proceedings and depositions to determine whether the problems raised in the letters were typical of those suffered by black textile workers generally.

"There Has Never Been No Colored Promoted Up"

One of the main complaints of the letters written to the EEOC was that black workers were restricted to the lowest-paying jobs and found it very difficult to secure promotions to higher-paying positions. This complaint was also a major issue in the proceedings of many lawsuits. In other cases where letters were written initiating proceedings, however, no records of depositions or trial testimony survived. The rest of this chapter will use depositions and trial testimony from the cases where these records were available to examine in greater detail the issues raised in the letters.

In the legal records, as in the letters, the most common grievance of black textile workers across the South was their restriction to low-paying jobs. What the legal testimony really highlighted, however, was that African Americans were not only refused promotions to higher-paying positions but also had to train inexperienced whites for these jobs. Richard T. Seymour, the attorney who represented the plaintiffs in most of the cases, told the court in *Sledge v. J. P. Stevens* that "the classic example" of discrimination in the textile industry was "that a black in a low-pay job is continually assigned to train whites, hired off the street, for higher-paying jobs; but is never promoted himself." Seymour used the pay differentials between black and white jobs to estimate the amount of back pay plaintiffs were entitled to because of being denied higher-paying jobs.[37]

The employment of white supervisors over all-black departments was a grievance for black workers in a variety of legal cases. In each situation, experienced black men felt aggrieved because they knew the work in their department well but were denied the opportunity to advance. In departments such as the dyehouse (*Adams v. Dan River Mills, Graniteville Company v. EEOC*, and *Galloway v. Fieldcrest Mills*) or the shipping department (*Ellison v. Rock Hill Printing and Finishing Company*), the textile industry's historic practice of using black men for heavy nonproduction work ensured that by the 1960s there was a large pool of black male workers with many years of seniority who were determined to secure better jobs and open up higher-paying job categories. In *Graniteville Company v. EEOC*, for example, black worker Edward Price explained that one of the chief grievances of black workers was that "in the Dyeing Department, they were all Negroes in this particular area, and the foreman who wasn't a Negro. . . . I am quite sure that some of these men who had been on the job for quite some time and knew the job quite well, I didn't understand why some of these men weren't offered the foreman's job. . . . I feel quite sure that some of them was qualified because there were several of them that had a high school education."[38]

In *Adams v. Dan River Mills*, a major class action suit, the central areas of complaint for black workers were their assignment to low-paying, undesirable jobs and the obstacles they faced in obtaining promotions to better-paying jobs. The case applied to the company's main group of plants in Danville, Virginia, where around 10,000 people were employed, of whom 23 percent were black by the time the case was filed in 1969.[39] Worker after worker gave vivid testimony describing how male African American workers were restricted to the lowest-paying jobs. When asked if she knew any black employees who were excluded from higher-paying jobs, one black worker replied, "Yes. . . . All black people. No black people have any higher paying jobs."[40]

One of the main issues in the *Adams* case was the difficulty that blacks faced in getting promotions to supervisory positions.[41] Most of the plaintiffs were experienced African American men who had worked in the company's dye-house for many years. They felt they were qualified to be supervisors but had been repeatedly passed over by the company. It was a particular grievance for these workers, many of whom had worked in the same department for over twenty years, to find the company hiring whites "off the street" to be their supervisors, especially as the black workers often had to train the whites for the job. As Harry Slade, who had worked in the company's dyehouse for thirty-two years, testified in 1973, "No white employees worked that job but they had white supervisors hired from out on the street to come in. They didn't know anything about the job and we would have to teach them the job. . . . They stood around and watched us and pretended. Anything that you showed them they appreciated." Slade told the attorney who was questioning him that their supervisors "didn't know a bit more about what I was doing than you do standing there."[42]

Dan River workers reacted strongly to violations of seniority, which was considered to be one of the most important principles that should have been applied in a plant. The promotion of a newly hired white to shift foreman, for example, moved black worker Robert Hereford to file an EEOC charge in 1969.[43] Hereford, who had worked in the dyehouse for thirty-two years, explained in his deposition that at Dan River, "there has never been no colored promoted up, but there has been more white come in and be promoted up. We stays at the same level. That's what we's arguing about." The promotion of a less qualified white was particularly galling because "we got to teach him what to do, then he going to be our boss man."[44] As Hereford added when he testified at the trial, "Well he comes in and you have got to learn him what to do and he turns around and tells you what to do."[45]

The records of *Adams v. Dan River Mills* show that the company used a variety of excuses to refuse black workers who asked for promotions. Black worker Edward Crews wanted to become a loom fixer but was told by his supervisor that he should "go to school." When Crews completed the necessary training classes and returned to ask for a fixing job again, he was told that he would "have to go back to school." This occurred despite the fact that whites were promoted to the fixer's job without going to training school at all. Indeed, black worker James Montgomery testified that many of the white supervisors placed over black workers "had less I.Q. than some of us." Another black worker, Harry Slade, went to the company's dye and operation school for an incredible nineteen straight years between 1953 and 1972 in an effort to secure a better job. He testified, however, that although the company made much of the fact that blacks had been admitted to training classes, "when they got ready to promote supervisors, it would be somebody out of this class, but it was never any black promoted out of the class."[46] Another black Dan River worker testified that his supervisor "laughed and walked off" when he asked for a promotion.[47] Black workers were also often told that they were "too old" for the jobs they wanted.[48]

Another common excuse given to black workers at Dan River was that they could only get a different position if they took a lower-paying one, or that the only positions available were less desirable than their present job. When Russell Dodson, who had worked for the company for thirty-three years, asked for another job, "they said they didn't have anything open but a janitor's job." Henry Wilson, who had been with the company for over twenty years, was told that "the only way I could transfer would be to go to a lower paying job." Like other black workers, however, Wilson refused to accept these excuses and continued to push his case.[49]

Although excuses were used, on some occasions company officials blatantly refused to consider blacks for promotions. When senior Dan River dyehouse worker Joe Marable asked his supervisor for an inspector's job after finding out that there was a vacancy, he was told that "he had a man trained for the job. . . . He said that he would much rather give the job to a white man than to give it to me because he had had training." Marable was even fired shortly after requesting this promotion. His discharge was clearly intended as a warning to other African American workers because he was the first black in his department to ask for the position of supervisor.[50]

In other cases, Dan River rebuffed black workers who wanted promotions by invoking the company's "right to manage." When some black workers protested the promotion of an inexperienced white to a supervisory job, they were told, "We have made up our minds, we pick who we want and as far as I am concerned it's over and that was it."[51] Black workers were not allowed to question the company's choice to promote whites. As one black worker remembered being told, "Garfield Harris is the drug room supervisor over y'all, and that is it."[52]

The case of *Ellison v. Rock Hill Printing and Finishing Company*, filed in 1972, closely resembled the Dan River case because it involved a group of male workers locked into nonproduction departments at a major southern textile company. Black workers complained that they were restricted to the lowest-paying jobs. Indeed, despite the companies' common defense that black workers were not qualified for better-paying positions, even when highly qualified blacks were hired, they were still placed in low-paying positions. Leroy Ellison described how African Americans with a college education were "working within the shipping department and not on one of the higher paid jobs." He added, "It has been with the blacks . . . that the higher educated you are, the lower I will put you on in employment."[53]

Plaintiffs in the *Ellison* case complained that it was impossible to receive promotions out of the low-paying departments where they worked. Chris Brown, who had been hired in 1946, remembered that "there wasn't no promotion. . . . The only ones that got a promotion was a white man, and when a white man come in the black fellows had to train him what to do. If a job was open for the white man all the blacks had to train him." This training of whites was a particular grievance. As Brown put it, "You know that man standing back there with a pencil, you trained him; sometimes you had to tell him what to do. He's supposed to have more knowledge. You trained him; now he's got your knowledge and gone."[54]

"We Were Able to Use Statistical Analysis to Demonstrate Discrimination"

One of the common features of class action lawsuits brought in the textile industry was the use of statistics by the plaintiffs' lawyers to prove the allegations of discrimination. Such statistics were collected directly from the companies' records, which lawyers gained access to through court orders, and thus provided quantitative proof of the validity of black workers' complaints. Statistics, indeed, clearly showed the extent of discrimination prevailing in the textile industry after "integration."[55]

In *Sledge v. J. P. Stevens*, the size of the class, together with the length of the case, ensured that an extensive body of statistics were collected that clearly illustrated the claims of job discrimination and pay disparities among male workers (see table 3). At the end of 1970, black men who worked on hourly paid jobs made $2.19 an hour, while white men earned $2.53 an hour. Statistics plainly showed that African Americans were assigned to lower-paying jobs than whites after being hired. Thus, for workers hired in 1975, white males were assigned to jobs averaging $2.48 an hour, while black males were assigned to jobs averaging $2.31.[56] As of October 1, 1972, statistics covering the company's hourly workers showed that 34.8 percent of black males earned less than $2.20 an hour, compared to only 10.4 percent of white males. However, only 2.7 percent of black males, compared to 35 percent of the white males, earned $2.81 or more.[57]

Statistical evidence used in *Adams v. Dan River Mills* also revealed consider-

Table 3. Racial Disparities in Pay Rates among All Male Employees at J. P. Stevens, 1967–1972

Date of Pay Rate Information	Average White Male Rate	Average Black Male Rate	Average Hourly Difference	Average Annual Difference
End of 1967	$2.12	$1.84	28.1¢	$584.48
End of 1968	2.26	1.95	30.6	636.48
End of 1969	2.40	2.08	31.9	663.52
End of 1970	2.53	2.19	34.5	717.60
End of 1971	2.67	2.33	33.4	694.72
Oct. 1, 1972	2.67	2.33	34.3	713.44

Source: Findings of Fact and Conclusions of Law, December 22, 1975, *Sledge v. J. P. Stevens*, p. 23.

able pay disparities between black and white men. In April 1969, a month before the suit was filed, white males at Dan River were paid $2.35 an hour, while black males made only $1.89. These "substantial disparities" in average pay rates still existed in April 1973 when the case was closed. Indeed, in the four years that the case was open there was no significant decline in the wage disparities between white and black males. (See tables 4 and 5.)[58]

The wage disparities between white and black men at Dan River Mills were demonstrated further by the proportions of blacks and whites at the bottom and the top of the wage scale. These figures show conclusively that African American men were overwhelmingly concentrated in the lowest-paying jobs (see tables 6 and 7). Despite the "integration" of the textile industry, all-white and all-black jobs were common at Dan River, and the wage rates of jobs increased dramatically as the proportion of blacks in the jobs decreased (see table 8). Thus, on January 31, 1972, the average rate of pay on all-white jobs was $2.66 an hour, while on all-black jobs it was a mere $2.10.[59]

At Dan River, as at other southern textile companies, African Americans were largely excluded from the better jobs at the plant, including supervisory jobs, salaried jobs, and craft jobs. In January 1967, for example, only one shift foreman out of a total of 196 was African American. Similarly, in January 1971, only 5 out of 817 salaried workers were black (0.61 percent).[60]

These statistics, however, did not take into account nonracial factors such as seniority or educational level, factors that textile companies insisted explained the pay disparities. According to the companies, blacks were not as qualified or experienced as whites, which was why they were concentrated in the lowest jobs. However, when wage rates of black and white men with the same seniority, education, and prior experience were compared, substantial pay disparities

Table 4. Average Pay Rates of Hourly Male Employees at Dan River Mills, Danville Division, April 1969

	Number	Average Hourly Rate
White males	3,436	$2.353
Black males	1,517	1.899
Hourly difference		.454
Annual difference (for 2,080 hours)		944.32

Source: Plaintiffs' Proposed Findings of Fact and Conclusions of Law, September 16, 1974, *Adams v. Dan River Mills*, p. 6.

Table 5. Average Pay Rates of Hourly Male Employees at Dan River Mills, Danville Division, April 1973

	Average Hourly Rate
White males	$2.77
Black males	2.36
Hourly difference	.413
Annual difference (for 2,080 hours)	859.04

Source: Plaintiffs' Proposed Findings of Fact and Conclusions of Law, September 16, 1974, *Adams v. Dan River Mills*, p. 7.

still persisted, both in the *Adams* case and in *Sledge*. Thus, race was clearly the factor that explained the pay disparities.[61]

Refuting the corporate argument that length of service explained pay disparities, plaintiffs' data from the *Adams* case showed conclusively that whites were initially assigned to higher-paying jobs when they were first hired by the company. Indeed, white males hired between 1951 and 1972 were consistently paid at a higher rate, varying from eighteen cents per hour up to seventy-six cents per hour (see table 9). Whites employed in January 1972 with less than one month's seniority still earned more than blacks hired before 1951. Thus, length of service had little bearing on the pay received by white or black workers.[62]

In *Sledge* the court gave the plaintiffs access to company records, thereby allowing them to expose patterns of racial discrimination similar to those in *Adams*. Indeed, the use of data to prove that seniority, experience, and educational level could not explain pay disparities was central to the arguments of lawyers such as Richard Seymour and Julius Chambers. In *Sledge*, for example, the company's bitter opposition to the charges of discrimination made it crit-

Table 6. Proportion of Male Employees at the Bottom and Top of the Pay Scale at Dan River Mills, April 1969

Pay Rate	Percent of All White Males	Percent of All Black Males
Less than $2.00 per hour	24.0	76.8
$2.25 per hour or more	60.1	6.9

Source: Plaintiffs' Proposed Findings of Fact and Conclusions of Law, September 16, 1974, *Adams v. Dan River Mills*, p. 8.

Table 7. Proportion of Male Employees at the Bottom and Top of the Pay Scale at Dan River Mills, April 1973

Pay Rate	Percent of All White Males	Percent of All Black Males
Less than $2.50 per hour	33.9	80.7
$2.80 per hour or more	50.0	6.2

Source: Plaintiffs' Proposed Findings of Fact and Conclusions of Law, September 16, 1974, *Adams v. Dan River Mills*, p. 9.

Table 8. Average Pay Rates of Male Employees in Racially Identifiable Jobs at Dan River Mills, January 31, 1972

Job Category	Number of Employees Assigned	Percent Black	Average Wage Rate of All Employees
All-white jobs	1,313	0	$2.66
Disproportionately white jobs	1,727	6.8	2.53
Disproportionately black jobs	1,198	68.7	2.17
All-black jobs	288	100	2.10

Source: Plaintiffs' Proposed Findings of Fact and Conclusions of Law, September 16, 1974, *Adams v. Dan River Mills*, p. 10.
Note: A department is considered "disproportionate" if more than 40 percent of its employees are of one race.

ical to prove the existence of racial disparities in pay. Statistics produced in the *Sledge* case revealed that black men consistently earned less than white men of the same educational level and seniority group, refuting company claims that these factors may have been responsible for the pay disparities. These patterns, moreover, held true throughout the 1970s. As late as December 28, 1980, for

Table 9. Average Pay Rates of Hourly Male Employees by Race and Year of Hire at Dan River Mills, January 31, 1972

Year of Hire	White Males	Black Males	Hourly Differential
Pre-1951	$2.68	$2.29	$.39
1952	2.58	2.29	.29
1953	2.66	2.19	.47
1954	2.60	2.08	.52
1955	2.68	2.25	.43
1956	2.61	2.16	.45
1957	2.71	2.20	.51
1958	2.73	2.18	.55
1959	2.81	2.22	.59
1960	2.68	1.92	.76
1961	2.73	2.20	.53
1962	2.73	2.30	.43
1963	2.66	2.32	.34
1964	2.73	2.36	.37
1965	2.71	2.28	.43
1966	2.65	2.21	.44
1967	2.57	2.26	.31
1968	2.72	2.23	.49
1969	2.60	2.19	.41
1970	2.55	2.19	.36
1971	2.43	2.15	.28
Jan. 1972	2.33	2.15	.18

Source: Plaintiffs' Proposed Findings of Fact and Conclusions of Law, September 16, 1974, *Adams v. Dan River*, pp. 20–21.

example, black males with a twelfth-grade education made less than white men with a first-grade education (see table 10).[63]

Many other cases also revealed stark pay disparities between black and white workers. In *Lewis v. J. P. Stevens*, for example, black males were consistently assigned to jobs paying ten cents an hour less than whites between 1966 and 1974. As in other plants, promotion tended to exacerbate rather than correct this differential. Thus, the average hourly pay rates of black males and white males at the end of each year from 1966 through 1974—reflecting the combined effect of initial assignments and promotions—showed racial differences between two and four times the amounts of the racial differences on initial assignments (see table 11).[64]

Data from companies not involved in lawsuits also indicate that substantial pay disparities existed between black and white workers. At Bemis Company in

Table 10. Comparison of Pay Rates of Hourly and Incentive Male Employees by Race and Education Level at J. P. Stevens Plants in Roanoke Rapids, N.C., December 28, 1980

Education Level in Years	Mean Salary, White	Mean Salary, Black	Hourly Difference	Annual Difference
0	$4.13	$3.71	$0.42	$877.07
1	4.67	4.01	0.67	1,388.40
2	4.20	3.90	0.30	632.67
3	4.53	3.90	0.63	1,310.56
4	4.48	3.75	0.73	1,524.50
5	4.77	4.04	0.72	1,502.50
6	4.64	3.97	0.67	1,388.37
7	4.64	4.04	0.60	1,249.42
8	4.69	4.11	0.57	1,189.25
9	4.76	4.20	0.57	1,180.29
10	4.57	4.08	0.49	1,025.47
11	4.54	4.13	0.42	864.82
12	4.66	4.26	0.40	839.63
13	4.47	4.13	0.34	714.13
14	4.83	4.27	0.56	1,174.51
15	4.82	4.17	0.65	1,343.68
16	4.02	4.00	0.02	41.60
Over 16	4.36	0	0	0

Source: Exhibit Data, December 28, 1980, *Sledge v. J. P. Stevens.*

Memphis, Tennessee, for example, an analysis of pay scales across the plant in September 1966 revealed significant disparities. Altogether the plant employed 40 blacks and 110 whites, but the whites received $1.94 an hour and the blacks only $1.51.[65]

Heavy and Hazardous: Black Workers Describe Their Jobs

In many ways, the central complaint of black workers was not about pay. Although their jobs were low-paying, African American men were equally concerned with the heavy and hazardous nature of their jobs, together with the fact that only blacks were assigned to them. In many mills, black men had traditionally been hired into nonproduction departments such as warehouses or shipping departments, where jobs were heavy and hard. When companies finished their own textiles, as was the case at Dan River Mills and Fieldcrest Mills, black men were also employed in finishing departments, in jobs that involved exposure to chemicals and high levels of heat and dust.

Table 11. Comparison of Pay Rates of Black and White Male Hourly Employees at J. P. Stevens, 1966–1974

Week Ending	Average White Male Rate	Average Black Male Rate	Hourly Difference	Annual Difference (for 2,080 Hours)
Dec. 25, 1966	$1.98	$1.65	$.33	$686.40
Dec. 24, 1967	2.15	1.77	.38	790.40
Dec. 22, 1968	2.16	2.00	.16	332.80
Dec. 21, 1969	2.32	2.08	.24	499.20
Dec. 20, 1970	2.48	2.26	.22	457.60
Dec. 19, 1971	2.58	2.33	.25	520.00
Dec. 24, 1972	2.71	2.48	.23	478.40
Dec. 23, 1973	3.01	2.71	.30	624.00
Dec. 22, 1974	3.22	3.03	.19	395.20

Source: Table, "Racial Differences in Average Hourly Pay Rates For Males, 1966–1974," Plaintiffs' Proposed Findings of Fact and Conclusions of Law, June 11, 1980, *Lewis v. J. P. Stevens*, p. 100.

In depositions and in trial testimony, black men often described the heavy and hazardous work they performed. In *Lewis v. J. P. Stevens*, a case brought in 1972 against Stevens's plant in Abbeville, South Carolina, the testimony of a group of black men who worked in the company's warehouse revealed much about the poor working conditions of African American men in nonproduction laboring positions. Contrary to Stevens's argument that warehouse workers wanted to work there, the testimony showed that many disliked the work and had repeatedly asked for other jobs. Most workers had not asked to work in the warehouse but were told by the company that the warehouse was the only job available. Robert Wharton, a high school graduate with vocational training, was placed in the warehouse because "they didn't have anything else."[66] James Roosevelt Williams had been told when he was hired "that I wouldn't be working in the warehouse no more than three weeks, and I would probably move up to another job." However, Williams "was still in the warehouse when I left there."[67]

Workers described how they had to perform a variety of sweeping and laboring duties, many of which exposed them to high levels of dust. All of them disliked the job. Asked how he liked his work, James Roosevelt Williams answered, "I didn't. It was too hot. The work and everything was too hard."[68] Others gave similar responses. Theodore Rollinson described his work as a cleaner in the warehouse as "nasty, filthy."[69] Many black men described the way that the company frustrated their attempts to escape the warehouse for a better job. Theodore Rollinson, for example, testified that "I told the foreman that

I needed a job making more money, and he told me the warehouse was the only thing they had."[70] All of the black workers also refuted the company's claim that working in the warehouse gave them more free time than on a production job.[71]

In *Adams v. Dan River Mills,* workers' depositions and trial testimony again revealed the hard working conditions and lack of opportunity facing African Americans in one of the South's biggest textile companies. Most of the Dan River plaintiffs described how African Americans were required to work in the dirtiest and most hazardous jobs, exposing them to dust and chemicals. James Montgomery claimed that "blacks always has the dirty work. Janitors. Cleaning. Blowing off. They always have it."[72] At the trial in 1972, Joseph R. Graves described how he had worked for Dan River since 1947 solely in cleaning and laboring work. Graves testified that he had tried for promotion on many occasions because his work was so hard. Asked whether he had been tired when he had taken the company's test to become a foreman following his shift, Graves replied, "Naturally. You're always tired when you leave Dan River."[73]

In many of the cases, black workers complained that their jobs were both heavier and more hazardous than those performed by whites. Because many African Americans worked in dyehouses, they were indeed exposed to more chemicals and dirtier working conditions. James Montgomery, who started working in the dyehouse of Dan River Mills in 1948, claimed that black jobs were more hazardous because "we have more dangerous things to come into contact with . . . Acids, different chemicals, we have had several serious accidents there." The job was also harder "because we have so much more lifting and things to do."[74] Robert Hereford described the all-black drug room as "dirty and dangerous," adding that the few whites who had been hired there had found it "too dirty" and "quit and went back on the machine."[75] The testimony of Wyllie Smyka, the white superintendent of the dyehouse where most of the plaintiffs worked, confirmed that the all-black job of drug room operator was much dirtier than the all-white job of machine operator.[76]

Many of the workers who testified in *Ellison v. Rock Hill Printing and Finishing Company* also described how black workers were made to perform much heavier jobs than whites. A strong sense of injustice came through when workers described these jobs. Chris Brown explained that he was in court because "every job that came along, the dirtiest job and the hardest job, Negroes were placed in them, regardless of education standard."[77] Charlie Ervin, who had worked at the company for over twenty years, similarly testified in 1973 that blacks were "always" assigned "the heaviest work, the most physical strain." Ervin added that even if there was overtime, the supervisor "will assign you to whatever is heavy and rough, that's what you get."[78]

Many of the workers' letters referred to the existence of segregated departments within the textile industry, and many lawsuits were brought because segregated job patterns persisted after the passage of the Civil Rights Act. Indeed, efforts to open up "white" departments probably constituted the most recurrent theme of all the lawsuits brought by black men.

Segregated jobs were an issue in many lawsuits.[79] In *Ellison v. Rock Hill Printing and Finishing Company*, for example, one of the major complaints was that the company maintained departments that were "segregated on a basis of race, so that when employees are hired, assigned, promoted, or demoted, they are placed in a job that is either a 'white job' or 'Negro job.'"[80] In *Ellison*, African American workers described their jobs as "black" jobs and claimed that the company did not want them to move into "white" jobs. Lead plaintiff Leroy Ellison testified in 1973 that "blacks were and are still doing what has been done as all black jobs. They have what they have called the white jobs and they are still being operated by white."[81]

When they did ask for promotions, Rock Hill workers ran into the problem of prescribed "black" and "white" jobs well past the passage of the Civil Rights Act. Waco Meeks, for example, explained that when a group of African American workers had asked for the "switch operator's job" in 1966, the supervisor "told us that was a white man's job."[82] On another occasion in 1967, a group of black workers who inquired about promotions were told by their supervisor "that we were not ready for the job and not prepared, and before he would see us go up there, he would die and go to hell. . . . He definitely said that that was a white man's job and I couldn't get it."[83]

In some cases, it was clear that complete job segregation was maintained well into the 1970s and beyond. In *Seibles v. Cone Mills*, a case brought in 1977, it was established that at Cone's power plant facility in Greensboro, North Carolina, the position of utility man, involving the moving of coal within the power plant to fuel the boilers in the plant, had always been filled by black men. In contrast, the higher-paying positions in the department, such as mechanics, boiler operators, and supervisors, had been filled only by white men. When black utility man Robert Seibles, who had been working in the power plant since 1937, applied for the "white" job of boiler operator, he was refused, leading to the filing of the lawsuit. Data collected from the company's records showed the complete segregation of jobs at the power plant in December 1971 (see table 12). Confronted with this evidence of "the rigorous segregation of job classifications," the company settled the case with a consent decree.[84]

The records of the largest lawsuits show that notions of segregated jobs were

Table 12. Racial Composition of Job Classifications in Cone Mills Power Plant, December 15, 1971

Job	Number of White Employees	Number of Black Employees
Boiler operator	3	0
Boiler operator	1	0
Mechanic	4	0
Group leader	2	0
Fuel material handler	0	11
Mender-loader	0	1
Plant maintenance	0	1
Utility pipe coverer	0	1
Machine operator trainee	0	1

Source: Order on Final Pre-Trial Conference, September 29, 1978, *Seibles v. Cone Mills*, p. 4.

held both by workers and management. In *Adams v. Dan River Mills*, black men described a segregated workforce where blacks held the lowest jobs and whites the highest. Many black workers even spoke of "black" and "white" jobs, showing how persistent the barriers of segregation were in their minds.[85] Joseph Graves, for example, testified in 1970, "Opening and blending cotton. All that's black jobs." As statistics suggested, black workers described clear segregation in the jobs that black and white workers were initially assigned to. According to Graves, "Well when they come from the employment office usually the blacks come across the tracks and white goes to No. 4 Spin or some other department. They don't hire whites for the jobs in 1 and 2 Opening and Blending." Graves even felt that it was "company policy" to maintain supervisory jobs as white only: "White men make supervisors." He claimed that supervisors "know better than to hire a negro on a job if they want to stay there."[86] Other Dan River workers produced similar testimony.[87]

Black men also claimed that supervisors used notions of "black" and "white" jobs when deciding who was to be promoted. In *Adams*, a variety of black Dan River workers testified that supervisors tried to keep jobs segregated even after the passage of the Civil Rights Act. Workers from the dyeing department, for example, testified that the job of machine operator was predominantly white and that as late as 1967, blacks who ran the machines "would be threatened to be fired if they didn't get off that job and take another job."[88] Black worker William Still testified that when he tried to get a production job in the late 1960s, one supervisor "came right out" and told him that the job he wanted was "the white man's job."[89]

Statistics from the *Ellison* and *Adams* cases support these notions of segregated jobs. At Dan River Mills, out of 139 departments in 1966, 53 were all-white and 8 all-black. Shift foreman was an all-white occupation, while the majority of jobs in the laboring category, such as sweeper-cleaner, trucker, and feeder, were performed exclusively by African Americans. Although the company made efforts to break down these patterns, a compliance review in February 1970 criticized the company for "not paying attention to the integration of job classifications," adding that "blacks are being channeled into black jobs, whites into white jobs." As a result, the Defense Supply Agency told Dan River that "somebody is sandbagging the Affirmative Action Program, that the Affirmative Action Program is dragging." In 1972, a lengthy study of the racial composition of departments showed that segregation was still prevalent, with 1,303 employees still working in all-white departments, and a further 2,592 working in departments with only token integration.[90]

Obstacles to Promotion: Seniority and Subjectivity

The letters written by African American workers describing how they were restricted to the lowest-paying jobs in the textile industry give a few hints as to the causes of this situation, including the fact that supervisors were clearly reluctant to promote African Americans. In many cases, however, more fundamental structural factors restricted the job opportunities of black workers. In the 1960s and 1970s, the overwhelming majority of black textile workers were men concentrated in nonproduction departments. Apart from white supervisors, the departments were generally all-black and the jobs undesirable and dirty. Two main factors helped to lock black men into separate departments and ensure that jobs were clearly "black" or "white." First, seniority agreements restricted African Americans to the departments in which they had been assigned. Second, a lack of job posting and reliance on the subjective decisions of supervisors ensured that few blacks were ever aware of, or considered for, promotion to "white" positions. The power of supervisors over promotions explains why it was so common for African American workers to complain that white workers had been arbitrarily brought into new positions by supervisors "off the street."

The large J. P. Stevens chain provided the best example of the way that textile companies frequently relied upon the subjective decisions of supervisors to decide who could be promoted. Because supervisors were overwhelmingly white, this practice allowed for a great deal of favoritism and discrimination when promotions were awarded. In *Sledge v. J. P. Stevens*, for example, the court found that Stevens's policy "of relying almost exclusively upon subjective conclusions of its all-white overseers and personnel officials in hiring and promotion is discriminatory." The company was also found to have discriminated by failing to "establish objective, formal guidelines for hiring, promotion and transfer" apart from "word of mouth." Confirming that there were "white" and "black" jobs, the court found that high-paying jobs had been reserved for whites and certain low-paying jobs for blacks. Similar findings were also made by the court in *Sherrill v. J. P. Stevens*. Warehouse worker Paul Gene McLean described how the lack of job posting destroyed any chances of promotion: "It has been a job open in the mill that I wanted and never know until somebody got the job."[91]

In *Adams v. Dan River Mills*, the trial also exposed the fact that the company had no objective standards for promotion and transfer. Black workers described how they worked in a segregated dyehouse and were completely unaware of vacancies occurring in their department or elsewhere in the plant. As one worker testified, "In the dye house you never known when a vacancy comes up, you never known anything."[92] At Dan River, as at many other southern textile companies, the lack of job posting meant that supervisory positions were filled before African American workers on the shop floor had a chance to find out about them. This problem was particularly acute because supervisors, who were all white, tended to recommend friends or relatives for these positions, thereby excluding blacks from consideration. African American worker Joseph Graves, for example, testified in his deposition that even when he knew of whites who were retiring, "each time somebody is already ahead from some other department. They put them on the job." The difficulty of finding out about vacancies for better jobs was well expressed by black worker Charlie Smith: "Every time we have a supervisor in No. 1 Dye he always has the job before we know it. Before I knew anything about it. Lots of times he's there 2 or 3 days. I says, 'Who's that fellow?' 'That's our new supervisor.'"[93]

In many mills, this lack of objective procedure was compounded by seniority policies that stipulated that workers who transferred out of their departments lost their seniority with the company. Since most black workers were assigned to low-paying, all-black departments, this provision made it very difficult for them to transfer to better jobs, because doing so would mean that they lost all their seniority with the company. White workers, who were usually assigned into higher-paying departments with much greater opportunities for promotion, did not face this problem because they could secure promotions to good jobs within their departments.[94] In *Ellison v. Rock Hill Printing and Finishing Company*, one of the main issues between the two sides was a departmental seniority system that hindered black promotion into production departments from the all-black shipping department. The plaintiffs' lawyer noted in 1980 that both the company and the union had continually fought to maintain a departmental seniority system as "something sacred."[95]

Many Rock Hill workers supported the lawsuit primarily because the company's discriminatory seniority system prevented them from being promoted out of the all-black shipping department. Lead plaintiff Leroy Ellison, for example, testified in 1972 that "I feel that the older employees of the blacks of the Printing and Finishing Company would have been glad to move up to any of the departments other than the Shipping Department if they had had the privilege to transfer without the possibility of losing their jobs the next day. . . . [T]his is one way that they are yet discriminating because we don't have the privilege to move up without losing our jobs."[96] Similarly, the main complaint of Bobby Johnson was "the seniority. If we were to get a transfer out of the Shipping Department to any other department, I would love to see that we get our seniority to take with us wherever we went in different departments."[97]

"White Supervisors Fail to Understand That 'Race' Makes No Difference"

It is clear that discrimination occurred frequently at the supervisory level, even where companies had nondiscrimination policies. Many of the letters written by workers to the EEOC complained about their supervisors, and other sources confirm that racist supervisors were a problem in many locations across the South.

Management sources themselves indicate that racist supervisors were often a problem. At Cone Mills, John Bagwill, a former industrial relations director, admitted in 1969 that although Cone had a nondiscrimination policy, "some of the old-line supervisors tried to sabotage it." As Bagwill put it, "A company like Cone has many units in small towns, and you know damned well there is discrimination."[98] At Dan River Mills, the company's private records show that upper-level management was concerned about the amount of discrimination practiced by supervisors. In a wide range of production jobs, supervisors exercised their departmental power to keep blacks locked into the lowest positions. Because supervisors controlled the assignment of work within their departments, blacks who were not rejected were simply placed in inferior jobs rather than in the ones they had been hired for by the personnel department. Supervisors often reassigned blacks who had been hired as white-collar workers. As personnel head Robert Gardiner admitted to a colleague in 1970, "We presently employ 594 individuals in the office and clerical group of which only 13 or 2% are black. There is absolutely no way in which I, as division compliance officer, can justify to the government our failure to make more progress in this area unless I flatly admit that our supervisors are discriminating and there is nothing I can do about it." Generally, supervisors were sent two or three well-qualified candidates, but, as Gardiner explained, "most supervisors find some reason to reject the black applicant regardless of rating."[99] Dan River's Robert

T. Thompson explained, "Applicants signed up by the employment office to fill specific jobs are frequently rejected or put on lesser jobs by particular supervisors." Figures collected by the company showed that around twenty blacks each month were either rejected by supervisors or put to work on less desirable jobs during the late 1960s.[100]

The fact that supervisors constituted one of the main obstacles affecting black progress at Dan River is confirmed by a lengthy internal memo written in 1970. This memo explored the problems facing the company's affirmative action program, and it offers insight into the amount of discrimination remaining at Dan River. More than half of the problems listed in the memo related to the actions of supervisors. Principal complaints included "the discriminatory treatment of minorities after employment with respect to their treatment by white supervisors" and "language used by supervisors to Negro employees." Indeed, many black workers were reported to be angered by "discussions with Negro employees using such terms as 'niggers,' 'boys,' etc." The memo showed that many supervisors held racial values widely removed from those put forward publicly by the company through the affirmative action program. They had "a complete unwillingness to make any effort to apply the company's affirmative action program, i.e., the oft repeated statement that 'You're employing too damned many niggers.'" It is clear that in this respect, the company was a victim of deeply rooted racial values where the inferiority of blacks was taken for granted. Racial attitudes could not be transformed overnight simply by instituting an affirmative action program. As the memo noted, "Many 'old time' supervisors have been brought up to look down on Negroes. Though times have changed, they have not and cannot change. The Negro, therefore, is treated as he was one hundred years ago. This creates problems."[101]

The memo highlighted the depth of these values by explaining how supervisors perpetuated a great deal of discrimination at Dan River without even realizing it: "White supervisors fail to understand that 'race' makes no difference, that the only criteria is the quality of performance. Thus, they discriminate without realizing that they are discriminating because they dislike blacks." Blacks were not encouraged to participate in training programs, were denied overtime, and were not told of openings by supervisors, who, "when they are sent a Negro prospect, automatically place him [or her] on the lowest paying, dirtiest job and move a white worker to the job on which the Negro has been placed. This cause problems." The memo thus dramatically confirmed the failure of increased black employment and affirmative action to fundamentally change the unequal working conditions of African American employees. As it candidly concluded, at Dan River "the Negro, at this point in time, is always placed in a lower position than the white. The problem is how this will be resolved."[102]

Notes that the company took based on conversations with black employees who filed complaints of racial discrimination with the EEOC further reveal the role played by supervisors in perpetuating discrimination on the shop floor. Black worker Russell Dodson, for example, claimed in 1970 that supervisors consistently assigned "more work to Negroes than to whites on the same job." Many workers recalled hearing racist statements made by individual supervisors, such as "supervisors are told not to hire colored on some jobs" and "certain people get certain jobs." Several black employees also accused supervisors of tokenism, claiming that they "hire perhaps one Negro in a higher paying job, rest in lower paying jobs."[103]

The memo also made clear, however, that one of the reasons supervisors continued to discriminate was "a subjective feeling on the part of the lower supervision that the higher echelon does not agree with the EEOC." Upper-level management was also criticized for failing to "adequately transmit to first line supervision the company's policy of EEO" and failing to "encourage supervisors to employ minority people."[104]

A variety of sources indicate that the textile industry had a tendency to employ "mean" white men in supervisory positions, and these men clearly did not adjust easily to the entry of African Americans into production jobs. Across the South, African Americans hired into the textile industry complained of discrimination from "mean" supervisors. It was particularly galling for black men that they frequently had to train uneducated, "mean" whites for supervisory jobs. In *Adams v. Dan River Mills*, black worker Robert Hereford described a white supervisor named Goebels, who was trained by black workers, as "plum mean. Didn't like nobody. Mean to everybody. . . . And he have cussed me many times. That's the truth. Not only me. A whole lot of them." Hereford claimed that the company had a preference for mean supervisors: "It looked like the ones that were good don't look like they stay there as long as those stay that are just mean. I don't know why. That's facts. I watched it."[105]

In *Sherrill v. J. P. Stevens*, most black workers who testified still performed heavy, nonproduction work in traditional black textile jobs. Workers complained that their white supervisors' attitudes also belonged to an earlier time period. Like other black workers, Dillard McDowell used the analogy of slavery to describe the way that the supervisor treated the black workers: "In my opinion he think he still back in slave time and don't have sense enough to talk to black people." The supervisor talked to black workers "in a nasty way. . . . I can't curse at him but its alright for him to curse at me." McDowell testified that the white supervisor also talked to the lone black supervisor in this way.[106]

Across the South, workers felt that supervisors treated black workers far more harshly than whites, forcing the blacks to work harder and denying them privileges such as overtime and breaks. Willie Long started working at the Eagle and Phenix Mill in Columbus, Georgia, in 1972. One of the first wave of blacks hired at the mill, Long remembered that "the white workers would have more of a break. White workers they were just treated totally different. The atmosphere was different—you could just see it, it was so obvious. They was arrogant with it—they didn't feel that they had to explain the reason why. A white worker was treated different when he was out, discipline was different, and he was talked different to. . . . They figured they had to watch us."[107]

Even where blacks were placed on jobs next to whites, evidence from across the South indicates that they were not treated equally and were made to work harder. Supervisors remained overwhelmingly white, and they gave white workers a variety of job privileges to ensure that they felt superior to blacks. Jacob Little, who was hired at another Columbus plant in 1966, expressed a typical view: "One thing, you know, if you was black you had to work twice as hard as the white worker. . . . You didn't get many breaks."[108]

Written sources confirmed these complaints of discriminatory treatment. In May 1968, for example, TEAM aide Lucion Waller reported that in Abbeville, South Carolina, it was usual practice that "when negroes get a fair job such as weaving, there Forman ride there back, give them a hard time and give them more work to do."[109] In Ellison v. Rock Hill Printing and Finishing Company, an experienced black worker, Chris Brown, described in vivid detail how the supervisors in the shipping department always expected blacks to be at their beck and call and perform extra jobs beyond their job classifications: "He didn't bother the whites. At times, the conveyor would jam up, you know, where the cases come round. If it jams up, the belt could be ready to break or break and he would never call a white man to ask him to help; it would always be a black. A white man could walk by there and cases be standing as high as this building, he wouldn't ask one of them to help unhang it. He always called the blacks to unhang it."[110]

Supervisors were usually responsible for discharging workers, and the complaint that African Americans were unfairly disciplined was common both in workers' letters and in a large number of lawsuits. In Woods v. Fieldcrest-Cannon, the main issue was the unfair discharge of black workers. Statistics produced in the case highlighted the fact that at Fieldcrest, blacks continued to be fired much more frequently than whites even as late as the 1980s. Between 1985 and 1988, for example, African Americans made up 37.8 percent of the workforce but received 52.9 percent of all involuntary discharges, a pattern that remained constant throughout the 1970s and 1980s. In 1985, African Americans received only 24.2 percent of voluntary discharges but 63.6 percent of involuntary discharges.[111] In a wide variety of cases, African Americans claimed that disciplinary rules were not applied equally between whites and blacks.[112]

Many black male workers also complained that supervisors fired them simply for talking with white female workers. Indeed, throughout the 1960s and 1970s, textile management was very sensitive about any links between black men and white women. In at least three lawsuits, black men complained that they had been discriminated against for conversing with white women.[113] In *Bean v. Star Fibers*, a black warehouse worker at a textile company in Edgefield, South Carolina, claimed that he was fired in 1970 for talking to a white female coworker even though "white people talk to the black [women] and they didn't terminate them." Highlighting the taboo that associating with white women still represented in the textile South, Bean explained that in order to get another job, he had to tell other companies he had resigned: "If I had told them that they had discharged me for a white woman, I would never have got a job so I didn't have much choice."[114]

In *Bean*, the plaintiff's lawyers claimed that the company had "a policy which disapproves inter racial social contact." Companies indeed attempted to prevent any contact between black male and white female coworkers. Many black workers remembered that it was clearly understood by all that they "did not go near" white women. Fear of such contact was also expressed by many executives in the 1960s and 1970s.[115] As Bean himself pointed out, the hypocrisy of the situation was that there was no such vigilance when it came to protecting black women from the attention of white men. Many workers recalled instances of sexual harassment of black women by white supervisors when African American women finally began to be hired in the 1960s.[116]

Inequalities in Job Classifications

In the *Sledge* case as well as several other lawsuits, African American men complained that they performed many skilled duties within textile plants but were only classified as unskilled workers or laborers. Blacks thus received the lowest pay available but often carried out jobs requiring higher skill levels than those performed by many whites. TEAM found that this practice was very common in the textile industry in South Carolina. In January 1968, TEAM director Mordecai Johnson wrote that one of the problems his agency discovered was that "Negroes tend to get lower salaries even when they are doing the higher jobs by simply denying them the classification for higher jobs." At the EEOC textile forum in January 1967, black workers and community leaders also described many cases of "higher wages going to whites for identical work."[117]

Black workers at J. P. Stevens continually complained about being paid less than whites for the same work. By August 1975, the EEOC in Atlanta had filed 178 charges of Title VII violations against Stevens, and unequal pay was one of the main areas of violation. Joe Moody, a local civil rights leader who helped gather workers' complaints in *Sledge*, remembered that "the way that J. P. Stevens had it, that white and black were working side by side, but the white were making more money than the blacks were on the same type of job." Plaintiffs' attorney T. T. Clayton recalled that "after getting employed, . . . the black employees, while doing the same job, were getting much less pay than whites." Clayton remembered that Stevens's records, which the plaintiffs' attorneys gained access to by court order, showed these pay disparities on the same job.[118]

Numerous EEOC charge forms describe individual examples of unequal pay. Many of Stevens's black truck drivers complained that they were paid less than their white counterparts. Timothy Harris, for example, wrote in 1974 that "white truck drivers receive at least $1.00 per hour more than black truck drivers doing the same job. I took a white driver's job when he was transferred to a road driving job, and was paid and am still being paid $1.00 less than the white driver was paid while on the same job." Other black truck drivers complained that they were made to handle a much greater workload than the white truck drivers they replaced.[119]

Not surprisingly, this practice of unequal pay was a major source of complaint from African American workers. It was in fact the main complaint in *Ellison v. Rock Hill Printing and Finishing Company*. In that case, the plaintiffs sued both the company and the TWUA for signing a contract that classified all black workers as janitors even though they performed a variety of semiskilled jobs. Lead plaintiff Leroy Ellison explained in his deposition that blacks were "hired in one classification, regardless to what their duties were." He had brought the lawsuit, he explained, because the union and the company "have done nothing about getting those people out of that trench." He added, "Certainly there was a discrimination there because . . . you could do anything they asked you to and you had no classification." As Ellison recalled, "We did skilled work but we were classified as cleaning. [Chris] Brown was a skilled fork-lift operator, but he was a janitor by classification."[120] Black workers often performed a variety of jobs but were only paid at the lowest pay scale for laborers.[121]

The lawsuit that Ellison initiated drew support from other African American workers frustrated by years of performing the same work as whites for less pay. Oscar Gill, another plaintiff in the case, explained why he supported the suit: "Well, now, there is several white fellows in the packing department that are operating an electric lift truck just like mine, the same make and produced by the same Company, but they are making more than I'm making . . . all the white drivers making more operating the same machinery produced by the same company."[122] Unequal pay was also a major issue among black workers at Cannon Mills.[123]

Conclusion: The Persistence of Discrimination

The striking conclusion that emerges from detailed written sources is that black textile workers who worked in the southern textile industry in the 1960s and 1970s faced massive discrimination in many areas of their working lives. Most black textile workers were men, and their main area of complaint was that they were restricted to low-paying jobs with no opportunity for promotion. Legal records also show that the problems faced by black workers did not diminish over time. The same complaints occurred in the late 1970s as in the early 1960s. Although the lawsuits forced companies to make many improvements in their racial hiring practices, it is clear that companies also failed to comply with many of the provisions of the various consent decrees, especially in the upgrading of black workers.

At Cannon Mills, for example, the EEOC wrote to the company in 1977 complaining about its failure to comply with consent decrees entered in 1971 and 1976. The EEOC pointed out that although more blacks were being hired, this increase "is almost entirely in the blue collar classifications which are the lower paying job titles. Additionally, these are the jobs in which blacks have traditionally been placed and the jobs in which there is the greatest concentration of black employees." Cannon still had ninety-four all-white job classifications, and thirty departments remained all-white after 1974. The EEOC also claimed that Cannon had made "next to no progress" in opening up white-collar jobs to blacks. The same was true with regard to supervisory jobs. Between 1971 and 1974, only two black supervisors had been hired even though there had been sixty-eight new supervisory vacancies during the period.[124]

In *Sledge v. J. P. Stevens*, data collected in the years after the consent decree of 1980 showed that pay disparities between black and white male workers actually got worse after the decree was entered. In January 1981, the plaintiffs' lawyers reported "strong patterns of substantial racial disparities in pay rates between black males and white males. . . . Compared with the showings of discrimination made at trial, the situation has become substantially worse for black males."[125] Even fifteen years after the passage of the Civil Rights Act, lawsuits were being filed by black textile workers that duplicated complaints made in cases a decade earlier.[126]

The failure of companies to comply with consent decrees typified the way that discrimination continued to be a serious problem in the textile industry throughout the 1960s and 1970s. It is clear that discrimination was not ended by black entry into the workforce. Indeed, in some cases companies discriminated more when blacks moved into production jobs in order to help white workers accept the change. The wide variety of records used in this study show conclusively that African American textile workers in the 1960s and 1970s worked in an industry that confined them to the least desirable jobs and severely restricted their opportunities for promotion. The EEOC forum on the textile industry, held in 1967, established clearly that although the industry was hiring more blacks, this hiring was occurring almost exclusively in the unskilled and semiskilled categories. It was also clear from the forum that little effort was being made to train or upgrade black workers.[127] The employment pattern was essentially one where blacks and whites were segregated to a large extent, despite the fact that the industry and the southern press heralded the "integration" of the mills.[128]

Getting Out of the
White Man's Kitchen

African American Women and the
Racial Integration of the Southern
Textile Industry

The experiences of African American women in the southern textile industry differed in many respects from those of African American men. In the 1960s and 1970s, black women, lacking a history of employment in the industry, found it very difficult to secure textile jobs and faced far more discrimination in hiring than their male counterparts. If black women were hired, however, they were usually able to move directly into production positions, avoiding the problems faced by long-term black male workers who were often locked into low-paying nonproduction jobs. Thus, the main grievance of black women in the 1960s and 1970s was discrimination in hiring, whereas the complaints of black men centered on discrimination in upgrading and promotion to better-paying jobs. The very different experiences of black men and women showed that gender as well as race was central to the way that workers were treated in the southern textile industry.

In the last twenty years, several excellent studies have explored the important role that women played in the southern textile industry. Led by *Like a Family*, which pioneered in gender-conscious history appropriate to an industry that relied heavily on women's labor, a number of other works have also explored aspects of women's participation in the southern textile industry. Few have looked at the 1960s and 1970s, however, especially the role that black women played as they were hired in increasing numbers in these years. This study attempts to extend the recent work of other historians by examining the experiences of women textile workers between 1960 and 1980, years of massive racial change. At the heart of this analysis is the argument that gender played a key role in shaping the course of racial integration in the southern textile industry. Indeed, black women's exclusion from the industry meant that they suffered from unique forms of discrimination. Entry into the industry thus had a very different meaning for them than for black men with a history of participation in textiles.[1]

Their history of exclusion from the textile industry meant that black women had different grievances from those of black men. As Kenneth Holbert, the EEOC's director of compliance, told the textile forum in January 1967, charges filed with the commission by black women alleged "refusal to hire . . . in an industry from which they felt traditionally excluded." For black men, many of whom already worked in the textile industry, charges filed were very different: "It is interesting to note that the primary basis of charges filed by Negro men alleged discrimination in conditions of work, such as unequal pay, unequal application of seniority, discharge, layoff, and segregated facilities."[2]

The role that gender played in shaping workers' complaints was reflected in several of the major class action lawsuits involving textile companies, especially the *Sledge v. J. P. Stevens* case. In his introductory remarks in the *Sledge* trial, for example, the plaintiffs' lawyer Richard T. Seymour explained how gender was responsible for different patterns of discrimination among African American men and women in the textile industry. For black women, the problem was not so much discrimination in the industry as it was getting hired: "One of the curious things about textile cases, including this one, seems to be that there is a very different treatment accorded to black females than to black males. We believe that black females find it more difficult to get hired and once hired, we think that their initial assignments tend to be much more like those of white females than the initial assignments of black males are like those of white males." Pay disparities between black men and white men were "very significant," whereas among women they were "insignificant."[3]

Data from *Sledge* and other cases confirms that there was little disparity between the pay of white women and black women who worked in the industry, but that black women had a much greater chance of being rejected for a job. Table 13, for example, shows that white females who applied for jobs at J. P. Stevens between May 1969 and June 30, 1972, were more than twice as likely to be hired as black females. White men had a hiring rate three times higher than that of black women. Black men were less likely to be hired than white women or men, but they still had almost twice the chance that black women did. In this period, moreover, Stevens's data show steadily worsening differences in the hiring rates of black females as compared to white females.

Table 13. Racial Hiring Rates at J. P. Stevens, Mid-May 1969–June 30, 1972

	Number of Applicants	Number of Hires	Percent Successful in Getting Jobs
White males	1,237	932	75.3
Black males	1,968	874	44.4
White females	1,260	684	54.3
Black females	1,918	442	23.0

Source: Findings of Fact and Conclusions of Law, December 22, 1975, *Sledge v. J. P. Stevens*, pp. 16–17.

Despite these hiring disparities, the court found that pay disparities between black and white women workers were much less than those between black and white men. Its 1975 decision noted, "Unlike the findings for male employees, the comparison of average hourly pay rates for current hourly female employees show few substantial differences between black females and white females. The differences shown are generally statistically insignificant." Data produced in the trial illustrated the point. Other cases also showed that pay disparities between black and white women were considerably less than those between men.[4]

"I Heard No Mention of Black Women Working in Textile Plants"

In the 1960s and 1970s, the American textile industry consistently employed more than half a million women workers, making it the biggest employer of women in basic manufacturing. The number of women employed in the textile industry greatly exceeded the average for American manufacturing industries as a whole. In 1977, 47 percent of textile workers were women, compared to 29 percent of workers in general manufacturing. The proportion of women in the textile industry increased, moreover, throughout the 1960s and 1970s. In 1977, 42 percent of J. P. Stevens's workforce were female, an increase of 23 percent since 1967.[5]

While the textile industry had traditionally been a large employer of women, almost all female textile workers before the 1960s were white. Indeed, the exclusion of African American women from the industry was striking. A study undertaken by TEAM in 1967 highlighted that while all blacks were underrepresented in the South Carolina textile industry, the problem was most acute among black women. As the report concluded, "The situation with regard to employment in the textile industry is even worse for Negro women than it is for Negro men." The study covered fourteen textile counties in the western

Table 14. Black Female Textile Workers Compared to White Female Textile Workers in South Carolina Piedmont Counties, 1967

County	White Female Textile Workers	Black Female Textile Workers	Percent Black Female Textile Workers
Spartanburg	6,370	208	3
Greenville	5,724	202	4
Anderson	4,241	178	4
York	3,341	141	4
Greenwood	3,266	221	7
Lancaster	2,913	56	2
Oconee	1,334	28	2
Union	1,555	152	9
Chester	1,166	18	2
Pickens	1,574	34	2
Cherokee	1,353	67	5
Laurens	1,440	40	3
Abbeville	903	58	6
Newberry	445	43	9
Total 14-county area	35,625	1,446	4

Source: *31st Annual Report of the Department of Labor of the State of South Carolina*, Table VI, "The Textile Industry and Negroes in Western South Carolina," TEAM Report, Reel 163, Southern Regional Council Papers, p. 2.

part of the state and showed that blacks held only 8 percent of jobs while making up 29 percent of the total population. Black women, however, held only 4 percent of all jobs occupied by women (see table 14). Among the largest eleven textile companies in South Carolina, black women held only 1,400 nonsalaried jobs, while white women held over 30,000. This was an acute problem in an area dominated by textile employment, with few other manufacturing jobs available.[6]

The gross underrepresentation of black women in the southern textile industry was confirmed by an EEOC study of the industry in the Carolinas. This study found that in 1960, women made up 43 percent of all employees in the Carolinas textile industry. There were, however, twenty-seven white female workers for each black female. There were only 2,792 black women compared to over 14,000 black men. The study concluded that "in the postwar period, the textile industry has provided blue collar jobs for an abundant supply of white females. . . . Negro women have not participated in these employment opportunities." Black women were also excluded from other southern industries. Indeed, only 5 percent of black women in the Carolinas worked in manufacturing industries in 1960. Over half of black women worked in personal services, mostly as domestic workers for white families.[7]

The exclusion of black women from the textile industry was a concern of civil rights leaders as well as the federal government. As early as 1945, the Southern Regional Council proposed that the labor shortage in the textile industry should be overcome by hiring black women who had been denied the opportunity to work in the industry.[8] Vivian W. Henderson, a black economist testifying at the EEOC textile forum in 1967, claimed that the "virtual exclusion" of black women from the textile industry was "the most glaring characteristic of textile employment." The status of black women in the industry was a major topic at the forum.[9]

While black men had always found some employment in the textile industry's heaviest jobs, the exclusion of African American women was almost total between the 1920s and the 1960s and showed few signs of changing. Indeed, the percentage of black women working in the textile industry in South Carolina actually declined from 1 percent in 1925 to 0.7 percent in 1965.[10] Data from EEOC reporting forms from the mid-1960s show that most textile companies employed at least some African American men but very few or no black women.[11] Black men often made up around 10 percent of male workers, but black women were usually only 1 percent or less of female workers. At Rock Hill Printing and Finishing Company, for example, 280 black men were employed in January 1966 out of 2,790 total male employees.[12] Only 3 black women, however, were employed out of 424 female workers. Another typical textile manufacturer employed only 2 black women out of 209 female employees in February 1966, while employing 81 black men out of 828 total.[13]

African American men who worked in textiles before the 1960s felt that women were not hired because they were not considered strong enough to perform heavy laboring jobs. Most black men believed that the only reason they themselves were hired was to perform strenuous jobs that whites would not do. Because black women were not seen as strong enough to perform these jobs, the industry had no use for them. Johnnie Archie, who worked in the shipping department at Rock Hill Printing and Finishing Company for more than thirty years, for example, felt that "they couldn't do a man's job. . . . The reason they hired us was to do work that the white man would not do, hazardous, dangerous jobs. . . . The black women didn't need to be out there on the trash truck, lifting heavy drums of trash about. She didn't need to be out there digging up trash for a pipeline, or running a jackhammer. The black woman was kept out of the plant because those jobs were off-limits to black people, period. We wouldn't have been there if it wasn't that we were doing the work that the white man didn't want to do. That's the only reason we were there."[14]

The only jobs that black women held in textiles before 1965 were a few clean-ing or janitorial positions.[15] Ollie Seals, who was one of the first black women to be hired at a textile plant in Columbus, Georgia, in 1969, remembered that "at first it was not easy for black women to get hired in textile plants. . . . When I was small I heard no mention of black women working in textile plants."[16] This restriction of black women to low-paying service positions was matched in other southern industries. Indeed, in industries such as lumber, service work was dominated by black women to a greater extent than in textiles. As historian James Cobb has concluded, "As of 1966 black women appeared to do little in southern industries except clean and maintain plant buildings."[17]

While discrimination in hiring was a problem for black men, it was far more acute for black women and continued to be a problem for them well into the 1970s. Data produced directly from the company's records in *Lewis v. J. P. Stevens* supports this assessment. From May 1969 through December 1974, the average hire rate for white females was between three and four times higher than that of black female applicants. The average white man had almost twice the chance of being employed as the average black male applicant (see table 15).[18] In *Adams v. Dan River Mills*, a statistical analysis undertaken in the early 1970s showed that the white male hire rate was 25 percent higher than the black male hire rate, but that the white female hire rate was 44 percent higher than the black female hire rate.[19] Standard deviation analysis undertaken in *Lewis v. Bloomsburg Mills* also revealed similar patterns of hiring discrimination.[20]

Black women who were hired also had to wait longer from the date of their first application to the date of their hiring. In *Sledge*, among female employees hired during 1972, the average time from the date of first application to the date of hire was 83.57 days for black females and 49.16 days for white females.[21] Some African American women returned to the Stevens personnel office as many as twenty times to check on their applications, waiting over three years to be hired.[22] Similarly, one of the chief complaints in *Lewis v. Bloomsburg Mills* was the imposition of "disproportionately long waiting periods" on black women applicants before they were hired.[23]

The Activism of Black Women against Hiring Discrimination

Many African American women were determined to protest against hiring dis-crimination in the textile industry. Indeed, the failure to hire black women was a central issue in the largest textile lawsuits. The largest case in the industry, *Sledge v. J. P. Stevens*, was actually initiated by a black woman, Lucy Sledge, fol-lowing Stevens's refusal to recall her after a layoff. Sledge initiated the lawsuit after watching the lines of job applicants at the mill. She complained that white women were hired to fill job vacancies similar to hers: "Every white that went

Table 15. Comparison of the Percentage of White Applicants and Black Applicants Who Were Hired at J. P. Stevens, 1969–1975

	Males		Females	
	Percent of White Applicants Hired	Percent of Black Applicants Hired	Percent of White Applicants Hired	Percent of Black Applicants Hired
1969	48.5	18.0	23.7	4.5
1970	42.9	7.9	20.8	3.8
1971	40.1	11.5	19.4	2.7
1972	64.4	30	54.5	20.3
1973	78.7	53.7	62.5	13.6
1974	59.0	43.0	36.4	9.4
1975	35.7	15.0	30.6	15.4
Total	53.5	28.9	36.3	10.9

Source: Plaintiffs' Proposed Findings of Fact and Conclusions of Law, June 11, 1980, *Lewis v. J. P. Stevens*, p. 7.

Note: For the period 1969–75, 43.2 percent of male applicants were black and 29.1 percent of male hires were black. For the same period, 45.9 percent of female applicants were black, and 20.3 percent of female hires were black.

in got hired. . . . Every black that went in didn't."[24] Another large case, *Adams v. Dan River Mills*, was based on two major complaints, which again demonstrated the different ways that discrimination affected black men and women: the assignment of blacks to the lowest-paying jobs, a complaint applicable largely to black men, and refusal to hire, a complaint from "female applicants for both production and clerical positions."[25]

EEOC statistics show that many black women filed charges to protest against hiring discrimination. In January 1967, the EEOC's compliance director, Kenneth Holbert, told the textile forum that the commission had received 197 charges from the textile industry since Title VII of the Civil Rights Act became effective in July 1965. Many of these charges alleged failure to hire and were "brought by Negro women who sought employment in an industry from which they felt traditionally excluded."[26]

African American women were often persistent in their efforts to get jobs in the textile industry. The lawsuits reveal an impressive record of activism by black women. In many cases women joined together to apply en masse at textile companies that had never hired black women before. When the companies refused to hire them, the women initiated lawsuits. The women's active confrontation of the textile industry's traditional bar on the employment of black women is particularly significant because little is known about the role of black women in protesting against employment discrimination.[27]

In three major lawsuits, *Lea v. Cone Mills*, *Lewis v. Bloomsburg Mills*, and *Lewis v. J. P. Stevens*, black women made a collective attempt to secure jobs at plants that had never before hired black females. The Civil Rights Act was a crucial turning point because it allowed determined African Americans to test these barriers of discrimination, knowing that federal law was on their side. Across the Piedmont South, African Americans began to push companies to end discrimination, and in many cases they initiated legal proceedings against the companies when they refused to take action. In *Lea*, a group of black women got together shortly after the passage of the Civil Rights Act and decided that it was time to put some pressure on the local Cone plant. On the morning of September 2, 1965, the group of women met in church and, with the help of their minister, drew up a list of plants that they would visit to try to get jobs. They planned to return to the church following the filing of the applications in order to sign complaints against companies which did not offer them jobs.[28] In *Lewis v. Bloomsburg Mills* and *Lewis v. J. P. Stevens*, a group of black women described how they carpooled and drove around the South Carolina countryside applying for jobs at various textile plants. They also filed charges against those companies that repeatedly refused to consider their applications.[29]

In *Lea v. Cone Mills*, a group of African American women tried to get jobs at a small Cone Mills plant in Hillsborough, North Carolina. The only manufacturing plant in that area of Orange County, the plant employed many white women as well as a small number of black men in laboring positions. On July 2, 1965, at the time the Civil Rights Act became effective, 346 people were employed at the plant. Of this workforce, 310 were white and 36 were black men. No black women had ever been employed in any capacity at the plant, and, aware of the company's policy, few black women applied for work before the spring of 1965.[30] The responses that the group of women received showed that the company had no intention of hiring black women even after the passage of the Civil Rights Act. One of the women, Annie Belle Tinnin, described at the trial what happened when she visited the plant in 1965: "Well, I didn't talk to anyone but the secretary. There was a little window like and she raised it up and my sister and I, we told her we was asking for a job and she said they didn't hire Negro ladies there."[31] Other black women also recalled being told outright that the company did not hire black women, even though the Civil Rights Act had already been passed and the plant was working on government business. Romona Pinnix described how she was told by the company when she went to the plant that they "never hired no colored women to do no industrial work."[32]

Black women who applied for jobs at other textile plants were also told outright that companies did not hire black women, even as late as the 1970s. In

Lewis v. Bloomsburg Mills, a group of African American women tried to get jobs at a Bloomsburg Mills plant in Abbeville County, South Carolina. The company was a small manufacturer of specialist textiles with two plants, one in Abbeville and one in Bloomsburg, Pennsylvania. Although the lawsuit was not filed until 1973, many of the plaintiffs in the case described how the company was still quite open about not hiring blacks. Carrie McIntosh, for example, described the company's response when she applied for a job in 1973: "Well, I went to apply for a job. I never filled out an application at that time. She said to me that they were only hiring whites, no black employees at that time."[33] Similarly, when Annie Calhoun applied in 1966, she was told there were "no openings for the colored."[34]

The records of the lawsuits describe rejection after rejection for black women who were trying to get jobs in the southern textile industry. Despite these setbacks, African American women showed remarkable courage and persistence in their efforts to get hired. It is clear that their main motivation was their overwhelming need for manufacturing employment. As the records of the lawsuits indicate, the only employment alternatives for black women were menial and backbreaking jobs with very low pay. Faced with these alternatives, African American women were determined to get jobs in textiles.

Their desperate need for industrial work, combined with companies' outright refusal to hire black women, moved many black women to action. Thus, in *Lewis v. J. P. Stevens*, lead plaintiff Sallie Pearl Lewis explained that because she could not get hired in textiles, she had to work "setting out pine trees" between February and April. Once this seasonal work was finished, she would pick peaches in the summer for $18 a day. This job meant leaving home at four o'clock in the morning and returning at ten o'clock at night in order to catch a bus to Spartanburg County, where the peaches grew. Lewis tried to get jobs at all of the textile plants in her area and filed EEOC charges because they refused to hire her: "I went to all the plants. . . . It's on there. Bloomsburg. All of them. . . . Calhoun Falls, Rocky River, J. P. Stevens, Abbeville Mill and the rest of them. . . . I just wanted a job and trying to get it, and nobody wouldn't hire me, so I had to write."[35] Lewis explained that it was the need for black women generally to find employment that had motivated her: "We went to all the plants and when I wrote that [the EEOC complaint] the colored folks had to live and I had to get some work to do." She also described how painful the constant rejection was: "You see, every time we go, we wonder why they'd let the white folks set back and the black folk had to leave with a hanged head down, aching heart and we had to wonder [where] we was going to get another meal at."[36]

Many black women needed textile employment because their only work was in seasonal agricultural jobs.[37] In *Lea v. Cone Mills*, for example, plaintiff Romona Pinnix explained that she needed work "very badly" because she had children to support.[38] Pinnix said that she sought a textile job because the farm work that she had been doing was seasonal: "Well, as I stated here on my application, I was a farm wife, and after farming season closed, there's nothing else we can do but try to find public work."[39] Lead plaintiff Shirley Lea described how she had been laboring in the tobacco fields at the time she applied to Cone Mills. She repeatedly tried to get jobs at Cone Mills but was told "that they didn't hire colored ladies." Lea then pleaded with the company, stressing her need for employment in a way that typified the persistence of black women: "I went there—I let him know I went there wanting employment. I didn't care if it was that day; I wanted it. And he let me know he didn't hire colored womens."[40] Another plaintiff in *Lea*, Annie Tinnin, described how she wanted a job at Cone Mills because she was working in a laundry pressing shirts for around $35 a week. Tinnin remembered that the need for better employment opportunities for black women in the community was very great because "there were a lot of Negro ladies in the community that didn't have work."[41]

In *Lewis v. Bloomsburg Mills*, plaintiff Janie Belle Ashmore explained that she had turned to the EEOC as a last resort after repeated failed efforts to get hired. Ashmore explained that her only work experience was "a little peach work" and "a little house work." She applied to Bloomsburg Mills on at least five occasions, as well as to many other plants. Typifying the tenacity of the black women, she explained in her deposition that she had visited a number of mills in Abbeville County. She went to one plant "more times than I've got fingers and toes," but a "big fat chunky man" told her that "we don't have anything for you to do." Not surprisingly, in the end Ashmore concluded "that they wasn't going to give colored people no job."[42] Similarly, Thelma Edwards recalled that in 1965 she went to "all" of the textile plants in Abbeville County: "I went to Abbeville Mills, Rocky River Mills, Bloomsburg, J. P. Stevens, Calhoun Falls Mills." She repeated her visits to every mill in succeeding years.[43]

Many black women described how they helped each other in their exhaustive search for textile jobs. In *Lewis v. Bloomsburg Mills*, women described how they borrowed money from each other or agreed to share cars so that they could make repeated trips to textile plants. Annie Calhoun, whose main work experience was, like Lewis's, in seasonal agricultural work, testified in her deposition that the women went to the mills in an overloaded car that they had borrowed: "Everytime I went out there there was a carload. . . . Loaded every time I went." The women went to plants of all the major textile companies, taking up a whole day in the process: "We would go and stay all day."[44] Similarly, Thelma J. Edwards testified that because so many black women were in need of textile employment, they joined together to try to help each other: "The majority of them over there was looking for jobs, so, when one knew that they was going, they would get in contact with the other one. We would chip in together with our little money and get some gas and all of us go in groups." Edwards explained that black women were desperate to penetrate the textile industry because of its dominant position in the local economy: "The only thing I know down here is textile."[45]

The stories that women told of their repeated attempts to get textile jobs were indicative of the determination and fighting spirit that African American women exhibited throughout the lawsuits. Rather than becoming discouraged by constant rejection, the women were determined to fight the injustice they met in the textile industry. The deposition of Sallie Pearl Lewis in *Lewis v. Bloomsburg Mills* typified this mood. It showed that Lewis decided to take on the companies and contact the EEOC on her own initiative. She emerged as a leader of a group of black women and encouraged them also to contact the EEOC. Lewis explained that she filed the suit against Bloomsburg Mills because she witnessed the wholesale rejection of black applicants by textile companies: "I just wrote to the Equal Employment and asked them about it, cause we went so much, the black folks, over there and they wouldn't never have nothing for them to do. But, the white folks would set back and they would turn us around at the window so we never did get no further than the windows. They'd just say, nothing for you all today and us will let you know." Lewis remembered that at all the mills, "they'd just be loads go there—colored folks. . . . Groups. Just carloads following the other one. Trying to get on."[46]

Some black women even reported that they had been rejected for textile jobs on the grounds of being too overweight or too short. In *Adams*, for example, Gracie Childress wrote on her EEOC complaint form that "the personnel office people said I was too fat and I know that there are fatter white people in the mill than me because I have seen them."[47] Like Childress, most African American women rejected the validity of these excuses. Josephine Jennings, for example, wrote on her EEOC form that "I was denied a position allegedly because of my weight. I believe that the real reason I was not hired was because of being too black rather than being too fat."[48] Textile companies were more likely to reject black women on physical grounds partly because they only wanted to hire those women who were capable of heavy exertion. Women who were hired frequently recounted how the company had asked how much they could lift or whether they could handle heavy work. The sheer number of black women applying for jobs meant that companies could afford to pick out those whom it thought could best handle "male" jobs.

Other companies placed moral requirements upon black women that were not applied to white applicants. In 1969, the EEOC even found one textile plant that refused to hire a black woman who had "borne children out of wedlock— although company officials admitted that they hired unwed mothers who were white."[49]

The lawsuits provide many individual stories that vividly illustrate what the statistics of hiring discrimination actually meant for black women who tried to get jobs in the textile industry in the late 1960s. There were many examples of women who tried for several years to get hired. In *Sledge v. J. P. Stevens*, the trial highlighted the case of Ellen Ellis, who had clerical qualifications and tried to get a job with the company for three and a half years. In all, Ellis made nineteen trips to the personnel office.[50] In *Adams v. Dan River Mills*, Loretta Harris explained in 1970 that she had been trying to get hired at the company for over three years: "March will be four years I been trying to get in the mill." Harris stated that "white applicants were hired in my presence on several occasions." Like most black women, Harris's persistence sprang from a desperate need for textile employment and a lack of alternative work. She explained that she had continued to apply because "I needed more money to begin with. With five children you need all you can get when you have to educate them. If you don't work in Dan River or somewhere paying money, there's no need to work. You can't make it off $25.00 a week for six days in domestic work."[51]

In *Sledge v. J. P. Stevens*, many African American women used their back pay questionnaires to describe their repeated efforts to secure textile work. The letters that *Sledge* plaintiffs attached to their questionnaires also highlighted the determination of black women to get textile work. Some told incredible stories of persistent visits to the mill. Pattie Kearney, for example, described in a 1981 letter how she had been trying to get a job at the mill since October 1967: "I was in and out of that office asking for work. And I wanted it and also needed it badly.... I went so much one lady in the office told me to stop coming so regular because I was paying people to bring me and just come every once in a while so I did." Despite never being hired, Kearney continued to try because she clung to the belief that it was not necessarily because of her race that she was being rejected.[52]

These letters reveal that many black women were lied to or misinformed in order to discourage them from applying at Stevens. Ruby V. Ward, for example, was told that "all of their vacancies are filled from within J. P. Stevens through promotions and job posting," even though the company's adamant refusal to post jobs was a major issue in the *Sledge* case. Not surprisingly, Ward suspected that the company's arguments represented "an act of stalling . . . to get rid of prospective employees."[53]

Some black women were not as patient as Kearney and became frustrated with the excuses that the company offered them. A mood of resistance came through in many letters as women questioned how they could ever satisfy the company's conditions for employment. As Annette Hawkins wrote in response to the company's argument that they preferred applicants with textile experience: "How can a person get experience if they dont have a chance."[54] Some women wrote in anger as they described what had happened to them because they had not been hired. The consequences of not being employed were often serious in textile-dominated towns such as Roanoke Rapids. Denise Johnson described how "I applied in '79' and I would check every Tuesday and Thursday for a good four month and always the same bull. I know for sure that they wouldn't call me so finally I just stopped going. . . . I really want a job I had no income whatsoever so I ended up on welfare! Where I am now, I am trying to get in the shipyard!" She ended her letter with the plea, "I hope someone gets some justice done."[55]

Some women used the back pay form to record how they really felt about J. P. Stevens. These forms illustrated that for some women, the company's history of racial discrimination had caused a great deal of resentment and hostility. Hattie F. Lewis, for example, wrote "they are prejudice" all over her back pay form and added a statement at the bottom: "I'm very glad to hear from you. I don't think they treat Blacks right. they treat Blacks like Slavery. They are Prejudice. I willing to answer any questions by the atorneys."[56]

Across the South, African American women showed the same determination to get hired in the textile industry, even in plants that had never hired a black woman.[57] In *Adams v. Dan River Mills*, many depositions were taken from women who had tried unsuccessfully to get hired at Dan River's plant in Greenville, Alabama, located between Montgomery and Mobile. Despite being located in an area with a large black population, the plant hired only white women as late as 1970. As in other cases, African American women tackled the problem collectively. A group of five women applied together in an effort to be the first black women hired. Most of the women were in desperate need of industrial employment, as their only previous work experience had been as domestics. Their testimony shows that when they were rejected, the women wanted to expose the company's discrimination and refused to accept company arguments that they were not qualified for a job. Marian Louise Epps testified that "when I came down there, the job was open and I didn't get it. He was looking for an experienced lady to run that job and I'm not that dumb, you know, I can catch on just as easy as anybody else." Elizabeth Millner told the company attorney that the company did discriminate "because every time you go over there they don't have nothing, so that leads up to something." She added, "If I was white I could go out there and you would hire me. . . . It just works that way. If my face was white and not being black I could go there and say—and ask for a job; and they would give me a job. But my face is black and they won't give me one."[58]

The validity of Millner's remarks was borne out by the testimony of John S. Crenshaw, a black man who worked for the company as a yardman. One of Crenshaw's tasks was to empty the trash from the company's office and take it to the dump. Crenshaw testified that while whites got hired or had their applications kept on file, he noticed that the applications of the five black women were thrown away the same day that they were filled out: "I was the yardman and cleaning up, you know, and I hauled the applicants to the dump, city dump, and burned them up. So, I felt like that they didn't want to hire them. I always have heard that you keep a application in the file for so long but they filled out theirs today and the next day I carried them away."[59]

The Experiences of African American Women in the Textile Industry

Although black women still faced considerable hiring discrimination in the 1960s and 1970s, they also began to enter production jobs in the industry in increasing numbers. Several large textile companies began to hire African American women in much greater numbers, opening up certain production positions that had previously been the domain of white women. Although the opportunities available to black women did not match their demand for textile work, the opening of some production positions was significant because of the traditional exclusion of black women from the industry. Indeed, the history of complete exclusion of black women from production jobs meant that even a small amount of hiring produced massive percentage increases. At J. P. Stevens's plants in Roanoke Rapids, North Carolina, for example, the *Sledge* case revealed that black women made significant progress into production jobs in the late 1960s. In mid-May of 1969, only 6 of Stevens's 120 female spinners were black. From this date until June 30, 1972, however, Stevens hired and assigned 45 women to the job of spinner, 22 of them black. In the same period, 40 black women out of a total of 116 assigned to the job of weaver were black, even though the weaver position had previously been only 1.9 percent black.[60] Similarly, the *Adams* case established that Dan River Mills had begun to assign many black women to the high-paying production job of weaver in the late 1960s, although few black men were given the same opportunity (see table 16).

By the late 1960s, black women were making more progress into some better-paying jobs than their male counterparts. As a result, data produced in a variety of lawsuits showed that pay disparities for black women were continually declining in the late 1960s and early 1970s, at the same time that they were static or increasing for black men. An analysis of pay disparities at Dan River Mills, for example, showed that there was a "noticeable decline" in the wage disparity between white and black females between 1969 and 1973, while at the same time the disparities between white and black males remained constant.[61] Similarly, in *Sledge v. J. P. Stevens*, a data analysis conducted in 1980 found that

Table 16. Assignment of New Hires to the Weaver Job by Race and Sex at Dan River Mills, January 1, 1969–March 31, 1971

	Males	Females	Total
White	305	501	806
Black	43	304	347
Total	348	805	1,153

Source: Plaintiffs' Proposed Findings of Fact and Conclusions of Law, September 16, 1974, *Adams v. Dan River Mills*, p. 29.

pay disparities were increasing between men but were decreasing among women.[62]

The entry of black women into textiles is an important change that merits further study, particularly as the historic exclusion of black women from southern industry has provided limited opportunities to explore the labor history of black women workers.[63] On the whole, black women interviewed for this study gave a balanced assessment of their experience as textile workers. Textile jobs represented a major economic improvement for them, but black women also found a great deal of discrimination in the mills.

Black Female Pioneers

While male pioneers were often promoted from within, the large-scale exclusion of African American women from the textile industry before 1964 meant that there was no pool of experienced women workers to upgrade to production positions. Consequently, female pioneers tended to have a somewhat different profile from their male counterparts, reflecting the very different problems that women faced in the southern textile industry. For black women, textile employment was a new experience, and the first production workers were very conscious of the fact that the success of their group depended on them. Companies, indeed, often hired the first group of black women as a deliberate experiment. As a result, the first black women were likely to be very well qualified or overqualified. In addition, the women were selected for their ability to withstand the pressure of being pioneers, including having the character and patience to withstand the possibility of racial abuse from white workers.

Companies' concerns about racial abuse from white workers meant that they tended to use their established contacts in the community to hire black women who were well known and respected by both the black and the white

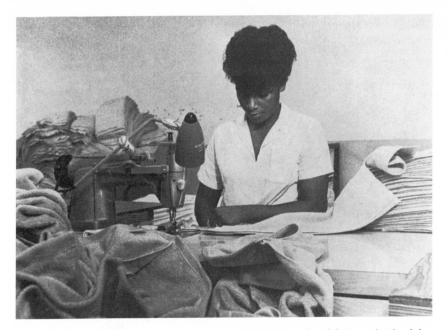

By the late 1960s, African American women were beginning to break into production jobs in the southern textile industry, particularly in plants with sewing operations. (*Textile Industries*, November 1968)

communities. Robert Lincks, the head of personnel development at Burlington Industries in the 1960s, for example, remembered that the first black women hired were usually referred by supervisors and were often "someone's maid."[64] At Cannon Mills in Kannapolis, North Carolina, the first black woman hired in the washcloth department, Kay Willis, was the daughter of the company president's long-serving domestic, who, after the successful hiring of her daughter, continued to recommend other blacks to the company.[65] Similarly, at the Alatex Company in Andalusia, Alabama, Gladys Trawick, the first black woman hired into a production job in 1965, felt that she was chosen because she had worked as a waitress at the Rotary Club, where mill executives frequently went. As she had catered to "the most elite crowds," they all knew her by name. Trawick felt that the three other women selected to go into the mill with her were also chosen for their family backgrounds and community reputations: "All four of us that was picked was people that went to church, and had family backgrounds that was good in all four of us." Like other female pioneers, all four Alatex women were asked if they wanted a job rather than applying to the company first.[66]

Similar stories emerge from other female pioneers across the South. Louise Peddaway was the first African American woman to be hired at Dixie Yarn in

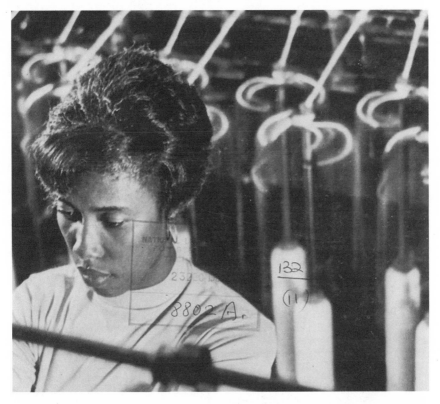

The entry of black women into spinning jobs, previously reserved for white women, was publicized by the industry, as this 1968 photograph used on the cover of a trade journal indicates. (*Textile Industries*, November 1968)

Tarboro, North Carolina, in 1964. Again, Peddaway did not apply to the mill but was approached by the personnel manager and his wife, who were close friends of her family.[67] Bobbie Harrison, who started working at Lee County Manufacturing Company in Leesburg, Georgia, in 1968, felt that the first black female, who was hired shortly before Harrison, had been selected because she was well known in the white community: "She got in there through somebody else. . . . She just didn't go there I don't think and just they hired her. . . . Her family was well known in Lee County, well known in Lee County, and they were sort of like a little mixed up there so . . . it was someone that knew her family real well that got her into that, and from that they began to hire black people."[68]

Another common feature of the black women's experiences was that companies often told the pioneers that they were an experiment and that the future of black employment at the plant depended on them. Companies took time to explain to the pioneers that they anticipated some reaction from white workers, but that if the women could withstand this and work successfully, the company would then hire other African American women. Louise Peddaway, for example, recalled, "I remember they said, 'Louise, we're going to put you in spinning, and we don't want you to be afraid, because we're going to work with you, and if it works out with you'—I think they were more afraid of how the whites were going to act towards me—and she told me that if it worked out okay, she told me that they were going to . . . hire somebody else. She didn't come right out and say another black, but I knew that's what she meant." About three weeks after Peddaway was hired, the company did indeed hire other African American women.[69] Corine Lytle Cannon, who was the first black woman hired at Cannon Mills in 1962, remembered what an embarrassed plant manager told her and another black woman when she went into the mill on the first morning: "He said, 'I'll tell you, you'll be an example. Everybody is going to be looking at you.' He said, 'But if anybody looks at you or says anything unpleasant, please don't answer back.' . . . And all this time he was standing with his back to us. He got up from the desk and turned his back to us and said, 'This is new and try to make the best of it. You have been chosen and you are going to be an example.'" The women were told to report any whites who gave them racial abuse.[70]

When the first black women entered the mills, they did in fact face a considerable amount of abuse from white workers. In many cases, white workers just stared at blacks. Kay Willis remembered that at Cannon Mills, "when I went in—I was very nervous and when I went in, all or the majority of the ladies, they would stand along the walls and watch me and just stand and stare at me."[71] Gladys Trawick recalled that in Andalusia, Alabama, the white workers would "call you names, but we were told that when they hired us, that we would be called names." Like other pioneers, she remembered vividly the experience of being watched by white workers on her first day: "It was weird, walking in there with everybody looking at you and everybody whispering. People would hear things in the community that was said about the four of us that would make our parents afraid." Illustrating the deep resentment that integration of the mills could arouse, in Andalusia it was rumored that the houses of Trawick and the three other black women would be burned down if they continued working there. Trawick felt that race relations in the mill were worse than in the town as a whole, and that many white workers "just didn't want you in because they felt that they was superior to you and you couldn't have the same jobs as they did."[72]

Bobbie Harrison also remembered that there was a lot of racial tension in the plant where she started working in Leesburg, Georgia, in 1968: "When I first started there in '68 we would be in the cafeteria and, you know, the black over here and the white over there, and I guess we were just checking out each other, just looking, because, you know, this was something that had never happened." Like Trawick, Harrison felt that white workers did not want blacks in the mill, although she believed that this had less to do with economic competition than with an aversion to social mixing: "It wasn't so much I don't think that they was worried about [blacks] coming in and taking their jobs. I just don't think they really wanted to be employed with the black man, I really don't. I don't think they wanted us there. . . . I felt like, and I still feel like, if some of them had a choice today we wouldn't be in a lot of places. . . . That's bad."[73]

Many other sources indicate that female pioneers faced hostility from white workers and had to endure isolation at work. At Burlington Industries, Geraldine Siler was the first African American to be employed in the company's executive offices in Greensboro, North Carolina. In December 1962, Siler described her experiences to an AFSC conference. She reported that many of her white coworkers had not really accepted her even though she had been working there for a year and a half: "None of the girls in the department have yet invited her to join them for coffee break." Siler had also not used the country club that Burlington maintained for its employees because the company had told her not to apply for membership "until she was fully accepted by the rest of the employees." Overall, the AFSC reported that "Ms. Siler finds her work satisfying, but would certainly enjoy it much more if there did not exist this reluctance on the part of the girls in the building to accept her as an individual."[74]

The AFSC conference found that this experience of isolation and alienation in the workforce was typical of other industry pioneers. Reporting on black pioneers in Greensboro, North Carolina, Sarah Herbin of the AFSC told the conference that "in spite of the fact that Negroes have moved into some of the non-traditional jobs in this area, these individuals remain pioneers. For the most part, there has not been the total acceptance and full participation of these persons into the mainstream of company activities. . . . [T]here is great reluctance on the part of white employees to initiate friendliness. This reluctance creates a defensive reaction on the part of Negroes who often seek to save themselves anxiety and embarrassment, and retaliate against white employees by isolating themselves from the group."[75]

The racism that the first African American women faced meant that they had to have strong temperaments in order to succeed. Pioneers, indeed, were often selected with these characteristics specifically in mind. Gladys Trawick, for example, felt that the company "chose the most bravest women then." She added that she would "try anything" as a young woman in the 1960s but would not go through the same experience now when she was middle-aged.[76] One of the main reasons that these women were able to overcome racism was the fact that they were conscious that they were pioneers and that their community depended on them. Gladys Trawick remembered that she was determined to succeed because she felt a responsibility to the local black community: "I felt that the community was depending on me and I had to, because a lot of them before I even went to take the test would come to me and ask me would I be considered as one of the first. A lot of the black community they just thought I could do it."[77] Similarly, at Cannon Mills, Kay Willis was conscious of being the first black woman in her department: "I felt myself as a pioneer." She was determined to succeed so that she and other black women could earn a decent living rather than relying on poorly paid work as domestics for white mill workers.[78] Bobbie Harrison was motivated to succeed because she felt strongly that the mill should be integrated and that African Americans should have equal opportunity: "I don't think we should be separate people. I think that we are human all of us, and I feel like what is good for the white man is good for the black man."[79]

The integration of Oneita Knitting Mills in Andrews, South Carolina, illustrated the virulent opposition that the hiring of black women could produce. The plant was integrated largely through the efforts of Rev. B. J. Gordon, a local civil rights leader and politician. Gordon used a bus from his church to take African American women to the plant gates to fill out application forms. Eventually, his pressure resulted in the company's agreeing to hire the first black women in 1965. Gordon remembered that the hiring of black women aroused strong opposition from the white community, especially from white workers who employed black women as domestic workers. For many years the plant manager, Frank Urtz, had refused to hire black women on these grounds. When the company finally agreed to hire them, Gordon selected women who were overqualified, so that the company could not refuse them, and women who had a good temperament, so that they could withstand intimidation from whites: "I selected . . . people who I knew who had good temperament, people who had an extra amount of patience, not knowing what they would run into, knowing and feeling that they would be intimidated in some way. . . . I made sure that I picked out the most temperate persons."[80]

Even though Gordon took great care in selecting the women, threats from white workers ensured that the women were still afraid when the day came for them to start work: "They were highly intimidated, I will never forget that, in those days, because the women were told about things by the folks they did work for, their jobs in the kitchens and keeping the white people's children. . . . The funny thing I'll never forget, always remember, is that the first group I took, people had made threats to them what was going to happen, what they were going to do to them, so I had to go in first and open the door and go in and come out and call them, because they were frightened because they were told all kinds of things." In the end, threats of violence did not materialize, although white workers still directed some racial abuse at the black women, telling them that they were not welcome and had "no business" in the plant. Whites also threatened a black barber who cut their hair, saying that they would boycott his business if he did not stop his pastor (Gordon) from pressuring the company to hire black women.[81]

Despite hostility from some workers, the first African American women who worked in the mills also felt that friendships they formed with particular white workers helped keep them going and ensured that they learned their jobs successfully. In some cases, companies carefully selected certain whites to train and look after the black pioneers, and these workers often formed lasting friendships. Louise Peddaway, for example, remembered that "the people there really cared. They acted like they really wanted me to learn, and I never forget there was a lady there named Miss Phelps, she was the one who worked with me, she was an older lady." In some cases, white workers were very understanding of the situation that the first black production workers were in and took it upon themselves to protect the blacks from any hostility. Ollie Seals, for example, started working at a textile plant in Columbus, Georgia, in 1969, when she was straight out of high school. Illustrating the way that integration could provide fond memories for some African Americans, Seals recalled that "at the time I was real young when I went to work into the plant, and most of the white people looked at me as being their baby.... White women took care of me. They looked out and made sure that none of the other people mistreated me."[82]

Both black and white women remembered forging close friendships for the first time with workers of the other race because of integration. It was clear that for most workers the integration of the mills changed established racial patterns and involved an adjustment period of getting used to dealing with each other on a new basis. Black worker Johnny Mae Fields, for example, who began working for Cannon Mills in the 1960s, remembered slowly getting to know the white woman who worked next to her. Fields recalled that after a few conversations, "she asked me one day, 'What would you rather me call you, black or colored?' And I said, 'black.' One day she said, 'Johnny, you're the first black woman I've ever really got to know.'" From this point on, the relationship between the two women began to flourish. As Fields explained, "She'd tell me stories that I wouldn't know had been said. For instance, black people's skin gets ashy in the winter time and she told me that white people always thought this was because we didn't have enough food to eat ... So there was all these tales and we'd sit in the bathroom and she'd tell 'em to me and we'd laugh. Now she had never liked black people, I knew that.... But this woman fell in love with me."[83]

Unlike black men who were upgraded into production positions, most of the first African American women who were hired had never been in a textile mill before. Many remembered that when they first went into the mill, they felt overwhelmed and scared by all the noise and machinery and doubted whether they could make it as textile workers. Angie Rogers, a tall African American woman who was hired at a textile mill in Columbus, Georgia, in 1968, remembered that her first feelings were that the mill was "scary . . . because when I first went in and started to work . . . it just seemed like you had to do so much work."[84] Ollie Seals recalled that when she went into the mill, "it was shocking because I really felt like I cannot do this, you know, this type of work . . . working with the hands and things, and at first I didn't think that I would succeed at working in a plant like that, but now I look back and say, 'I made it, all those years.'"[85] Like Seals, most black women did successfully adapt to plant work and took pride in their long service in the mill. Most were determined to do a good job because this was their first opportunity to work on a production job. Reverna Crittenden was hired in 1972 at Columbus Towel Mill in Columbus, Georgia, and was proud to still be on the same job twenty-four years later. She summed up the determination of many other black women who were interviewed: "I was happy that I had gotten hired there. . . . I was real excited when I went for this job, and I was determined to make the best of, you know, the best out of what I did."[86]

Textile companies soon realized that black women made excellent workers. In 1969, a manager from the large West Point Pepperell chain declared that "the Negro woman is a better, more responsible employee than the Negro male," a view repeated by several other companies.[87] Many union officials and black women themselves felt that textile companies turned to hiring more African American women because they were such good workers. Some argued that companies knew that recruiting black women would reduce turnover because they had less opportunity to leave the industry for better jobs elsewhere. In addition, many black women supported families with their textile wages and thus were unlikely to quit. Sammy Glover, who was hired into a textile mill in Andalusia, Alabama, and later became the director of the union, remembered being told by one mill owner that he had started to hire black women because, unlike white women, they were often the "primary breadwinner." They were less able to quit and also tried to work harder so as to make more money. There was, as Glover recalled, a perception that a black woman "would work harder because there was a greater need for her to work harder."[88]

Data collected by Dan River Mills proved the point, showing that black women had the lowest quit rates and absenteeism levels of any group of workers (see table 17). Dan River data also showed that black women were usually better educated than their white counterparts. In 1969, black women, who

Table 17. Comparison of Turnover by Race and Sex at Dan River Mills, Danville Division, 1969

	Employees Hired in 1969	Employees Hired in 1969 Who Quit in 1969	Percent
White male	1,937	904	46.6
Black male	1,751	745	42.5
White female	1,595	614	38.5
Black female	1,041	346	33.2

Source: R. C. Gourley to R. M. Stephens, May 1, 1970, "Affirmative Action—Statistical Information on Black Employment, Promotions, etc. 1968–1972" folder, Dan River Mills Company Papers.

were the lowest-paid group of workers, had the most education, 9.76 years on average, while white men, the higher-paid workers, had the least, with only 7.99 years. Company data show that this pattern was maintained into the 1970s.[89]

Coming Out of the White Man's Kitchen: The Significance of Black Women's Entry into the Textile Industry

Before the 1960s, the main source of income for African American women who lived in textile towns was working as domestics in the homes of white textile workers. As black mill worker Katie Geneva Cannon explained, in the mill town of Kannapolis, North Carolina, "most of the white people ... didn't clean their houses. That was what black women were for. That was how black women would get their income, how they survived." Wages paid to black domestic helpers were very low and kept the economic level of the black community well below that of white mill workers.[90] Indeed, many African American women who worked as domestics for white textile workers felt that white women made a collective decision to limit the pay of their black "help." As Blanche Willis, who worked as a domestic in Kannapolis, recalled, "The white women would get together and they had clubs. And they made a rule that all of 'em would pay $15, whatever they paid. . . . Wouldn't do no good to stop one and go to the other, because they had already made this rule that whoever hired a black domestic servant, they weren't gonna pay 'em over $15. And they all stuck to that."[91]

Because domestic employment was the only work available to black women in many southern communities dominated by the textile industry, it was essential to open up jobs in textiles and other manufacturing industries. In August 1966, for example, Kelly Alexander, president of the NAACP in North

Carolina, wrote to one textile manufacturer that "we certainly want to keep the lines of communication alive as to job opportunity for our people. There is a great demand from our women for employment in the manufacturing industry. We are having a problem of placing women with less than a high school education and they need to work where they get more than domestic pay." Alexander established an NAACP Job Market Information Bureau and corresponded with textile and other manufacturers in an effort to help African Americans get jobs in industry.[92]

The common practice of black women working as domestic helpers for white workers made many textile managers and workers particularly opposed to black women entering the industry. Indeed, one of the biggest obstacles African American women faced in many towns was the resistance of the white community to employing black domestics in textile plants. In *Hicks v. Cannon Mills*, for example, one of the main complaints in the case was that "Negro females employed as housemaids may be refused employment on that account."[93] Similarly, in *Lewis v. Bloomsburg Mills*, lead plaintiff Sallie Pearl Lewis complained that she had been refused a job at Bloomsburg Mills in Abbeville, South Carolina, on these grounds: "I believe they don't want to hire me because I do house work for white families who don't want me working in a mill."[94]

Black women who applied for clerical work with textile companies were sometimes told by white managers that there were no clerical jobs available, but that they knew whites who needed domestic help. At one company in Gaffney, South Carolina, for example, a TEAM aide reported that "2 black girls had applied but then said that they were in the wrong office according to the manager's assistant, and the manager's assistant tried to hire them to do her personal domestic work."[95]

On many occasions the employment of black domestics aroused strong opposition from the white community and put companies under pressure to refuse applications from black women. In Andrews, South Carolina, Rev. B. J. Gordon, a local civil rights leader, pressured the local Oneita Knitting Mills to hire black women throughout the 1960s. The plant provided the only manufacturing jobs in the area but employed only white women in a coastal region of South Carolina that was predominantly black. Gordon remembered that the plant's manager, Frank Urtz, was frightened to hire black women because his workers employed them as domestic help: "Urtz's thing to me was that it was pressure from the community, it wasn't him, it was community pressure. . . . I think the head officials, Urtz, meant good, but as he told me, well you know he got pressure from the community, and that pressure was not to hire their cooks, not to hire their workers."[96]

Some civil rights activists also found that textile companies gave black women the hardest jobs in the mills and treated them unequally in order to force them to quit and go back to being domestics. TEAM aide Alice Gallman, for example, reported that in Union County, South Carolina, "some overseers are careful not to overload their Negro women workers, but they talk mean to them to make them give up their jobs and go back to domestic work."[97]

The fact that African American women had this background of low-paying domestic work made their entry into textile jobs particularly significant. Their employment in the textile industry brought a huge change to southern textile communities where black women had always been restricted to domestic work and had frequently worked for white textile workers. Black women who were hired in the 1960s and 1970s remembered that the opportunity to enter the mills and earn comparable wages to white women was a great economic improvement. Laura Ann Pope was hired at Oneita Knitting Mills in Andrews, South Carolina, in 1970. The plant, whose workforce was around 85 percent women, began hiring its first black women in the mid-1960s, a few years after it had first moved to Andrews. Pope explained the large improvement that this entailed for black women who had previously been restricted to domestic or agricultural labor: "The majority was ladies, and they would be so glad to get out the white man's kitchen and out the cotton field, and out the tobacco, and all this. They was just glad to have anything, because they were cooking for the whites and cleaning up and all this sort of stuff. . . . See, after Oneita came here the whites had their own food to [do], had their own cooking to do, their laundry to do, and their housecleaning to do, because they were, the ladies was out right with them on the job . . . but until Oneita, until they started hiring a lot of blacks, they were in their houses, you know, cleaning up for them. . . . Yes, that was an improvement."[98]

Across the South, African American women felt that the textile work was an economic advance. Bobbie Harrison, who was hired at a textile plant in Leesburg, Georgia, in 1968, explained that the mill was an improvement "because at least they were going to pay you minimum wages. . . . In '68 I left out of a white woman's kitchen, working for her for $15 a week, and I went there and I made minimum wage. . . . It was a big difference. . . . We started buying our homes, because that year I bought my home. It was a great difference, sure was."[99] In Eden, North Carolina, Joan Carter, who was one of the first black women hired at the local Fieldcrest Mill in 1965, remembered that the mill was "*the* place to work, if you were going to really do anything. . . . You know, at the time they were paying like $1.25 an hour, I really remember that. When I got my paycheck I thought that I really had some money. In 1965, it was good money, it was the better paying jobs in that area. Stayed there for 25 years."[100] In Columbus, Georgia, black women hired into the area's textile mills also recalled that mill jobs were a big improvement over "cleaning up people's houses."[101]

Civil rights groups were acutely aware of the massive improvement that textile jobs could offer African American women. Indeed, one of the primary goals of TEAM was to open up the textile industry for black women.[102] In communities dominated by the textile industry, the economic impact of black women entering the industry was obvious and dramatic. Sammy Glover, who started working at a textile plant in Andalusia, Alabama, in 1966, later quit the plant and ran the textile union in Andalusia. A tall, amiable black man, Glover felt that the entry of black women into the local mill was "a boon for the community" because it gave them much more "spending power" than they had as maids. As a result of textile employment, black women bought items that they never had before: "They could buy insurance, they could buy more groceries, they started to buy cars. Prior to then, back in the mid '60s, there were very few Afro-American women that drove their own car. . . . When the Afro-American woman started to earn a paycheck in the mid '60s, she started to create her own buying power and . . . she was less dependent on the Afro-American male. So it affected the black community and the community as a whole. . . . It was an economic stimulus, I would say, to the entire community." Thus, while the mill was an economic improvement for all African Americans, this improvement was greatest for African American women who had never held manufacturing jobs before.[103]

Similarly, the role of textile employment in stopping out-migration was magnified for black women who got textile jobs in the 1960s. Sammy Glover remembered that with black women able to work in the mill, "there was no need for the dependents to have to leave home to go north to find a good paying job. They could always find it here."[104] In Andrews, South Carolina, women hired in the 1960s remembered that the number of women who headed north after high school graduation depended entirely on how many women Oneita Knitting Mills hired. Oneita worker Carmela McCutchen went to New York after graduating from high school in the 1960s because the mill was not hiring at the time. She explained that "if they were hiring black people, I would never leave home, you know. I would have stayed home, because I didn't really want to leave to go to New York, but I didn't have a choice." The migration north after high school graduation was so ingrained in local culture that the train to New York was referred to as "the chicken-bone special." As McCutchen explained, "You get your diploma, and a bag, and a chicken. . . . Then you gone. . . . The chicken-bone special, that's the name we really gave it. . . . The train, it stopped in every little town, we called it the chicken-bone special because you had your lunch in a brown bag."[105] Similarly, Charlene June, a black woman hired at Oneita in 1967, remembered that she went to work in New York immediately after leaving high school until she heard that the mill was hiring: "There were a lot of black women that came out of school right before I did that was working there. . . . But then like the year that I came out, and a couple of years later, then those people went north, because just there was nobody hiring here during that time, because when I went there I met several of my classmates living in New York."[106]

The racial integration of the textile industry thus represented a profound change in the lives of many African American women, bringing them much closer to economic equality with whites. This change had far-reaching consequences for textile communities across the South, as black women achieved a standard of living and economic independence in sharp contrast to their traditional lowly status as white workers' domestic "help."

Black Women and Male Jobs

The testimony of company officials in a variety of lawsuits showed that jobs in the textile industry were clearly categorized by gender. Heavy jobs, such as those in the card room, were identified as male jobs, while lighter jobs requiring more dexterity, such as spinning, were viewed as women's jobs. In *Lea v. Cone Mills*, for example, Otto King, the personnel manager of Cone's Eno plant, explained how jobs were classified by gender: "Spinning is considered a female job, spooler tenders, quiller operators are women." At the same time, the card room was considered a male department: "I can't think of any full-time job in the carding department that a woman could safely run."[107] Similarly, the overseer of the carding department claimed that "all of the jobs in the carding department are too heavy for female employees to run."[108] These classifications, moreover, were industry wide, as the same basic job structure operated in all southern textile mills even if the material being processed varied.[109]

When the industry began to hire black women in the 1960s, however, it altered its notion of male and female jobs, as African American women were frequently placed on jobs previously reserved for men. Since pay disparities between black and white women were not so great as those between black and white men, it is easy to assume that black women were given the same job assignments as white women. In fact, however, many black women hired into the textile industry complained more about having heavier workloads than white women and about being assigned to "male" jobs than about unequal pay. This assignment of black women to "male" jobs is particularly significant because it showed that companies did not view black women as deserving of the same protection as white women. Companies indeed seemed to view black women as a convenient way of getting heavy "male" jobs performed cheaply. A comment made by a manager of the large Deering-Milliken textile company in 1969 clearly illustrated the point that, driven by the labor shortage, companies were seeking to hire black women as a way of getting heavy "male" jobs filled:

"The emphasis now is on trying to change 'male' jobs to 'female' jobs to bring in Negro females, the only labor supply."[110]

The field aides of TEAM frequently encountered the attitude from textile companies that they were only interested in hiring black women for heavy "male" jobs. In Cherokee County, South Carolina, aide Juanita Harrison described a visit to Limestone Manufacturing Company in 1967. The company's personnel manager told her that "he had no jobs for black women except jobs that were for men."[111] A TEAM report in January 1968 found that this was a common problem: "Negro women tend to get the harder jobs with few exceptions."[112] Aides described many examples of supervisors giving black women much heavier workloads than the white women they worked with. At Abbeville Manufacturing Company in Abbeville, South Carolina, aide Lucion Waller described how "in one case they took six sets of Loom from the Supervisor wife and gave it to a Negro women which gave her more than usual. . . . Later they had so much work to do that they decided to quit working."[113]

Black women hired into the industry felt that they were being placed on the hardest jobs and that the companies were using their hiring to increase workloads. Lottie Staton, a quiet, pleasant black woman who worked for Burlington Industries between 1967 and 1992, recalled that black women were regularly assigned to "running combs," which entailed lifting heavy rows of cotton for a full eight-hour shift. Staton felt that this was "a man's job. I thought that was too hard for a woman especially, but they had black women running it. They didn't put no white women on it."[114]

The most vivid insights into the way that companies treated African American women, however, came from the letters aggrieved workers wrote to the EEOC or to lawyers. In many cases, black women described how they had been hired into "men's" jobs. In these letters, indeed, many women also showed a keen awareness and moral sense of what constituted a woman's job in the industry, and they protested when they were forced into "male" jobs. From Cannon Mills in Kannapolis, North Carolina, for example, Ida Mae Caldwell wrote in 1969 explaining that "I feel that I am being discriminated against because I am black and a female. My job consist of sweeping and opening waste machines, it has been a man's job all along." She added that this work was "to heavy work For a woman." White women who came into the department were assigned to "better jobs than the Negro." Indeed, Caldwell described how "I have been working on this job for three (3) years and have never seen a white woman doing this work."[115]

Many other letters from Cannon Mills workers described how African American women had been placed on men's jobs and were struggling to keep up with the workloads. A letter from a Mrs. Crowder written to a district court judge gave a telling insight into the way that the company had used the hiring of black women to increase workloads and fill "male" jobs. It also gave graphic evidence of the toll that these jobs took on African American women. The letter began with a heartfelt plea: "Dear Mr. Stanley, just a few lines to let you know something going on in Cannon Mills in this town of Kannapolis, NC, we are suffering . . . the work is so hard until people are having hart atacks and some are having strokes and some are under the doctor all the time, some people are cracking up over their jobs for being over worked." Crowder explained that most of the white women who had been in her department had left, and the company was using the hiring of black women to increase workloads: "The jobs we are doing now two peoples have done them. Since the black peoples been in there they have put them to doing two and three peoples work." Crowder begged Stanley to do something to reduce the workloads because there were "so many women under the doctor." The workload was so heavy that "when the night is over you are to tired to go to sleep, after a week work you are tired to go to church on Sunday, oh lord we need your help."[116]

Many of the same complaints were expressed in other letters that women from Cannon Mills wrote to the district court judge in *United States v. Cannon Mills*. Mary Black, for example, also pleaded for help to relieve women from men's jobs: "Is it anything you could possible do, to get the black women off these air blowing jobs? It is a dirty job. And it is a man job." The job entailed pulling a heavy air hose over the looms to clean them, as well as installing iron pipes. White male mechanics refused to help the black women but "sit back and watch us work." Because the women received no male help, the workload of the job was exacting a heavy price upon their health: "We are over worked. One person is during enough work for three people. Some have had strokes, heart attacks, and some have even died. We need help very badly."[117]

In *Lewis v. Bloomsburg Mills*, a case involving a small textile plant in Abbeville, South Carolina, numerous black women described how the company refused to consider them for clerical or well-paid production jobs, instead placing them on hard, dirty, "male" jobs. Willie Sue Johnson, for example, asked for a better-paying job but was told "if I didn't like my job to just quit." When asked if she thought black and white women were treated equally at the plant, Johnson replied, "Compared to the white ladies, the black ladies got the more masculine type jobs and the white ladies got the more feminine." Johnson had replaced a white man on a job that involved steaming yarn in a dyehouse and then pushing it back through the warehouse. The yarn then had to be "racked up," a heavy task that her predecessor had received help with.[118] Luella Gunter, like most of the black women, worked in the low-paying, dirty job of unifil creeler for four years between 1974 and 1978. She asked for the job of cloth grader "because cloth grader was a much cleaner job." Gunter only found out about a vacancy on that job, however, after it "was filled with a unifil creeler that I trained, a white girl. . . . [T]hey hired that white girl out there on the job when I had more seniority than she did."[119]

Many other lawsuits provide evidence of black women being hired into heavy jobs that had previously been performed by men. One of the central complaints in the class action suit of *Adams v. Dan River Mills* was "the assignment of Negro women to arduous work to which white women are not assigned." The official charge of discrimination in the case listed as its major complaints "placing many Negro females in positions previously occupied by males" and "refusing to place Negro females in positions comparable to those occupied by white females." Numerous plaintiffs described how they were hired into the hardest jobs and had to work harder than white women. Leroy Johnson, a long-term black male worker, testified that "in the finishing department, second floor, they got colored women sorting rags and sweeping them big cement floors. I don't see no white doing it. Never."[120]

The testimony of workers such as Johnson was often particularly revealing because they had worked for Dan River for many years and knew whether jobs had traditionally been performed by men or women. Thus, when experienced black worker Henry Wilson was asked if he knew of any situation where black women had been placed in harder jobs than whites, he replied, "Yes. . . . Sweeper. Colored woman, taking a man's job. Colored sweeper. It was a man's job for 17 years, as long as I been there."[121]

In *Adams v. Dan River Mills*, many black women themselves described how they performed hard, dirty jobs that the company would not give to white women. Janie Hunt worked in the company's card room as a loom cleaner. She described how "you have to take and clean that loom all over. You get just greasy and dirty. . . . Then I sweep and scrub up under some of the looms. I ain't wanted that job since I had it. I didn't want it when he gave it to me. I told them." Describing how other black women were also arbitrarily assigned to similar jobs, Hunt added, "They wouldn't dare give a white woman them nasty jobs."[122]

"They Gave the White Women Help"

African American women who were hired into the southern textile industry in the 1960s and 1970s were subjected to a great deal of discrimination in the workplace. In addition to being hired for heavier jobs than white women, black women also faced a variety of other discriminatory practices that together affected virtually every aspect of their jobs. Although pay disparities were not as great as for black men, black women suffered from particularly unfair treatment in areas such as layoff, job security, and favoritism.

Black women complained that many textile companies had a blatant disregard for their maternity rights. Many described how the companies fired them when they asked for maternity leave or refused to give them their jobs back after the birth of a baby. TEAM aide Alice Gallman claimed in a lengthy report from Union County, South Carolina, that textile companies repeatedly refused work to black women when they returned from maternity leave. She felt that companies picked out black women in this way as a means of reducing the number of blacks in the workforce "without firing them."[123]

In *Sledge v. J. P. Stevens*, many women attached letters to their back pay claim forms describing their grievances against the company. These letters revealed that many pregnant black women had been unjustly treated by the company. Indeed, the company seemed to regard pregnancy as a chance to harass women or eliminate them altogether from the workforce. A typical letter came from Marion Brown Mason, who had worked at J. P. Stevens in 1973–74: "I got pregnant and I told them that I was have problem and I couldn't work until I had the baby. But they told me I was fired, and I lost the baby July and went back to try and get my job back, but them wouldn't hiring me back."[124]

Many women found it very hard to continue working when they were pregnant because of the heavy jobs they were expected to perform. Lena Harris Dowtin described how she got sick on her job at Stevens because she continued working after she became pregnant: "I went to the doctor and the doctor said I was having a threatened miscarriage. After I told him what type of work I was doing he said it was too heavy a job. He made me stop work for a month. And told me I needed a lighter job. I went back and my employer and they wouldn't give me a lighter job."[125] A woman at another Stevens plant described how the heavy "male" jobs that black women were expected to perform often caused problems during pregnancy: "Two pregnant women went into labor early, at about 6 or 7 months. One lost her baby. They could have been given easier jobs. But they had to do jobs that men should do."[126]

The violation of women's maternity rights was such a common complaint of African American women in the textile industry that in 1975 the TWUA filed a sex discrimination class action suit under Title VII of the Civil Rights Act. The suit was based on statements collected from women workers at J. P. Stevens plants in Roanoke Rapids, North Carolina, and Wallace, South Carolina. The union backed the suit because it thought that it provided "a good issue around which to organize women workers."[127]

Black women were also much more likely than men to complain that they had been unjustly fired for working too slowly. Again, companies often seemed to view black women simply as a way to increase workloads and denied them the same protection that was given to white women. Those who could not keep up were simply removed. At Fieldcrest Mills in Columbus, Georgia, for example, Fayetta Kendrix filed a charge in 1975 claiming that she had been discharged for "working to slow," even though white women who also worked at the same pace had not been fired. Voicing another common complaint, Kendrix also complained that the supervisor "would give the black the worst machine . . . to work with, that is discrimination by being Black work."[128]

In general, the letters that African American women wrote described how companies were particularly ruthless in their treatment of black women. Often the women were told when they were hired that failure to meet production goals would mean immediate firing, and they were generally made well aware that they had absolutely no job security. In *Sledge*, for example, one plaintiff described how the supervisor told her when she was hired "that if I made one mistake that I would be fired."[129] Another woman described how she was fired for not being fast enough, even though no one had told her there was anything wrong with her performance.[130] In *Lewis v. Bloomsburg Mills*, plaintiff Mary Coleman testified that a supervisor threatened her when she clocked in a few minutes late, saying, "Nigger, hit the damn clock."[131] Some workers described with desperation how the company would not move them from their job or help them with a simple request to improve their conditions. One black sweeper, for example, reported that Cannon Mills would not replace her stick broom with a wooden broom even though the stick broom had made her hands "so worn I cant hardly sweep."[132]

Across the South, African American women complained that they were fired more frequently than whites. At a Fieldcrest Mills plant in Laurinburg, North Carolina, for example, a black worker, Anna F. Bethea, was fired in 1976 for "not making production." She claimed that her firing actually represented the culmination of a campaign of harassment against her by her supervisor. She filed a charge with the EEOC, adding that "it has been my observation while employed at Fieldcrest under Mr. Martin's supervision, that many fine people have been fired. All of the people fired, with the exception of one, an Indian, were Black. This has been my experience during the past three years."[133]

Many letters written by women expressed support for the lawsuits because of the harsh treatment they had received in the workforce. In many cases, black women wrote simple letters of support to their attorneys, thanking them for taking up their cases. In *Hicks v. Cannon Mills*, black plaintiff Rachel Houston wrote, "I dont have a lawyer of my know so I will be glad to let those appointed for us Blacks to do the best they can on this because I know I wasnt treated right."[134] A letter written by Mary Boyd in *Galloway v. Fieldcrest Mills* reflected the harsh treatment that many black women suffered, and the way that this experience made them grateful that a lawsuit was taking place. Boyd described how she had worked for Fieldcrest between 1973 and 1978 but had been fired for "not making rates." Despite repeated attempts, Boyd had been unsuccessful in getting her job back. Her letter ended with a thank-you to the lawyer for bringing the case: "I have 4 children to take care of by myself and it is hard not being able to work. This that happening with those black people is like a prayer being answer by God for me."[135]

Many black women who came into the industry tried to secure promotions out of their hard jobs but usually came up against outright resistance from their supervisors. Indeed, their complaint forms show that many companies limited black women to a defined number of production jobs. In *Hicks v. Cannon Mills*, for example, Elaine McCree described how "I ask for a transfer in October of 1969 and was told there was no openings and that I should be glad to have the job I have. I asked for a transfer to the Cloth Room. There are no black females in this department. In October my foreman told me when I asked for a transfer that Black Females hadn't been considered to work in the Cloth Room."[136] Another black woman who asked for a promotion to the cloth room was also put off by being told "that openings only occurred in the Cloth Room every 3–4 years or longer."[137]

In *Lewis v. Bloomsburg Mills*, many black women described in detail the barriers that prevented them from obtaining higher-paying production positions. Like their male counterparts, black women came up against rigidly applied notions of white and black jobs well into the 1970s. Mary Coleman testified that in the early 1970s she had asked her supervisor about getting the better-paying position of cloth grader, but "he told me that they only hired whites."[138] Women also faced problems in finding out about job openings and with training whites for positions that they themselves wanted.[139]

Unlike black men, however, who were often denied supervisory positions, black women complained about being denied clerical jobs. Throughout the 1960s and 1970s, the inability to secure clerical jobs was one of the central grievances of black women. The lawsuits provide repeated examples of highly qualified black women who were placed in low-paying production jobs after applying for clerical positions. This refusal to place black women in clerical positions confirms that many companies were only interested in hiring them for hard, menial jobs. In *Sledge v. J. P. Stevens*, for example, Cathy Lou Long applied for a clerical job, but despite a degree in "General Office Technology," she felt that she "was not consider for clerical work. My first job was a low paying job and I was not promoted because of my race."[140] In *Lewis v. Bloomsburg Mills*, Phyllis Dunlap described the company's reaction when she applied for a clerical position in May 1974. She was a well-qualified applicant, having completed two years of business college and possessing all relevant qualifications for the job. When she applied at the personnel office, however, the company immediately told her that she was not qualified. It was clear that the company, which employed all whites in its clerical positions, was shocked to see a black applicant for a clerical job. Dunlap testified that as she walked through the personnel office, "everyone seemed to stop what they were doing and stare." Although she had been stared at before, Dunlap added that this "was the first time I ever noticed it to that extent."[141] Having witnessed the failure of black clerical applicants, some resigned themselves to production positions. Thus, plaintiff Paretha Clinkscales, who was a high school graduate, had accepted a production position at the company because "it was hard for blacks to get any kind of jobs in offices, so I just didn't even bother."[142]

Another common complaint of black women was that supervisors granted white women various job privileges to make their work much easier. In particular, African American women claimed that white women were given more help on the job to ensure that they got higher production rates. At Cannon Mills, Johnny Mae Wilson complained that "they gave the white women help and wouldn't give us the blacks any so I just got tired of it."[143] An especially common complaint was that supervisors prevented black women from producing more than white women. At Cannon Mills, Ruth B. Leazer complained in 1971 that her supervisor "would cut off my spinning frames to prevent me from making production. He would put two white spinners on the same job, and expect me to run the job alone. If I asked for any help he would tell me that he could not give me help."[144]

In *Adams v. Dan River Mills*, black women workers claimed that supervisors took production work away from fast black workers and gave it to white women who were slower.[145] Dan River worker Erma Garland claimed that throughout the mill, "the material (sides) is made available to the whites before the Negroes which increases their opportunity for production pay."[146] Garland, who was one of the first blacks to be hired as a spinner in 1967, also described how, although all the white spinners had lockers, black spinners who came onto the job were not given lockers. As a result, black women had to try to persuade white women to share a locker or else carry their tools home with them every night.[147] Other Dan River workers complained that supervisors gave them heavier workloads than white women. Helen Crews testified that she was "required either to perform a job by myself that is performed by two white girls on another shift or to run three twisting machines while the white girl runs only two at the same rate of pay." Many other black women at Dan River complained that white women were given overtime hours and more production pay.[148]

In *Lewis v. Bloomsburg Mills*, black women testified that in the job of unifil creeler, white women were consistently treated better by supervisors and did not have to handle as heavy a workload. The supervisor would ask the weavers to help the white women, but black women had to run the job on their own. Black plaintiff Fannie Mae Williams testified that black women had to run twice as many machines as whites. White women "had less machines and they could break; and I had to go all the time on mine. I couldn't break; I had to work along with my cup or whatever I had in my mouth and run the job right on."[149] One black worker, Josie Mae Johnson, described how she had let her job run out because she was determined to have a break the same as the white women did: "Cause the whites have a break I figure we could too."[150]

Black women who were hired into textile jobs were also far more likely to be the victims of layoffs than white women. Some African American women had witnessed so many layoffs of blacks that they were even unaware that the companies they worked for had seniority policies governing layoffs. In *Adams v. Dan River Mills*, for example, creeler Gracie Childress had an interesting exchange with the company's attorney, Homer Deakins, who tried to argue that Dan River only laid off in accordance with seniority:

Deakins: Do you know how seniority affects lay-offs at the company?
Childress: I don't know.
Deakins: You don't know that the most junior employees are layed off first?
Childress: Not the most junior. The most colored is layed off in Danville Mills.
Deakins: The most what?
Childress: Most colored people. Negroes.
Deakins: What do you base that on?
Childress: They the ones gets layed off the most.
Deakins: Why do you say that?
Childress: 'Cause it's true.[151]

As with black men, black women who participated in civil rights activities were subjected to particular harassment on the job. In 1976, a major case against Cannon Mills involved the discharge of two women workers who had been active in previous litigation against the company and in other civil rights activity in the community. In *Crawford and Leazer v. Cannon Mills*, both plaintiffs had been discharged after agreeing to serve as witnesses in the separate case of *Hicks v. Cannon Mills*. The case described how the company had "subjected Daisy Crawford and other Cannon employees who participated in these investigations to disparate treatment, harassment, and intimidation."[152] The foreman of Crawford's shift, Jay Campbell, testified that "when I started work as a foreman I was told by my overseer, Norman Pethel, to watch Daisy Crawford because she is a member of the NAACP and a trouble maker; she has been giving information to the NAACP." Crawford, indeed, had initiated a 1969 Justice Department suit against the company by writing to President Lyndon B. Johnson alleging racially discriminatory housing practices by Cannon Mills. After she wrote this letter, Crawford's looms were tampered with and her production was cut. She was also harassed by Johnny High, a white loom fixer in her department. Crawford's lawyers claimed that High had been specially picked to lead the campaign of harassment, because the company repeatedly refused to discipline him after each incident. On two occasions, High put live mice in Crawford's weaving alley, knowing that she had a phobia concerning mice. High was not disciplined for these actions. Crawford was discharged in 1975 for slapping High after he had walked past her, "rubbing her breast and calling her a 'nigger.'" High had also told Crawford that "all of you look alike." High was suspended for four days following this incident, while Crawford was discharged. The Crawford case illustrated the extent of the harassment that black workers who complained often had to endure.[153]

Despite the risks of harassment, many black women continued to be very outspoken about the discrimination facing African American textile workers. Legal records show that even when their jobs were at stake, many women were eager to expose their company's discriminatory practices. In *Adams v. Dan River Mills*, for example, Gracie Childress told the company's attorney that the company's policy of nondiscrimination meant nothing: "They got that sign up, but they certainly don't go by it." Childress recited many other examples of discrimination even though the company attorney frequently tried to dismiss her testimony as hearsay.[154]

Black Women and Workplace Activism

Just as black women fought together against hiring discrimination, those women who were hired into the industry were also determined to act together to end discrimination and improve workplace conditions. Most black women who came into the textile industry found themselves working in demanding jobs with little protection against layoff and other injustices. These conditions made many determined to form unions. Addie Jackson, a textile worker in Statesboro, Georgia, stated that she had played a leading role in the organizing campaign at her plant because "at J. P. Stevens, before we started organizing, it wasn't too much different than slavery. No lunch hour. Just eat your sandwich while running your machines. I thought that was the most terrible thing I ever heard of."[155]

Many African American women who were hired into textile jobs in the 1960s and 1970s soon became tired of the industry's low pay and discrimination and organized to improve conditions. A good example of the activism that black women brought to the workplace occurred at Oneita Knitting Mills in Andrews, South Carolina, where the TWUA won an election in 1971. At the time of the election, the company's workforce was 85 percent women and 75 percent African American. Following fifteen months of fruitless negotiations for a contract, the workers embarked on a six-month strike in January 1973. Workers struck a plant that made men's and boy's knitted underwear for major department stores such as K-Mart and J. C. Penney. Oneita had two plants in a coastal area of South Carolina, one in Andrews and the other in the small town of Lane. Together these plants employed more than 1,000 workers.[156]

Women had always made up the majority of the company's workforce, but black women had only been hired since the mid-1960s. The difference that black women brought to organizing is apparent when the successful 1973 strike is compared to a failed strike in 1963, when the company employed no black women. The 1963 strike failed when workers broke ranks, but in 1973 they held firm and won. African American women who were active in the strike had no doubt that the change in the racial composition of the workforce was responsible for the 1973 victory. Laura Ann Pope, a bright, vivacious African American woman who played a key role in organizing the union in the 1970s, felt that the 1963 effort failed because "it wasn't enough black."[157]

Union leaders also attributed the success of the strike to the overwhelming support and militancy of the black women strikers. They sustained the strike for over six months, refuting the common belief in the industry that any strike was lost if it went on for more than two or three months. The TWUA's southern director, Scott Hoyman, remembered that "in Oneita, the fact that there was a big black majority there was very, very helpful. . . . The fact that we had black people, a substantial number of black people, was one of the considerations that helped us win the strike, because the union's experience was that once a strike in an unorganized plant ran for more than a couple of months, the statistics were that that was a goner."[158]

Although the composition of the workforce was the key element in the strike's success, the union also owed its victory to the financial support given the strike by the rest of organized labor and to a boycott of Oneita products that was widely publicized and supported.[159] The success of the boycott, in fact, was also related to the composition of the workforce. The TWUA publicized the preponderance of black women in the workforce as a way of building support for the strike. In mobilizing support for a boycott of Oneita products, the union highlighted the fact that "approximately 85% of the strikers are women and 75% of them are Black. They live and work in one of the nation's most poverty-ridden counties. So while this strike is in protest of the company's unfair labor practices, it also is significant from the standpoint of civil rights, women's rights and the war on poverty." In another appeal for support, the national union called the main issue in the strike "fair and equal treatment of workers regardless of race and sex."

Such publicity was successful, because the strike attracted attention from women's rights organizations as well as civil rights groups. As was the case in the J. P. Stevens campaign, women's rights groups such as the National Organization for Women (NOW) supported the Oneita boycott and helped to exert pressure on the company to settle.[160] On May 1, 1973, Oneita strikers marched through the center of New York City to the headquarters of J. C. Penney in order to publicize the strike. Joining the march were members of women's liberation and civil rights organizations, including Gloria Steinem, editor of *Ms.* magazine, and Bayard Rustin, executive director of the A. Philip Randolph Institute. Rustin later traveled to Andrews and made a documentary film about the strike entitled *Contract, Contract.*[161]

The way that a workforce of black women held out to win a union contract was one of the most positive stories of the 1960s and 1970s. For the TWUA, a union accustomed to painful strike defeats in the South, it was truly inspiring. TWUA staffer George Perkel wrote that "the Oneita strikers demonstrate the truth and relevance of the adage, in union there is strength." Perkel recommended using the Oneita story in other campaigns because "their determination to prevail against great odds is a tribute to the growing awareness of textile workers that they don't have to take the bosses' crap any more. . . . The victory over Oneita is a harbinger of the coming victory over the entire textile industry." Civil rights leader Bayard Rustin called the strike "a giant step for the half million unorganized southern textile workers."[162]

The Oneita strike was an important victory for southern labor. It showed that black and white textile workers could unite effectively, and it illustrated the positive impact that the entry of black workers, especially black women, could have on organizing efforts. For the black women who took part, success was particularly appreciated because it showed that a union could be organized by black women. As Laura Ann Pope put it at the end of *Contract, Contract*, "Now we felt great because the majority of us was ladies and we really held out and we tried to do everything we could to win, and we did." Other black strikers also took pride in their militancy. As Glora Jean Robinson explained, "It makes you feel pretty good to know that you stayed out for six months and you got what you went out for."[163]

The Oneita victory was crucial to the union's survival in the South. In the 1950s and 1960s, TWUA leaders had increasingly referred to a "southern conspiracy" among mill owners to prevent unionization. Indeed, the union put forward this concept because it suffered repeated defeats in the South and had a miserable organizing record. TWUA leaders felt that the Oneita victory was proof that this conspiracy could be overcome with militant workers and support from the labor movement. In particular, it showed that a strike could force a company to sign a contract. As TWUA southern director Scott Hoyman declared during the strike, "The strike is part of the struggle to organize southern textile workers in face of the continuing conspiracy of employers to deny them the benefits of collective bargaining. This showdown is being carefully watched by nine other Southern companies, with a total of 6,000 employees, whose plants were recently organized by TWUA. If Oneita succeeds in destroying the union, the other employers are bound to embark upon the same kind of union-busting campaign."[164] The TWUA's president, Sol Stetin, claimed that the outcome of the strike "is also bound to have a strong effect upon the efforts of many thousands of other workers in the same area to form unions. If Oneita succeeds in smashing this strike, it will be the cue for other employers to invoke the same union-busting tactics."[165]

In a letter written to all TWUA locals shortly after the strike settlement, Stetin emphasized the significance of the Oneita victory. He detailed a settlement that included a seventy-five-cent wage and fringe benefit increase, a company-paid pension plan, and the voluntary check-off of union dues. For the national union, however, more significant than these specific gains was the fact that the union had proved its power to other employers in the area and could now negotiate contracts with these companies: "Had the Oneita strike been lost, the obstacles to winning contracts for these workers would have been truly formidable."[166]

Laura Ann Pope embodied the determination and spirited resistance that many African American women brought to the textile mills. An NAACP member and community leader, Pope took a job at the mill in 1970 in order to organize the plant. She had become tired of hearing about the discrimination in the mill from her two sons who worked there: "I was hired in '70, and I went. I had two children working there, two boys, and I got sick of them coming home telling me about, you know, the condition, and I decided to go and apply for a job, and I did, but I went in there intentionally to organize that plant, because I heard [plant manager] Frank Urtz name called so much in this house with my two boys until I said, 'Well, this is enough.'"[167] Pope set about her task equipped with a special dress that had numerous pockets cut into it. In the pockets were placed union cards. Pope succeeded in getting a majority of the workers signed up by passing out cards on her shift: "I would just go by and pat them on the shoulder and say, 'How your machine running?' And you asked them, 'When you get time, go in the ladies' room and sign this card, and I'll pick it up this afternoon.' And I just went all through. . . . I would get my machine running real good, and I would go next door, which is another set of machines, to that person, and the next, and I just keep on going down the line real fast and giving them these cards, and I would go back and pick them up in the afternoon. And I never was caught; I was smart."[168]

Pope summed up the way that for many black women, the satisfaction of having a textile job quickly gave way to dissatisfaction with the industry's poor working conditions. She felt that while the opening up of textile jobs was a big

Laura Ann Pope, 1973.

improvement for black women who had been restricted to working as domestics for whites, this sense of improvement did not last: "They were so glad to get out of the white man's kitchen. But after a while you want something better, because $1.60 an hour isn't nothing, and no security."[169]

The organizing efforts at Oneita led to an election on November 19, 1971, which the union won by a vote of 380 to 287. The company refused to sign a contract, however, leading to the strike in January 1973.[170] The main reason for organizing had been to win some protection against the exploitative labor conditions that the women were hired into. Laura Ann Pope felt that most women supported the union because of "unfair labor practices." In particular, the discrimination and favoritism practiced by supervisors made the women determined to organize.[171] Carmela McCutchen, hired in 1968, remembered that she supported the union because of the discrimination in the plant, especially the lack of opportunities for promotion: "We were ready, because we didn't have nothing to look forward to. . . . You didn't move up, you didn't like rise up from one position to the next, going higher. You didn't have a chance, black people didn't have a chance. You didn't have a chance but to do one thing, sit right at that machine and sew, and I used to see white ladies every vein in their legs shored from sewing all their life, and I said, 'I don't want that to happen to me or my children if they had to work in there.' There had to be a better way, and it was."[172]

Seniority and the right to bid for promotions were basic aims of the Oneita strikers, but wages were also important. Most black women at the plant were hired into similar production positions and were paid only $1.40 an hour. Charlene June, who was hired in 1967, summed up the way that many strikers wanted both more workplace democracy and more money: "I wanted to change where like if there was a grievance, that I could be heard and something could be done about it. And I wanted to change wages, because like I say I had worked there from '67 until '73 without a raise, and I mean you really worked, and I really felt like we could do better if we was working for more money."[173] Carmela McCutchen remembered that she was never satisfied with her $1.40 an hour: "You couldn't make it off a dollar and forty cents. You imagine a family of six and seven trying to make it off a dollar and forty an hour. That's no money."[174]

Most black women held out in support of the strike because they were determined to improve their pay and win some benefits. Like McCutchen, most felt they had little to lose because they could not provide properly for their families on what they were paid. Striker Mary Lee Middleton explained why she was on strike: "What can you do for your family on a $1.60 an hour? When these kids get sick I can't afford a doctor. When they get a toothache, I can't afford a dentist. . . . This strike is for my babies and I'm not going back until we win a decent contract."[175]

In *Contract, Contract,* the documentary film about the strike, it is clear that many of the strikers were determined to win a contract because of anger and resentment over the discrimination they faced in the mill. Seniority was the primary aim of many black strikers because it would prevent supervisors from bringing in whites from outside to take higher-paying jobs. As Carmela McCutchen put it, "They'd hire whites off the street. They didn't even have seniority when we went in there."[176] Many white workers also supported the strike because they shared the same goals as blacks. Many had been victims of favoritism, and they wanted seniority. As Mary Cox, a white striker, declared, "If you don't have seniority in a mill where you work with a lot of different people, then you don't have anything. I think that's one of the main reasons I was out there. . . . I made pretty good, but it was mostly seniority and to have a say in what was going on in the mill, because if you don't have a say, you just don't have anything in a mill."[177]

The Oneita strike provides a close look at how black and white unity in strikes was possible, yet fragile. White support was very important in the strike because although whites only made up around 25 percent of the workforce, their support was still needed to keep the strike solid. Many whites responded to the militancy and leadership of blacks and were happy to follow someone whom they felt could achieve common gains. Laura Ann Pope remembered that she received a lot of support from whites because "they wanted to see somebody and follow somebody that had the guts to stand up to them [the company], and they saw that in me. And they would always say, 'Now, you are brave, I know you will do it,' you know, and I said, 'Oh yes, as long as y'all stay out of the plant.' . . . We really had 75 percent black when we organized, when we began organizing. . . . But I'm so proud of my white strikers, oh I'm so proud of them. They said they were proud of me, but I was so proud of them."[178]

The strike experience of cooperating with blacks was also educational and beneficial for many white women. They came to respect blacks more and formed lasting friendships. As white striker Mary Cox declared, "One thing that I thoroughly enjoyed when I was out, I didn't know a lot of the women, especially the colored women, and I learned to know them, and I learned to like a lot of them that I really didn't think I could like. But I found out that they're colored people and that doesn't matter at all, they're just like we are."[179]

At the same time, it was difficult for some blacks to accept the fact that whites would not take an active role in the union. Interviewed during the strike, Carmela McCutchen stated that "only a small number [of whites] were actually active in the organizing, but a larger number are out on strike now. It's still a minority of the white workers. A lot of them said they were for the union, that we needed a union, but to actually get out and help well they wouldn't." Whites responded slowly to the union, and some only joined it after the strike to remedy specific grievances.[180]

As in other strikes and organizing campaigns, the Oneita dispute sent a complicated message about interracial cooperation between workers. Cooperation was possible, but there was also a feeling that whites refused to pull their weight during the strike, expecting blacks to take risks for them. Nevertheless, the cooperation that was achieved was especially notable given the fact that the 1963 strike had failed because of racial division. The Andrews area had a strong Ku Klux Klan, and the Klan had actually led the 1963 strike among white workers. Oneita had started to hire blacks during the 1963 strike as a way of breaking it. Thus, the 1973 strike actually united blacks with some of the white racists who had led the previous unsuccessful unionization effort. The race issue failed to divide strikers, however, partly because both scabs and strikers were a mixture of both races. As the TWUA's Bruce Raynor recalled, "Hostility was reserved for the strikebreakers who were unknown and thought of as outsiders. Due to the multiracial makeup of both strikers and scabs, the racial issue played no major role during the six-month shutdown."[181]

The Oneita strike was also important because it showed the benefits that the civil rights movement could have for the union movement. Black strikers admitted that they were inspired by the events of the civil rights protests that they had watched on television. When black scabs went into the mill, strikers reminded them of the indignities of segregation and the fact that plant manager Urtz had only recently started to speak to blacks. The strike was marked by mass meetings and songs, and both white and black regularly sang the civil rights anthem, "We Shall Overcome." Strikers themselves wrote their own song, "Contract, Contract," and this was performed throughout the dispute, led by a black striker who sang in a church choir. One black striker remembered that they had invented their own songs because they had not known the songs in the TWUA songbook that had been given to them. TWUA representative Bruce Raynor wrote that the strikers "turned the struggle into an exciting, vibrant affair, complete with original songs and several mass marches. Unity became the theme of this strike and resulted in success which has established the Oneita local union as one of the strongest in the entire South."[182]

The long-term impact of the Oneita strike, however, was not as great as union leaders hoped. While it was an important victory, its success proved difficult to replicate, largely because mills like Oneita, which were majority black and were able to draw upon black militancy and civil rights support, were rare in the textile South of the 1970s. Indeed, many companies were aware of the union potential of a majority black workforce and tried to limit the proportion of blacks in the mills, especially after the Oneita strike.

Gender clearly played a central role in shaping the racial integration of the southern textile industry. The main reason for this was the fact that black women, unlike black men, had always been excluded from the textile industry. This exclusion explained the economic advance that textile jobs represented for black women as well as the continued resistance of some companies to hiring them. When they were hired, black women complained that supervisors practiced a variety of different types of on-the-job discrimination in order to ensure that white women continued to have a better deal. Unlike black men, black women complained more about workloads and favoritism than they did about promotions and unequal pay, and they claimed that companies were forcing them to perform "male" jobs that were not given to white women.

Before the last twenty years, very few historians had explored the history of women workers, especially in the South. As Jacquelyn Dowd Hall noted in 1986, "Until recently, historians of trade unionism, like trade unionists themselves, neglected women, while historians of women concentrated on the Northeast and the middle class."[183] Although recent scholarship has corrected this neglect by uncovering "an impressive record of female activism" among women workers, most of it has concentrated on the period before the civil rights era, especially the late nineteenth and early twentieth centuries.[184] Similarly, within the southern textile industry, there have been excellent studies of women workers and union activists in the Progressive Era and in the 1930s, but very little has been written on the civil rights era, especially with regard to black women.[185]

This study has found a considerable degree of collective activism among black women who were determined to protest against hiring discrimination in the southern textile industry. Black women made a persistent effort to break down hiring discrimination, carpooling and relying on groups of female friends to challenge the companies. Black women in the Oneita strike also organized themselves, even signing up the membership necessary before the TWUA committed an outside organizer to the plant. Black women's activism was based mostly on financial necessity, the desire to support their families and provide them with a better life. As Kelly Alexander of the NAACP told the textile forum in 1967, those workers who needed textile jobs the most were "mothers who are breadwinners of families, who go to work at 7:00 o'clock in the morning and come home late at night."[186]

Community Activism and Litigation

The Role of Civil Rights Organizations in the Racial Integration of the Southern Textile Industry

seven

The existing literature of the civil rights movement has tended to bypass the impact of the movement on the small towns of the southern Piedmont, especially in the period after 1968. Indeed, because the main protests largely occurred in towns and cities in the Deep South, most historical studies have concentrated on these areas. In so doing, however, these studies have overlooked a whole section of the South, the industrial Piedmont, where textiles was the dominant industry and social and political structures were very different from those of the Deep South. It is important to explore the movement's impact in this area of the South because there was in fact considerable civil rights activity in the area, much of it, moreover, occurring after the conventional "heroic period" of activism.[1]

One such major civil rights initiative was TEAM, a project which aimed to improve the employment opportunities of African Americans in the South Carolina textile industry in the late 1960s. The extensive records of TEAM offer an opportunity to examine the impact of civil rights initiatives on an area that has received little historical attention, the Piedmont region of South Carolina. It is particularly useful to find out what impact major civil rights initiatives such as TEAM had on small towns in the state, as most existing studies have concentrated either upon large Deep South cities or small towns outside the industrial Piedmont.[2]

The TEAM initiative is important because it was a major drive aimed at addressing the economic inequality of African Americans rather than political or legal inequality. Historians have argued that the civil rights movement's attempts to tackle economic issues were much less successful than its drive to overcome the legal barriers of segregation, partly because the drive for economic equality went beyond "American ideals." As William H. Chafe has written, the movement was successful only when its goals were "compatible with the traditional values of individualism and competitiveness." Thus, demands for liberty for blacks were granted, but the aim of material equality was resisted. Abandoning Jim Crow in public accommodations and voting was also relatively easy compared to attacking economic inequality, which required much greater sacrifices from whites.[3]

The failure of the civil rights movement to improve the economic situation of African Americans has usually been illustrated by examples of campaigns in the North, especially in Chicago. Less is known, however, about how such demands for economic equality were treated in the South, particularly in the Piedmont, the region's industrial heartland. TEAM, moreover, was at its most active in 1968, the very time that historians have marked as the end of the civil rights movement, a time when the climate seemed very unfavorable for any civil rights activity. The experiences of TEAM can thus be used to assess the validity of arguments advanced on the basis of studies in other areas of the country. Did the experience of TEAM indicate that demands for economic equality in the late 1960s were doomed to failure, as the northern experience suggests? Or did the agency show that civil rights initiatives in the economic arena could have some success, even in the late 1960s?

TEAM

TEAM grew out of the EEOC textile forum held in Charlotte, North Carolina, in January 1967. The forum, which explored racial employment patterns in the textile industry, indicated a "widespread under-utilization of Negroes in textile manufacturing, numerous discriminatory situations, and a general failure by the industry to make use of affirmative action programs." This unsatisfactory picture was partly responsible for pushing six private agencies to join together after the forum in a joint project to improve job opportunities for African Americans in the textile industry. The six agencies included major civil rights groups such as the National Urban League, the NAACP Legal Defense and Educational Fund, and the Southern Regional Council.[4]

Although the TEAM project involved six agencies, records show that the most important role in setting up TEAM was played by the NAACP Legal Defense Fund. The idea for a textile industry project began in 1965 with discussions within the Legal Defense Fund on the subject of employment. These talks were part of the fund's general concern with attacking racial discrimination in employment, although "high priority was given to the textile industry." The Legal Defense Fund gradually attracted the support of other private agencies and of the EEOC for its idea of a special textile industry project. The Legal Defense Fund also received the cooperation of the Office of Federal Contract Compliance, which agreed to give special attention to contract compliance in the southern textile industry. Through the lawsuits that the NAACP Legal Defense and Educational Fund brought against textile companies, and through its central role in TEAM, the NAACP played a central role in the integration of the southern textile industry in the 1960s and 1970s.[5]

By March 20, 1967, the private and federal agencies had decided to concentrate a textile program on the important textile state of South Carolina. Funding of $25,000 was obtained from the Field Foundation for a one-year project to be carried out in the state. The goals of TEAM were ambitious. Indeed, the agency declared that it wanted "to eliminate all forms of discrimination in the textile industry." TEAM aimed to achieve a substantial improvement in the numbers of African Americans hired in entry-level jobs as well as "a wide scattering" of blacks in the higher-level white-collar and managerial jobs, which at that time were overwhelmingly white. The ambitious nature of the project was shown by the fact that TEAM set a target of providing 25,000 new jobs for African Americans in the South Carolina textile industry, an optimistic estimate for a project only scheduled to run for one year.[6]

Because of the far-reaching aims of the agency, the records of TEAM provide revealing insights into the barriers operating to limit blacks in textile communities in the late 1960s. The agency's ambitious program meant that it directly challenged established employment patterns, and the responses from textile companies revealed a great deal about the attitudes of the white power structure toward African American demands for greater economic equality, as well as the problems that civil rights activists encountered in textile communities.

TEAM established its headquarters in the textile center of Greenville, South Carolina, in September 1967. The project's director was Mordecai C. Johnson, a young black lawyer who had graduated from South Carolina State College in Orangeburg before going on to law school at Howard University. Until taking up his position with TEAM, Johnson worked in the Office of General Counsel of the U.S. Commission on Civil Rights. Jean Fairfax of the NAACP Legal Defense and Educational Fund headed the TEAM committee that supervised the project's field activities.[7]

TEAM's main method of increasing black hiring was to conduct site visits to textile plants, and staff aides were chosen for this purpose. Each aide was responsible for a particular county. The aide who figured most prominently in the records was Patrick Flack, a local civil rights leader from Anderson, South Carolina, who led efforts to increase black hiring in Anderson County. Other TEAM aides were also local leaders in the black community.[8]

The area that TEAM selected covered fourteen counties in the western part of South Carolina that were dominated by the textile industry. Textiles, indeed, provided around two-thirds of all manufacturing jobs in the fourteen counties. Blacks made up 29 percent of the overall population but occupied only 8 percent of all textile jobs. (See tables 18–20.) Across America, civil rights leaders in the late 1960s were becoming increasingly aware of black poverty, and TEAM's leaders shared this concern. They were eager to publicize the poverty that resulted from blacks being underrepresented in the textile industry. TEAM's leader, Mordecai C. Johnson, wrote that in none of the fourteen counties did the median income for black families in 1960 approach the federal nonpoverty level of $3,000. At the same time, the median income for all families was above $3,000 in all the counties. Johnson thus argued that black exclusion from textiles explained black poverty.[9] He recognized that the textile industry was crucial because, while wages in the industry were low, they could still lift black families out of poverty and prevent out-migration. As Johnson explained, "In the final analysis, all of this boils down to the one thing that matters. It is not the number of angels that can dance on the head of a needle, it is not integration; it is money. Three out of four black families in our state are officially poor—with incomes of less than $3000—while the average textile wage-earner makes some $4500 per year." Johnson, indeed, portrayed textile employment as central to eradicating black poverty and realizing the dream of Dr. Martin Luther King Jr.[10]

The creation of TEAM showed once more that civil rights leaders recognized the central importance of the textile industry in advancing civil rights in the Piedmont. They knew that while initiatives to desegregate schools and public places or to get the vote were important, it was also crucial for blacks to have more employment opportunities in the South's biggest industry. For civil rights activists, the industry was important not simply because of its size, but also because textile jobs could be easily learned by inexperienced workers, meaning that the industry had the potential to absorb thousands of unemployed African Americans.[11] One TEAM report effectively summarized why the decision had been made to concentrate on textiles: "The industry is big; it often provides the only industrial jobs; it is important to local communities; it influences social patterns; and it serves as an introduction to industrial work." When the project began, TEAM's director Mordecai Johnson emphasized the industry's dominance of South Carolina's economy, with textile plants located in thirty of the state's forty-six counties, employing over 140,000 nonsalaried workers in more than 300 plants.[12]

Table 18. Racial Composition of South Carolina Piedmont Counties Covered by TEAM, 1960

County	Nonwhite Population	Total Population	Percent Nonwhite
Greenville	36,978	209,776	18
Spartanburg	34,729	156,830	22
York	22,554	78,760	29
Anderson	19,242	98,478	20
Laurens	14,039	47,609	30
Greenwood	13,119	44,346	30
Chester	12,378	30,888	40
Lancaster	10,617	39,352	27
Newberry	10,437	29,416	36
Union	8,887	30,015	30
Cherokee	7,400	35,205	21
Abbeville	6,854	21,417	32
Pickens	4,642	46,030	10
Oconee	4,145	40,204	11
Total 14-county area	271,334	908,326	29

Source: U.S. Census of Population, 1960, in Reel 163, Southern Regional Council Papers.

Table 19. Textile Employment Compared to Total Manufacturing Employment in South Carolina Piedmont Counties, 1967

County	Total Manufacturing Employment	Textile Employment	Percent Textile Employment
Spartanburg	29,158	17,864	61
Greenville	35,588	17,413	49
Anderson	17,517	13,152	75
York	12,910	10,541	82
Greenwood	12,213	9,116	75
Lancaster	7,988	7,127	89
Oconee	8,410	5,272	63
Union	5,491	4,874	89
Chester	5,185	4,394	85
Pickens	9,841	4,387	45
Cherokee	5,777	4,210	73
Laurens	7,783	4,203	54
Abbeville	3,803	2,741	72
Newberry	3,128	1,936	62
Total 14-county area	164,792	107,193	65

Source: 31st Annual Report of the Department of Labor of South Carolina, Tables IV and XXI, in Reel 163, Southern Regional Council Papers.

Table 20. Black Textile Workers Compared to Total Textile Workers in South Carolina Piedmont Counties, 1967

County	Total Textile Workers	Black Textile Workers	Percent Black Textile Workers
Spartanburg	17,864	1,585	9
Greenville	17,413	1,064	6
Anderson	13,152	1,034	8
York	10,541	829	8
Greenwood	9,116	1,237	14
Lancaster	7,127	551	8
Oconee	5,272	163	3
Union	4,874	788	16
Chester	4,394	220	5
Pickens	4,387	282	6
Cherokee	4,210	437	10
Laurens	4,203	341	8
Abbeville	2,741	398	15
Newberry	1,936	162	8
Total 14-county area	107,193	9,091	8

Source: *31st Annual Report of the Department of Labor of the State of South Carolina*, Table VI, in Reel 163, Southern Regional Council Papers.

In an overview report written at the end of the project, Johnson admitted that TEAM had been unable to make substantial progress in many of these counties. He described how one important county, Abbeville, like many others in the textile belt of South Carolina, was a very hard environment in which to try to bring about racial change: "I think that gaining substantially on jobs will be a long hard pull in Abbeville County. This is tough country." The same kind of environment hindered TEAM in other Piedmont counties of South Carolina. As Johnson wrote, "My comments about the toughness of Abbeville County could be made about any of our counties." Overall, the TEAM records illustrate clearly just how difficult it was to promote civil rights in Piedmont textile communities.[13]

One of the central problems that faced TEAM staff aides who conducted plant visits was the fierce resistance of many textile executives to changing their hiring practices. Many managers had a keen perception of power, realizing that there was little that TEAM could do to affect job assignments. Therefore, the most common response was that companies were polite to TEAM aides but totally noncommittal. At a TEAM board meeting on March 8, 1968, for example, it was reported that all the executives visited had been "vague and non-committal." A typical visit to the large Springs Mills saw TEAM representatives greeted in a "cordial" fashion by the head of personnel, "but with no specific commitments." Similarly, the large Abney Mills and Riegel Mills were both described as "cordial but non-specific and non-committal." Overall, Johnson wrote that he had made very little progress in plant visits: "In general, I found most of the plants would let me in their doors but they varied in the extent to which they would say anything and very few of them were willing to enter into a sustained cooperative arrangement with TEAM to improve their EEO pictures."[14]

Other companies were evasive. Many refused to meet TEAM representatives. Aide Robert Ford, operating in Greenville County, wrote in an activity report covering four months that "I got the impression that none of the plant managers were willing to talk to TEAM. I had no interviews in any mills." Many companies used "avoidance tactics" in which they referred TEAM representatives to their headquarters, claiming that individual plants were not allowed to discuss equal employment opportunity. Trips to company headquarters, however, proved frustrating because companies made general statements but claimed that they could not discuss individual plants.[15]

Some companies were more openly hostile to TEAM's efforts. After a futile visit to the Abbeville Mills, a TEAM aide wrote, "These gentlemen state that they neither need nor want any help from TEAM. They were pretty uncooperative. I don't think we'll get much here on a voluntary basis." Large chain companies were often the most difficult to crack. The large Westpoint Manufacturing Company refused to talk to TEAM, claiming that "we comply with the law." In Abbeville County, Johnson described visits to the biggest textile company, Deering-Milliken, as "horrible. . . . The plant manager was unavailable and the personnel director and the equal employment director were both uncommunicative and uncooperative."[16]

In several counties, one major textile company dominated the local economy and maintained the racial status quo. This was especially true of Greenwood County, which was an area "largely controlled" by Greenwood Mills. The company owned ten plants as well as a hospital and had a controlling influence in banks and other corporations. The company rejected all of TEAM's efforts to increase its hiring of African Americans, thereby ensuring the failure of TEAM in the county. As Johnson wrote, Greenwood Mills "must be broken, if only because it's big and a leader in local industry and otherwise." This task, however, was beyond TEAM's capabilities: "Breaking Greenwood Mills is a major undertaking requiring skills and resourcefulness which I don't see here."[17]

Similarly, in Greenville County, J. P. Stevens was the largest textile company and set a pattern of resistance on race. As Johnson explained, "Stevens is one of the biggest textile companies [employing some 30,000 people in the Greenville area] and one of the worst. The textile firms stand or fall together and the larger companies, such as Stevens, set the pace." At Stevens, personnel hiring and promotions were "arbitrarily handled by supervisors," a policy that tended to lock blacks into the lowest positions.[18]

In general, the reluctance of textile executives to work with TEAM confirmed the industry's dislike of outsiders putting pressure on its racial hiring practices. The industry was hiring a great number of blacks in these years, but it resented efforts from either the federal government or civil rights workers to interfere in black hiring, especially with regard to upgrading.

Textile management presented a formidable adversary for TEAM. Johnson, for example, wrote of the state's major textile center, "The Textile Industry in Greenville is sophisticated and tough." Part of this toughness came from the extensive experience that textile companies had in working together to devise strategies to prevent unionization. Union leaders had complained for years about the way that companies acted together to defeat organization, robbing the union of any economic appeal by deciding wage patterns. Similarly, Johnson described how in every county, TEAM came up against personnel managers' associations. These associations were part of a larger statewide organization. Although employers claimed that they were only "lunch-sitting groups," aides described how these associations actually controlled hiring and other personnel matters on a countywide basis and were crucial in setting a policy of resistance to TEAM. In Anderson County, for example, aide Patrick Flack reported that "there is personal clubs that is formed by industry and they meet once a week at the Anderson Country Club. Purpose is to discuss Black folks and Blacks jobs. There is a Executive Club that do the same things and at the same place. This is the thing that makes Negro or Black folks jobs limited." Managers in Union County were also said to have formed "some kind of pact along the lines of the personnel association referred to by Pat Flack in Anderson County." This pact involved limiting blacks to a small number of low-paid jobs.[19]

The biggest problem was that textile companies continued to dictate the extent and the pace of integration, finding various ways to keep blacks in an inferior position in the industry. Many TEAM aides claimed that companies were acting together to frustrate the agency's efforts and resist real integration. Across South Carolina, aides described how management acted together to keep integration on its terms. In Union County, aide Alice Gallman wrote that companies were ensuring that blacks were only being hired in the least desirable plants: "There are four air-conditioned plants in Union, and even though I have no way of knowing for sure, I believe that some kind of agreement has been made, in the power structure of Union, to relegate most Negroes into the cotton mills and steer the whites into the air conditioned plants because the work in these newer plants is easy and the buildings are clean, while in the older mills, the work is hard and the buildings are dirty, and hot." This presented a major dilemma for TEAM, because while the program in Union County was successful in getting blacks hired for the first time, companies turned this hiring to their advantage by using eager blacks for their least desirable jobs. Thus, TEAM was actually in danger of helping companies discriminate. As one TEAM aide commented at a meeting, "We should be careful not to build in a new kind of discrimination under which the black man gets the hot dirty jobs while the good jobs, say, with air conditioning go to whites." Despite this warning, this was exactly what happened. Similarly, it was reported that across South Carolina the "more glamorous," higher-paying plants were more likely to use "culturally biased tests as a condition to employment."[20]

Fear among the black community was another major problem reported by TEAM aides. Many black workers were unwilling to sign charges of discrimination, fearing the loss of their jobs or other retaliation. In Cherokee County, for example, aide Juanita Harrison reported that "a problem in this county is that the Black people are unwilling to sign complaints even when they are discriminated against." In a report reviewing her experiences with TEAM, she explained that the failure to overcome fear had been a serious problem: "In my work I have found plenty complainers, and the complaints were justifiable, but just as soon as the one complaining found out he or she had to sign the complaint and maby have to go to court they said drop it or Ill let you know later. Most of them are afraid of loosing their jobs and when you explained to then what TEAM would [do] for them they seem not to believe it or they were just afraid."[21] TEAM aides were especially frustrated to find that many black workers did not seek advancement. As Johnson noted, "In one case, a high school graduate who was sweeping and mopping indicated that she was afraid to apply for a higher job because she might lose the job she has. This feeling developed to be fairly widespread."[22] Other aides explained that elderly black workers were particularly reluctant to file complaints of discrimination.[23]

Such fear was very damaging for TEAM because it meant that the agency was unable to put pressure on companies by threatening them with investigations by the EEOC or other federal agencies. Indeed, most blacks would not talk to federal representatives, and many mistook TEAM aides for federal officials. As Johnson noted, "Most Negroes are afraid to talk with a Federal man." TEAM found that it was unable to cooperate with federal agencies as it had planned to because very few blacks were willing to file official complaints.[24] The 1968 assassinations of Martin Luther King Jr. and Robert Kennedy were reported to have worsened the fear in the Piedmont's African American community.[25]

This fear was partly explained by the fact that the Ku Klux Klan was very active in Piedmont communities at that time. Johnson, for example, explained that "the Ku Klux Klan still rides in Abbeville County. A flare-up occurred in Dec. 1967 around the issue of police brutality. Generally speaking, fear in the black community is the order of the day." Fear was so prevalent in Abbeville County that black churchmen were afraid to let the NAACP meet in black churches. TEAM's aide in Abbeville County described it as "a rural county adjoining Greenwood where fear among blacks and oppression by whites is rampant." Similarly, Anderson County was described by TEAM as "KKK country."[26]

Textile companies also effectively sustained fear among blacks by their treatment of those who did file charges. Indeed, the experiences of several workers who filed charges justified the fear of many African Americans. Ruth Witcher, for example, who filed a complaint of discrimination after failing to become the first black office worker at the Dow Badische Company in Anderson, was unable to secure any job afterward. She became the victim of what TEAM called a "non-employment conspiracy" in Anderson County, and the agency ended up paying her rent and giving her enough money to live on. Aide Patrick Flack reported that the Witcher case had helped stop TEAM's progress in Anderson County, making it "extremely hard to get anyone to file a complaint." He added that blacks "simply are afraid. This is one way TEAM will loose its effectiveness in the piedmont."[27]

TEAM aides themselves were singled out for harassment and discrimination as a warning to prevent other African Americans from filing complaints or seeking better jobs. Johnson described how Anderson County aide Patrick Flack was subjected to "tremendous pressure" because of his activities for TEAM. Companies with which he had made progress gave him "cold treatment" after they found out that TEAM was affiliated with the NAACP Legal Defense Fund. Johnson wrote that Flack's work was hindered as he became "an untouchable in the black community particularly with the established leaders," while "the white power structure is beginning to gang up on him." Flack was subjected to repeated visits from state tax officials and was refused short-term loans. Creditors began to demand weekly rather than monthly payments. As Flack himself wrote, he felt that "the 'noose' is getting a bit tighter each day." Other TEAM aides were subjected to similar treatment, especially those who were more militant and active.[28]

The fear prevailing in the African American community was reflected in the weakness and conservatism of established black leaders in Piedmont textile communities. TEAM aides claimed that white leadership was successful at preventing racial change by working with collaborationist local black leadership. TEAM aide Patrick Flack described how, shortly after the start of the project in Anderson County, "the white industrial group called a meeting at the Chamber of Commerce with five of the so called 'Uncle-Toms' Negroes this week. . . . They called this meeting secretly." Flack explained that the purpose of the meeting "was to udermind all the Civil Rights groups and get the Negros hired by the white man's rules. It will not be up-grading jobs only low-rate jobs." Flack reported that all the plant managers attended this meeting and that it was responsible for effectively thwarting TEAM in Anderson County. He described TEAM as "lost in this area" because of the meeting.[29]

In several counties, aides complained that local black leaders cooperated with the white power structure to thwart TEAM's efforts. Johnson wrote that in Spartanburg County, TEAM had not been successful because of the fact that "the original group of 'Negro leaders' still have their fingers in the pie." He explained that TEAM had made a mistake by choosing one of these leaders as its aide. This had limited progress because local black leadership had a tendency to compromise with the white power structure: "A pattern in this county is that the white power structure likes to talk with the black power structure on an 'off the record' don't tell anybody basis, meaningful commitments in a few cases and follow through in fewer cases." Companies claimed that they could not openly cooperate with TEAM because this would "alert the white rednecks." Johnson became frustrated that local black leaders accepted this excuse for inaction. TEAM, indeed, never became an open operation in Spartanburg County because companies would only discuss black employment confidentially, so that, as Johnson wrote, "the whites won't find out what they are doing for Negroes."[30]

TEAM aides described the weakness of local black leaders as one of the biggest problems that they encountered. Johnson called the NAACP and other civil rights organizations in Anderson County "singularly ineffective." In many areas of Piedmont South Carolina, the NAACP was a fragile, fledgling organization. In Greenwood County, for example, a chapter was not organized until March 1968, making the county one of the last two in the state to join the NAACP movement.[31] Although TEAM was largely a product of NAACP initiative, aides became increasingly critical of the inaction and conservatism of leaders at the local level in South Carolina. In Anderson County, aide Patrick Flack was particularly critical of the local NAACP, which he described as "doing nothing but talk. Afraid to take a stand and call for a type of action."[32]

Although some of Flack's criticism of the local NAACP was valid, much of it also revealed the frustration of a militant young leader with the more conservative wing of the civil rights movement. Reflecting the division in the civil rights movement at the national level, Johnson described Flack as "coming to believe the black power boys may have something."[33] Flack's reports, indeed, showed that the experience of dealing with textile companies had the effect of radicalizing him and convincing him that companies had to be forced to change. This shift itself was a testimony to the strength of opposition that TEAM representatives faced from textile companies. In August 1968, for example, Flack claimed that "the ony thong U.S. employers respect is power and authority other than that, they don't care."[34] Slow-moving NAACP leaders did not seem to be the ones to force this kind of change. Flack, indeed, claimed that "the NAACP . . . was always PROMISE and Never-Dealing with the Common Working Man. Not helping him with his many problems." By July 1968, Flack felt that "the county of Anderson, South Carolina, is in need for leadership and assistance in the Black man and his problems."[35]

One of the most striking features of the TEAM records was the way that other aides also went through this process of education and self-development as they investigated race relations in textile communities. While many did not become as militant as Flack, staffers increasingly realized that the problems of African Americans were complex and broad-ranging and required more staff and more money than TEAM possessed. In many reports, aides described the complex web of forces that worked to keep blacks in poverty in the southern Piedmont.

The reports of Alice Gallman, TEAM's aide in Union County, reflected the way that TEAM staffers increasingly realized that black poverty would not end even if the textile industry hired African Americans in much greater numbers. As Gallman wrote, "Heretofore, I thought that once Negroes could have the earning power, some of the other problems would be automatically solved. Nevertheless, my thinking was wrong." She explained that even if blacks got good jobs, it would be very difficult for them to find good housing. No new housing had been built for blacks in Union County for over fifty years, leading to severe overcrowding: "Some household count are fifteen to twenty-five living under one roof. Most of the time there are no bathroom facilities or running water." These living conditions in turn led to chronic health problems. The lack of child-care facilities meant that many black women were unable to work, forcing down family income and keeping blacks in poverty. Black women who got jobs in the textile plants were able to take them only if they rotated their children in school, meaning that their children missed a great deal of schooling. Blacks also found it difficult to secure loans on new homes because of the large down payments required, and it was almost impossible for blacks who got jobs in textile plants to buy plots of land in order to build their own homes. As Gallman explained, "Now, I have another problem. LAND, all the land in Union, except maybe some far back place, belong to white people, and they won't sell to Negroes. There are some property collectors here who exploit Negroes with high rent for run down homes."[36]

TEAM aides also argued that meaningful progress in the textile industry would be limited as long as segregation persisted in other areas of life. The

South Carolina Piedmont counties that TEAM described in 1968–69 were, indeed, overwhelmingly segregated. An overview report written in September 1968, for example, concluded that schools in Anderson County were "substantially segregated." The police force was also "all-white." A major mill followed the pattern. Even in 1968, it had "dual water fountains, restrooms, absence of black women and black men employed in only 1 department, dyeing." In the major textile center of Greenville County, where textiles provided 49 percent of all jobs, there were segregated schools and an all-white school board, and TEAM noted that there was fierce resistance to school integration.[37]

The TEAM reports are important because they describe the textile industry as part of a regional Piedmont culture that was fiercely resistant to civil rights. Rather than viewing the industry in isolation, TEAM aides saw it as a major component of an area that was segregated in nearly all areas of life. Their reports highlighted the extremely tough environment that Piedmont communities presented to civil rights groups. The dominance of a "sophisticated power structure," led by the "sophisticated and tough" textile industry, meant that civil rights leaders faced an uphill struggle to bring real racial change. All of the factors that aides described as hindering their efforts sprang from the resistance of this culture, which made black workers too fearful to file charges, led black leaders to compromise with the power structure rather than fight it, and made the textile companies themselves afraid to go out on a limb and implement any more racial change than was agreed upon by the major companies.[38]

Despite the opposition it faced, TEAM was successful in forcing concrete improvements in the hiring practices of many textile companies in South Carolina. The main success of the project lay in the large numbers of African Americans that it helped to get hired. Overall, TEAM's aides secured jobs for over 500 African Americans in the South Carolina textile industry. In addition, over eighty complaints were filed with federal agencies, and in some of these cases companies took remedial action to avoid a lawsuit.[39]

While TEAM struggled to operate in some counties, in others the aides seemed to be accepted by textile companies, who increasingly used them as a source of recruitment with the black community. For example, Johnson described Union County aide Alice Gallman, who was a local nurse, as "one of the best, if not the best, aide we have. She is a master at manipulating the system." Gallman had been successful in greatly increasing black employment in several mills in Union County. Johnson reported that "in one case, Mrs. Gallman was able to get a truckload of Negroes employed at Buffalo Mills," which was one of the largest mills in the area.[40]

TEAM also made considerable progress in many other areas of civil rights activity. Its records show that it helped to identify a new generation of civil rights leaders and produced an upsurge of community activism. TEAM both initiated and encouraged a wide variety of civil rights efforts. In Greenville County, TEAM worked with new local leadership to set up a chapter of the Black Awareness Coordinating Committee (BACC). The BACC became active in identifying targets in the community that were refusing to integrate. It launched a selective buying campaign against Kash and Karry, a major grocery store that refused to hire black clerks. Charges were also filed against the store with the EEOC. Following these activities, the store hired nine black clerks in a week. K-Mart, the other large grocery chain in the area, also increased its hiring of black cashiers following the pressure put on Kash and Karry. TEAM also became involved in the Poor People's Campaign, and it "gave local politics a badly needed shot of blackness in its arm." A TEAM report concluded that because of these civil rights efforts, "whether or not TEAM stays in operation, Greenville will not be the same again."[41]

Important civil rights activity was carried out in other counties as well. In Union County, for example, TEAM aide Alice Gallman was successful in obtaining a daycare center for children of black mothers who worked. A TEAM summary report in September 1968 claimed that the agency had produced "continuing gains from community organization, the stimulation of groups to act on their own, and the goading of public agencies to enforce laws or to carry out their duties equitably."[42]

In the textile industry, however, TEAM felt that it had been unable to cause fundamental changes in racial hiring practices. In particular, aides expressed the belief that the textile industry was staying in control of the pace of integration. The feelings of many TEAM aides were summed up by aide Alice Gallman, who claimed in 1968 that the textile companies that she came in contact with "want to do just enough to get by. They don't want the majority of the Negro race to think that times are changing."[43] Patrick Flack complained that TEAM was able to get blacks hired, but only in low-paying jobs, jobs that the industry wanted blacks in rather than vice versa: "Speaking of jobs in Anderson County. There is no job shortage; but there is a shortage of up-grading jobs. This is a general picture of the entire area. Jobs, yes, but service types. . . . Oh, there is one or two that have taken jobs but there is a picture of not up-grading Black folks." Although Flack had succeeded in getting seventy-eight blacks hired, he added, "We feel that this 78 would have been hired anyway. They were the fellows and girls out of school and they had to work somewhere." All the jobs that blacks got were entry-level positions with pay of only $1.60 an hour. The experience of TEAM thus reflected the mixed achievement that the racial integration of the textile industry represented for African Americans—satisfaction that blacks were hired, yet frustration that the jobs available were low-paying and the least desirable.[44]

In assessing what TEAM had achieved, Mordecai Johnson also expressed mixed feelings. He claimed that the agency had "made our presence felt" but also cited the failure to achieve more high-paying jobs as a major failure. Johnson pointed out that the picture for African Americans was "not much better at higher skill levels" and added that "the industry still has not hired a single Negro salesman in the entire state despite its 900,000 black people and six senior black colleges."[45]

The Contribution of Civil Rights Organizations to Textile Lawsuits

The records of TEAM and the AFSC indicate that these agencies were partially successful in contributing to the racial integration of the textile industry. Other civil rights groups, particularly the NAACP, also played important roles, both at the local and national levels. Indeed, there were strong links between the textile lawsuits and civil rights activity in the communities in which the cases were filed.

Although TEAM aides expressed frustration with the NAACP in South Carolina, a great deal of evidence suggests that the association played a key role in helping African Americans fight discrimination in the textile industry, especially in North Carolina, where NAACP branches were much stronger than in South Carolina. The association particularly targeted the southern textile industry from the earliest days of the civil rights movement, continually seeking to increase black representation in the industry. In April 1961, even before the President's Committee on Equal Employment Opportunity had been set up, the NAACP had filed charges of discrimination against a number of textile companies, including Burlington Industries and J. P. Stevens. In July 1961, the NAACP's labor secretary Herbert Hill filed affidavits with the committee alleging discrimination in seven leading textile companies. The organization's concern was black exclusion from the South's "basic manufacturing industry," in which blacks constituted "less than 2 per cent of the total work force." Between 1961 and 1964, the NAACP filed more than 900 complaints of discrimination with the predecessor of the EEOC, over eighty of them directed against large textile plants in the South.[46]

In July 1968, the NAACP Legal Defense and Educational Fund mapped out a new strategy to fight job discrimination, with "heavy emphasis" being put on the southern textile industry, which the fund recognized as crucial to reducing black poverty in the South and stemming out-migration from the region. The NAACP's emphasis on textiles led to many lawsuits. As the *New York Times* explained in March 1969, "The NAACP has been suing the textile companies for years." The most publicized lawsuit occurred in April 1969, when the association filed suit against Burlington, J. P. Stevens, and Dan River, claiming that these companies continued to discriminate against blacks in recruitment, hiring, and promotion. The two largest textile cases, *Sledge v. J. P. Stevens* and *Adams v. Dan River Mills*, both resulted from this consolidated case.[47]

The NAACP Legal Defense Fund also represented black plaintiffs in the vast majority of the huge number of Title VII textile cases brought in the 1960s and 1970s, including *Hall v. Werthan Bag*, *Hicks v. Cannon Mills*, *Sledge v. J. P. Stevens*, *Galloway v. Fieldcrest Mills*, *Lea v. Cone Mills*, *Lewis v. Bloomsburg Mills*, *Ellison v. Rock Hill Printing and Finishing Company*, and *Adams v. Dan River Mills*. Most plaintiffs were represented by the Charlotte-based law firm of Chambers, Stein, and Ferguson, who were cooperating attorneys for the Legal Defense Fund in New York. Julius Chambers was also chairman of the NAACP's Regional Legal Committee in the Southeast.[48]

In the textile South, NAACP branches played an important role in informing blacks of their rights under the Civil Rights Act and encouraging them to file charges. Throughout the 1960s, workshops were held in southern textile communities urging blacks to seek more specialized jobs at textile plants. Blacks were acquainted with equal employment opportunity and informed of their rights under the new civil rights legislation. If African Americans were refused jobs because of their race, they were urged to report their cases to the nearest NAACP branch, which then helped them to file charges with the EEOC. The association filed numerous EEOC charges for workers or initiated class actions on their behalf where appropriate. The local NAACP worked closely with many of the lead plaintiffs of the *Sledge* and *Sherrill* lawsuits that were brought against J. P. Stevens.[49]

A 1965 NAACP report highlighted the important role that local branches played in helping workers file charges. In other industries, as in textiles, NAACP branches served as the first point of contact for many workers who felt they had been discriminated against. As the report put it, "NAACP Branches in the Southeast were primed to move immediately that Title VII under the Civil Rights Act became effective." Thousands of EEOC complaints were handled through NAACP branches across the South. In 1967, North Carolina led the nation in the number of EEOC complaints filed, and most of these were reported to have been "initiated on the local level" and then passed to the NAACP's regional and national leaders.[50] Indeed, in 1967 North Carolina had more NAACP branches than any other state. Julius Chambers was very active in the North Carolina NAACP, and he brought a large number of cases against textile, furniture, and tobacco firms in the state.[51]

Many textile lawsuits would never have occurred without the vital support provided by the NAACP at both the local and national levels. Attorney James Ferguson remembered that the NAACP played a crucial role in bringing many cases to trial. The association often provided encouragement and support for black plaintiffs, as well as negotiating with textile companies to encourage them to change. Ferguson felt that "the NAACP was a very, very valuable resource in this whole fight to desegregate the workforce and to desegregate the textile industry."[52]

Many lawsuits were the product of broader civil rights activity in the local community. Ferguson emphasized that textile lawsuits were often formulated along with other community-wide civil rights protests: "In many instances these cases would grow out of a total community effort, and within that community effort would be a number of groups, sometimes SCLC, sometimes other groups." Ferguson added that employment lawsuits were often filed at the same time as other civil rights activities were going on, such as voting rights campaigns and protests against the segregation of schools and public facilities.[53]

Julius Chambers also remembered that civil rights organizations were "very active" in communities where he brought lawsuits against textile companies. In *Lea v. Cone Mills*, a case against the company's plant in Hillsborough, North Carolina, the local NAACP helped to bring a lawsuit for desegregation of the schools at the same time as the textile case: "The NAACP was active in both of those cases, and it was great that it was, because someone has to provide some support for people who understandably are scared to death about stepping out to assert their rights, and the NAACP provided that kind of support." In other cases, such as *Sledge v. J. P. Stevens*, Chambers remembered the assistance of Southern Christian Leadership Conference (SCLC) chapters. Both SCLC and the NAACP were helpful in providing support for plaintiffs and for assisting in bringing suits in other areas besides employment.[54]

The records of the textile lawsuits illustrate how local civil rights organizations often played a crucial role in helping workers file suit. In *Broadnax v. Burlington Industries*, for example, a case was brought by a black woman, Betsy Ann Broadnax, who complained that she was discharged because of her race. Broadnax also claimed that the company was engaged in other, broader discriminatory practices at its plant in Madison, North Carolina. The way that the case was brought to court illustrates how workers often relied on local civil rights organizations to take up their cases for them. Following her discharge, Broadnax explained her case to Arthur Griggs, a representative of the NAACP in nearby Reidsville. Griggs wrote a letter to the company attempting to settle the matter but was unable to do so. Following this, he supplied Broadnax with the relevant forms from the EEOC and assisted her in drawing up a formal charge of discrimination.[55]

There were also other connections between the textile lawsuits and broader civil rights activity. In class action lawsuits involving broadly based complaints of discrimination, the leading plaintiff was often a local civil rights leader active in the NAACP or other organizations. In *Ellison v. Rock Hill Printing and Finishing Company*, for example, the workers were represented by Rev. Leroy Ellison, a local minister and NAACP activist. Ellison was described by an attorney in the case as "an intelligent black leader in the community" who was pastor of one of the largest churches in York County, South Carolina.[56] Ellison had played a key role in local protests in support of the civil rights bill in 1963. In initiating *Ellison v. Rock Hill Printing and Finishing* in 1972, he had contacted the EEOC personally and arranged a meeting for aggrieved black workers which had been attended by over 300 people. Interviewed more than twenty years after the case, Ellison remembered well how he filed the charge and initiated the lawsuit: "I started this on my own. . . . See, what happened in 1966, there was a statement in the local paper that Rock Hill Printing and Finishing Company was doing nothing to comply with the civil rights laws, and this gave me the idea that they didn't intend to. So I got the form from the post office for EEOC and filed a complaint, and they sent in a representative, and they saw that everything I complained about was true, and then they wrote me and told me that we had a right to sue. . . . We set up a class action, 13 men, and we started moving forward."[57]

The close links between the textile lawsuits and broader civil rights activity were also illustrated by the important role that the black church played in both. Several of the key plaintiffs, such as Leroy Ellison in *Ellison* and Sam Adams in *Galloway v. Fieldcrest Mills*, were ministers, and plaintiffs often met in church. In *Adams v. Dan River Mills*, for example, plaintiff Mae Crews remembered that the original case was put together at a meeting called for black Dan River workers at a local church. In *Lea v. Cone Mills*, a group of black women were persuaded to apply at the local textile mill, which had never hired a black woman, by a "Reverend Felder." Before applying as a group, the women met at Felder's chapel in Efland, North Carolina. At the chapel, black ministers advised the women on how to make an application.[58]

Civil rights leaders also played a key role in the largest and most important textile lawsuit, that of *Sledge v. J. P. Stevens*. In the early stages of the case, before a formal complaint had been made, a local NAACP activist and civil rights leader, Joe P. Moody, was instrumental in getting workers to sign EEOC complaint forms and in passing the names and other information on to civil rights attorneys. Moody's wife, Mable Moody, was one of the lead plaintiffs in the *Sledge* case. Joe Moody remembered that the lawsuit first began with thirteen workers that he brought together at his house in Roanoke Rapids: "The lawsuit started in my living room, right here, where we got together here, and I followed the case on up to Raleigh. . . . Richard T. Seymour, he just had come out of law school and then he came up here, and myself at my house, and we met with some of the group straight after then. Then I done a lot of investigation for him all over Halifax County and Northampton County." Moody continued to work for Washington attorney Seymour until more than 3,000 African Americans had signed charges of discrimination against J. P. Stevens. He was helped by other members of the local NAACP, which he described as "real active" at the time of the case.[59]

Black Activism and the Filing of Lawsuits

Although the NAACP helped many blacks initiate lawsuits, the amount of litigation brought in the textile industry was ultimately a reflection of a considerable degree of grassroots activism and courage. Numerous workers initiated lawsuits themselves by writing letters of complaint to the EEOC. Testimony showed that in many mills, black workers had tried for years to fight discrimination within the plant but had eventually concluded that only outside help could effect change.[60]

Indeed, one of the striking features of the lawsuits is the amount of activism among black workers and their determination to break down segregated job classifications. The major case of *Adams v. Dan River Mills*, filed in 1969, began when a group of black workers in the dyehouse got together and decided to protest about the promotion of an inexperienced white man, Garfield Harris, to be supervisor of their all-black department. They met as a group and decided to challenge the company. As Russell Dodson, one of the plaintiffs, recalled, "It was back in 1969 at the time that Garfield Harris was made a supervisor, all the blacks requested a meeting with the department heads and we were granted that meeting. . . . [A]t the time he was appointed supervisor we wanted to know why someone that was in the department that had been there longer and taken courses, why it was that some black was not given the job."[61]

This decision to file a lawsuit came after many years of trying to get promotions within the plant. The strong desire of Dan River workers to secure promotion was epitomized by Leroy Johnson, who had worked in the dyehouse as a pipefitter for over twenty years. Johnson testified that he had taken the job on the understanding that if he learned "everything about the job, it would be progressive and I could move on this job." As a result, Johnson described how for years, "I had learned through some correspondence courses and studying day and night, so hard sometimes I couldn't sleep, I had learned the job so that I knowed I could take care of anything that would come into Dan River and I couldn't get any promotion." Indeed, utilizing a wide range of excuses, the company told Johnson: "You are doing a good job, you doing the work, we want you to stay where you are, we don't have anybody to replace you, we will see what we can do." In court after twenty years of trying to secure a promotion, Johnson stuck to his dream of a better job.[62]

A mood of confidence and determination was apparent in all the Dan River plaintiffs. Many used the example of untrained white workers who had been made foremen to refute the company's argument that untrained blacks could not be made into foremen. The Dan River workers, most of whom had been working at the company for over twenty years, also derived their confidence from their close knowledge of many jobs in the mill, as blacks had frequently been assigned to run machines for whites who were out sick or on leave. Thus, Robert Hereford, who started working at the mill in 1935, refuted the suggestion that he was not qualified to be a shift foreman by citing the example of whites and his detailed job knowledge: "The white boys are took off the machines and trained for shift foreman. I feel like I could do the same thing. . . . Let's put it this way, anytime anybody is out I runs the machine right now. It is thirty-five people and I does that now. When anybody is out I take over." Hereford also claimed that he would "love to" be a mechanic and felt that he was qualified.[63]

In *Sherrill v. J. P. Stevens*, a case brought against the company's plant in Stanley, North Carolina, African American plaintiffs also showed a strong desire to challenge discrimination. Paul Gene McLean, for example, summed up the mood of many workers who wanted a chance to know about higher-paying jobs: "I'm testifying for one simple reason. I want a better job and when it comes open I want to know about it."[64] Warehouse worker Robert Costner had gone to work for Stevens in 1949. For twenty-seven years he had been restricted to "pushing hand trucks, loading trucks, things like that" and had never received a promotion. Costner told the company's attorney that "I'd like an office job, section man, you know, make more money but I never saw no sign up about no job like that." Determined not to be denied, Costner eventually filed charges with the EEOC. Like many black workers, his motives for filing sprang from a feeling that he had a right to advance in the mill: "I wanted to check it out, blacks rights, what's going on. I been there 27 years and I haven't advanced a bit, the same old thing." His deposition ended with the simple assertion that "I want a better job outside of pushing hand trucks."[65]

Workers generally supported litigation because they believed that it was the only way to fulfill their goal of promotion. Having tried for years to get promotions from their supervisors, these workers felt that they had to file charges so that their case could become known to officials higher up in the company. William Still, a Dan River worker who had taken various courses and asked for promotion "so many times," testified that he had supported the *Adams* case because "at the time I couldn't get the job I wanted and I thought that was the only way I could get to the big man."[66]

In bringing the lawsuits to court, many of the black workers involved showed a great deal of courage, particularly since they risked losing their jobs. Workers had to testify confronted by hostile company attorneys who were determined to try to force them to drop the case. In *Ellison v. Rock Hill Printing and Finishing Company*, for example, black worker Jerry Williamson, who had worked at the plant since 1953, was asked in his 1973 deposition how he felt the company treated its black workers. He explained that "you can see that everybody is not treated the same. It's right there before you. If you go in there, you can see that." Pressured by one of the defense's white attorneys who claimed that there was no discrimination, Williamson added, "I don't think no white man can understand how I feel by the way I've been treated because of the difference of the two skins. My skin is black and yours is white. You never had to suffer for anything and I have. . . . [Y]ou've always had freedom. You was free to do things.·There have been so many things we actually couldn't get because we was colored."[67] Like Williamson, other black workers had a deep personal knowledge of discrimination that sustained them when the defense attorneys tried to push them into denying that discrimination existed.[68] They claimed that they were in court because they were determined to end this discrimination. Lead plaintiff Leroy Ellison, for example, testified that "I brought the lawsuit because I believe in justice and equality to all people . . . to correct all of the discriminatory issues."[69]

Civil Rights Activity in Piedmont Communities

Although the textile belt does not have a reputation for activism, the area did experience some civil rights activity, including a major protest movement in the textile town of Danville, Virginia.[70] The town of Rock Hill, South Carolina, was at the center of the sit-in movement that swept across the South in 1960–61. The Rock Hill movement began on February 12, 1960, when approximately 100 African Americans sat down at two Rock Hill stores—Woolworth's and McCrory's. This began more than a year of sustained demonstrations in Rock Hill, leading to scores of arrests. The Rock Hill protests were part of a large effort led by the local black community in coordination with national civil rights leaders. In February 1961, a year after the first protests, over 300 local blacks heard speeches and advice from national civil rights leaders. Among the speakers were Ella Baker, James Ivory, and James T. McCain, Congress of Racial Equality (CORE) field secretary. On February 13, 1961, more than 600 blacks took part in a motorcade to the county prison, where those arrested in the sit-ins were held. When the demonstrations began, the local *Rock Hill Evening Herald* described the town as "a focal point in the segregation vs. integration tug of war." As they continued, the *Herald* became increasingly worried about the damage that the protests might do to the town's "progressive" image.

With demonstrations still continuing in 1961, the *Herald* described Rock Hill as "the key spot for lunch counter sit-in demonstrations in the South."[71]

The Rock Hill protests also had the effect of mobilizing white and black textile workers against one another. Some of the African Americans who took part in the protests were textile workers, including Leroy Ellison. Conversely, it is clear that white textile workers played a central role in mobilizing the opposition of the white community to the demonstrations. A White Citizens' Council was formed in response to the sit-ins, and its first meeting took place at the union hall of one of the local textile plants. More than 125 "tense white adults" heard an address by Farley Smith, son of former South Carolina senator "Cotton Ed" Smith. The next day Smith spoke at a "heated Rock Hill rally of white residents," and the White Citizens' Council was organized. A subsequent meeting of the council drew an attendance of around 600.[72]

Local press accounts show that civil rights demonstrations in other Piedmont communities often made local headlines yet failed to capture national attention. Many of these protests were concerned with employment.[73] In Greenville, South Carolina, a town at the heart of South Carolina's textile belt, more than 250 African Americans protested outside the Greenville Municipal Airport in 1960 against "the stigma, the inconvenience and stupidity of racial segregation." The protest had been organized in response to an incident at the airport in October 1959, when former baseball star Jackie Robinson, who had been the first black major league player, was forced to use the airport's "colored" waiting room. The demonstrators were addressed by regional NAACP director Ruby Hurley, who urged further civil rights protests in South Carolina. Many other members of NAACP branches from across South Carolina were also present. Another protest occurred in April 1960, when seven black students were charged with disorderly conduct for entering the white library in Greenville.[74]

The largest protest movement in a textile community, however, occurred in Danville, Virginia, in 1963. These demonstrations deserve further study, as they have not received the same amount of historical attention as other civil rights protests. The Danville protests drew the involvement of all the leading civil rights groups, including the NAACP, SNCC, CORE, and SCLC. Moreover, as in other major demonstrations, Martin Luther King Jr. visited the town to give leadership to the protesters. At the time of King's visit, more than 100 blacks had just been arrested for violating a city injunction. He tried to revitalize the demonstrations by calling on local blacks to "fill the jails for freedom."[75]

In the protests that King led, emphasis was given to Dan River Mills, the textile company that dominated the town's economy. In July 1963, SNCC demonstrators picketed outside Dan River's offices in New York City. The logic behind these demonstrations was that Dan River had such a dominant influence over Danville that it could easily force the whole town to integrate. Indeed, in 1963 Dan River was by far the biggest employer in the town, employing more than 10,000 people in a community of around 47,000. One of the leading demonstrators, Rev. Lawrence Campbell, claimed that "Dan River Mills can, if it wanted to, integrate Danville tomorrow." In a letter to ninety U.S. senators written in July 1963, the Danville Christian Progressive Association claimed that "the shame of Danville can end immediately with a phone call from the president of Dan River Mills." SCLC also charged Dan River with a discriminatory hiring policy, claiming that the 900 African Americans who worked for the company held "the most menial jobs."[76]

Other civil rights activities also targeted Dan River. SNCC selected the company for a boycott, which it hoped would become worldwide. Arguing that a boycott was necessary because the company dominated the "power structure" of the town, SNCC claimed that the mills were responsible for the terrible economic standards of Danville's black population because Dan River discriminated against blacks in hiring. Those blacks who were hired were limited to "the back breaking dirty jobs that no one in the white community will take." SNCC also claimed that the protests that had erupted in 1963 were caused by this economic situation: "Due to these economic reasons the people decided to move to the streets and demonstrate for change in the existing status quo."[77]

The Danville protests were largely a failure, due mainly to the violent opposition of the local police department and the wider white community. The Danville movement was essentially defeated when demonstrations were brutally dispersed by the police on June 10 and June 13, leading to widespread injuries among the protesters.[78]

The failure of the Danville demonstrations invites comparison with Albany, Georgia, where demonstrations led by King in 1962 failed partly because of astute police tactics.[79] King himself claimed that the opposition he encountered in Danville was greater than in any other campaign. Speaking at a rally in Danville in August 1963, he called the city's resistance to black demands "the worst in the United States, closely followed by Gadsden, Ala., and Savannah, Ga." The way that the police effectively crushed the movement also threw some doubt upon King's nonviolent methods and showed that they could not succeed against well-planned, aggressive policing. Indeed, officials from cities across the South were reported to be visiting Danville to learn its strategy for "successful resistance to Negro demonstrations." Danville's police captain, Juby E. Towler, even obliged by producing a handbook, *The Police Role in Racial Conflicts*, describing how he had successfully defeated the demonstrators. In contrast to the Birmingham experience, the Danville strategy was based on quiet and efficient mass arrests to prevent television dramatizing police treatment: "Rough stuff makes police look bad." In addition, the city effectively utilized an old Virginia statute making it an offense to "incite the colored population to war and violence" to arrest and control demonstrators. Such was the effectiveness of the tactics that King's call to "fill the jails" reputedly produced only 82 volunteers to march out of 2,000 who heard King speak. Of these eighty-two, all but fourteen were routed by the commands of the police chief. The *New York Times*, which gave extensive coverage to the Danville demonstrations, called Danville's strategy "the most unyielding, ingenious, legalistic and effective of any city in the South."[80]

Although the demonstrations in Danville were crushed by what SNCC described as a "brutal" police that used "nazi like tactics" on the people, the civil rights group claimed that the protests had led to a number of important achievements. Many of these improvements occurred at the mill, with the company's night and trade schools being opened to blacks for the first time. The demonstrations also pushed the segregated textile unions in Danville to merge. There was some token integration of the city's schools and upgrading of blacks in the local tobacco plant. A variety of positions in retail stores and in the city government were also opened to blacks.[81]

The most important achievement, however, was what SNCC leaders called "the Reborn Negro in the Community." The protests had led to a "new sense of dignity" among African Americans, "a new sense of civil responsibility," and "the refusal to accept segregation in any form." This mood of increased assertiveness was shown by a large increase in the number of blacks who registered to vote between 1961 and 1964. Indeed, the voter registration projects of SNCC, SCLC, and CORE in Danville tripled the number of blacks who were registered to vote.[82]

This spirit of community activism clearly influenced the filing of the *Adams* case some six years after the 1963 demonstrations. Julious Adams himself had worked at the mill for many years before the demonstrations, but after playing a key role in the protests, he emerged as a leader for a large group of black workers who were determined to improve the status of black workers at Dan River. Adams participated in various efforts to end segregation in Danville. He was a plaintiff in the school desegregation suit filed against the local school system as well as in the suit to desegregate restaurants in Danville. He had also taken part in the 1963 civil rights demonstrations. As treasurer of the local chapter of SCLC, he had accompanied Martin Luther King Jr. when he visited Danville to lead the demonstrations. He had been arrested on five or six occasions, most notably after leading an effort to desegregate a Howard Johnson's restaurant. Adams was also treasurer of the Danville Christian Progressive Association, a local group set up to lead the 1963 demonstrations. He clearly had a reputation as a civil rights leader in the community and in the mill. In *Adams v. Dan River Mills*, for example, the plaintiffs' attorneys claimed that

Adams's civil rights activities "establish that Adams has drive, aggressiveness and leadership potential."[83]

Adams's leadership of black workers seeking to gain entry into white jobs was an extension of these civil rights efforts. Many African American workers described how they turned to Adams to help them file charges when they felt they were being discriminated against.[84] When Helen Crews, for example, wanted to file an EEOC charge, she "went to Julious Adams and I told him I felt I was being discriminated against, that I wanted to write the Equal Employment Opportunity Commission. He told me I'd have to get some blanks from Jerry Williams [a local black lawyer]."[85] Having received a large number of complaints, Adams set about initiating the lawsuit. In March 1969, he held a meeting at a local black church for all African American workers "who were treated unfairly at Dan River Mills." Around seventy-five workers attended and filed EEOC charges, forming the basis of the lawsuit. The charges were signed and notarized at a later meeting at Adams's house.[86]

The company was well aware of Adams's civil rights activities, and Adams claimed that he was victimized as a result. He described how he was harassed on his job and fired on five different occasions.[87] Donald R. Aichner, the former superintendent of the finishing division, described Adams as someone who was "working for his race" and admitted that this attitude caused "some negative feelings by supervisors towards Mr. Adams." Aichner said that workers and supervisors knew about Adams's civil rights activities and that this "would have been a factor in regard to some white people there." He argued, however, that because Adams was so militant, supervisors treated him with extra caution, and he got away with more than other workers. Supervisors were "afraid of him . . . they treated him with kid gloves."[88] Adams "had access to people way up high, including Washington and everything else. The average supervisors didn't know how to handle this."[89]

The American Friends Service Committee, TEAM, and Piedmont Civil Rights Activity

Another civil rights group that played a key role in the racial integration of the textile industry was the American Friends Service Committee. Through more than twelve years of pressuring textile companies, the AFSC's Merit Employment Program clearly achieved some results in helping African American entry into the textile industry. In the early days of the program, employer visits played an important role by simply confronting managers with integration and making them think about an issue that many were unaware of.[90]

Between 1953 and 1965, the AFSC carried out hundreds of employer visits to textile mills across the South, pushing companies to hire blacks in nontraditional positions. Nationally, more than 4,000 visits were made between 1953 and 1959. Some companies clearly responded to AFSC pressure and encouragement. In 1957, for example, the AFSC reported that as a result of the Merit Employment Program, "some progress toward job equality has been made." In textiles, the program secured a small number of placements for blacks in clerical and technical jobs. In 1958, the AFSC reported proudly that it was responsible for the appointment of a black supervisor at "one of our larger textile mills in Greensboro." In 1959, a textile manufacturer in High Point, North Carolina, agreed to hire five black men into production jobs. The black workers were trained on Sundays in a locked plant so that they knew the job when they were placed in the plant. Some white workers left the mill when the blacks were introduced, but the mill owner held firm and the experiment worked.[91]

Although it produced some results, in general the AFSC faced a tough battle to overcome the opposition of textile executives to merit employment.[92] The resistance encountered by civil rights organizations such as TEAM and the AFSC, together with the way that the Danville protests were crushed, was indicative of the problems facing the civil rights movement as a whole in the Piedmont South. While there was in fact considerable civil rights activity in the region, strong resistance from the white community and power structure made the Piedmont a very difficult region in which to promote civil rights.

The records of other civil rights groups such as SNCC indicate that they found the Carolinas to be just as resistant to civil rights activity as the Deep South. South Carolina was repeatedly described as a tough environment by civil rights workers.[93] In North Carolina, reports from civil rights workers described the state's liberal image as a myth. In 1965, for example, SNCC representative Eric Morton wrote a "Proposal for a SNCC Project in North Carolina." Morton noted that "North Carolina has carved out for itself a liberal image, yet in numerical membership its Ku Klux Klan is stronger than any other state." Morton found that the major problem was North Carolina's black belt, located in the northeastern part of the state. Many textile plants were located in this area, including the huge Stevens complex in Roanoke Rapids. Morton described this area as comparable to the black belt of Mississippi and Alabama: "The facts are simple and clear. The northeastern region of North Carolina is made up of roughly 25 black belt counties comparable to any area in Mississippi or Alabama. In Alabama the polls are open 3 to 4 days a month; in North Carolina, the polls are open for registration 6 days every 2 years. All the usual segregationist tactics are used to keep the black people of this region from exercising their natural and basic rights in determining their own political destiny: violence, intimidation, harassment, fear, economic reprisal, etc." The area was 50 percent black but elected white congressmen who were "segregationist and reactionary." In North Carolina's Second Congressional District, an area covering a range of counties in the northeastern part of the state, 83 percent of blacks earned less than the federal poverty level of $3,000 per year.[94]

It is clear that civil rights organizations played an important role in the racial integration of the textile industry in the 1960s and 1970s. Both TEAM and the AFSC had some success in pushing companies to improve their hiring records, even though they came up against determined corporate opposition. More success was achieved by the NAACP and its Legal Defense Fund, especially in initiating important Title VII litigation against most of the major textile companies. This litigation played a central role in reducing discrimination in the textile industry.

In a recent overview of civil rights historiography, historian Adam Fairclough has noted that one of the largest gaps in historical knowledge of the movement is the neglect of the NAACP and the Legal Defense Fund: "The NAACP is virtually uncharted territory, and the same is true of the NAACP Legal Defense Fund." If there is one theme that runs through this story of the efforts of civil rights groups to integrate the textile industry, it is the central role played by the NAACP and the NAACP Legal Defense Fund. The Legal Defense Fund was the driving force behind TEAM, a major civil rights initiative that produced important results, and it played a key role in many major textile lawsuits. NAACP branches also played a central role in many communities, especially by encouraging workers to file charges. This conclusion supports other recent research that has suggested that the NAACP formed the backbone of the civil rights movement in states such as Louisiana and South Carolina.[95]

This study also suggests that the civil rights movement should not be defined too narrowly. Most historians now argue that the movement was a mass movement, and this study supports this conclusion. Civil rights activism extended into a wide variety of Piedmont communities, often led by groups about which we know relatively little. The drive to integrate the southern textile industry was led not by SCLC or SNCC, but by groups such as TEAM and the AFSC. The efforts of TEAM, the AFSC, and the Legal Defense Fund, together with the activism of black workers such as Julious Adams in Danville and Leroy Ellison in Rock Hill, are not among the movement's classic protests, but they show that textile communities experienced their own version of the civil rights movement.[96]

A Mixed Blessing

The Role of Labor Unions in
the Racial Integration of the
Southern Textile Industry

eight

In May 1967, Wilton E. Hartzler of the AFSC wrote of his experiences at the EEOC textile employment forum held in Charlotte, North Carolina, in January of that year. The forum, which explored the position of black workers in the industry, included extensive testimony from union and civil rights leaders. Hartzler wrote that the forum had established that "the textile industry is discriminatory against both the non-white worker and the union member and that the union is also discriminatory against the non-white worker." In view of this, Hartzler called the union "a mixed blessing" for black textile workers.[1]

In many ways, the "mixed blessing" metaphor sums up the contradictory and ambiguous role that labor unions played in the racial integration of the textile industry. On some occasions, unions were sued along with companies in racial discrimination lawsuits; in others, they supported workers' efforts in the suits. The seniority provisions of union contracts could also be either a blessing or a burden for African American workers. In some cases, black textile workers complained about the discriminatory impact of seniority agreements; in others, they claimed that the seniority provisions of a union contact played a central role in overcoming discrimination and allowing black workers to bid on better-paying jobs. Black workers themselves often had ambiguous and complicated attitudes toward unions, frequently supporting unions that they knew discriminated against them.

This chapter will explore the role that labor unions played in the racial integration of the textile industry and attempt to explain these ambiguities. One of the central areas to be examined is the role of cooperation between white and black workers in the workplace. In recent years, an "emerging revision" has looked at the history of interracial unionism in close detail. In particular, many historians have emphasized interracial organization among various workers in the late-nineteenth and early-twentieth-century South. This scholarship, however, has not been carried forward into the 1960s and 1970s. The influx of black workers into the textile industry provides an excellent opportunity to do this, especially as the entry of blacks carried with it the expectation that unionization would increase. This study has found that although there is considerable evidence of racism among white union members, in many cases black and white workers still showed the ability to cooperate effectively.[2]

Can This Hurt Us with Our Present Southern Membership?

The two major unions in this period were the Textile Workers Union of America (TWUA) and the United Textile Workers of America (UTWA). The TWUA was by far the larger of the two, with between two and four times the membership of the UTWA in the 1950s and 1960s. In 1976, the TWUA merged with the Amalgamated Clothing Workers of America (ACWA) to form a new union called the Amalgamated Clothing and Textile Workers' Union (ACTWU).[3]

In the 1950s and 1960s, textile unions, like textile companies, failed to take a strong stand in favor of civil rights partly because they feared a negative reaction from their white southern members. The minutes of a special staff meeting called by the TWUA leadership in December 1966 to discuss the union's statement for the forthcoming EEOC textile forum offers insight into the union's fears of alienating its white members and reveals the caution of its leadership. The main issue at that meeting captured the union's dilemma well: "The key question is 'shall we state our strong position on civil rights or can this hurt us in organization and with our present Southern membership?'" Because of its fear of alienating whites, the union decided to downplay its support for civil rights, arguing that "the industry should be blamed for discrimination and/or civil rights problems." When the question was raised of "whether we shall spearhead the civil rights fight or simply continue to take a positive position," it was the "consensus of the group" that the latter position should be taken. This decision meant that the union would continue to make statements supporting civil rights but would not push the issue of civil rights in the South. Indeed, the union developed this position in the written statement it submitted to the forum, arguing that management had the "responsibility for existing racial patterns" because they had "the unilateral right to hire—in unionized plants as well as in non-union plants."[4]

The union's minority position in the industry also explains why the TWUA failed to take a strong stand in support of civil rights. In the mid-1960s, no more than 10 percent of textile workers in the Carolinas were unionized. Attempts to organize southern textile workers in the 1950s and 1960s met with repeated failure.[5] With so little of the industry organized in the South, the TWUA feared that supporting civil rights would further jeopardize its vital task of organizing. Textile employers sometimes used racial propaganda against the union during organizing campaigns, further strengthening the union's reluctance to support civil rights. One report of a southern union staff training seminar in which TWUA participated explained the union's position: "Faced with . . . bitter employer resistance and a low ratio of already organized workers, TWUA field men appeared to feel that successful organization is the number one objective; the development of favorable membership attitudes on civil rights was considered important but subordinate."[6]

The implementation of Executive Order 10925[7] in April 1961 revealed much about the caution of the TWUA over the race issue. A flurry of correspondence took place within the union emphasizing that the TWUA should avoid making any bold statement of nondiscrimination. When one company asked where the union stood over the issue, president William Pollock warned that "although our union, as such, does not practice any discrimination, I would like to avoid any official letter going out from the International Office at this time." Pollock feared that such a statement would be used against the union if it tried to organize that company: "They have several plants in the south that we tried to organize from time to time, so I am not at all certain what use they make of any official statement coming from us."[8] In another memorandum, a union official urged caution because integration "is a very touchy subject and I did not want our union going on record before it was absolutely necessary for us to do so."[9]

The TWUA anticipated considerable resistance from white workers when integration took place. A staff conference called in May 1961 informed all southern staff members that integration was probable in many mills and that even though companies were likely to handle the issue "in a way so as not to arouse antagonism," there would still be "great uneasiness" among white workers. Union staff members were instructed to stress to white workers "the inevitability of hiring and the need for unity to build strong unions."[10]

The leadership of the UTWA was also reluctant to give open support to civil rights. In 1962, the union debated how to respond to a proposal by Vice President Lyndon Johnson that called for a nondiscrimination clause in all collective bargaining contracts. The union took the position that although it was sympathetic to the proposal, it preferred that "the Government itself introduce legislation that would make this a matter of law, rather than simply a voluntary program." The union acted on the advice of its southern staff members that openly supporting civil rights would alienate workers and allow management to stir up the race issue by publicizing the union's stand, thereby destroying any organizing prospects.[11] Johnnie E. Brown, a southern vice president, reported that in many towns where UTWA locals were located, the issue of civil rights was very divisive. In South Carolina, local white leadership still insisted on segregated union meetings. With such tension, Brown warned that supporting civil rights would benefit the companies: "In our organizational campaigns unscrupulous Companies have used the race issue without hesitation to defeat us. I am sure that if we are the prompter and insist on paving the way for the inclusion of these clauses, they will not hesitate to use this again to attempt our destruction." He concluded that "I do not feel that we should make ourselves vulnerable to the sadistic employers of the South by giving him scrap iron to fire back at us."[12]

Faced with such caution, civil rights organizations began to realize that organized labor would not cooperate effectively with them in the South. A report drawn up by CORE in 1964 highlighted the fact that civil rights organizations knew that the backing of the labor movement at the national level would not be translated into action at the local level. The report, surveying North Carolina, concluded that "at the national level there is more or less an alliance of civil rights and labor. As long ago as August 1963, labor contributed a very large percentage of the participants in the March on Washington. Yet the development of a meaningful coalition has not penetrated to the state and local levels to any significant extent. Especially in the South, organized labor is often more foe than friend. In North Carolina it will not be easy to work with the state AFL-CIO."[13]

White Resistance

To a certain extent, the reaction of many white workers to integration justified textile unions' fears and caution. Between the 1950s and the late 1970s, many white textile union members consistently used their local union as a vehicle with which to oppose civil rights and integration. Indeed, many whites clearly expected their local union to take a stand against integration.

Sources indicate that many textile locals became strong centers of Ku Klux Klan and White Citizens' Council activity, especially during the peak of the councils' popularity in the late 1950s. In 1957, TWUA staff expressed concern "that in some textile locals an unhealthy majority of the workers were council or Klan members."[14] In the same period, the TWUA's Julius Fry explained that there was considerable opposition to integration among TWUA local unions in the South and that "Hate organizations" were active in several locations.[15]

These comments reflected the fact that textile workers generally were considered to be overrepresented in the Klan and other pro-segregation groups. In 1957, two top officials of the TWUA in the South were reported to feel that "Textile Workers and other rank and file workers would supply the bulk of the reaction to any move for desegregation."[16] In January 1957, the Southern Regional Council, reporting on the growth of pro-segregation "resistance" organizations in the South, found that there was a Klan revival in North Carolina centered around the company-owned textile town of Kannapolis. It felt that the Klan "may be successful, since a potential Klan membership exists there."[17]

One close look into the racial mood among white textile union members in the late 1950s was provided by detailed questionnaires sent to local unions across the South by Emory Via, the labor consultant of the Southern Regional Council. The questionnaires asked a series of questions about the attitudes of local union members to integration and the race issue. The survey took place in 1956–57, providing a good opportunity to observe the reaction of white textile workers to the 1954 *Brown v. Board of Education* school desegregation decision and civil rights demonstrations such as the 1956 Montgomery bus boycott.

A clear pattern emerges from the surveys. It is evident that the vast majority of white textile workers were strongly opposed to integration. Those completing the surveys had a choice of filling in categories of "most," "many," and "few" to indicate the proportion of their members that held certain views on the race question. In locals across the South, "most" white workers were reported to be very opposed to school integration and to hold "antagonistic feelings toward Negroes." "Most" or "many" were also said to be in favor of "putting public schools under private control." It was also commonplace for white workers to be "in favor of segregation in general." Many white workers had taken an organized stance against school integration and supported the White Citizens' Council or the Klan. At the Granite local of Cone Mills in Haw River, North Carolina, for example, it was reported that "there is a strong Citizen's Council. . . . Some of our members and many nonmembers belong to this organization." A picture of Walter Reuther donating money to the NAACP had "caused an uproar among our white membership mainly in the finishing department. Although we had a special meeting to discuss this matter, the result was that the stewards and dues collectors in this department resigned. They have not been willing to reenter the Union since then."[18]

The reaction of the Granite workers typified that of other white textile workers. Of the local unions included in the survey, all of those who gave a response to the question claimed that "most" of their members were "strongly opposed to school integration." One local in Columbia, South Carolina, even deleted "most" and replaced it with "all" to indicate that there were no workers who were not strongly opposed to school integration. This local claimed that 30 percent of its members belonged to the White Citizens' Council. Another local wrote that "the race issue has become important in this local since the school decision." Illustrating the way that white workers often expected the local union to lead the opposition to the school question, it was reported that at this same textile local, "not all members are aware of the position of the Union on segregation. One young leader in a department invited the other workers in his group to have a combined meeting of union and 'Klu Klux' near his house because as he said 'I'm not in favor of my children going to school with niggers.'"[19]

In addition to school integration, the other issue that white workers were strongly opposed to was equal opportunities in the plant. In most surveys, "most" or "many" whites were said to be "opposed to Negroes having the same economic opportunities on the job as white workers have." From one local, for example, it was reported that "friction here is mostly as to what jobs are white and what are colored. . . . In several cases where negroes bid to a better job or even to a different job which they had not previously held, the white workers reaction was such that the Company did not award them the job."[20]

The surveys provide clear insight into why the national TWUA wanted to avoid strong public support for integration. Surveys from mills that the union was trying to organize showed that many white workers were very opposed to any association of the union with integration. From a Burlington Mills plant in Chattanooga, Tennessee, for example, a survey noted: "Organizers report that about one person in six approached about joining the union brings up the school desegregation question. These people say 'they don't blame the organizers but don't like the big boys at the top trying to force them to send their children to school with negroes. Won't have their dues going to NAACP.'" Organizers themselves recommended that the national union should minimize the damage caused by this issue by being reticent about its support for civil rights: "Organizers say national unions can help best by, to put it succinctly, 'keeping quiet.'"[21] Similarly, from a TWUA local in Clifton, South Carolina, it was reported that the *Brown* decision had caused many members to consider withdrawing from the union. The leadership of the local recommended that the national union should not take a position, "because we have to organize the South. We feel that it will hurt us in organizing by taking a position."[22]

Many TWUA members did withdraw after the union passed a resolution condemning the White Citizens' Council at its 1956 convention. Union records show that the passage of the resolution had caused damaging fallout in local unions. Charles Auslander reported from Spray, North Carolina, that the leadership of one of the major locals was very angry about the resolution, and "there was much talk of a general resignation of members. Only by some tedious work were we able to limit the resignations to about a dozen." Across the South, business agents felt that the resolution had made the job of organizing more difficult.[23]

The Via surveys show that organized labor throughout the South was struggling to deal with a backlash of white resistance to civil rights in the 1956–57 period. In a wide variety of industries, it was reported that the *Brown* decision and the Montgomery bus boycott had angered white workers and caused race relations to become more tense. Textile workers shared this reaction, although reports from other industries show that other workers had similar feelings. Reports from rubber and steel locals in Alabama show that white workers had been stirred up by civil rights activity in their state, especially the Lucy riots at the University of Alabama.[24] A large steelworkers local in Birmingham, Alabama, was reported to be "considerably worked up" over the Lucy case and other recent civil rights disturbances: "The situation here is quite explosive and would certainly respond to capable leadership by white supremists."[25] At a large rubber workers local in Tuscaloosa, Alabama, it was reported that relations between black and white workers were "now strained. . . . [T]here is indisputable evidence that many members participated in the Lucy riots at University of Alabama. It is also true that many members belong to the WCC and are adamant segregationists."[26] Locals in several other industries were reported to have a "heavy membership in WCC."[27]

The resistance of white textile union members to integration continued into the 1960s and 1970s. TWUA representatives who were in the field when companies decided to integrate in the early 1960s often had to deal with a backlash of white resistance directed at them. The strength of the feelings described in written reports confirms how white workers often looked to the union to make a stand against integration. In April 1961, for example, David Terry, a business agent at DuPont's plant in Old Hickory, Tennessee, wrote an emotional letter to his southern director describing how white workers were strongly opposed to a company announcement to integrate the plant. Terry felt that, with the contract about to run out, the company had made the announcement as a way of weakening the union: "Our feeling is that the Company made this move at this particular time with a purpose in mind; to get our members to withdraw from the union." Describing how he had become unpopular because he had refused to oppose integration, Terry wrote, "I am the bastard of the community right now as the membership is blaming me for the change in policy. . . . If you hear of a lynching in Old Hickory—it will be me on the rope."[28]

Other reports showed that white workers often looked to the local union to oppose integration and used it as a way of organizing white workers against the introduction of blacks. At a Celanese plant in Rome, Georgia, the local union called a wildcat strike when the company tried to integrate certain departments. At another Celanese plant in Rock Hill, South Carolina, a local chapter of the White Citizens' Council was organized at the union hall in response to civil rights demonstrations occurring in Rock Hill in 1960–61.[29]

As at Old Hickory, one of the complaints that was often made by TWUA representatives in the 1960s was that management exploited the racism of white workers to weaken local unions. Although companies claimed that they took a firm stand against those who opposed integration, it is clear that in reality, workers' opposition was often encouraged by management as a way of encouraging workers to leave the union. At a meeting of TWUA leaders called in 1966 to discuss civil rights, for example, it was reported from southern union leaders that "some of our members have revolted against our policy of non-discrimination because they knew they had the bosses' support."[30]

Most local unions did little to combat discrimination. In December 1966, the TWUA undertook a survey of its southern locals to determine how much local unions were doing to end discrimination. The replies showed that very little was being done. The survey revealed that only 2.6 percent of all TWUA contracts contained a nondiscrimination clause.[31] In this sense, textiles was far worse than American industry as a whole, where around 20 percent of major collective bargaining agreements contained specific bans against discrimination in 1961.[32] Very few locals had African American stewards or officers, yet they felt they did not discriminate.[33] The survey also showed that the grievance machinery was not being used to help blacks advance, even when they had significant representation in the plant. Indeed, 86.8 percent of local unions had never filed grievances on behalf of black workers seeking better jobs.[34] This survey confirms the observation of TEAM in 1967 that unionization made no difference to the racial make-up of plants: "A check of union plants indicates that the racial mix is no better."[35]

Union representatives who were active in the South remembered a great deal of resistance from white union members to the racial integration of local unions. This resistance lasted well into the 1970s. Bruce Raynor started working in the education department of the TWUA in the South in 1973, going on to become southern director of ACTWU and the new Union of Needletrades, Industrial, and Textile Employees (UNITE!) in the 1980s and 1990s. Raynor remembered that within many southern local unions, African Americans were held back: "In the early days that I worked, I was in education. . . . There were emerging black activists in the local unions, resisted in many cases by the whites, so you had in a number of cases the whites trying to hold on to the power in the union. The textile union in 1973 in the South was a heavily white-led union, and the locals were led by whites, even though by that time there were lots of blacks in the plants." In some cases whites resigned from the union en masse when the first African Americans were elected to positions of responsibility. As in organizing, the union found it very difficult to run mixed locals, finding its locals becoming either heavily black or staying all-white.[36]

Other organizers and union staffers remembered similar experiences. Some recalled that most local union leaders were white men who reacted badly to the integration of the workforce. These whites tried to hold on to leadership positions even when blacks became a majority in the plant.[37] Joe Gaines, an African American organizer for TWUA and ACTWU, remembered that generally whites accepted black membership but were unwilling to let African Americans hold any leadership positions: "For the purpose of them coming as membership to make the organization stronger, yeah, that was welcome by the white because that gave them more power. But as far as giving the minorities speaking power, they wouldn't have that. They would have positions where they were just members and not in a decision-making role."[38]

Many black workers who tried to secure leadership positions within local unions remembered the resistance they encountered from the established white leadership. Joan Carter started working at Fieldcrest Mills in Eden, North Carolina, in 1965, and was an enthusiastic union supporter. A bright, vivacious woman, she recalled that the local union leadership was all white males, who fiercely resisted blacks gaining leadership positions in the union. Carter felt that racism in the local union was greater than in the plant as a whole: "I felt like there was more racism in the union than in the workforce. . . . It was all male. It was a fight just to be a woman, and then to be a black woman. In reality, the fight was really in the union, because they really didn't want to see black women accomplish anything." One union president, who was later appointed the joint board manager in Eden, was "a card-carrying member of the Ku Klux Klan." Carter concluded from this experience that "a Ku Klux Klansman can move up quicker in the union than a Negro." Overall, she felt that white union leadership felt threatened by the entry of militant blacks into the workforce.[39] Other African Americans who tried to secure leadership positions within local unions shared Carter's opinion that resistance was greater among union leaders than in the plant as a whole.[40]

Black Attitudes to Unions

Across the South, the textile lawsuits revealed complaints by black workers that unions were failing to represent them. The records show that many black workers tried to file grievances in order to remedy discrimination, yet they complained that unions would not process these grievances. African American workers often described how they had repeatedly tried to secure representation from their local union, only to be continually frustrated and abused. Many of the black workers in *Ellison v. Rock Hill Printing and Finishing Company* claimed that the union failed to process their grievances and represent them properly.[41] Black worker Chris Brown testified in 1972 that the local union had never been willing to take up his grievances. Brown testified that he had been to the union hall on many occasions, but that the union's representative had told him "that when the Union was set up, it was set up against the Negro. . . . Set up against the Negro and nothing he could do about it."[42]

Lead plaintiff Leroy Ellison shared the feeling of many black workers that the union had a responsibility for the discrimination that existed in the plant. Ellison felt that the union was partly responsible for the segregation of jobs: "Well, the jobs I think there is a lack of representation that causes these jobs to exist in a segregated manner. . . . We, the blacks in the plant have not been represented fairly by the union." Ellison even described how black workers had stopped telling the union about their grievances for equal pay "to save embarrassment. . . . [W]e have had so many problems that were ignored until you don't feel like going through the same embarrassing situation." Ellison claimed that when the international union had sent in a representative who had tried to help the African American workers, the white workers complained and got the representative transferred.[43]

Other black workers also described how the union ignored their grievances. Jerry Williamson, who worked in the shipping department, testified that he waited eighteen months without hearing what had happened to his grievance: "My shop steward told me when they get to my grievance, the president would let him know and he would let me know what day to be there. Everytime they would have a grievance meeting, I would ask him about mine. He said mine wasn't coming up." Williamson was in no doubt as to why the union had ignored his complaints: "My honest opinion, I would say it was because of my color."[44] Another shipping department worker, James Barnes, was critical of the local union's performance since he had started working at the plant in 1949. Questioned by the TWUA's attorney, Barnes claimed that "I don't think they have did as much for the blacks as they did for the whites."[45]

White workers who were active in the local Rock Hill union confirmed that these allegations were accurate. Fletcher Beck, a white worker who sat on the TWUA's shop committee in the 1960s, remembered that "when I went on that shop committee I would hear language that . . . the blacks wouldn't hear by the all-white committee about some of the grievances: 'Well, you don't have to push that one too hard, they're black.'"[46]

This lack of representation, however, did not stop the same black workers from supporting the union. In *Ellison*, lead plaintiff Leroy Ellison explained why black workers supported an institution that had failed to help them. Like other black workers, Ellison explained that he was a firm believer in unions and still supported them because he felt that union representation could be very beneficial to black workers. Ellison, however, was able to distinguish between the principle of union representation, which he supported, and the practice of discrimination against black workers by the local union in Rock Hill, which he was protesting against. Thus, Ellison still supported union representation even though black workers themselves had not been properly represented in Rock Hill: "I wouldn't place this on Textile Workers of America. I would have to say the Local Union that I had dealings with refused to represent us properly because of our skin." Ellison had even worked as an organizer for the TWUA shortly before bringing the case against it. He rejected the union attorney's claim that this made him a "hypocrite" by pointing out that "I was trying to get members, and I felt that a new organization would be a good organization because it would be set up right to start with." In sum, "It would be the same organization but different representation."[47]

Other black workers also supported the principle of union representation even though the local union had discriminated against them. Another plaintiff in the *Ellison* case, Johnnie Archie, remembered that throughout the case, "everything the local union did was to throw stumbling-blocks in the way of the blacks who had suffered discrimination and [been] deprived of jobs." Nevertheless, he felt that union representation was still beneficial because it had provided a measure of job security: "We wanted job security. If the supervisor didn't like the way I looked . . . he'd say, 'Don't you come back tomorrow,' but with a union, although we didn't get the representation that we thought we should have, we had job security. He couldn't run me off because he didn't like my looks. If the blacks had got out of the union, it would have been, to my opinion, to the company's advantage. . . . By staying in the union we had some protection, some protection." Other Rock Hill workers also stressed the protection against unfair discharge that the union gave them. They claimed that the union represented them on disciplinary issues, even though it was unwilling to take up their grievances about unequal pay. Willie A. Simpson, for example, testified: "I'll tell you, the Union represents you for being fired or something like that, but as far as coming to get more money, they don't do very much representing towards the blacks."[48]

The attitude of many black workers was summed up by *Ellison* plaintiff Henry Wiley. After working for the company for twenty years on the same job, Wiley complained in his 1972 deposition that the white shop stewards had done nothing to help African American workers who wanted better jobs: "Our representatives didn't do no good jobs for us because they haven't even represented us." Despite this, Wiley felt that black workers were in "better shape" because they had a union, and that "I wouldn't want to work over there without a Union."[49]

More than twenty-five years later, former *Ellison* plaintiffs still defended their position of support for a local union that "would not represent us." Leroy Ellison remembered that "we went through all of this lawsuit, suing the union, paying our union dues, helping to pay them to fight us, and we realized our money was being used against us as well as for us, but we never got out of the union." Ellison felt that he had stayed in the union because "the union helped us in some ways," and he again cited the protection that the union offered against arbitrary and unfair company actions.[50]

Many black workers in *Adams v. Dan River Mills* had similar attitudes toward unionism. Generally, black workers in that case also described how the union had consistently failed to represent them and fight against discrimination.[51] Testimony from the case shows that the union did protect African American workers against unfair discharge and other noneconomic issues.[52] It failed, however, to tackle structural problems of discrimination, especially the complaints of unequal pay and segregated jobs. Edward Crews, for example, claimed that the union had never helped him when he had filed grievances about unequal pay: "Whites working on production get more pay than Negroes for the same or less production. I have brought this to the attention of Local 248 of United Textile Workers of America (AFL-CIO) about the lower pay rate but nothing was ever done."[53]

As in *Ellison*, this inadequate representation did not deter most of the black workers in *Adams* from being union members and even officeholders. Leroy Johnson, for example, testified that he had been a shop steward for twenty years even though the union had failed to take up his claims of discrimination. He had complained to the union "every chance I have. . . . Attending shop steward meetings I'd speak about it frequently. Every chance I can get. . . . [W]hen I bring it up, they promise they're going to do something about it. Never do nothing." Despite this, Johnson directed most of his resentment against the company rather than the union, feeling that they were more responsible for discrimination.[54]

Throughout the 1960s and 1970s, the main complaint of black textile workers was their inability to move into the better-paying jobs. Many blacks appreciated union protection because it provided seniority, meaning that jobs were awarded to the most senior worker who was qualified for the job. Plantwide seniority allowed senior African Americans the opportunity to secure higher-paying jobs that had previously been awarded to more junior white workers. Before the 1960s, most textile contracts provided department seniority, which discriminated against blacks because it only provided seniority within their own departments, which were likely to be all black. When unions had been organized before the 1960s, as in *Adams* and *Ellison*, inadequate representation and the dominance of white leadership meant that they failed to fulfill their potential to overcome discrimination. Indeed, as in *Adams* and *Ellison*, unions often signed departmental seniority agreements that effectively prevented blacks from being promoted out of their low-paying, all-black departments.

When local unions were organized by black workers themselves in the 1960s and 1970s, however, they often played a key role in allowing African Americans to gain better-paying jobs through seniority. In these cases, seniority was not restricted to departments but was plantwide, allowing blacks to be awarded jobs on the basis of experience that previously supervisors might have given to less experienced whites. Across the South, African American workers who organized local unions in the 1960s and 1970s saw the union as a major improvement because of the role it had played in overcoming discrimination through seniority. Earl Moore, an African American worker who helped to organize a union at a Fieldcrest plant in Columbus, Georgia, in the 1970s, expressed a typical view: "With the coming of the union it opened the door for blacks to make a significant gain into the workplace on jobs other than sweeping or menial jobs."[55]

The lawsuits themselves reflected the way that a local union could be a foe or a friend to black workers. In cases involving unions organized before the 1960s, local unions were often sued along with the companies because they had signed discriminatory seniority agreements. Where the union was organized after integration, however, especially if there was a large amount of black involvement, the union often supported the black workers' litigation. This occurred in *Sledge v. J. P. Stevens* and in several smaller cases.[56]

African American workers who organized unions after 1964 claimed that by providing seniority, the union could be a vehicle for racial justice. Many described how, before the union, supervisors had relied on favoritism and promoted whites into positions regardless of seniority. Black workers felt that it was only when they had union representation that they were able to get good jobs. James McGhee, who started working at a textile plant in Andalusia, Alabama, in 1956, for example, summed up how the opportunities for black workers had changed with the arrival of the local union in 1965: "Union made all the difference in the world, when union came in there, period. . . . You had seniority, see. It improved the integration."[57]

Black workers who came into the industry after 1965 gave strong support to unions. In most cases, blacks supported unions as a way of overcoming discrimination in the mills, and seniority was seen as the most important way of achieving this. The amount of support for unions from black textile workers was indicative of the amount of discrimination prevailing in the industry. As Angie Rogers, a tall black woman who was hired in a textile mill in Columbus,

Georgia, in 1968, explained, "I think that blacks support the union because it would mean that you will have equality in the workplace. Okay, you get this union in . . . If it comes down to a layoff, I've been there twenty years, and you see this white girl over here been here five years, you going to lay me off to let her work. You see stuff like that. That's the reason why black people would vote for the union, just to get fair treatment."[58]

Two major events of the 1960s and 1970s—the civil rights movement and the Vietnam War—helped to radicalize black workers and change their views of unions. Vietnam often had an important radicalizing influence on African Americans who took part, many of whom came back from the war and became union leaders. Jacob Little, for example, remembered that he was transformed by his service in Vietnam. After growing up in the segregated Columbus, Georgia, of the 1950s, Little had worked in a local textile mill before serving in the army. His military experience changed his life because he was placed in charge of white soldiers, giving him an unprecedented amount of self-esteem and confidence. Upon returning from Vietnam, Little helped organize a union at his plant and served in a variety of leadership positions, including president. Roosevelt Broadnax, who worked at the same plant as Little, went through a similar experience, returning from Vietnam to become a union activist and organizer.[59]

Nick Builder, who worked as ACTWU joint board manager in Columbus in the 1970s, remembered that Vietnam had a radicalizing effect on a whole generation of black workers who became union leaders. The war "did do a number of things to African American workers. It gave them frequently an experience of being equal to if not superior to whites, something that would never have happened if they'd stayed in the South. It also gave them a powerful, you know, demonstration of what was wrong with the society that they lived in, of exploitation and the fact that there were more of them forced to serve in Vietnam than white people . . . and it occurred at the same time as the Civil Rights Movement, so . . . it did have an effect on radicalizing people."[60]

The civil rights movement also played a major role in radicalizing black workers, and it is clear that this militancy affected union activity. The *Philadelphia Inquirer*, for example, reported in 1986 that "in North Carolina . . . many black textile workers have come to regard unions almost as they viewed protest marches and sit-ins in the 1960s." The union was seen as a support by black workers who filed equal opportunity and discrimination complaints, and by the 1990s more black workers (21 percent) were union members than white workers (15 percent).[61]

Many African American workers remembered how the civil rights movement affected union activity in the 1960s and 1970s. Macy Adkins, who was hired at Columbus Towel Mill as a young man in 1968, was active in organizing a union at the plant and became president of the local in 1978. Adkins felt that "the momentum from the civil rights movement was something that . . . moved a lot of union activists throughout the South." The union became a "vehicle" that enabled African American workers to end racial discrimination in the workplace.[62] Similarly, black worker and union leader Joe Gaines felt that the civil rights movement played a crucial role in the formation of his textile local in Sylvester, Georgia: "The civil rights movement affected me more or less by strengthening me. . . . Basically that's how we got our union started, from civil rights organizations, that we had a right to form a union."[63] Earl Moore, who worked at the Eagle and Phenix plant in Columbus, Georgia, played an active role in organizing a union at that mill in 1979. Like other African Americans, he supported the union because he saw the union and civil rights as bound together: "When the union came into the plant, so came civil rights with that. Basically you might say that the two were inseparable, you know, the ideology of the union and civil rights. They both worked together."[64]

Written records also provide examples of the way that civil rights and union activity often occurred together. In the late 1960s and 1970s, the TWUA employed former SCLC staffer James Orange as one of its organizers in the South, and many of his union campaigns also involved voter registration drives and other civil rights activity. In 1978, for example, Orange was placed in charge of a campaign to organize J. P. Stevens's plants in Great Falls, South Carolina. It was reported that Orange "has developed a 'civil rights movement' in Great Falls, with extensive voter registration activity and social service assistance."[65] At Cannon Mills, a lawsuit brought by TWUA against the company in 1975 involved the discharge of Daisy Crawford, a black worker who was involved in both civil rights and union activities. The case described how Crawford's union and civil rights work went hand in hand. Crawford was eventually reinstated as a result of legal action.[66] Leading civil rights leaders frequently gave their support to union campaigns in which black workers were involved, particularly the J. P. Stevens campaign.[67]

"Southern Textile Workers Are Ready to Organize"

The attitude of unions toward the integration of the textile industry was not entirely one of caution and fear. Once African Americans were being hired in significant numbers in the industry, unions became optimistic that their entry would make the industry easier to organize. Observing how black workers had been radicalized by the civil rights movement, textile unions began to welcome the entry of blacks into the workforce. A TWUA report from 1961 captured the way that fear and caution about integration gradually gave way to optimism. The report noted that as black workers were first brought into the mills, the race issue might be used against the union. When this period of "heightened emotions" was over, however, the TWUA anticipated that black workers would be easier to organize than whites had proven to be: "One of the classic reasons advanced in the past as to why southern workers would not organize was their homogeneous anglo-saxon background. To the extent that the entrance of the Negro on equal terms destroys this pattern, the workers may turn from personal controls and relationships to organized controls and relationships such as unions." The union was very optimistic about black entry, feeling that it would transform its organizing prospects in the South: "The entrance into textile plants of a substantial minority of Negro workers may have great benefits in terms of future organizing campaigns."[68]

The records of the TWUA show that its southern staff felt that the organizing climate in the late 1960s was very favorable. Organizers produced a document entitled "Recommendations for an Expanded Southern Organizing Program" that was received at the TWUA's convention in 1970. The document claimed that "southern textile workers are ready to organize" and that organizing activity should be immediately increased because "the workers are ready now." The organizers claimed that "the increased number of blacks in textile plants makes organizing more successful" but added that white workers had also been affected by the mood of dissatisfaction produced by the youth and civil rights movements: "Those eligible to vote in our organizing targets are on the whole younger, more exposed and more sophisticated than in the past and finally seem to be infected with the general discontent with the status quo which is so evident in the United States."[69]

It is important to determine the extent to which unions were able to capitalize on this favorable organizing climate. It is particularly interesting to see whether white workers were radicalized by black entry as TWUA organizers claimed. The entry of blacks into a white workforce indeed provides an excellent opportunity to explore how much cooperation was achieved between the races over workplace issues and to measure the limits and possibilities of interracial unionism.

In many ways, the optimism of the TWUA organizers was not misplaced. The entry of black workers did lead to an upsurge in unionization. Union records offer many examples of campaigns that were won largely because of the overwhelming support of black workers. At Kenlon Mills in Allendale, South Carolina, for example, a 1970 election victory was attributed to the fact that the "majority of workers were black and were self organized and the company could not crack their solidarity."[70] Major victories at Oneita Knitting Mills in Andrews, South Carolina, in 1973 and at J. P. Stevens in Roanoke Rapids, North Carolina, in 1974 were also due in large part to black militancy and support.[71]

Such was the extent of black support for unions that in many campaigns organizers relied on complete support from all the blacks in the workforce. TWUA organizer Clyde Bush remembered that throughout the 1960s, he knew that he could always count on black support: "Anywhere back in the '60s when we were having campaigns in the South at that time . . . you could go into a plant and you'd find out how many blacks was in there, that give you a pretty good assurance. If you had fifty blacks that worked in that plant, you could count yourself fifty votes, automatic. Every black in that plant would vote 'yes' for the union."[72] The written record of many campaigns confirmed that the union was able to secure 100 percent support from black workers. In one campaign in July 1970, for example, the organizer wrote, "About 40% of the plant are black workers and we should get their vote."[73]

The entry of blacks into the workforce benefited the union in other ways. In several union campaigns, the fact that large numbers of African Americans were in the workforce broadened the support base for the union. A wide variety of groups expressed support for unionization as a way of overcoming racial discrimination. This was especially true of the J. P. Stevens campaign.[74] The union successfully publicized Stevens's record of racial discrimination as a way of building support for the campaign. In January 1978, for example, Sol Stetin of ACTWU wrote the AFL-CIO Department of Civil Rights asking for more information on EEOC charges pending against Stevens, because the publicizing of the *Sledge* decision had proved favorable to the union: "The court decision finding the company guilty of illegal discriminatory hiring and promotion practices in Roanoke Rapids, N.C. has been a major feature of our boycott campaign."[75]

The Stevens campaign was successful at mobilizing a variety of groups that saw the struggle for civil rights as inextricably linked with unionization. Indeed, the end of the civil rights movement of the 1960s brought with it an increased realization that the gains of the 1960s could only be protected if African Americans achieved more economic equality. One group which gave active support to the Stevens workers was Southerners for Economic Justice (SEJ), formed in 1976 by a group of prominent southerners including Atlanta mayor Maynard Jackson. SEJ's board declared that "unless individual civil rights were carried into the workplace the victories of the sixties would remain partial." SEJ recognized that unions were essential to giving African Americans workplace rights, and it supported organized labor's efforts to strengthen the powers of the NLRB.[76] The Southern Organizing Committee for Economic and Social Justice (SOC) was another broadly based civil rights group that was born in the 1970s and gave extensive support to the J. P. Stevens campaign. Again reflecting the increased emphasis that civil rights groups placed on economic issues in the 1970s, the SOC aimed to re-unite the civil rights coalition of the 1960s around the idea that "the poor and working people of the South hold the key to social and economic change."[77]

It is clear that in some cases the entry of blacks did not automatically alienate white workers and prevent organizing. Many whites watched blacks demand their rights and came to admire them. Across the South, white workers
showed a willingness to allow blacks to take the lead in organizing efforts
because they recognized that black militancy could organize a union that
would benefit all workers, black and white. One white worker at J. P. Stevens in
Roanoke Rapids, for example, expressed a typical attitude in 1977: "I really
admire the black folk. They stand up for their rights. I think the whites have a
lot to learn about that."[78]

Many white workers even welcomed the entry of blacks into the workforce because they felt that black militancy could help all workers achieve
more justice in the workplace. Nick Builder, a tall, articulate man who
worked for the TWUA and ACTWU as an organizer and staff representative in
the 1970s and 1980s, felt that the civil rights movement had produced a
"myth" among whites "that somehow, as they would put it, 'Black people
know how to stick together,' which you used to hear a lot."[79] In Erwin, North
Carolina, the white president of the local union declared in 1969 that he
welcomed the entry of African Americans into the workforce because he felt
that this would revitalize the local, which only had around 50 percent membership in the plant. He explained that "I think within the next few years
we'll have many more Negroes. Whites hate to organize. They want to 'get
along' with management. But Negroes know it's not on their side. They've
known that kind of thing all the way back to slavery times." Other white
workers in Erwin were also reported to be "hoping that Negroes will
strengthen the union."[80]

Union records also show that many white workers were themselves radicalized by the civil rights movement and the entry of blacks into the workforce. In
1970, TWUA southern director Paul Swaity sent a detailed memo to union president William Pollock describing how "the climate for organizing textile workers in the south is better today than it's been since the early '40s." Swaity
explained that the mood in the industry was very favorable to organization
largely because of the entry of black workers, who saw union activity as an
extension of the civil rights movement: "The black workers pride themselves
on what they've achieved through unity and confrontation in the civil rights
field. They know these same techniques are applicable to economic progress.
Their attitude to a union is, therefore, generally favorable." Swaity claimed,
however, that black militancy had also produced militancy among whites:
"The confrontations and civil rights progress of the black people has had an
impact on white textile workers. The entry of blacks into textile plants and the
manner in which blacks stand up for their rights, has made the docile textile
workers sit up and take notice." Thus, the workforce as a whole was "much

more prone to rebel against low wages and employer paternalism, which their parents took for granted."[81]

A similar situation was also reported at the large Cone Mills in Greensboro, North Carolina. Here, organizers claimed that in the late 1960s, defunct local unions had been revitalized by militant black workers. They also argued that black militancy had begun to radicalize whites: "Fear of the Negro encroaching on 'white jobs' is giving way to the acceptance on the part of white workers of the fact of Negro employment and the necessity of united effort; even a grudging admiration of the Negroes' sense of unity and the feeling that the Negro people 'got what they wanted by sticking together.'"[82] In many cases, white textile workers who were outspoken union advocates saw the civil rights movement as proof that grassroots activism could be successful in bringing about positive change. One militant white worker interviewed in 1974 in Carrboro, North Carolina, reported that she was "glad" when the civil rights movement came about. She felt that textile workers should begin asserting their rights and uniting in order to win improvements as blacks had done.[83]

While some white workers were inspired by the example provided by the civil rights movement, others drew more pragmatic lessons, reasoning that because blacks were more militant, whites could sit back and allow them to organize unions. In these cases, whites were willing to cooperate with blacks, but only on their own terms. Nick Builder, who worked as an organizer across the South in the 1970s, remembered that whites often let blacks take the lead in organizing unions because they realized that the blacks were more militant. White workers would often support a union once it was organized, but they wanted the black workers to take the risks of organizing it. He remembered one major union campaign at Wellman Industries in Johnsonville, South Carolina, where the TWUA won an election in the 1970s. Just before the election, Builder was anxious because so few white workers supported the union in a plant that was around 50 percent white. He was reassured, however, by one of the white union supporters who claimed that whites would vote for the union: "Hardy Godwyn was one of two or three white workers who was involved in supporting the union in Wellman Industries in Johnsonville, South Carolina, big plant. . . . And I asked Hardy one time, you know, what kind of kept him coming to meetings, and I also asked him what, you know, where he thought the heads of white workers were. And he said not to worry about white workers, that when the meal was served they'd be there ready with their knifes and forks, but they wanted the blacks to go in the kitchen and cook the meal. And I used that analogy so many, many times because it is true."

Builder remembered several campaigns in which white workers supported the union once it was organized because of the workplace protection it offered, but they wanted blacks to organize or "cook" it for them.[84] After the union was organized, moreover, whites tended to take up the prominent leadership positions, which offered them extra prestige, power, and perks. Thus, whites wanted blacks to "lead in the sense of once again go into the kitchen and stand in the steam and peel the potatoes, but when it came to lead like cutting a ribbon or getting some honors or something, getting credit, the ceremonial aspects . . . they wanted that for themselves."[85]

It is clear that whites accepted black participation if it helped them to secure their own goals. Many union representatives remembered that it was common in the 1970s for local unions to have a white president and a black vice president. The white leadership often encouraged black leaders to run as a way of strengthening the union, especially if militant blacks could "go to bat" and win concessions from management.[86] Other examples of whites accepting black leadership also occurred, especially if it helped whites to secure economic gains.[87]

The victory that the TWUA won over J. P. Stevens in 1974 depended upon a similar unity of interests between black and white workers. The Stevens plants were about 40 percent black at the time of the election, and black support for the union was reported to be a decisive factor in the victory.[88] At the same time, however, it was clear that the campaign could not have been successful without a great deal of white support. African American organizers remembered that they were able to get many whites to vote for the union because of the economic benefits that it promised. The economic appeal of the union was particularly powerful at the time of the election because many white workers were upset by a company pension scandal in which workers who had paid into the scheme witnessed declining returns. The union capitalized on this issue by promising to negotiate a pension plan that would show an increase every year. As black organizer Bennett Taylor remembered, this kind of basic economic issue united black and white workers: "When you start talking facts like that, whether you're black or white, you know, people understand when you start taking my money." Once the union was organized, it was hard-hitting economic issues that continued to mobilize white support, especially at times of contract negotiations. As Taylor put it, "They know that anytime that you go to the table and negotiate a wage increase, we're increasing their pocketbooks as well as increasing ours, and that's the name of the game, that's why you work."[89]

Unity was thus possible where blacks and whites had common economic interests. Numerous examples show that black and white workers were able to unite effectively over economic workplace issues even when cooperation was not extended in other areas. Cooperation was especially notable when the survival of the contract was at stake.[90] The unity that the two races achieved over workplace issues could often be considerably greater than any that existed outside of the plant. Joe Gaines, who was president of a local union in Sylvester, Georgia, for many years, remembered that his local always struggled to get white support "because there was still that old southern, racist-type ethic that was going on, not only there in the shop but in the community as a whole. . . . They viewed it as a black union because of the leadership." This attitude was especially strong in the community, where black and white workers had little social contact. At one time, the Sylvester local only had two white members in a plant that was 40 percent white. When the future of the union was threatened at key points in contract negotiations, however, Gaines remembered that white workers expressed their support and willingness to strike with blacks: "If you get to the point, and we've got to this point a couple of times when we were going into contract negotiations or a controversial issue about insurance or something like that, then they would unite, but of course there had to be something that they were going to get out of it . . . and as soon as that was accomplished, it's like back into their own world. They didn't really want to be a part of the organization."[91]

White workers thus revealed contradictory attitudes to uniting with blacks. They would often call the union a "black union" and refuse to join it, but they would support it at key times out of economic self-interest. In Sylvester, Georgia, Joe Gaines felt that this behavior could be explained by the fact that African Americans had a much more permanent need for a union: "My interpretation of the reason they did was because basically the whites got what they wanted, so they had no real interest in forming an organization to force the company to give them what they wanted. The company always treated them better than they did the blacks. . . . The only way that you could get some of that so-called catering if you were black was to have a strong organization to help force that type of thing."[92]

Those active in the textile labor movement remembered many examples of such an attitude among whites. Nick Builder recalled one campaign which illustrated clearly how workers could unite at work in ways that they would not do socially. In a plant in Cornelius, North Carolina, the TWUA was approached by three or four workers who identified themselves as Ku Klux Klan members. The workers wanted a union to be organized, and they promised a majority of white support. They were aware, however, that they themselves could not take any part in the campaign if it was to reach out to black workers: "They understood that for the union to be successful and get in, it was going to have to have black support, and . . . they understood that if they played a prominent role in it in any way it would not have black support, so they said, "We'll be with you but out of the picture.'" The union was eventually organized through this method, showing that it was possible for black and white workers to organize even when they held extreme racist views.[93]

At Fieldcrest-Cannon in Columbus, Georgia, black union activists claimed that the union had always managed to unite black workers and Klan members over workplace issues.[94] In one 1974 strike, white Fieldcrest workers even boasted, "We're going to win this strike because we have the black workers with us." The union's southern director, Scott Hoyman, remembered that many of these whites "were driving in from their homes in Alabama with Wallace stickers on their cars; but they joined blacks to support the union."[95]

Nick Atkins, who started working as an organizer for TWUA in 1965, recalled countless examples of white workers holding similar contradictory attitudes to unions: "You always have some Klan element in there, such a schizophrenia. The workers believe they can be a member of the union, particularly the whites who control the leadership, and at the same time be a part of the Klan—really screwy." Atkins added, "That schizophrenia is common. We had a guy who claimed to be a captain in the Klan and walked the picket-line with a guy that he selected himself . . . black guy, big, strong. This Klansman wouldn't walk the line with anybody except this guy. So how schizophrenic can you get? At one point he demonstrated to some of our people that he had Klan sheets under his bed, and all the Klan paraphernalia, and on the other hand he has this view about how you work in the union, you've got to stick together."[96]

Why Does Black Entry Not Lead to Lasting Unionization?

The introduction of large numbers of African Americans into production positions in the textile industry was accompanied by predictions that widespread unionization would follow. Textile companies themselves sought to restrict the hiring of blacks because they feared that they would be more prounion. Nevertheless, the integration of the industry failed to lead to a marked increase in unionization, and textile unions continued to hold a minority position in the industry. Indeed, the number of workers covered by TWUA contracts was around 25 percent less in 1976 than it had been in 1950. In 1976, less than 10 percent of southern textile workers were unionized.[97]

The failure of unionization in the 1960s and 1970s must be viewed in the context of the textile industry's historic resistance to organized labor. Throughout the twentieth century, the southern textile industry has resisted unionization, and the failure of repeated efforts to organize the industry has constituted a major defeat for organized labor. As historian Thomas Terrill has noted, "Organized labor's failure to unionize the southern textile industry was one of its most critical defeats."[98] The industry was very adept at fighting unions and possessed a large number of weapons to defeat organizing drives. Public policy in the South was historically supportive of employers' positions in labor disputes. The competitive economic structure of the textile industry hindered unionization efforts, as plant size was small and any union victories that were won were incremental. Economic fluctuations often meant that unions were unable to exert any pressure on companies during strikes. Above all, southern textile management was vehemently anti-union and cooperated closely in fighting unions. Managers were adept at putting pressure on workers by issuing anti-union propaganda on the eve of union elections. Their most potent threat was that the company would close the plant if the union were elected, a threat that was carried out at a Deering-Milliken plant in Darlington, South Carolina, in 1956. The Darlington closure was highly publicized in the South and clearly helped to prevent unionization.[99]

In the 1960s and 1970s, predictions of unionization were overly optimistic given textile management's proven track record of defeating unions. Indeed, the main reason that the entry of blacks into the industry did not lead to lasting unionization was that the racial composition of the workforce did not alter the economic balance of power in the industry. The entry of blacks into the workforce did not change the strongly anti-union environment of the American South. In fact, the strength and variety of employers' weapons made worker militancy largely irrelevant. In previous strikes, many white textile workers had shown great militancy but had still been defeated, often because chain companies hired strikebreakers or switched production to nonunion plants. At bottom, unions were simply not powerful enough to force recognition, especially given the pressure that employers could exert on union supporters during organizing campaigns.[100] Although black workers were often militant, the union was aware that this was not enough to produce lasting gains. As TWUA southern director Scott Hoyman put it, "The basic reason for the minority position of the union in the South is employer opposition and the ineffectiveness of the American labor acts. They are such that if an employer decides to delay or to stop union organization, they can do that no matter how good the people in the plant may be. . . . The labor law is the main problem—that's an issue more important than the composition of the workforce."[101]

This point was made by Hoyman in a detailed analysis of the union's position in the J. P. Stevens campaign. Writing to union president Sol Stetin shortly after the Roanoke Rapids election victory in 1974, Hoyman recognized that the struggle to gain a contract would be much more difficult than winning an election had been, because the union was at a disadvantage in a strike situation. Hoyman argued that the union had been able to win the Oneita Knitting Mills strike not simply because of black workers' militancy but because a strike was only effective against a small company like Oneita that could not switch production.[102] Against chain companies such as J. P. Stevens, the strike lost this power. Thus, even though black workers had been crucial to the Roanoke Rapids election victory, there was nothing they could now do to win recognition of the union: "The resources of J. P. Stevens and its size are much greater than those of TWUA. During the Oneita strike last year, we occasionally took comfort from the thought that here we had a fight with a company that was no bigger than we were. . . . The opposite is true with J. P. If there was an effective strike in Roanoke Rapids which could shut those plants down and keep them down, the impact of that loss of production which would represent about $\frac{1}{16}$ of their total work force would be roughly comparable to a drop in sales of only $\frac{1}{16}$ or 6% of their roughly one billion dollars in annual sales. So in effect, assuming a perfect strike, there would be 15 Stevens workers producing in other locations for each Roanoke Rapids striker in spite of a stoppage in Roanoke Rapids."[103]

Hoyman's advice was to avoid a strike at all costs and instead launch a boycott of J. P. Stevens products, which the union hoped would be more effective at putting pressure on the company to sign a contract. Without a strike weapon, the union was maneuvering from a position of weakness. As Hoyman recalled, the company even tried to goad him into calling a strike: "Stevens had kept saying, 'Why don't you strike, Mr. Hoyman?' We said, 'We don't want a strike.' . . . They had 35,000 people; they would have loved it if we had gone out on strike. Now in Oneita, that was a different thing. They had a plant in Alabama and a couple of little things up here, but we had the guts of the company."[104]

Most union leaders and organizers who were active in the South stressed that the introduction of blacks did not alter the union's lack of bargaining power in the textile industry. To them, organizing was still as difficult as before because of the ineffectiveness of federal labor laws. Nick Atkins, a southern organizer active since the 1960s, stressed the very difficult environment that unions operated in: "You know the expression in America, a level playing field? What is permissible to an employer in terms of propaganda is so broad that to compete with them, it's like it boils down to who's got the most money, who can hire the consultants. The consultants are experts—they can hold two-hour meetings—the level of propaganda . . . You're suddenly put in an environment where if you support the union you're the stupidist fucker on the face of the earth." The union was struggling "not because we're sitting on our hands and knees" but because "the job is so damn difficult, you have to be a virtual kamikaze to succeed."[105]

A second reason for the continued failure of textile unionization in the 1960s and 1970s was the fact that the black influx allowed textile employers to use the race issue against the union. Textile employers had historically played the race card as a way of defeating unions. In the 1940s and 1950s, white workers were told that unions favored integration, implying that a union victory would lead to whites being replaced by blacks.[106] The influx of black workers into the textile industry twenty years later allowed employers to exploit white workers' racial fears in order to divide white and black workers during unionization campaigns. Although racial propaganda had been used before, it clearly had more force once blacks had begun to work in production positions. Union sources placed considerable emphasis on employers' use of the race card. According to Bruce Raynor, the southern director of ACTWU, the union lost elections in the 1970s and 1980s because companies successfully used racial propaganda against it. Speaking in 1995, Raynor felt that "to this day every campaign we run the company makes race an issue, every single one. The company will tell the whites, 'The union's going to force us to give the good jobs to blacks.' . . . It's still a big weapon against us."[107] Raynor's observation is supported by accounts in the contemporary press that described how employers were using the race issue to defeat unions.[108]

Thus, in many ways the actual effect of integration was to make organizing harder, not easier. Unions had to struggle to unite black and white workers into a common organization in an industry that was able to utilize damaging racial propaganda against the union as well as its considerable experience in fighting unions. In many cases, the union was unsuccessful in overcoming racial division among workers. As Raynor admits, although the union has been successful in organizing some mills with a mixed workforce, "it's a lot easier in this day and age to organize a mill that's one or the other than it is the split ones."[109]

Written records show that racial division led to serious problems in organizing. Across the South, companies continued to try to divide workers by arguing that the union was a black union. Organizers wrote from a campaign to organize a J. P. Stevens plant in Goldsboro, North Carolina, for example, that "Co. spread rumors of black unionism."[110] Many black and white textile workers recalled that such propaganda was successful in dividing them. At Fieldcrest Mills in Columbus, Georgia, workers remembered the racial divisions that occurred when the union tried to organize in the 1970s. Ollie Seals, a black pro-union worker, remembered that the supporters of the union were predominantly black, with very few whites willing to join. White workers "would often speak their opinions. Sometimes they would say, 'Well, it's a black union, . . . I don't see nothing but black people in this department that is in the union.'"[111]

In the 1960s and 1970s, the most important organizing campaign carried out in the textile industry was directed against the large J. P. Stevens chain. The TWUA made a deliberate decision to concentrate its resources on Stevens, arguing that as the company was one of the largest, a victory would lead to unionization elsewhere. Beginning in 1963, and continuing throughout the 1960s and

1970s, the vast majority of the union's resources were directed at Stevens. Illustrating how much the union invested in the campaign, organizing director Paul Swaity wrote a colleague in 1974 that "I don't have to tell you how important a breakthrough in J. P. Stevens would be to all unions not only in North Carolina, but in the entire United States as well. Approximately half of all manufacturing workers in North Carolina are employed in the textile industry and only a very small percentage of these are organized. Giant textile chains like Burlington, J. P. Stevens and a host of others lead the conspiracy to keep the south non-union." In assessing how the entry of blacks affected organizing, a great deal of attention must therefore be given to the Stevens campaign.[112]

J. P. Stevens frequently sent a letter to workers on the eve of an election that specifically associated the union with black rights. This letter was used repeatedly, being modified slightly to meet the needs of the occasion. The letter illustrated well the way that companies appealed to white fears of black domination: "We would at this point like to say a special word to our black employees. It has come repeatedly to our attention that it is among you that the Union supporters are making their most intensive drive—that you are being insistently told that the Union is the wave of the future for you especially—and that by going into the Union in mass, you can dominate it and control it in this Plant, and in these Roanoke Rapids Plants, as you may see fit."[113]

Racial division contributed to the union's failure to organize J. P. Stevens. Although the TWUA won an election at the company's Roanoke Rapids plants in 1974, it failed to extend organization to any other Stevens mills, despite great organizing efforts. Reports written by ACTWU organizers showed that one of the key problems faced by the union was uniting black and white workers. It was this problem that prevented the union from extending the organizing gains it had made at J. P. Stevens's Roanoke Rapids plants to other mills in the chain. This was a significant failure because it left the Roanoke Rapids plants as an isolated beachhead of unionism in a fervently anti-union company. Union staff admitted that the racial cooperation they achieved at Roanoke Rapids was unusual. As a *Nation* correspondent put it in 1976, "Roanoke Rapids is a beachhead, not only of unionism but of racial co-operation among Southern working-class people. Organizers concede they had never before been able to keep the races together as they did in the seven plants there."[114]

In many Stevens campaigns, the union easily signed up black workers but found it difficult to find support among whites. At an abortive Stevens campaign in Pamplico, South Carolina, for example, organizers reported that the main problem was that "the plants are about 40% black but this is an all black campaign." The union had assigned an extra white organizer to the campaign "to try to build some white support," but the campaign was still a failure.[115] From a J. P. Stevens campaign in Wagram, North Carolina, organizer Vonnie

Hines described in 1978 how "we need white organizers in Wagram, our black participation is much greater than our white. My white contacts are working hard in the plant, but I can't seem to get them involved in our committee work like I know they should be."[116] When Hines worked on another campaign in Wallace, South Carolina, two years later, she described similar problems. The union campaign was faltering because the vast majority of supporters were black, while white workers refused to join: "We are still having trouble getting the whites involved. . . . Most of the 125 cards we have signed are from the black workers. We still have some departments that don't have a committee person."[117]

Organizers in a wide variety of Stevens campaigns described similar problems. In May 1980, organizer Robert Ross recommended against starting a campaign at a Stevens plant in Walterboro, South Carolina, because only black workers would support it: "After house calling about 25 new white employees I have been unable to get new committee members. . . . There is as usual a great deal of interest in organizing coming from the blacks. Unless some of the whites that I have house called during the past couple of weeks decided to help, I do not see any use in starting a campaign in Walterboro at this point. I feel that many of the whites here still see this as a black campaign."[118] Similarly, organizer Mel Tate described how a campaign at J. P. Stevens plants in Tifton and Milledgeville, Georgia, "stalemated" in January 1977 because of lack of white participation. In Milledgeville, as elsewhere, the problem was that blacks signed up en masse as soon as the union campaign started, alienating whites who immediately associated the union with black rights.[119]

Even in Roanoke Rapids, the records of the campaign show that it was difficult to unite black and white workers. Just a few months before the 1974 election, union meetings were being attended by an overwhelming majority of blacks but few whites. TWUA's Paul Swaity reported that "the spirit and morale of Stevens' workers prior to Sunday's meeting was not high, largely because many key workers, primarily the black workers, felt they had exhausted their potential in signing up additional workers. They were discouraged because the whites were not signing up or taking part." Swaity explained that the company had successfully "built antagonism between many black and white workers in the plant. The company discourages white participation in the campaign by pointing to the preponderant activities of the blacks, and stating that it will get a black union and blacks will be telling the whites what to do in the plant." Blacks made up around 45 percent of the workforce, yet they accounted for 80 percent of the union's strength.[120] Workers who were active in the Roanoke Rapids campaign remembered that racial divisions were very damaging. Black worker Jettie Purnell remembered that many white workers refused to support the union because they believed the company's propaganda that it was a pro-black institution: "That's the reason the whites resented the union, because they was told that union would elevate black above them, and they believed that."[121]

Another way that employers played the race card was revealed in a 1994 ACTWU publication, "Ball and Chain for African-American Workers?: An ACTWU Report on B & C Associates," in which the union claimed that companies negated its appeal among black workers by employing a black public relations firm during organizing campaigns. The firm, B & C Associates, was started in High Point, North Carolina, in 1960, making it, as it described itself, "one of the oldest and most respected public relations firms in the nation." Set up by Robert J. Brown, the son of a textile mill worker, by 1994 the firm was a major public relations consultant whose clients included several Fortune 500 companies. B & C had also been retained by Woolworth's at the height of the 1960 sit-in for advice on how to overcome its negative image in the black community.[122]

One of B & C's central techniques was to use the power of the civil rights movement's legacy as a way of breaking union solidarity among African Americans. Indeed, ACTWU called the firm's tactics "union-busting with a civil rights twist."[123] In a union campaign against Cannon Mills in 1974, B & C utilized two black ministers with ties to the 1960s movement to stage a rally for management just before the election.[124] In other campaigns, B & C agents claimed that they had worked with Martin Luther King Jr. and were members of the Southern Christian Leadership Conference. They then proceeded to disseminate anti-union material with a civil rights flavor. In several campaigns, for example, black workers were told that "Dr. Martin Luther King Jr. Died in Memphis, Tennessee While Helping Workers Form A Union." B & C also used songs of the civil rights movement but changed the words to give them an anti-union meaning. As many of the civil rights songs had their origins in well-known spirituals, song leaders often localized them by adding lyric lines appropriate to their particular situation. B & C thus changed the traditional civil rights song "Ain' Gonna Let Nobody Turn Me 'Round," which was used during the 1962 demonstrations in Albany, Georgia, giving it a new, anti-union meaning.[125]

Original Civil Rights Version	*B & C Version*
Ain' gonna let nobody turn me 'round,	Ain't gonna let no union turn me 'round,
turn me 'round, turn me 'round.	turn me 'round, turn me 'round.
Ain' gonna let nobody turn me 'round.	Ain't gonna let no union turn me 'round.

I'm gonna keep on a-walking,   I'm gonna keep on a-working,
  keep on a-talking,   keep on a-fighting,
  marching up to freedom land.   kicking the union down the drain.

In its 1994 report, ACTWU claimed that B & C had effectively thwarted the union in many campaigns in the South. It had been successful because it had persuaded black community leaders to speak out against the union, and because it had frequently used the threat of plant closings at a time when textile plants were shutting down as a result of foreign imports and mergers. The fact that the firm's agents were all African American also had an impact. As one union official commented, "When you put black on black, a black consultant against a group of black workers, they will have some credibility, just as a black union organizer has an impact with a group of black workers."[126] The 1974 Cannon Mills election, in which B & C was very active, was lost by a vote of 5,982 to 3,530, and union leaders blamed last-minute black defections for the severity of their defeat.[127] One textile executive admitted that B & C had been effective in keeping a union out of his company's plant: "We consider that we are buying protection. [Brown] can communicate with Negro employees and keep them quiet and keep trouble from generating with that group. . . . We just give him a payoff to keep down trouble."[128]

Union organizers and officials also claimed that companies used the race issue against them through the use of black supervisors. When companies began to promote blacks into supervisory positions in the 1970s, they were denied the same authority as white supervisors and tended to be used to discipline black workers. It was rare for a black supervisor to be placed over large numbers of white workers.[129] Union representatives who worked in the South claimed that companies became very effective at controlling or firing militant black workers by appointing African American supervisors. As ACTWU organizer and business agent Nick Builder recalled, companies promoted black supervisors because of "the feeling that African American supervisors were going to be much more successful at controlling or influencing African American workers and the whole fear about African American workers being more militant or more rebellious, or more open to unions." Builder remembered that when white supervisors fired militant black workers, the union often won the arbitration case, but that this was not true when black supervisors did the firing. Militant black workers could thus be more easily removed when black supervisors did the firing.[130]

Builder also remembered that he had witnessed the disillusioning effect that the appointment of black supervisors had upon militant black workers. Black workers had "always been fighting a power structure that was pretty redneck," so when the first black supervisors were promoted, workers felt that it was really "going to make a difference." Builder even remembered cases of black workers who went on strike when obvious black candidates were passed over for supervisory jobs. These workers had hoped to receive better treatment from black supervisors who would have more understanding of what it was like to be a black worker. In fact, the opposite was often true. In order to keep their jobs, black supervisors usually had to treat black workers worse.[131]

The promotion of black supervisors was especially damaging for unions because those promoted were often workers who would have made successful union leaders. Even in the 1940s, when the textile workforce was all white, companies had fought unions effectively by promoting promising union leaders into supervisors. In the 1960s and 1970s, textile companies used the same technique to negate the militancy of promising black activists.[132] TWUA organizer Clyde Bush explained in 1980 how the organizing climate had altered since black entry in the 1960s: "You can't take anything for granted anymore. Back in the late 1960s, whenever you went into one plant the first thing looked to was how many blacks are there working in here. And if there were forty blacks you could count on forty votes. Today, you can't count on that. Management some way has got to them. They're going in and hiring the best-liked, the best black they have in the plant, and they're making a damned supervisor out of him."[133]

Textile union officials also claimed that companies used racial hiring as a way of overcoming pro-union support among black workers. Organizers complained that when a company was subject to an organizing campaign, it hired white nonunion workers, often using contacts in the white community to build up "loyal" support in the plant. Organizers claimed that this technique had helped to defeat the union in several campaigns in the 1970s and 1980s. Interviewed in 1995, UNITE! southern director Bruce Raynor felt that racial hiring was "still a problem." He added, "It's always been a problem. Racial hiring went on all through the '70s and '80s, and even today when a company is fighting us, their hiring pattern will be to hire whites. . . . You know the blacks are much more union-minded, so they'll hire overwhelmingly whites when they're fighting us." UNITE! organizer Joe Gaines thought that racial hiring was one of the employers' "most effective weapons. . . . In certain areas it's a big problem."[134]

In recent years, an "emerging revision" among labor historians has begun to explore the relationship between black workers and organized labor. This scholarship has concentrated either on the racial policies of organized labor in the early twentieth century or on the role that African American workers played in the labor upsurge of the 1930s and 1940s, especially in CIO unions.[135] Two views have emerged from existing scholarship. While many new labor historians have stressed the ability of certain unions to be "thoroughly integrated," critics, led by Herbert Hill, have portrayed unions as little more than white job trusts aimed at shielding their members against competition from black labor.[136] The present study, while recognizing the strength of working-class racism, shows that this racism did not necessarily doom biracial unionism. Workers could be racist and still recognize the need to cooperate in the workplace. The failure of organization was ultimately caused by the overwhelming power held by employers, who possessed so many weapons that the racial composition of the workforce became largely irrelevant.

The influx of African Americans into production jobs in the textile industry brought with it high hopes that unionization would occur. In fact, however, unions found it difficult to turn the militancy of blacks into lasting organizational gains. Overall, organizers felt that the integration of the industry was both a help and a hindrance. Black workers were clearly militant, and many had been affected by the civil rights movement. Many whites were also radicalized by black entry into the industry and were often happy to provide support for, or tolerate, black efforts to organize. At the same time, however, the black influx also helped companies by providing them with a new, divisive issue that could wreck organizing campaigns. TWUA organizer Nick Atkins, who had worked in the South continuously since 1965, summed up the complex impact that black entry had for union organizers: "If we get a call from a plant and they say there is interest, I have to go on what we call a probe, and generally I would contact black workers first. Almost universally that's where I would start. I would get a much more sympathetic hearing." At the same time, Atkins felt that employers had hired blacks in just enough numbers to effectively divide workers. Thus, integration also favored companies because "they drew advantages in the sense that they had a natural division that was introduced into the mill. It benefited them; they knew what effect it would have upon organizing. They're still playing blacks against whites."[137]

epilogue

In November 1969, Robert Gardiner, the personnel manager of Dan River Mills, reacted with astonishment to a newspaper article in which a textile executive claimed that blacks had proved themselves to be good textile workers. Illustrating the wide gap between what the industry said about black employment publicly and privately, Gardiner wrote to a colleague, "When I read Howell's comment quoted above, I was curious because, from all I have heard, the Negroes we are employing are shiftless, lazy, don't want to work and leave as fast as they are hired." Dan River's white workers and management shared the attitudes prevalent across the South that blacks "lay down on the job," suffered from higher rates of absenteeism, and were generally lazy. Indeed, it was common for line managers to report these views based on their own observations of black and white performance.

Determined to find out the truth, Gardiner and his colleagues undertook a detailed analysis of Dan River data, comparing the performance of black and white workers in the same jobs. The results showed conclusively that blacks had lower turnover and absenteeism rates than whites, and slightly higher productivity. During the first nine months of 1969, the company hired 2,579 white workers and 1,971 black workers. In this period of labor shortage, both groups had high turnover, but white turnover was considerably higher than that of blacks, refuting the prevailing view that blacks did not stick to textile jobs as well as whites. The data showed that 79.4 percent of whites quit, compared to

69 percent of blacks. A comparison of absenteeism between black and white workers in the same jobs also disproved the widely held view that blacks had trouble maintaining the discipline necessary to perform an industrial job. For the year 1969, a comparison of "extensive samples" showed that the absenteeism rate for white workers was 7.8 percent, compared to 6.3 percent for African American workers. Detailed comparisons of productivity between black and white workers showed that there was "no discernible difference in performance" between the races, although in a number of job classifications black workers scored marginally higher than their white counterparts. These figures showed conclusively that blacks had adapted well to "white" production jobs such as spinning, doffing, and weaving.[1]

Despite the overwhelming proof of black ability, Dan River's managers found it hard to believe what their own statistics told them. The company reacted with bewilderment and disbelief to the notion that black workers were better performers than white workers. As Dan River's Ray Gourley remarked about the data showing that blacks had a higher educational level than whites, "As far as I can tell, these are valid facts. You can draw your own conclusions." Reacting to the absenteeism figures, meanwhile, Robert Gardiner wrote, "The above figures would seem to prove that Negroes, at least on better jobs, are more reliable than white employees." Similarly, the figures on turnover "appeared" to show that "we actually lost less of the colored than we did the white." Gardiner ended by predicting that these figures meant that blacks would continue to enter the southern textile industry in increasing numbers: "The one thing this does indicate is that, if the trend continues, the mill is going to get darker and darker."[2]

This episode illuminated many of the themes that characterized the racial integration of the southern textile industry in the 1960s and 1970s. Above all, African Americans adapted well to running textile jobs, and the racial integration of the southern textile industry was successful. For the black workers who were hired into the industry, textiles represented a major improvement, and they worked hard to hold on to their new jobs. Across the South, companies found that blacks made good textile workers, and they struggled to change deep-seated prejudices about black work habits. Many African American textile workers who were hired in the 1960s and 1970s felt that companies "learnt a lot" about the true work performance of blacks in these years. The way that Dan River executives struggled to accept black competence was typical of textile integration in these years.[3]

As the first book-length account of the racial integration of the southern textile industry, this study has covered new ground in a number of areas. It found that many companies had widespread fears about hiring a greater proportion of black workers. Like Dan River executives, many mill managers were fearful that hiring blacks would cause a loss of efficiency, lead to unionization, and cause whites to leave, so that the industry would end up with the executive's nightmare of a predominantly black workforce. It also examined in detail the racial discrimination that remained in the mills after integration. The amount of discrimination that prevailed is important to recognize in order to have an accurate and complete picture of textile integration. The persistence of discrimination tempered the economic advance that blacks had originally hoped textile jobs would bring. Discrimination, indeed, was most acute in the confinement of African Americans to the lowest-paying jobs, resulting in large disparities in pay. This study also found that companies used black hiring as a way to increase workloads for blacks. Even if "white" jobs were relatively desirable when blacks were first placed in them, black workers felt that companies used that opportunity to increase workloads and make these jobs heavy and undesirable.[4]

The type of discrimination faced by black workers also varied greatly according to gender, with black women facing far more hiring discrimination than black men. Gender distinctions are crucial to understanding how the textile industry treated its workforce. While the main grievance of black men was their difficulty in securing promotions out of lower-paying textile jobs, black women suffered from unique problems securing even these low-paying positions. When they were hired, moreover, black women were treated more harshly than white women by the industry. Letters written by black women workers showed that their experience of integration was unique and that they had completely different grievances than black men. Black women rarely complained about promotions but rather about heavy workloads and favoritism practiced by supervisors toward white women. Summarizing the unique problems that still faced black women in the industry, UNITE! director Bruce Raynor declared in 1995, "There's still racial discrimination in the industry on a day by day basis. . . . There still is more difficulty getting black women than white women in the mills, things like that. There's a lack of respect shown the black women that's not shown the white women. Black women are still the bottom of the ladder in the eyes of southern mill management."[5]

It was not just companies who resisted black entry into textiles. Records show that there was considerable resistance from white workers to the hiring of blacks. Extensive interviews with black pioneers reveal a history of resentment and resistance to black participation in the workforce from white workers and supervisors. This resistance ensured that pioneer black workers often had to show considerable bravery to succeed. The situation in the textile industry invites comparison with school integration, where the first black children who attended all-white schools faced resistance and often had to exhibit a great deal of courage to succeed.[6]

A central conclusion of this account is that the racial progress made by African Americans in the textile industry between 1960 and 1980 would not have been possible without the Civil Rights Act. This finding refutes existing studies that have argued that the labor market would have forced integration regardless of the Civil Rights Act.[7] It challenges recent studies that have emphasized the federal government's ineffectiveness in the civil rights era as well as the current pessimistic climate about the inefficacy of central government activity.[8] Most companies only began to hire blacks in large numbers after the act was passed. Besides pressuring companies to hire blacks, the Civil Rights Act also gave many companies an excuse to integrate because they could appease their white workers by saying that the law was forcing them to hire blacks. The act also produced a new sense of confidence among African American workers across the Piedmont. These workers were encouraged by the act's passage to challenge discrimination for the first time. Their efforts to end discrimination led to class action lawsuits that were themselves made possible by Title VII of the Civil Rights Act. These lawsuits forced the company involved to improve its racial record and made other companies do the same for fear of becoming involved in costly litigation. The extensive Title VII litigation carried out in the textile industry, with most major companies being sued at least once in these years, was a central reason for the progress in black hiring that was made by the industry.

Thus, rather than symbolizing the end of the civil rights movement, the Civil Rights Act stimulated protest across the South. The story of the civil rights movement did not end with the enactment of federal laws; in some ways that was just the beginning of a new phase of protest and organization. Few existing studies have examined the lasting impact of civil rights initiatives, especially into the 1970s. Historians have tended to concentrate on the movement's main protests between 1954 and 1968. If studies have been carried out outside this framework, the trend has been to go back in time rather than forward, searching for the origins of the civil rights movement. Many historians, for example, have traced the origins of the civil rights movement back to World War II and even the Great Depression.[9] This study shifts attention to the consequences of the era's civil rights legislation and shows that the Civil Rights Act had a significant impact on textile workers across the South. It affected their lives in many communities that did not experience an organized civil rights movement. Indeed, while the major protests were confined to a small number of communities, the impact of the law was felt in textile communities throughout the South.

Lawsuits brought under Title VII of the act occurred throughout the 1960s and the 1970s in towns across the South, many of them located outside of the conventional pale of the "civil rights movement." This study found that the

NAACP and local civil rights groups often played a central role in bringing these cases to court, demonstrating that there was considerable civil rights activity in many textile communities that did not have a reputation for it, and that this activity continued well into the 1970s. The efforts of the AFSC and TEAM to integrate the southern textile industry were also explored in some detail, highlighting a chapter of civil rights activism that has previously gone largely unrecognized.

If there is one theme that emerges throughout this story, it is indeed the activism of black workers across the South. African American workers consistently played an active role in the integration of the textile industry, and it could never have integrated to the extent that it did without their determination and courage. Black workers expressed their activism in a variety of ways. Some, such as the Gladys Trawick in Andalusia, Alabama, or Corine Lytle Cannon in Kannapolis, North Carolina, played a key role by agreeing to be the first blacks hired, thereby accepting the responsibility for the future success of black employment at their plants. Others, like Leroy Ellison in Rock Hill, South Carolina, or Julious Adams in Danville, Virginia, took the lead in initiating important class action lawsuits against companies that were not complying with the Civil Rights Act. These lawsuits forced companies to improve their treatment of African American workers and accelerated the integration of the industry. Many black women, epitomized by Sallie Pearl Lewis in South Carolina and Shirley Lea in North Carolina, fought against the industry's reluctance to hire black women and initiated lawsuits that helped to open up the industry to black women. Some black workers, such as Bennett Taylor and James Boone in Roanoke Rapids, North Carolina, responded to discrimination by turning to the labor movement, aware that the seniority provisions of a union contract could prevent the favoritism and discrimination they witnessed around them.

All of these workers exhibited bravery and determination. Indeed, many black pioneers were subjected to racial abuse and threats. Those who led the efforts of black workers in lawsuits, such as Julious Adams, were often fired or harassed on their jobs. Union supporters also risked losing their jobs or being blackballed if they took a prominent role in organizing efforts. Despite this, many African American workers were determined to eliminate discrimination and secure a better deal for African Americans in the textile industry. Sammy Alston, a worker at J. P. Stevens in Roanoke Rapids, North Carolina, who played a leading role in both the *Sledge* case and the union's efforts, summed up the mood of many others in explaining his activism: "It couldn't have gotten no worser, because we were right down at the bottom anyway. . . . I don't think we had nothing to lose, because the only thing he could do was fired you, that's all, and you couldn't have went no lower because you was working at the last level right there, and they constantly come and hired people over the top of you, come in there and create jobs for people."[10]

With hindsight, it is clear that at the very time when blacks began to enter textiles in large numbers, the industry began a serious decline from which it has yet to recover. Since 1980, dozens of mills have closed and the apparel and textile industries have lost half a million jobs. This economic decline makes the black struggle to enter the southern textile industry bitterly ironic. In the 1960s, civil rights leaders concentrated particular attention on the textile industry because they anticipated that it would continue to dominate the southern economy for many years to come. The president of the NAACP in North Carolina, Kelly Alexander, for example, declared in 1967 that it was important to increase black opportunity in the textile industry because "the textile industry will continue for a long, long time. . . . It will be here for a long, long time and it will be a major industry."[11] In fact, no sooner had black activism helped to secure a foothold in the industry than jobs began to be eliminated on a widespread basis. Problems became especially acute in 1993 when the North American Free Trade Agreement provided for the gradual elimination of tariff and quota protections.[12]

In many ways, this decline has hit blacks particularly hard. As in other industries, deindustrialization has had a disproportionate impact upon blacks. Many of the textile plants that have closed are located in rural, heavily black areas where they constituted the only source of manufacturing employment. The closure of such plants had catastrophic consequences for blacks who depended on them, exacerbating rural black poverty. A good case in point was Oneita Knitting Mills in Andrews, South Carolina, which closed its main sewing operations in 1996. African American women had fought long and hard to get hired at Oneita, and many supported families from the wages they made sewing underwear and T-shirts. The large-scale layoff hit Andrews hard and has left many African Americans pondering leaving South Carolina to get work, the only option available before Oneita opened its doors to blacks in the 1960s.[13]

Even for those who continue to work in the industry, the outlook appears bleak. Economists predict that if the southern textile industry does recover, it will need to utilize increasingly sophisticated technology that will offer fewer opportunities for employment to unskilled, poorly educated workers. In many ways, the ironies of black entry into textiles are mirrored in other southern industries. As Robert Norrell has written of black advancement in the steel industry in Birmingham, "Most of the jobs to which they [black workers] had just gained access now disappeared."[14] In many American industries, mechanization and automation have had a disproportionate effect on African American workers, who were concentrated in the labor-intensive jobs that have been progressively eliminated.[15]

Despite plant closings, the outlook for black workers is not entirely negative. In the 1980s and 1990s, the textile industry continued to offer opportunities to black workers, especially as many plants became predominantly black. Both black and white workers felt that the industry had gone full circle and would soon become all-black in production jobs. In some mills, this had already occurred by the mid-1990s. Often the workforce had changed from all white to predominantly black within the working life of particular workers. Louise Peddaway was the first black worker hired at the Dixie Yarn Company in Tarboro, North Carolina, in 1964. Interviewed in 1995, Peddaway summed up how the plant had changed during the thirty years that she had worked there: "It's an overturn, it's a total overturn, because when I went in there, there was nothing but white. Now you walk in Dixie Yarn you don't hardly see a thing but black. There are very few whites that's out there working on the machines."[16]

Like many black workers, Peddaway had mixed feelings about the integration of the mill. Textile jobs were a "great improvement" and had allowed many African Americans to leave the farm or jobs as domestics. At the same time, Peddaway was frustrated by the fact that the upper echelons of the industry remained white. For many black workers, integration carried with it feelings of exploitation and frustration that blacks were hired for the harder production jobs but were still refused skilled jobs and management positions. Blacks described an industry where the production jobs were increasingly becoming "black work," leaving whites to work in other industries or in the best jobs in the textile industry. As Peddaway put it, "It's turned all around, yet still the opportunity for us is not that great. Even if I was on a job making spinning, I would not expect them to give me a supervisor's job. . . . Sometimes you look at it and it's like they're trying to get back to slaving you back again, even though you're not slaves."[17] Many black textile workers envisioned a future of all-black production jobs with white supervisors and management. As Nellie Tarver, a worker at Fieldcrest-Cannon in Columbus, Georgia, put it, "I think overall the black and white people are working more together now than we did back then, but also I would have to say that most of the white people are getting out of the mills. They're going on to easier jobs like the banks. . . . They're still leaving, and I feel before the end of time that the mills are going to be all, all, predominantly black except for white supervisors. I think that's the way we're heading now."[18]

notes

Abbreviations

ACTWU-NCJB Papers   Amalgamated Clothing and Textile Workers' Union—North Carolina Joint Board Papers, Southern Labor Archives, Georgia State University, Atlanta

ACTWU-SRO Papers   Amalgamated Clothing and Textile Workers' Union—Southern Regional Office Papers, Southern Labor Archives, Georgia State University, Atlanta

AFL-CIO Papers   AFL-CIO Southern Area Civil Rights Department Papers, Southern Labor Archives, Georgia State University, Atlanta

AFSC Papers   American Friends Service Committee Papers, American Friends Service Committee, Philadelphia, Pa.

Alexander Papers   Kelly Alexander Papers, University of North Carolina at Charlotte

Andrews Papers   Mildred Gwin Andrews Papers, Southern Historical Collection, University of North Carolina at Chapel Hill

Cannon Papers   Cannon Mills Papers, Perkins Library, Duke University, Durham, N.C.

Dorn Papers   William Jennings Bryan Dorn Papers, Modern Political Collections, University of South Carolina, Columbia, S.C.

DRMC Papers   Dan River Mills Company Papers, Dan River Mills, Danville, Va.

Ervin Papers   Samuel Ervin Papers, Southern Historical Collection, University of North Carolina at Chapel Hill

LBJ Papers   Civil Rights during the Johnson Administration Papers (material microfilmed from the Lyndon Baines Johnson Library, Austin, Tex.), Cambridge University Library

Pope Papers	Laura Ann Pope Papers (private collection of Laura Ann Pope), Andrews, S.C.
SNCC Papers	Student Non-Violent Co-Ordinating Committee Papers, Martin Luther King, Jr., Center for Non-Violent Social Change, Atlanta, Ga.
SOHP	Southern Oral History Project, Southern Historical Collection, University of North Carolina at Chapel Hill
SRC Papers	Southern Regional Council Papers (microfilm), National Archives, Manuscripts Division, Washington, D.C.
Thurmond Papers	Strom Thurmond Papers, Strom Thurmond Institute, Clemson University, Clemson, S.C.
TWUA Papers	Textile Workers Union of America Papers, State Historical Society of Wisconsin, Madison
Uprising Papers	Uprising of '34 Papers (tapes and records accompanying *The Uprising of '34*, a documentary film about the 1934 general textile strike), Southern Labor Archives, Georgia State University, Atlanta
Via Papers	Emory Via Papers, Southern Labor Archives, Georgia State University, Atlanta
Wharton Papers	Wharton School's Industrial Research Unit Papers, University Archives and Records Center, University of Pennsylvania, Philadelphia

Note on court cases: Repositories are not provided in individual citations of court cases. Records of *Adams et al. v. Dan River Mills* are at the Federal Records Center, Philadelphia, Pa., and records of *Sledge et al. v. J. P. Stevens* are at the U.S. District Court, Eastern District of North Carolina, Raleigh. Records of all other cases, unless otherwise indicated, are found at the Federal Records Center, East Point, Ga.

Introduction

1. The historiographical emphasis on protest is brought out well in Norrell, "One Thing We Did Right." As Norrell writes, "The literature of the civil rights movement so far has dwelled primarily on the protest efforts" (p. 65). The neglect of economic aspects of the movement has been highlighted by Wright, "Economic Consequences." Two recent studies that have explored the links between organized labor and the civil rights movement are Honey, *Southern Labor and Black Civil Rights*, and Draper, *Conflict of Interests*.

2. Lyndon Baines Johnson to Franklin D. Roosevelt Jr., January 6, 1966, Part 1, Reel 8, LBJ Papers; Hubert H. Humphrey, address of August 19, 1965, in "Report of the White House Conference on Employment Opportunity," ibid.

3. King quoted in Charles J. Levy, "Scripto on Strike: The Race-Wage Picket Line," *Nation*, January 11, 1965, pp. 31–32, quote on p. 32.

4. Stokely Carmichael summarized this approach when he declared: "If a black man is elected tax assessor, he can collect and channel funds for the building of better roads and schools serving black people—thus advancing the move from political power into the economic arena." Carmichael quoted in Goldfield, *Black, White, and Southern*, p. 206. King quote is drawn from Martin Luther King Jr., "Freedom's Crisis: The Last Steep Ascent," *Nation*, March 14, 1966, pp. 288–92, quote on p. 288.

5. Goldfield, *Black, White, and Southern*, pp. 168–69, 202.

6. Gavin Wright, in an overview of civil rights historiography, has called for more re-

search into the black breakthrough into textiles in the 1960s. Wright, "Economic Consequences," pp. 178–79.

7. "Negro Employment in the Textile Industry," ATMI Press Release, April 1969, in Folder 39, Box 12, Wharton Papers; Defendant's Proposed Findings of Fact and Conclusions of Law, 1975, *Adams v. Dan River Mills*, p. 9; *Textile Hi-Lights*, December 1971, p. 3, and June 1978, p. 3; Frederickson, "Four Decades of Change," p. 62; Goldfield, *Black, White, and Southern*, p. 204.

8. Peter Byrne Baxter, "Across the Lake in Kannapolis," *Textile Industries*, January 1975, p. 47, copy in Folder 566, Andrews Papers; "Fact Sheet, Cannon Mills Company," November 1983, Folder 565, ibid.

9. "Unionization of the Textile Industry: A Case Study of J. P. Stevens," *Backgrounder* (Heritage Foundation Publication), August 3, 1977, p. 13, clipping in Folder 886, ibid.; Decision of Fourth Circuit Court in *Sledge v. J. P. Stevens*, October 4, 1978, in Box 2, ACTWU-SRO Papers, p. 61.

10. The complete exclusion of blacks from production jobs in textiles marked the industry out to black leaders as unique in the intensity of its racism. See, for example, the transcript of the EEOC Public Forum on Employment Patterns in the Textile Industry, Charlotte, North Carolina (hereafter cited as EEOC Textile Forum), January 12–13, 1967, Part 2, Reel 2, LBJ Papers, p. 26. Historians, too, have emphasized the industry's absolute exclusion of blacks from production positions before the 1960s. See, for example, Hall et al., *Like a Family*, p. 66.

11. Rowan, "The Negro in the Textile Industry," p. 115. Rowan also calls black entry into textiles "a virtual revolution in employment in the southern textile plants." Rowan quoted in Frederickson, "Four Decades of Change," p. 71.

12. Wright, "Economic Consequences," pp. 178–79.

13. Mary Frederickson describes how black workers called the mid-1960s "the change" and emphasizes the "innumerable changes" that have taken place in southern textile communities since the 1960s. Quotes are drawn from Frederickson, "Four Decades of Change," pp. 71, 74.

14. Gavin Wright mentions the change as part of a short article on the economic consequences of the civil rights movement. Wright, "Economic Consequences," pp. 178–79. Mary Frederickson's article, "Four Decades of Change," pp. 62–82, provides a good overview of the change. Richard Rowan's 1970 study, "The Negro in the Textile Industry," covers the change in more detail and contains a great deal of valuable data illustrating the entry of blacks into the industry, but it does not explore the experiences of black workers in the workforce, especially the important issue of how much discrimination remained in the industry. Conversely, the experiences of black workers in the industry are given excellent coverage in the oral history interviews in Byerly, *Hard Times*, esp. pp. 123–60, and Conway, *Rise Gonna Rise*, pp. 90–128.

15. "Discrimination Suit Settled by Cannon," *Daily News Record*, January 13, 1982, clipping in *Hicks v. Cannon Mills*.

16. The argument that integration was caused by a labor shortage is made by Richard Rowan. See Rowan, "The Negro in the Textile Industry," p. 135.

17. For an overview of this debate, see Halpern, "Organized Labor."

Chapter 1

1. Biographical details of Johnnie Archie drawn from Exhibit A-1, *Ellison v. Rock Hill Printing and Finishing Company*; Archie interview.

2. "Employment of Negroes in the Southern Textile Industry," TWUA Research Department Report, May 19, 1964, Box 316, TWUA Papers.

3. Rowan, "The Negro in the Textile Industry," p. 54; Dewey quoted in ibid., p. 66.

4. *Textile Hi-Lights*, December 1973, pp. 1, 3; ibid., April–June 1965, p. 4.

5. Glass, *The Textile Industry in North Carolina*, p. 100.

6. "Textile Earnings Reported Rising," *Greensboro Daily News*, February 25, 1964, p. A12, clipping in "Textile Industry Background Data" folder, Box 7, ACTWU-NCJB Papers.

7. "Fieldcrest Has Record Year," *Greensboro Daily News*, February 4, 1965, p. D10, clipping in ibid.

8. See, for example, "Burlington Sets Record," *Greensboro Daily News*, October 27, 1965, clipping in ibid.

9. *Textile Hi-Lights*, November 1966, p. 1.

10. "Textile Production in South Soars," *Greensboro Daily News*, April 17, 1963, clipping in "Textile Industry Background Data" folder, Box 7, ACTWU-NCJB Papers; Rowan, "The Negro in the Textile Industry," pp. 20, 22.

11. The states referred to are North Carolina, South Carolina, Georgia, Virginia, Florida, Tennessee, Alabama, and Mississippi.

12. Henry P. Leiferman, "Trouble in the South's First Industry: The Unions Are Coming," *New York Times Magazine*, August 5, 1973, p. 10.

13. In December 1966, North Carolina was 22.3 percent black and South Carolina 30.5 percent black. EEOC Press Release, December 14, 1966, copy in Box 316, TWUA Papers.

14. Ibid.; Phyllis A. Wallace and Maria P. Beckles, "1966 Employment Survey in the Textile Industry of the Carolinas," EEOC Research Report 1966-11, December 19, 1966, copy in ibid., p. 1.

15. Glass, *The Textile Industry in North Carolina*, pp. 96–101.

16. *Textile Hi-Lights*, April–June 1965, p. 4; November 1966, p. 2; March 1969, p. 3; September 1969, p. 3; December 1973, p. 3; June 1978, p. 3. Rowan, "The Negro in the Textile Industry," p. 22.

17. "Cannon Chief Tells What's Right About Textiles," *Charlotte Observer*, October 22, 1978, clipping in Folder 566, Andrews Papers; Glass, *The Textile Industry*, p. 106.

18. Rowan, "The Negro in the Textile Industry," pp. 13–14.

19. Ibid., p. 15. Unlike J. P. Stevens, Burlington had a tendency to settle cases immediately out of court, meaning that these cases did not generate the voluminous records of other cases.

20. Ibid., pp. 11–13, 24.

21. Ibid., pp. 7–11.

22. Hall et al., *Like a Family*, p. 66.

23. Ibid., p. 66.

24. Transcript of EEOC Textile Forum, January 12–13, 1967, Part 2, Reel 2, LBJ Papers, pp. 26, 32.

25. Theodore R. Suggs interview.

26. Alston interview.

27. Quarles interview.

28. Little interview.

29. Theodore R. Suggs interview.

30. Deposition of Durwood William Costner, September 19, 1972, *Ellison v. Rock Hill Printing and Finishing Company*, pp. 27–28; Boger interview; Complaint, n.d., *Ellison v. Rock Hill Printing and Finishing Company*, p. 6.

31. Carter interview.

32. Jackson interview.

33. Ibid.

34. Alston interview.

35. Adkins interview.

36. Purnell interview.

37. Robert Lee Gill interview.

38. Walter N. Rozelle, "The Mill and the Negro: Let's Tell It Like It Is," *Textile Industries* 132, no. 11 (November 1968): 70.

39. Mayes Behrman visit with Scott Hoyman, TWUA-CIO Organizer for Seven Cone Plants in North Carolina, September 20, 1955, "Merit Employment Program Visits to Businesses, Southeastern Regional Office 1955" folder, "Southeastern Regional Office 1947–56" box, AFSC Papers.

40. Ibid.; Mayes Behrman visit to Cone Mills, April 15, 1953, "Merit Employment Program Visit to Businesses, Southeastern Regional Office 1953–1954" folder, ibid.

41. Mayes Behrman visit with Scott Hoyman, TWUA-CIO Organizer for Seven Cone Plants in North Carolina, September 20, 1955, "Merit Employment Program Visits to Businesses Southeastern Regional Office 1955" folder, ibid.; Mayes Behrman visit to Cone Mills, April 15, 1953, "Merit Employment Program Visit to Businesses, Southeastern Regional Office 1953–1954" folder, ibid.

42. Mayes Behrman visit with Emanuel Boggs, September 12, 1955, "Merit Employment Program Visits with Community Leaders and Organizations, July–December 1955" folder, ibid.

43. Report on Merit Employment Program, January 1963, "Southern Program, High Point, Employment on Merit 1963" folder, "Community Relations Division 1963, Southern Program" box, ibid.

44. Noyes Collinson to Tartt Bell, October 9, 1962, "Southern Program—High Point—Atlanta—Employment on Merit" folder, "Community Relations 1962 Southern Program" box, ibid.

45. Noyes Collinson to Tartt Bell, October 25, 1962, ibid.

46. Employment on Merit, An Interim Report, "Atlanta Civil Rights Program, Employment on Merit Program Reports, Southeastern Regional Office 1966" folder, "Southeastern Regional Office 1966" box, ibid.

47. Mayes Behrman visit to Barnhardt Brothers, June 28, 1955, "Merit Employment Program Visits to Businesses, Southeastern Regional Office 1955" folder, "Southeastern Regional Office 1947–1956" box, ibid.

48. Mayes Behrman visit to United Mills, January 8, 1953, "Merit Employment Program Visit to Businesses, Southeastern Regional Office 1953–1954" folder, ibid.

49. Visit to Harris and Covington Hosiery Mills, November 6, 1958, and Visit to Randolph Mills, November 26, 1958, "Merit Employment Program Visits to Businesses, Southeastern Regional Office 1957–1958" folder, "Southeastern Regional Office 1957–1959" box, ibid. Like the AFSC, the Southern Regional Council found that textile management usually cited opposition from white workers as the main reason they could not hire blacks into production jobs. As the council reported in 1945, "Mill management is prone to say that it is impractical and undesirable to allow Negroes to come into the cotton mills to work, that the white workers would strike, and that there would be trouble." "A Statement on the Textile Labor Situation," n.d., Reel 67, SRC Papers.

50. Mayes Behrman to Thelma Babbitt, December 9, 1955, "Merit Employment Program Visits to Businesses, Southeastern Regional Office 1955" folder, "Southeastern Regional Office 1947–1956" box, AFSC Papers.

51. Visit to Cone Mills, June 4, 1958, "Merit Employment Program Visits to Businesses, Southeastern Regional Office 1957–1958" folder, "Southeastern Regional Office 1957–1959" box, ibid.

52. Visit to Tip Top Hosiery Mills, November 25, 1958, and Visit to Randolph Mills, November 26, 1958, ibid.

53. Visit to Randolph Mills, November 26, 1958, ibid.

54. Visit to Standard Hosiery Mills, November 10, 1958, ibid.

55. Visit to Cone Mills, June 4, 1958, ibid.

56. Visit to Jordan Spinning Company, November 26, 1958, ibid.

57. Transcript of the EEOC Textile Forum, January 12–13, 1967, Part 2, Reel 2, LBJ Papers, p. 34.

58. Mayes Behrman visit to United Mills, January 8, 1953, "Merit Employment Program Visit to Businesses, Southeastern Regional Office 1953–1954" folder, "Southeastern Regional Office 1947–1956" box, AFSC Papers.

59. Sarah Herbin to Jean Fairfax, June 26, 1962, "Southern Program: High Point, Employment on Merit, 1962" folder, "Community Relations 1962, Southern Program" box, ibid.

60. William Allison to Tartt Bell, April 14, 1964, "Southern Program Projects, Employment on Merit, High Point 1964" folder, "Civil Rights Department, Southern Program 1964" box, ibid.

61. William Allison to Tartt Bell, August 10, 1964, ibid.

62. Noyes Collinson to Tartt Bell, September 7, 1962, "Atlanta, Georgia Office, Employment on Merit Program Visits to Businesses 1962" folder, "Southeastern Regional Office 1960–62" box, ibid.

63. Mayes Behrman visit to Burlington Mills, December 15, 1955, "Merit Employment Program Visits to Businesses, Southeastern Regional Office 1955" folder, "Southeastern Regional Office 1947–1956" box, ibid.

64. Mayes Behrman visit to Blue Bell, Inc., October 7, 1954, "1954 Visits to Businesses" folder, ibid.

65. Mayes Behrman visit to Cone Mills, January 19, 1953, "Merit Employment Program Visit to Businesses, Southeastern Regional Office 1953–1954" folder, ibid.

66. "Summary of Visits Received in Philadelphia Office, June 1–June 29, 1956," "Job Opportunities—Summaries of Visits Made by National and Regional Office Staff 1956" folder, "American Section 1956 Community Relations" box, ibid.

67. Noyes Collinson to Tartt Bell, September 7, 1962, "Atlanta, Georgia Office, Employment on Merit Program Visits to Businesses 1962" folder, "Southeastern Regional Office 1960–62" box, ibid. *AFSC Employment News*, "Employment on Merit—High Point 1965" folder, "Civil Rights Department, Southern Program 1965" box, ibid.

68. Report of Merit Employment Program Southeastern Region—American Friends Service Committee, September 25, 1958, "Southern Program—High Point, Employment on Merit Reports 1958" folder, "American Section 1958 Southern Program" box, ibid.; 1956 Annual Report of Mayes Behrman, February 13, 1957, "Merit Employment Program General, Southeastern Regional Office 1957" folder, "Southeastern Regional Office 1957–1959" box, ibid.

69. Rowan, "The Negro in the Textile Industry," pp. 49–58; Carlton, *Mill and Town*, pp. 158–60; Hall et al., *Like a Family*, p. 66.

70. Visit to Tip Top Hosiery Mills, November 25, 1958, "Merit Employment Program Visits to Businesses, Southeastern Regional Office 1957–1958" folder, "Southeastern Regional Office 1957–1959" box, AFSC Papers; Mayes Behrman visit to United Mills, January 8, 1953, "Merit Employment Program Visit to Businesses, Southeastern Regional Office 1953–1954" folder, "Southeastern Regional Office 1947–1956" box, ibid.

71. Mayes Behrman visit to Cone Mills, January 19, 1953, ibid.

72. Mayes Behrman visit with Ross Groshong of the United Textile Workers–AFL, February 9, 1954, "Merit Employment Program: Visits with Community Leaders and Organizations, Southeastern Regional Office 1954" folder, "Southeastern Regional Office 1954–1956" box, ibid.

73. Mayes Behrman visit to Barnhardt Brothers, June 28, 1955, "Merit Employment Program Visits to Businesses, Southeastern Regional Office 1955" folder, "Southeastern Regional Office 1947–56" box, ibid.

74. Rufus M. Dalton to Mildred Andrews, March 24, 1978, Folder 1324, Andrews Papers; "Templon-Chemspun Expansion Will Mean 50–75 Jobs for Town," *Mooresville Tribune*, November 16, 1961, clipping in ibid.

75. Ginny and Buddy Tieger to Mrs. Sutherland, August 12, 1965; Joseph H. Tieger to E. Frank Outland, August 12, 1965; Elizabeth Sutherland, "Report on Discussion with L. V. Miles Co."; Virginia Tieger to Sidney M. Miller, September 2, 1965, all in Folder 5, Box 105, SNCC Papers.

76. Virginia Tieger to Sidney M. Miller, September 2, 1965; Ginny Tieger to Mrs. Sutherland, September 3, 1965; Ginny Tieger to Mrs. Sutherland, n.d., all in ibid.

77. Rowan, "The Negro in the Textile Industry," p. 54.

78. Harriet L. Herring to Guy B. Johnson, March 29, 1945, Reel 67, SRC Papers; Harriet L. Herring to Forrest Shuford, March 20, 1945, ibid.

79. W. M. Thomas to Dr. Ira De A. Reid, March 3, 1945; A. L. Thomas, "Report on Bibb Mill No. 1," n.d., both in ibid.

80. Aubrey Clyde Robinson to Charles S. Johnson and Howard W. Odum, April 13, 1945; "Negroes in the Textile Industry—Augusta, Georgia," report signed by H. H. Carter, R. C. Calhoun, M. J. Whitaker, both in ibid.

81. "Remarks on Textile Policies Affecting Negro Employment at Points in Alabama," n.d., ibid.

82. Aubrey Clyde Robinson to Charles S. Johnson and Howard W. Odum, April 13, 1945; Harriet L. Herring to Guy B. Johnson, March 29, 1945, both in ibid.

83. W. M. Thomas to Dr. Ira De A. Reid, March 3, 1945, ibid.

84. "Remarks on Textile Policies Affecting Negro Employment at Points in Alabama," n.d., ibid.

85. Noyes Collinson to Tartt Bell, October 25, 1962, "Southern Program—High Point—Atlanta—Employment on Merit" folder, "Community Relations 1962 Southern Program" box, AFSC Papers.

86. Visit to Tip Top Hosiery Mills, November 25, 1958, "Merit Employment Program Visits to Businesses, Southeastern Regional Office 1957–1958" folder, "Southeastern Regional Office 1957–1959" box, ibid.

87. Minchin, "'The Union Was Our Only Voice,'" pp. 6–7; Mayes Behrman plant visit to Dan River Mills, September 12, 1955, "Merit Employment Program Visits with Community Leaders and Organizations, July–December 1955" folder, "Southeastern Regional Office 1947–1956" box, AFSC Papers.

88. "Southern Mills Supplying U.S. Fear New Hiring Rules," *Daily News Record*, April 6, 1961, clipping in "Equal Employment Opportunity 1961" folder, Box 316, TWUA Papers.

89. "Conferences on the Textile Labor Situation," March 19–24, 1945, Reel 67, SRC Papers.

90. EEOC Press Release, December 28, 1966, copy in Box 316, TWUA Papers.

91. Nathan, *Jobs and Civil Rights*, pp. 13–16.

92. Chambers interview.

93. Transcript of EEOC Textile Forum, January 12–13, 1967, Part 2, Reel 2, LBJ Papers, pp. 43–44, 99–104.

94. Statement of Emory F. Via at the Textile Employment Forum, January 12–13, 1967, copy in "EEOC Textile Employment Forum, January 1967, Commission Proceedings" folder, Box 316, TWUA Papers; "EEOC Chief Shulman Is Seeking to Cut Thru Tolerance Platitudes," *Daily News Record*, January 9, 1967, clipping in "EEOC Textile Employment Forum, 1/67, General" folder, ibid.

95. "A Statement on the Textile Labor Situation," n.d., Reel 67, SRC Papers.

96. "8 House Negroes Write President," *New York Times*, April 4, 1969.

97. "Pentagon Weighs Textile Contract," *New York Times*, February 1, 1969.

98. "Dirksen Upbraids Rights Aide at Hearing," *New York Times*, March 28, 1969, p. 31.

99. Butler, Heckman, and Payner, "The Impact of the Economy," p. 240.

100. "The EEOC Probe," *America's Textile Reporter*, June 22, 1967, clipping in Box 316, TWUA Papers; Daniel Jordan to George Perkel, April 7, 1967, ibid.

101. "Information on Efforts to Reduce Racial Discrimination and Create Equality of Job Opportunity in the Southern Textile Industry," January 30, 1969, Reel 163, SRC Papers.

102. *America's Textile Reporter*, September 21, 1967, clipping in Box 316, TWUA Papers.

103. Statement of Senator Walter F. Mondale before the Subcommittee on Administrative Practice and Procedure of the Senate Judiciary Committee, March 27, 1969, Reel 163, SRC Papers.

104. Statement of Senator Edward M. Kennedy, Chairman, Subcommittee on Administrative Practice and Procedure of the Senate Judiciary Committee, March 29, 1969, ibid.

105. "Brief for Plaintiffs," n.d., *Lea v. Cone Mills*, pp. 1–2.

106. Peddaway interview.

107. Gaines interview; Davis interview.

108. Reese Cleghorn, "The Mill: A Giant Step for the Southern Negro," *New York Times Magazine*, November 9, 1969, p. 35; "The Textile Industry and Negroes in Western South Carolina," Reel 163, SRC Papers, p. 5; William Suggs interview.

109. Boone interview.

110. Broadnax interview.

111. Pharr interview.

112. Ibid.

113. "Textile Plants Hiring More Blacks," *Charlotte Observer*, August 17, 1969, p. 1, clipping in Folder 46, Box 13, Wharton Papers.

114. "Industry in South Woos Negro Labor," *New York Times*, May 19, 1969, p. 1.

115. "Textile Plants in the South Now Woo Negro Workers Seeking Better Jobs," *New York Times*, May 19, 1969, p. 42; Reese Cleghorn, "The Mill: A Giant Step for the Southern Negro," *New York Times*, November 9, 1969, p. 156.

116. Reese Cleghorn, "The Mill: A Giant Step for the Southern Negro," *New York Times Magazine*, November 9, 1969, pp. 34, 35, 142, 144, 145, 147, 156. Illustrating the break from long-standing hiring practices that the entry of African Americans represented, Cleghorn wrote that "until the early nineteen-fifties a visitor to Erwin would have seen very much the same kind of mill town that had been here from the start. But change has come steadily since then" (p. 34).

117. "Textile Plants in the South Now Woo Negro Workers Seeking Better Jobs," *New York Times*, May 19, 1969, p. 42.

118. "The New South: Negroes in the Textile Industry," *Daily News Record*, December 1, 1965, clipping in Box 652, TWUA Papers.

119. Transcript of *McNeil/Lehrer Program*, December 22, 1976, Box 51, ACTWU-SRO Papers; Rowan, "The Negro in the Textile Industry," p. 15.

120. "Crystal Lee: The Plight of the Real Norma Rae," *Atlanta Journal and Constitution Magazine*, June 10, 1979, p. 13.

121. Decision of Fourth Circuit Court, October 4, 1978, *Sledge v. J. P. Stevens*, p. 2; Complaint for Injunctive and Other Relief, October 2, 1970, ibid.

122. Plaintiffs' Proposed Findings of Fact and Conclusions of Law, June 11, 1980, *Lewis v. J. P. Stevens*, p. 1; "J. P. Stevens and Company, Inc. Textile Plants and Warehouses in the U.S.," TWUA Research Department Data, April 21, 1976, Box 22, ACTWU-SRO Papers.

123. Paul Swaity to Charles Buff, February 21, 1974, ibid.; Jonathan R. Harkavy to William Finger, April 28, 1977, Box 2, ibid.

124. Minchin, *What Do We Need a Union For?*, p. 135; Minchin, "'The Union Was Our Only Voice,'" pp. 6–7; Rowan, "The Negro in the Textile Industry," p. 15.

125. Complaint, October 24, 1969, *Adams v. Dan River Mills*, pp. 3–5; Frank Talbott to Robert T. Thompson, January 20, 1970, "Adams v. Dan River: Correspondence 1970 January–March" folder, DRMC Papers.

126. Brown, *A City without Cobwebs*, p. 259; Complaint, n.d., *Ellison v. Rock Hill Printing and Finishing Company*, pp. 3–6.

127. "J. P. Stevens and Its Record of Discrimination in Employment Practices," ACTWU Fact Sheet, Box 47, ACTWU-SRO Papers; Fourth Circuit Court Decision, *Sledge v. J. P. Stevens*, p. 14, copy in Box 2, ibid.

128. Cannon interview.

129. Ferguson interview.

130. Douglas, *Reading, Writing, and Race*, pp. 108–9; Ferguson interview.

131. Transcript of EEOC Textile Forum, January 12–13, 1967, Part 2, Reel 2, LBJ Papers, p. 94; Project Report for Year Ending September 1968, September 12, 1968, Reel 163, SRC Papers, p. 7.

132. 1966 Summary Sheet of Callaway data, Folder 70, Box 12; 1966 Summary Sheet of Deering-Milliken data, Folder 70, Box 12; Table A, Folder 11, Box 14, all in Wharton Papers.

133. Statement by Clifford L. Alexander Jr., Chairman, EEOC, before the Subcommittee on Administrative Practice and Procedure of the Senate Judiciary Committee, March 27, 1969, Reel 163, SRC Papers.

Chapter 2

1. Rowan, "The Negro in the Textile Industry," p. 135.

2. Mary Frederickson, for example, argues that "by 1969, the transition was over and management in most Southern textile communities feverishly sought to hire black workers, literally to keep the mills running." Like Rowan, she argues that the need for labor influenced companies to seek blacks. Frederickson, "Four Decades of Change," p. 73. Gavin Wright makes a similar conclusion to Frederickson, claiming that "by 1970 most firms were actively seeking black workers, often using black recruiters." Wright, "Economic Consequences," p. 178.

3. As historian Hugh Davis Graham has documented, the civil rights movement destroyed the basis of the Jim Crow system in a relatively short time: "By the end of the 1960s Jim Crow was dead. The black mobilization for civil rights was a revolutionary social movement that utterly destroyed the biracial caste system in the South." Graham, *The Civil Rights Era*, p. 452.

4. Northrup, "The Negro in the Tobacco Industry," p. 90.

5. Northrup, "The Negro in the Paper Industry," p. 129.

6. Northrup, "The Negro in the Automobile Industry," pp. 76–78; Northrup et al., *Negro Employment in Basic Industry*, pp. 721–23.

7. Minchin, *What Do We Need a Union For?*, pp. 48–68, 141–49; "Textile Plants Hiring More Blacks," *Charlotte Observer*, August 17, 1969, p. 1, clipping in Folder 46, Box 13, Wharton Papers; "Industry in South Woos Negro Labor," *New York Times*, May 19, 1969, p. 1; Butler, Heckman, and Payner, "The Impact of the Economy," pp. 328–30.

8. "The New South: Negroes in the Textile Industry," *Daily News Record*, December 1, 1965, clipping in Box 652, TWUA Papers.

9. "Staff Meeting in President Pollock's Office," December 21, 1966, Box 90, ibid.

10. Lincks interview.

11. Richard Rowan plant visit to Russell Mills, March 13, 1969, Folder 18, Box 13, Wharton Papers.

12. "Textile Plants in the South Now Woo Negro Workers Seeking Better Jobs," *New York Times*, May 19, 1969, p. 42.

13. H. S. Williams to William Pollock, January 2, 1962, Series 3, Box 316, TWUA Papers; "Employment of Negroes in the Southern Textile Industry," TWUA Report, May 19, 1964, ibid.

14. Report on Merit Employment Program, January 1963, "Southern Program, High Point, Employment on Merit 1963" folder, "Community Relations Division 1963, Southern Program" box, AFSC Papers.

15. Butler, Heckman, and Payner, "The Impact of the Economy," pp. 239–40, 328–29.

16. Jean Fairfax to Mordecai Johnson, August 7, 1967, Reel 163, SRC Papers, p. 16.

17. George L. Holland to Southerland Dyeing and Finishing Mills, April 13, 1966, Folder 479, Box 177, Ervin Papers.

18. Bloomsburg's Statement of Defenses in Response to Court's April 8, 1980, Order, June 17, 1980, *Lewis v. Bloomsburg Mills*, p. 14.

19. "Negroes Advancing Slowly into Better Southern Jobs," AFSC Employment News, "Employment on Merit—High Point 1965" folder, "Civil Rights Department, Southern Program 1965" box, AFSC Papers.

20. Plaintiffs' Proposed Findings of Fact and Conclusions of Law, February 18, 1975, *Sherrill v. J. P. Stevens*, p. 5.

21. Waldrep interview.

22. Deposition of Fred Cisson Jr., February 26, 1968, *United States v. Southern Weaving*, pp. 3, 78.

23. Summary of Southern TWUA Staff Survey, December 15, 1966, Series 3, Box 316, TWUA Papers.

24. Roxbury Southern Mills Questionnaire, Southern TWUA Staff Survey, December 15, 1966, ibid.

25. Chase Bag Company Questionnaire, Southern TWUA Staff Survey, December 15, 1966, ibid.

26. Boulware interview.

27. Phyllis A. Wallace and Maria P. Beckles, "1966 Employment Survey in the Textile Industry of the Carolinas," EEOC Research Report 1966–11, December 19, 1966, copy in Box 316, TWUA Papers, pp. 13–17.

28. "The Textile Industry and Negroes in Western South Carolina," Reel 163, SRC Papers, p. 4. There was also a sharp jump in black employment during World War I, although from a very small base. Between 1910 and 1920, black employment doubled from 1.3 percent to 2.6 percent. Rowan, "The Negro in the Textile Industry," p. 54.

29. "Plaintiffs' Post-Trial Findings of Fact and Conclusions of Law," filed as part of "Plaintiffs' Rule 52 and Rule 59 Motions that the Court Amend Its Findings, Make Additional Findings, and Alter or Amend the Judgement," January 7, 1973, *Lewis v. Bloomsburg Mills*, pp. 30–52.

30. Uniroyal plant visit, June 1969, Folder 18, Box 13, Wharton Papers.

31. Riegel Textile Corporation plant visit, n.d., ibid.

32. Bibb Mills plant visit, June 17, 1969, ibid.

33. Fulton Cotton Mills plant visit, June 3, 1969, ibid.

34. "Textiles: Blacks in the Mills," *Newsweek*, November 2, 1970, p. 50.

35. Plaintiffs' Proposed Findings of Fact and Conclusions of Law, September 16, 1974, *Adams v. Dan River Mills*, p. 5. Executive Order 11246 was issued in 1965 by President John-

son and strengthened the federal government's commitment to eliminating discrimination by federal contractors.

36. Hearing of February 24, 1976, *Sledge v. J. P. Stevens*, pp. 95–96.

37. *America's Textile Reporter*, September 21, 1967, clipping in Box 316, TWUA Papers; Project Report for Year Ending September 1968, September 12, 1968, Reel 163, SRC Papers, p. 9.

38. "The Mills Are Hiring More Negroes," *Winston-Salem Journal*, May 26, 1968, clipping in Folder 58, Box 13, Wharton Papers.

39. Walter N. Rozelle, "The Mill and the Negro: Let's Tell It Like It Is," *Textile Industries* 132, no. 11 (November 1968): 65, 70.

40. Lincks interview; "Textiles: Blacks in the Mills," *Newsweek*, November 2, 1970, pp. 50–51.

41. William C. Little to M. A. Cross, April 25, 1962, "Government Contracts—Correspondence 1961–1962" folder, DRMC Papers.

42. Ibid.

43. "Textiles: Blacks in the Mills," *Newsweek*, November 2, 1970, pp. 50–51. Dan River was also sent a copy of *The Mill Whistle*, the company newspaper of Fieldcrest Mills, a major southern textile company based in Eden, North Carolina. In the *Whistle*, Fieldcrest workers were told that integration was occurring because "it is the policy of the company to obey the law, whatever the laws are." *The Mill Whistle*, June 28, 1965, "Civil Rights Act—Fair Employment Practices (Correspondence) 1964–1966" folder, DRMC Papers.

44. File Memo—Hylton Hall Cafeteria, July 11, 1963, "Government Contracts—Compliance Survey—June 1963" folder, ibid.

45. Lincks interview.

46. Rozelle, "The Mill and the Negro," p. 65.

47. Chambers interview.

48. Trial testimony of Otto King, September 17, 1968, *Lea v. Cone Mills*, pp. 110, 121–24.

49. Quarterly Reports of J. P. Stevens, Plaintiff's Exhibit 133, *Sledge v. J. P. Stevens*.

50. "Negro and Labor Leaders Vent Wrath on Dixie Mills," *Greensboro Daily News*, January 13, 1967, p. 1, clipping in "EEOC Textile Employment 1/67 General" folder, Box 316, TWUA Papers.

51. Cannon interview.

52. Trawick interview.

53. Seals interview.

54. Pharr interview.

55. Collins interview. Similarly, Jettie Purnell, who worked at J. P. Stevens in Roanoke Rapids in the 1950s and 1960s, when asked whether integration would have occurred without the Civil Rights Act, responded, "No, no, no, no, never would have. . . . They wouldn't give up nothing if it hadn't been for the Civil Rights." Purnell interview.

56. Bush interview.

57. Glover interview.

58. Beck interview.

59. Smith interview; Dawson interview.

60. Deposition of Durwood William Costner, September 19, 1972, *Ellison v. Rock Hill Printing and Finishing Company*, pp. 62–65; Oscar Gill interview.

61. Archie interview.

62. Ibid.

63. Robert Lee Gill interview.

64. Archie interview.

65. Jesse Broadnax et al. to the EEOC, March 11, 1971, *Galloway v. Fieldcrest Mills*.

66. Moody interview.

67. Clayton interview.

68. Deposition of Bertha Louise Farrow, February 23, 1970, *Adams v. Dan River Mills*, pp. 28–32.

69. "Uphill Bias Fight," *Wall Street Journal*, April 12, 1967, clipping in Box 316, TWUA Papers.

70. In *Adams v. Dan River Mills*, for example, one of the first blacks to be hired at the company's Greenville, Alabama, plant testified that the company had started to hire more blacks, as one worker put it, "since you all or whoever it is started checking with them. Because when I first went there there wasn't but two there, that was me and the old fellow who retired." Deposition of John S. Crenshaw, February 25, 1970, *Adams v. Dan River Mills*, p. 34. In *Sherrill v. J. P. Stevens*, records showed that the mill was integrated shortly after the EEOC charges were filed. Plaintiffs' Proposed Findings of Fact and Conclusions of Law, February 18, 1975, *Sherrill v. J. P. Stevens*, p. 25.

71. Deposition of Leroy Ellison, August 17, 1972, *Ellison v. Rock Hill Printing and Finishing Company*, p. 18.

72. Brief for Plaintiffs, n.d., *Lea v. Cone Mills*, p. 39; United States Court of Appeals for the Fourth Circuit Decision, January 29, 1971, ibid., p. 4.

73. Trial transcript, July 10, 1975, *Lewis v. J. P. Stevens*, pp. 576–79.

74. As plaintiffs' attorney Richard T. Seymour described it, "The company's performance went way up in the year after the trial and way down when there was no decision." Thus, in the immediate year after the trial, the proportion of blacks hired rose to 60.9 percent, but in 1974 and 1975, when there was no decision from the court, the hiring rate fell to 35 percent and 38 percent respectively. Hearing of February 24, 1976, *Sledge v. J. P. Stevens*, pp. 92–93, 114.

75. Memorandum from Project Director to TEAM Aides, July 12, 1968, Reel 163, SRC Papers.

76. Plaintiffs' Reply Memorandum, February 13, 1975, *Adams v. Dan River Mills*, p. 3.

77. Hearing of July 8, 1971, *Lea v. Cone Mills*, pp. 9–11.

78. "Factory-Bias Fight," *Wall Street Journal*, January 5, 1967, clipping in "EEOC Textile Employment Forum 1/67 General" folder, Box 316, TWUA Papers.

79. Deposition of John H. Marshall, November 21, 1972, *Ellison v. Rock Hill Printing and Finishing Company*, pp. 81–82.

80. Brown interview; Pharr interview; Boger interview. Johnnie Archie, another plaintiff in the case, also felt that it had achieved a great deal: "There were skilled labor departments, mechanics, electricians; they kept you out of it, period, until this court decree was passed." Archie interview.

81. Deposition of Leroy Ellison, August 17, 1972, *Ellison v. Rock Hill Printing and Finishing Company*, p. 22.

82. "Outline of the Decree Entered by the United States District Court on June 25, 1976," in Box 2, ACTWU-SRO Papers; Taylor interview.

83. Alston interview.

84. "Discrimination Suit Settled by Cannon," *Daily News Record*, January 13, 1982; "Cannon Mills, Workers Happy with Settlement," *Greensboro Daily News*, January 13, 1982, p. B10; "Black Plaintiff: Conditions Are Better at Cannon," *Salisbury Post*, January 12, 1982, p. 1B; "Workers Pleased with Cannon Settlement," *Charlotte News*, January 13, 1982, p. 1, all clippings in *Hicks v. Cannon Mills*.

85. Transcript of Trial Testimony, June 6–7, 1973, *Adams v. Dan River Mills*, p. 246.

86. Ferguson interview; Chambers interview.

87. Jacob Little, a black worker hired at a mill in Columbus, Georgia, in 1966, felt that companies started to hire more blacks because "they became afraid of suits." Little interview.

88. Young interview.

89. Johnson interview.

90. Alston interview.

91. Crittenden interview.

92. Defendant's Discovery Deposition of Ray Tate, March 29, 1966, *Hall v. Werthan Bag,* pp. 40–41; Intervenor's Complaint, March 12, 1966, ibid.

93. Minutes of TEAM Meeting, August 16, 1968, Reel 163, SRC Papers, pp. 1–2.

94. Project Report for Year Ending September 1968, September 12, 1968, ibid., p. 31.

95. Long interview.

96. Young interview.

97. Fairclough, "State of the Art," pp. 395–96.

98. Ibid., pp. 387–90; Norrell, "One Thing We Did Right," p. 66. The work of implementing civil rights legislation has not been completely neglected. See especially Graham, *The Civil Rights Era.*

99. Many historians have traced the roots of the civil rights movement back to the New Deal and World War II. See especially Sitkoff, *A New Deal for Blacks,* and Korstad and Lichtenstein, "Opportunities Lost and Found." For an overview of this literature, see Fairclough, "State of the Art," pp. 387–90.

100. Norrell, "One Thing We Did Right," pp. 74–75; Woodward, "What Happened to the Civil Rights Movement," p. 167.

Chapter 3

1. Examples of this literature include Hall et al., *Like a Family*; Griffith, *The Crisis of American Labor*; Fink, *The Fulton Bag and Cotton Mills Strike*; Carlton, *Mill and Town in South Carolina*; Newby, *Plain Folk in the New South*; Hodges, *New Deal Labor Policy*; Flamming, *Creating the Modern South*; Minchin, *What Do We Need a Union For?*; and Salmond, *Gastonia 1929.* The best overview of this literature is Zieger, "Textile Workers and Historians," pp. 35–59.

2. As Jacquelyn Dowd Hall has noted, "The South's textile barons left few paper trails." Hall, "Private Eyes, Public Women," p. 244.

3. Frederickson, "Four Decades of Change," p. 73. Similarly, in his study Gavin Wright notes that "by 1970 most firms were actively seeking black workers, often using black recruiters." Wright, "Economic Consequences," p. 178.

4. Graham, *The Civil Rights Era,* pp. 456–58.

5. Walter N. Rozelle, "The Mill and the Negro: Let's Tell It Like It Is," *Textile Industries* 132, no. 11 (November 1968): 68; Plaintiffs' Proposed Findings of Fact and Conclusions of Law, September 17, 1974, *Adams v. Dan River Mills,* p. 25.

6. Trial testimony of Wyllie Smyka, July 24, 1973, ibid., pp. 42–44, 49, 50, 60.

7. Trial testimony of Norman Hall, July 24, 1973, ibid., p. 104.

8. Trial testimony of Fred S. Evans, July 24, 1973, ibid., pp. 114–15, 126.

9. Trial testimony of Robert Gardiner, January 11, 1974, ibid., pp. 366–67, 427.

10. Defendant's Proposed Findings of Fact and Conclusions of Law, n.d., ibid., pp. 22–23.

11. Trial testimony of Robert L. Cann, July 9, 1975, *Lewis v. J. P. Stevens,* p. 231.

12. General Manager Durwood Costner, when asked to explain why blacks were concentrated in the laundry and shipping departments, answered, "That I really couldn't say. But I do understand that there are requests along that line." Deposition of Durwood William Costner, September 19, 1972, *Ellison v. Rock Hill Printing and Finishing Company,* p. 30; Deposition of Samuel Boyd Roach, September 20, 1972, ibid., p. 28; Deposition of John W. Simpson, September 19, 1972, ibid., p. 26.

13. Deposition of C. A. Rhyne, August 28, 1973, *Sherrill v. J. P. Stevens*, pp. 20–21.

14. Juanita Harrison, "My Activities with TEAM," n.d., Reel 163, SRC Papers.

15. Deposition of C. A. Rhyne, August 28, 1973, *Sherrill v. J. P. Stevens*, pp. 60–68, 70.

16. Deposition of Jack Human, November 15, 1973, ibid., pp. 4, 38.

17. Deposition of C. A. Rhyne, August 28, 1973, ibid., p. 70.

18. Deposition of Jack Human, November 15, 1973, ibid., p. 44.

19. Plaintiffs' Proposed Findings of Fact and Conclusions of Law, September 16, 1974, *Adams v. Dan River Mills*, p. 111.

20. Deposition of C. A. Rhyne, August 28, 1973, *Sherrill v. J. P. Stevens*, pp. 4–5.

21. Trial testimony of James B. Miller, November 6, 1972, *Sledge v. J. P. Stevens*, p. 522.

22. Trial testimony of Edwin Akers, November 6, 1972, ibid., pp. 666–67.

23. Ibid., pp. 823–24.

24. Trial remarks of Whiteford Blakeney, November 6, 1972, ibid., pp. 973–76.

25. Trial testimony of Boyce E. Crocker, July 8, 1975, *Lewis v. J. P. Stevens*, p. 171.

26. Trial testimony of Robert L. Cann, July 9, 1975, ibid., pp. 215, 227, 239.

27. Defendant's Proposed Findings and Conclusions and Memorandum in Support Thereof, March 14, 1981, ibid., p. 17.

28. Trial remarks of Whiteford Blakeney, November 6, 1972, *Sledge v. J. P. Stevens*, pp. 976–77.

29. Reply Brief for Defendant, March 3, 1975, *Adams v. Dan River Mills*, pp. 26–28; Defendant's Proposed Findings of Fact and Conclusions of Law, n.d., ibid., p. 35. Dan River also claimed that there were no black supervisors because of a shortage of qualified applicants: "There is a lack of minority applicants who possess the skills required." Trial testimony of Robert Gardiner, January 10, 1974, ibid., p. 366.

30. Trial testimony of Edwin Akers, November 6, 1972, *Sledge v. J. P. Stevens*, pp. 670–73.

31. Ibid., pp. 684–90.

32. Sarah Herbin to Jean Fairfax, November 9, 1962, "Southern Program: High Point, Employment on Merit 1962" folder, "Community Relations 1962 Southern Program" box, AFSC Papers.

33. Transcript of trial testimony, January 8, 1974, *Adams v. Dan River Mills*, p. 86.

34. At Russell Mills in Alexander City, Alabama, for example, the company claimed in 1969 that it had been unable to appoint black clerical workers because "even though the Negro high school gives typing courses and they have the latest equipment, apparently the girls are graduated without knowing how to type. The Company would hire qualified Negro girls today if they could find them." Memo to Russell Mills Files, March 13, 1969, Folder 18, Box 13, Wharton Papers.

35. Hearing of February 24, 1976, *Sledge v. J. P. Stevens*, pp. 38–41.

36. Ibid., p. 65.

37. Ibid., p. 73.

38. Deposition of Jerry McKinsey, September 20, 1972, *Ellison v. Rock Hill Printing and Finishing Company*, p. 61.

39. Defendant's Discovery Deposition of Ray Tate, April 18, 1966, *Hall v. Werthan Bag*, pp. 39, 54–55; Plaintiff-Intervenor's Reply in Opposition to Defendant's Motion for Order to Compel Deponent Ray Tate to Answer, May 27, 1966, ibid., p. 2; Memorandum of Law in Support of Plaintiff-Intervenor's Reply in Opposition to Defendant's Motion to Compel Ray Tate to Answer, May 27, 1966, ibid., p. 3.

40. Mordecai C. Johnson to Jean Fairfax, August 28, 1968, Reel 163, SRC Papers, p. 4.

41. A. J. Maino to Sam J. Ervin Jr., March 25, 1964, Folder 327, Box 120, Ervin Papers.

42. C. O. Ellis to Sam J. Ervin Jr., August 16, 1963, Folder 403, Box 103, ibid.

43. B. Frank Miller to Sam J. Ervin Jr., July 8, 1964, Folder 379, Box 122, ibid.

44. C. Almon McIver to Sam J. Ervin Jr., July 17, 1963, Folder 373, Box 102, ibid.

45. Russell Gant to Sam J. Ervin Jr., August 7, 1963, Folder 393, Box 103, ibid.

46. C. L. Cammack to Sam J. Ervin Jr., April 10, 1964, Folder 339, Box 120, ibid.

47. Charles E. Hicks to Sam J. Ervin Jr., May 19, 1964, Folder 366, Box 121, ibid.

48. J. J. Norton Jr. to William Jennings Bryan Dorn, March 6, 1964, Folder 2, Box 67, Dorn Papers.

49. Randal R. Craft to Strom Thurmond, July 19, 1963, Box 3-1963, Thurmond Papers.

50. W. C. Whitman to William Jennings Bryan Dorn, December 15, 1970, Folder 3, Box 89, Dorn Papers.

51. Joseph T. Allmon to William Jennings Bryan Dorn, November 4, 1970, ibid.

52. Ralph P. Jackson Jr. to Strom Thurmond, April 3, 1968, Box 3-1968, Thurmond Papers; Nathan Mandell to Strom Thurmond, March 27, 1968, ibid.

53. Annette Duchein to William Jennings Bryan Dorn, September 14, 1971, Folder 56, Box 95, Dorn Papers; J. W. Greene to Strom Thurmond, June 1, 1966, Box 2-1966, Thurmond Papers.

54. Walter Montgomery to William Jennings Bryan Dorn, September 15, 1971, Folder 56, Box 95, Dorn Papers.

55. John G. Wellman to William Jennings Bryan Dorn, November 20, 1970, Folder 3, Box 89, ibid.; N. Browne Glenn to Strom Thurmond, July 13, 1967, Box 3-1967, Thurmond Papers.

56. William C. Lott to William Jennings Bryan Dorn, November 16, 1970; Ronald Wood to William Jennings Bryan Dorn, November 18, 1970; S. C. Thomas to William Jennings Bryan Dorn, November 18, 1970; Frank E. Harling to William Jennings Bryan Dorn, November 19, 1970, all in Folder 3, Box 89, Dorn Papers.

57. William Jennings Bryan Dorn to Robert Stevens, June 1, 1966, Folder 22, Box 77, ibid.; Frederick B. Dent to William Jennings Bryan Dorn, May 30, 1966, ibid.

58. *Charlotte Observer*, August 20, 1969, August 17, 1969.

59. "Textiles: Blacks in the Mills," *Newsweek*, November 2, 1970, pp. 50–51.

60. E. W. Gould of Pacific Mills, Halifax, Virginia, to M. A. Cross, June 5, 1961, "Government Contracts—Correspondence 1961–1962" folder, DRMC Papers; Handwritten notes, "Government Contracts—Correspondence 1963–1965" folder, ibid.; Frank Talbott to M. A. Cross, June 23, 1965, "Civil Rights Act—Fair Employment Practices (Correspondence) 1964–1966" folder, ibid.

61. *America's Textile Reporter*, April 27, 1961, pp. 28–29.

62. "Govt. Hiring Rules May Force SC Mills to Look Elsewhere," *Daily News Record*, April 19, 1961; Solomon Barkin to William Pollock, April 11, 1961, Series 3, Box 316, TWUA Papers.

63. *America's Textile Reporter*, April 27, 1961, pp. 28–29; "So. Mills Supplying U.S. Fear New Hiring Rules," *Daily News Record*, April 6, 1961, clipping in Series 3, Box 316, TWUA Papers.

64. See, for example, the testimony of Dr. Vivian W. Henderson, Transcript of the EEOC Textile Forum, January 12, 1967, Part 2, Reel 2, LBJ Papers, pp. 39–43.

65. Crown Cotton Mills Questionnaire, Southern TWUA Staff Survey, December 15, 1966, Series 3, Box 316, TWUA Papers.

66. Roxbury Southern Mills Questionnaire, Southern TWUA Staff Survey, December 15, 1966, ibid.; Bemis Company Questionnaire, Southern TWUA Staff Survey, December 15, 1966, ibid.

67. "Employment of Negroes in the Southern Textile Industry," TWUA Report dated May 19, 1964, ibid.

68. *New York Times*, October 20, 1985, quoted in "Ball and Chain for African-American Workers?: An ACTWU Report on B & C Associates," ACTWU Civil Rights Committee Publication, July 1994, p. 20.

69. Ferguson interview.

70. "ATMI to Snub Airing of Industry Job Woes," *Daily News Record*, January 9, 1967; *America's Textile Reporter*, June 22, 1967, both clippings in Box 316, TWUA Papers.

71. *America's Textile Reporter*, June 22, 1967, clipping in ibid.

72. "Straining a Gnat's Heel," *Southern Textile News*, December 19, 1966, p. 4, clipping in ibid.

73. Motions hearing, March 4, 1968, *United States v. Southern Weaving*, pp. 11, 32.

74. Proceedings, filed October 14, 1968, *Graniteville Company v. EEOC*, pp. 6–7.

75. James P. Wilson and Horace Hill to Sen. Sam J. Ervin Jr., April 14, 1967; Sam J. Ervin Jr. to Horace Hill and James P. Wilson, May 5, 1967, both in Folder 479, Box 177, Ervin Papers.

76. George L. Holland to Southerland Dyeing and Finishing Mills, April 13, 1966, ibid.

77. F. M. Southerland to Sam J. Ervin, April 26, 1966, ibid.

78. F. M. Southerland to Sam J. Ervin, February 2, 1967, ibid.

79. Sam J. Ervin Jr. to F. M. Southerland, May 13, 1966, ibid.

80. *Daily News Record*, December 1, 1965, in Box 652, TWUA Papers.

81. John A. Bynum to Richard L. Rowan, February 14, 1967, Folder 55, Box 12, Wharton Papers.

82. Plant visit to Burlington Industries, July 22, 1969, Folder 18, Box 13, ibid.

83. Robert W. Armstrong to Richard L. Rowan, June 17, 1970, Folder 4, ibid.

84. Fieldcrest visit, June 20, 1969, Folder 18, ibid.

85. R. M. Gardiner to R. M. Stephens, March 21, 1969, "Affirmative Action Correspondence 1969 January–March" folder, DRMC Papers; Gerald C. Adcock to W. C. Jackson, February 3, 1968, "Affirmative Action—Statistical Information on Black Employment, Promotions etc., 1968–1972" folder, ibid.

86. Hearing of February 24, 1976, in Raleigh, North Carolina, *Sledge v. J. P. Stevens*, p. 142.

87. Ibid., p. 145.

88. Lincks interview.

89. Noyes Collinson to Tartt Bell, September 7, 1962, "Atlanta, Georgia Office, Employment on Merit Program Visits to Businesses 1962" folder, "Southeastern Regional Office, 1960–62" box, AFSC Papers.

90. Bibb visit, June 17, 1969, Folder 18, Box 13, Wharton Papers.

91. Indian Head visit, November 17, 1966, Folder 17, ibid.

92. Plaintiffs' Proposed Findings of Fact and Conclusions of Law, June 11, 1980, *Lewis v. J. P. Stevens*, pp. 29–31; Trial testimony of Richard R. Rice, July 25, 1975, ibid., p. 1243.

93. Henry C. Woicik to William Pollard, May 19, 1976, Box 2, ACTWU-SRO Papers.

94. Plaintiffs' Proposed Findings of Fact and Conclusions of Law, September 16, 1974, *Adams v. Dan River Mills*, pp. 31–33.

95. Deposition of Paul Gene McLean, October 8, 1973, *Sherrill v. J. P. Stevens*, p. 6; Deposition of Robert H. Costner, October 8, 1973, ibid., p. 12.

96. Deposition of Ronald Furr, August 29, 1973, ibid., p. 28.

97. Ibid., p. 46; Deposition of Riley Skidmore, August 28, 1973, ibid., pp. 43–48.

98. Mordecai Johnson to Jean Fairfax, January 1968, Reel 163, SRC Papers, p. 5.

99. John C. Cauthen to Mordecai C. Johnson, March 29, 1969, ibid.

100. Hearing of February 24, 1976, *Sledge v. J. P. Stevens*, pp. 27–29.

101. Ibid., pp. 71–72.

102. Transcript of Trial Proceedings, January 8, 1974, *Adams v. Dan River Mills*, pp. 36–37, 65–66, 73.

103. Ibid., pp. 84–85; Transcript of Trial Proceedings, July 24, 1973, ibid., p. 97. The discrimination carried out by Dan River supervisors is discussed in Chapter 4.

104. Deposition of William Lowndes, February 26, 1968, *United States v. Southern Weaving*, pp. 27, 37, 46, 62.

105. West Point Pepperell plant visit, July 14, 1969, Folder 18, Box 13, Wharton Papers.

106. "Yet to Come: Negro Textile Supervisors," *Charlotte Observer*, August 19, 1969, clipping in Folder 46, ibid.

107. Deposition of Birdie Ruth Harris, February 23, 1970, *Adams v. Dan River Mills*, pp. 9–10.

108. Deposition of Ray Lewis McDowell, October 10, 1973, *Sherrill v. J. P. Stevens*, pp. 21, 31.

109. Trial testimony of Robert Costner, August 28, 1974, ibid., p. 159.

110. R. M. Gardiner to J. C. Spangler, May 9, 1972, "Affirmative Action Program—Correspondence 1972" folder, DRMC Papers.

111. Motions hearing of March 4, 1968, *United States v. Southern Weaving*, p. 33.

112. Randal R. Craft to Strom Thurmond, July 19, 1963, Box 3-1963, Thurmond Papers.

113. D. H. Shuttleworth to Strom Thurmond, September 19, 1967, Box 3-1967, ibid.

114. D. B. Barlow to Strom Thurmond, August 7, 1967, Box 3-1967, ibid. "Rat" Brown is a corruption of the name of the radical black leader H. Rap Brown.

115. Reactions of Labor and Defense Departments Representatives to Company's Proposed Affirmative Action Program—May 14, 1968, "Affirmative Action Correspondence 1968 May–August" folder, DRMC Papers; R. M. Gardiner to R. M. Stephens, May 15, 1968, ibid.

116. Hearing of February 24, 1976, *Sledge v. J. P. Stevens*, p. 139.

117. Supplemental Memorandum for the Defendant, June 4, 1976, ibid., p. 3; Defendant's Reply Brief in No. 76-1988 and Answering Brief in No. 76-2150, December 17, 1976, ibid., copy in Box 2, ACTWU-SRO Papers, pp. 2–8, 29–30; Hearing of February 24, 1976, *Sledge v. J. P. Stevens*, pp. 49, 82–83, 139.

118. Ferguson interview.

119. Jean Fairfax to Mordecai C. Johnson, August 7, 1967, Reel 163, SRC Papers, pp. 18–19.

120. Paul Swaity to Stephen N. Shulman, March 21, 1967, Folder 10, Box 2857, AFL-CIO Papers.

121. Minchin, *What Do We Need a Union For?*, pp. 40–41.

122. Bibb Manufacturing Company plant visit, June 17, 1969, Folder 18, Box 13, Wharton Papers.

123. EEO-1 Form for Bibb Manufacturing Company Plant No. 2, January 1969, in Folder 49, Box 12, ibid.

124. *The Bibb Recorder* 49, no. 19 (May 9, 1969), copy in ibid.

125. EEOC Review Report of Russell Mills, March 13, 1968, in Folder 3, Box 14, ibid.

126. Rowan, "The Negro in the Textile Industry," p. 15; Mayes Behrman visits to Cone Mills, January 19, 1953, and April 15, 1953; Mayes Behrman visit with J. Spencer Love, November 20, 1953, "Merit Employment Program Visit to Businesses, Southeastern Regional Office 1953–1954" folder, "Southeastern Regional Office 1947–1956" box, AFSC Papers.

127. Mayes Behrman visit to Cone Mills, January 19, 1953, ibid.

128. Mayes Behrman visits to Cone Hospital, January 23, 1953, and February 11, 1953, ibid.

129. Mayes Behrman visit with Scott Hoyman, TWUA-CIO Organizer for Seven Cone Plants in North Carolina, September 20, 1955, "Merit Employment Program Visits to Businesses, Southeastern Regional Office 1955" folder, ibid.; Mayes Behrman visit to Cone Mills, April 15, 1953, "Merit Employment Program Visit to Businesses, Southeastern Regional Office 1953–1954" folder, ibid.

130. Mayes Behrman visit with J. Spencer Love, November 20, 1953, ibid.

131. Mayes Behrman visit to Dr. George D. Heaton, June 16, 1954, "Merit Employment

Program: Visits with Community Leaders and Organizations, Southeastern Regional Office 1954" folder, ibid.

132. Mayes Behrman visit to Burlington Mills, December 15, 1955; Thelma Babbitt to Mayes Behrman, December 20, 1955; Thelma Babbitt to Mayes Behrman, August 9, 1955, all in "Merit Employment Program Visits to Businesses, Southeastern Regional Office 1955" folder, ibid.

133. Mayes Behrman visit to Cone Mills, April 15, 1953, "Merit Employment Program Visit to Businesses, Southeastern Regional Office 1953–1954" folder, ibid.; Mayes Behrman visit to Burlington Industries, August 2, 1955, "Merit Employment Program Visits to Businesses, Southeastern Regional Office 1955" folder, ibid.

134. Mayes Behrman visit to Shuford Mills, July 15, 1955, ibid.; Mayes Behrman to Thelma Babbitt, July 21, 1955, "Merit Employment Program Visits with Community Leaders and Organizations, July–December 1955" folder, ibid.

135. Mayes Behrman visit to Cone Mills, January 19, 1953, "Merit Employment Program Visit to Businesses, Southeastern Regional Office 1953–1954" folder, ibid.

136. Mayes Behrman visit to Burlington Industries, August 2, 1955, "Merit Employment Program Visits to Businesses, Southeastern Regional Office 1955" folder, ibid.; "Summary of Visits Received in Philadelphia Office—March 1 to 30," April 2, 1956, "Job Opportunities— Summaries of Visits Made by National and Regional Office Staff Project Section 1956" folder, "American Section 1956 Community Relations" box, ibid.

137. Mayes Behrman visit to J. P. Stevens, July 29, 1955, "Merit Employment Program Visits to Businesses, Southeastern Regional Office 1955" folder, "Southeastern Regional Office 1947–1956" box, ibid.

138. Richard Rowan plant visit to Burlington Industries, July 22, 1969, Folder 18, Box 13, Wharton Papers.

139. "Development of an Affirmative Action Program—Harassment by Federal Agencies," November 23, 1970, "Affirmative Action Correspondence 1970 October–November" folder, DRMC Papers.

140. Graham, *The Civil Rights Era*, p. 456.

141. "Reaction of Labor and Defense Department Representatives to Company's Proposed Affirmative Action Program, May 14, 1968," "Affirmative Action Correspondence 1968 May–August" folder, DRMC Papers; Defendant's Proposed Findings of Fact and Conclusions of Law, n.d., *Adams v. Dan River Mills*, p. 10.

Chapter 4

1. Title quote comes from Kay Willis interview, interview G8/G9, Uprising Papers, p. 16.

2. Reese Cleghorn, "The Mill: A Giant Step for the Southern Negro," *New York Times Magazine*, November 9, 1969, p. 35; "Negroes Gain Foothold in South's Mills," *New York Times*, January 12, 1969, p. F17; "Textile Plants in South Now Woo Negro Workers Seeking Better Jobs," *New York Times*, May 19, 1969, p. 42; "Blacks in the Mills," *Newsweek*, November 2, 1970, p. 50; Henry P. Leifermann, "Trouble in the South's First Industry: The Unions Are Coming," *New York Times Magazine*, August 5, 1973, p. 26.

3. Rowan, "The Negro in the Textile Industry," p. 132.

4. Mary Frederickson, for example, notes that "although integration within the mills made white workers more aware of the skills and abilities of black workers, few employees totally forgot the past." Frederickson, "Four Decades of Change," p. 74. Mimi Conway, meanwhile, describes some examples of continued discrimination and white resistence after integration. Conway, *Rise Gonna Rise*, pp. 104–5, 109–13.

5. The only detailed information about a black pioneer that the author is aware of is an

oral history interview with a pioneer black worker published in Byerly, *Hard Times*, pp. 143–60. Frederickson's article provides an overview of integration, while Rowan's focus is essentially on the reasons for the shift in management thinking rather than exploring the experiences of black workers.

6. Glover interview.

7. Alston interview.

8. Little interview.

9. Deposition of Donald R. Aichner, September 19, 1973, *Adams v. Dan River Mills*, pp. 72–73.

10. West Point Pepperell visit, July 14, 1969, Folder 18, Box 13, Wharton Papers.

11. Fulton Cotton Mills visit, June 3, 1969, ibid.

12. DuPont visit, May 16, 1969, Folder 75, Box 12, ibid.

13. "Employer Experiences in Dublin, Georgia," Folder 57, Box 13, ibid.

14. EEOC Charge Form of Edward Price, March 26, 1968, *Graniteville Company v. EEOC*; Order on Final Pre-Trial Conference, September 28, 1978, *Seibles v. Cone Mills*, p. 2; Deposition of Henry Wilson, February 10, 1970, *Adams v. Dan River Mills*, pp. 13–14; Transcript of Trial Proceedings, June 6 and June 7, 1973, ibid., pp. 245–46, 259. Robert Ford, a TEAM representative, found separate bathrooms at a textile company in Greenville, South Carolina, in September 1968. Robert Ford, Four Months Activity Report, September 1968, Reel 163, SRC Papers. TEAM also found "de facto segregation in rest rooms" at Ace Sweater Company in Union County, South Carolina, in 1968. See Minutes of TEAM Meeting, August 28, 1968, ibid., p. 4. In an NLRB case against J. P. Stevens in 1966, the trial examiner severely condemned the company's practice of maintaining segregated toilet facilities, which was revealed at the hearing. Statement of the Textile Workers Union of America at the Textile Employment Forum, January 12–13, 1967, Box 316, TWUA Papers, p. 4.

15. Complaint, October 24, 1969, *Adams v. Dan River Mills*, p. 3.

16. Complaint, April 10, 1969, *Georgia Hall v. George P. Schultz*, copy in Box 2, ACTWU-SRO Papers, p. 11.

17. Long interview.

18. "Powerful C. A. Cannon Rules Kannapolis, N.C., But He Faces Challenge," *Wall Street Journal*, April 29, 1969, clipping in Folder 46, ibid.

19. Gaines interview.

20. McGhee interview.

21. Etheridge interview.

22. Johnson interview.

23. Long interview.

24. Moore interview.

25. Johnson interview; Waldrep interview.

26. Davis interview.

27. Deal interview.

28. Gaines interview.

29. "Negro Not Advancing to Mill Middle Posts," *Daily News Record*, February 9, 1968, clipping in Reel 163, SRC Papers.

30. In February 1968, for example, a TEAM aide undertook a detailed plant visit with Greenwood Mills of Greenwood, South Carolina. The company was the largest one in the area, and the aide talked at length with Connor Stewart, who was the director of industrial relations. Stewart described how the company had been unsuccessful in promoting the first black into a supervisor's job because of opposition from white workers. "Stewart stated that in one case which he would not detail, they tried to promote a Negro to a supervisory job and 'all hell broke loose.' 'We almost had a mutiny on our hands.' He went on to explain that

they had given this Negro full company backing and had made it clear that he was the boss and that the issue was not race and that this was a good man. However he hinted without saying so that they would not try this again." "Interview with James H. Self, Jr., Feb. 16, 1968—Greenwood County, [and] Connor Stewart, Dir., Industrial Relations, Greenwood Mills, Executive Building," Reel 163, SRC Papers. Similarly, in the 1960s the Riegel Corporation refused an invitation to test South Carolina's state law about integration because "there's no use to stir up the red necks." Riegel plant visit, Folder 18, Box 13, Wharton Papers.

31. "Memo to Russell Mills Files," March 13, 1969, ibid.

32. Alston interview.

33. Waldrep interview.

34. Celanese visit, July 28–29, 1969, Folder 18, Box 13, Wharton Papers.

35. Lincks interview; Waldrep interview.

36. Waldrep interview.

37. Ibid. An EEOC report on textile integration explained how the federal government had given white workers who opposed integration few options: "By increasing the extent to which governmental regulations prohibiting racial discrimination in employment cover employment alternatives . . . Federal programs have reduced the chance that a worker will be able to 'escape' multiracial associations." Donald D. Osburn, "Negro Employment in the Textile Industries of North and South Carolina" (1966), Part 2, Reel 2, LBJ Papers, p. 30.

38. H. S. Williams to William Pollock, January 2, 1962, Series 3, Box 316, TWUA Papers.

39. Deposition of James Montgomery, March 11, 1970, *Adams v. Dan River Mills*, p. 20.

40. W. T. Cheatham to Samuel J. Ervin Jr., March 27, 1964, Folder 329, Box 120, Ervin Papers.

41. Chambers interview.

42. Johnnie E. Brown to George Baldanzi, September 4, 1962, Folder 3, Box 960, United Textile Workers of America Papers, Southern Labor Archives, Georgia State University, Atlanta.

43. Trial testimony of Robert Costner, August 28, 1974, *Sherrill v. J. P. Stevens*, pp. 158–61; Deposition of Ray Lewis McDowell, October 10, 1973, ibid., p. 21.

44. Transcript of Trial Proceedings, January 11, 1974, *Adams v. Dan River Mills*, pp. 420, 423.

45. R. M. Gardiner to R. M. Stephens, March 4, 1969, "Affirmative Action Correspondence 1969 April–May" folder, DRMC Papers; R. M. Gardiner to J. C. Spangler, May 9, 1972, "Affirmative Action Program—Correspondence 1972" folder, ibid.

46. Answers to Defendant's First Interrogatories to Plaintiff, May 31, 1977, *Foster v. Fieldcrest Mills*, pp. 2–3; Robert H. Foster to Harris A. Williams of EEOC, November 20, 1975, ibid.

47. Geraldine Lindsay to The Equal Employment Opportunity Commission, January 3, 1974, *Lindsay v. Cone Mills*.

48. Joann W. Calhoun to Mr. Foster, n.d., *Lewis v. Bloomsburg Mills*.

49. Complaint, December 1, 1976, *Harris v. Golden Belt Manufacturing Company*, p. 3.

50. Transcript of Trial Proceedings, June 5, 1973, *Adams v. Dan River Mills*, pp. 67, 70–71.

51. Deposition of Leroy Johnson, January 23, 1970, ibid., p. 26.

52. Amended Complaint, February 8, 1978, *Mark v. Burlington Industries*, pp. 2, 3; Jerdean A. Mark to The Equal Employment Opportunity Commission, April 1, 1970, ibid.; Conciliation Agreement, March 13, 1974, ibid.

53. Findings of Fact and Conclusions of Law, November 10, 1975, *Sherrill v. J. P. Stevens*.

54. Deposition of A. C. Sherrill, March 18, 1974, ibid., pp. 93–98, 104.

55. Court Reporter's Transcript of Proceedings, August 28, 1974, ibid., p. 147; Deposition of William Luckey, October 24, 1973, ibid., pp. 17, 47.

56. Plaintiffs' Proposed Findings of Fact and Conclusions of Law, February 18, 1975, ibid., p. 17.

57. Ibid.; Deposition of A. C. Sherrill, March 18, 1974, ibid., pp. 58, 116–17.

58. Plaintiffs' Proposed Findings of Fact and Conclusions of Law, February 18, 1975, ibid., p. 18; Deposition of A. C. Sherrill, March 18, 1974, ibid., p. 50; Court Reporter's Transcript of Proceedings, August 28, 1974, ibid., p. 88.

59. Deposition of A. C. Sherrill, March 18, 1974, ibid., pp. 80, 111–12, 153–55; Court Reporter's Transcript of Proceedings, August 28, 1974, ibid., pp. 143–44.

60. EEOC Charge of Discrimination of Dell Carter, November 7, 1979, in Box 48, ACTWU-SRO Papers.

61. These were consent decrees or conciliation agreements that companies and plaintiffs agreed to as a way of avoiding further litigation. Many cases were settled in this way, and they usually contained specific agreements to allow blacks to move into white jobs.

62. Young interview; Johnson interview.

63. Beck interview.

64. Pharr interview.

65. Deposition of Leroy Ellison, October 31, 1973, *Ellison v. Rock Hill Printing and Finishing Company*, pp. 9–20.

66. Ellison interview; Archie interview.

67. Robert J. Lenrow to Eugene T. Bost, May 10, 1977, Box 79, Cannon Papers.

68. Bench Brief, n.d.; Complaint, May 25, 1979; Affidavit of Norman Youngblood, June 29, 1979, *Youngblood v. Rock Hill Printing and Finishing Company*.

69. "Fair Employment Practices in Cone Mills," May 15, 1961, Box 638, TWUA Papers, pp. 2–3.

70. Mildred Edmond and Mattie Shoemaker interview, SOHP, H-46, p. 33.

71. Latham interview.

72. Gaines interview.

73. Crittenden interview.

74. Uniroyal visit, n.d., Folder 18, Box 13, Wharton Papers.

75. Riegel Textile Corporation plant visit, ibid.

76. Bibb visit, June 17, 1969, ibid.

77. Smith interview.

78. This pattern emerges from my reading of the more than two hundred interviews with mill workers that make up the Southern Oral History Project in Chapel Hill, North Carolina, many of which discuss the integration of the textile industry.

79. Eula Durham interview, SOHP, H-64, pp. 17–18; Carrie Yelton interview, SOHP, H-115, p. 64.

80. "Relevant Pages from Robertson Deposition Transcript," n.d., *Millner v. Fieldcrest Mills*, pp. 28, 32.

81. Lincks interview; Deposition of Thomas McCorkle, October 9, 1973, *Sherrill v. J. P. Stevens*, p. 44; Deposition of Miles Luckey, October 24, 1973, ibid., pp. 7–8.

82. Deposition of Tom Waters, April 24, 1968, *United States v. Southern Weaving*, pp. 19–20.

83. Deposition of Fred Cisson, February 26, 1968, ibid., p. 79.

84. Deposition of James Bloxsom, *Sledge v. J. P. Stevens*, p. 9.

85. EEOC Review Report for Russell Mills, March 13, 1968, in Folder 3, Box 14, Wharton Papers.

86. Memorandum by field representative William C. Erler, February 11–13, 1964, Folder 26, Box 13, ibid.

87. Deposition of Miles Luckey, October 24, 1973, *Sherrill v. J. P. Stevens*, pp. 7, 10, 16–30, 34.

88. Deposition of Thomas McCorkle, October 9, 1973, ibid., pp. 1–30.

89. Plaintiffs' Proposed Findings of Fact and Conclusions of Law, February 18, 1975, ibid., p. 5.

90. Riegel plant visit, June 30, 1969, Folder 18, Box 13, Wharton Papers; "The New South: Negroes in the Textile Industry," *Daily News Record*, December 1, 1965, clipping in Box 652, TWUA Papers.

91. "The New South: Negroes in the Textile Industry," *Daily News Record*, December 1, 1965, clipping in ibid.

92. Buck interview.

93. Deposition of John H. Marshall, November 21, 1972, *Ellison v. Rock Hill Printing and Finishing Company*, p. 16.

94. Transcript of trial testimony, June 5, 1973, *Adams v. Dan River Mills*, pp. 67, 91.

95. Project Report for Year Ending September 1968, September 12, 1968, Reel 163, SRC Papers, p. 20.

96. Mordecai Johnson to Jean Fairfax, September 22, 1967, Reel 164, ibid., p. 2.

97. Project Report for Year Ending September 1968, September 12, 1968, Reel 163, ibid., p. 34; clipping entitled "Textile Leaders Say: To Get Management Position Negro Needs More Education," n.d., ibid.; "Textile Companies Slow," *Charlotte Observer*, May 28, 1969, clipping in Folder 46, Box 13, Wharton Papers.

98. Noyes Collinson to Tartt Bell, April 18, 1962, "Southern Program—High Point—Atlanta—Employment on Merit" folder, "Community Relations 1962 Southern Program" box, AFSC Papers.

99. Walter N. Rozelle, "The Mill and the Negro: Let's Tell It Like It Is," *Textile Industries* 132, no. 11 (November 1968): 61.

100. H. S. Williams to William Pollock, January 2, 1962, Series 3, Box 316, TWUA Papers.

101. Cannon interview.

102. Sarah Herbin to E. T. Kehrer, February 3, 1967, Folder 10, Box 2857, AFL-CIO Papers.

103. *Charlotte Observer*, July 7, 1968.

104. At Oneita Knitting Mills in Andrews, South Carolina, for example, several of the first African American women hired into production positions had attended college. Gordon interview.

105. Sarah Herbin to Jean Fairfax, April 18, 1963, "Southern Program, High Point, Employment on Merit 1963" folder, "Community Relations Division 1963 Southern Program" box, AFSC Papers; Sarah Herbin to Jean Fairfax, September 25, 1962, "Southern Program: High Point, Employment on Merit 1962" folder, "Community Relations 1962 Southern Program" box, ibid.

106. Transcript of EEOC Textile Forum, January 12–13, 1967, Part 2, Reel 2, LBJ Papers, pp. 24, 36–37, 43.

107. Lincks interview. Jackie Robinson was the first black major league baseball player, and in order to enter the majors in 1947 he had to be an exceptional talent. Indeed, Robinson proved that he was better than most whites, leading the National League batting averages in 1949 and entering the illustrious Hall of Fame in 1962. The Jackie Robinson story was used repeatedly as a metaphor by those who remembered the integration of the southern textile industry. *The Baseball Encyclopaedia: The Complete and Official Record of Major League Baseball* (New York: Macmillan Publishing Company, 1974), pp. 157–58, 752.

108. Sarah Herbin's remarks at EEOC Textile Forum, sent to E. T. Kehrer, February 3, 1967, Folder 10, Box 2857, AFL-CIO Papers.

109. Purnell interview; Lucy Sledge quoted in Conway, *Rise Gonna Rise*, p. 109.

110. Taylor interview.

111. Alston interview.

112. Builder interview.

113. Taylor interview.

114. Boone interview.

115. Gaines interview.

116. Bush interview.

117. Project Report for Year Ending September 1968, September 12, 1968, Reel 163, SRC Papers, p. 65.

118. Long interview.

Chapter 5

1. Mary Frederickson, for example, points out that by 1978 black workers held 31 percent of all operative jobs in the Carolinas and Georgia. Frederickson, "Four Decades of Change," p. 71.

2. Gaines interview.

3. Transcript of EEOC Textile Forum, January 12–13, 1967, Part 2, Reel 2, LBJ Papers, p. 33.

4. "Job Discrimination Ending Quickly, ATMI Reports," *Greensboro Daily News*, February 12, 1969, clipping in Folder 33, Box 90, Dorn Papers.

5. "Burlington Bucks Policy of Silence On Negro Hiring," *Charlotte Observer*, August 19, 1969, Folder 46, Box 13, Wharton Papers; "Textile Companies Slow to Upgrade Their Blacks," *Charlotte Observer*, May 28, 1969, pp. 10–11, clipping in ibid. For the industry's willingness to promote overall statistics, see F. S. Love to Richard L. Rowan, July 30, 1969, Folder 39, Box 12, ibid.

6. The reasons for this employment pattern are explained in greater detail in Chapter 6.

7. Taylor produced data to show how stark patterns of discrimination persisted well into the 1970s. In April 1972, out of 212 office and clerical jobs, only 2 were held by blacks. Between 1968 and 1972, Stevens always had over 200 officials and managers, all of whom were white. Thus, according to Taylor, Stevens refused to give out information on what their black workers really did "because it would show that at Stevens almost nothing has changed." Bennett Taylor quoted in *Mountain Life and Work*, September 1978 (special issue on Southern Textile Workers), p. 11, copy in Box 58, ACTWU-SRO Papers.

8. Sarah Herbin to E. T. Kehrer, February 3, 1967, Folder 10, Box 2857, AFL-CIO Papers.

9. The report found, for example, that "not only do large numbers of blacks feel they are being treated unfairly, but close to forty-three percent believed that they are not allowed to advance on the job as fast as their fellow white workers. . . . The overriding theme that comes out of this section is the perception on the part of blacks of seemingly willful exclusion of blacks from equal promotional opportunities." Indeed, many African American workers made the cynical statement, "Man, you know white folks will not let blacks get ahead as fast as white folks." They also complained about the use of racial epithets by supervisors and poor relationships with white textile workers. "Changes in Minority Participation in the Textile Industry of North and South Carolina, 1966 to 1969," Department of Economics and Center for Manpower Research and Training, North Carolina Agricultural and Technical State University, March 15, 1972, pp. 102, 105. Report held at North Carolina State University Textile Library, Raleigh, North Carolina.

10. Two accounts do cover discrimination in the mills after integration in some detail—Conway, *Rise Gonna Rise*, pp. 90–128, and Byerly, *Hard Times*, pp. 137–60. Because these accounts are largely individual oral history collections, they offer insights into individual stories of discrimination but do not provide the same overview as class action lawsuits involving hundreds or thousands of workers. For the excellent use that historians have made of letters written to President Roosevelt during the New Deal, see Hall et al., *Like a Family*, pp. xv, 293–302. The quote comes from p. xv of *Like a Family*.

11. Rowan, "The Negro in the Textile Industry," p. 15.

12. Willie L. Johnson and Rev. Sam Adams to the Equal Employment Opportunity Commission, February 1, 1971, *Galloway v. Fieldcrest Mills*.

13. Jesse Broadnax to the Equal Employment Opportunity Commission, March 11, 1971, ibid.

14. Exhibit 3, ibid.

15. Edward Price and James C. Walker to "The Equal Employment Opportunity," February 9, 1968, Exhibit A, *Graniteville Company v. EEOC*.

16. Ibid. For background information on the Graniteville Company, see Hall et al., *Like a Family*, pp. 56–57.

17. Affidavit of David W. Zugschwerdt, EEOC attorney, June 10, 1968; Attachment XXIX, *Graniteville Company v. EEOC*.

18. In 1965, for example, black textile worker Charles Brown initiated a class action lawsuit against his employer, a North Carolina company involved in the finishing of textiles, by writing a formal complaint letter to the EEOC. His complaints, which formed the basis of *Brown v. Southern Dyestuff*, again centered around the segregation of jobs. The promotion of inexperienced whites over blacks with seniority was a major grievance. Brown wrote that "Negro employees with twenty years of service are never promoted to foremen, although they are well qualified to perform the job. Instead they are required to teach a new white foreman the job, to qualify him as the superior." Brown also described a system of complete segregation of job assignments. The EEOC investigated Brown's letter, finding that the company had violated the Civil Rights Act by restricting promotions to whites. This finding cleared the way for a class action lawsuit. "Complaint of Unfair Employment Practices Under the 1964 Civil Rights Act Title VII," March 13, 1965, filed as Exhibit A, *Brown v. Southern Dyestuff*; EEOC Decision, October 31, 1966, ibid.

19. William [illegible] to "Civil Rights Commission," copy in Folder 46, Box 13, Wharton Papers.

20. EEOC Charge of Discrimination of Dexter Law, November 24, 1970, *Galloway v. Fieldcrest Mills*.

21. Rowan, "The Negro in the Textile Industry," p. 15.

22. Donald Ray Hicks to Sir, June 4, 1969, *Hicks v. Cannon Mills*.

23. Complaint, June 1, 1970, ibid., p. 4.

24. Charge of Discrimination, April 16, 1970, ibid.; "Powerful C. A. Cannon Rules Kannapolis, N.C., But He Faces Challenge," *Wall Street Journal*, April 29, 1969, clipping in Folder 46, Box 13, Wharton Papers; Complaint, April 8, 1969, *United States v. Cannon Mills*.

25. Ferguson interview.

26. The complaint letter claimed that "the Company assigns Negro employees to the lowest-paid and least desirable jobs, being generally the jobs demanding the most strenuous and continuous physical exertion." Charge of Discrimination, April 16, 1970, *Hicks v. Cannon Mills*.

27. Ibid.

28. Ibid.

29. Rowan, "The Negro in the Textile Industry," p. 15.

30. Clayton interview.

31. The problems facing African American women in the southern textile industry will be discussed in the next chapter.

32. "Findings of Fact and Conclusions of Law," December 22, 1975, *Sledge v. J. P. Stevens*, p. 18.

33. Back Pay Questionnaire and Claim Forms of Larry Cornelius Dowton, February 16, 1981, and William Milton Lee, May 11, 1981, ibid.

34. Back Pay Questionnaire and Claim Forms of James Richard Person, June 4, 1981; Willie McKinley Green, July 27, 1983; John Thomas Lashley, n.d.; Alphonzo Richardson, March 27, 1981; and Thomas Young, February 10, 1981, all in ibid.

35. Back Pay Questionnaire and Claim Form of William Milton Lee, May 11, 1981, ibid.

36. Back Pay Questionnaire and Claim Forms of David L. Burnette, March 5, 1981; Orlando Johnson, February 17, 1981; Denise Johnson, April 12, 1981; and William Milton Lee, May 11, 1981, all in ibid.

37. Hearing of May 4, 1976, ibid., p. 15.

38. Transcript of Trial Proceedings, July 2, 1969, *Graniteville Company v. EEOC*, p. 34.

39. Defendant's Proposed Findings of Fact and Conclusions of Law, n.d., *Adams v. Dan River Mills*, p. 10.

40. Deposition of Mae Crews, January 7, 1970, ibid., p. 37.

41. See Chapter 1, table 1.

42. Transcript of Trial Proceedings, June 6–7, 1973, *Adams v. Dan River Mills*, pp. 282, 288, 291.

43. Robert W. Hereford, EEOC Charges of Discrimination, June 2, 1969, January 7, 1970, ibid..

44. Deposition of Robert Hereford, January 22, 1970, ibid., pp. 18, 30.

45. Transcript of Trial Proceedings, June 6–7, 1973, ibid., pp. 221–22.

46. Transcript of Trial Proceedings, June 5, 1973, ibid., pp. 2–3, 8, 30–31; Deposition of James Montgomery, March 11, 1970, ibid., p. 8.

47. Transcript of Trial Proceedings, June 6–7, 1973, ibid., p. 225.

48. Ibid., p. 229.

49. Wilson's testimony epitomized the refusal of the Dan River workers to accept the excuses that the company gave them: "I went to see Mr. Winn in the maintenance Department. He said he would let me know something if he got an opening. He didn't say anything else. I didn't hear anything so I went back again. He said if he gave me a job he might have to lay me off later. I told him I didn't mind taking a lay-off, if I could get a job in this department I could work myself up to a better paying job. He said he would let me know. Since then a lot of people has been hired." Transcript of Trial Proceedings, June 5, 1973, ibid., pp. 75, 125–26.

50. Deposition of Joe Marable, March 11, 1970, ibid., pp. 8–10.

51. Transcript of Trial Proceedings, June 5, 1973, ibid., p. 98.

52. Transcript of Trial Proceedings, June 6–7, 1973, ibid., p. 292.

53. Deposition of Leroy Ellison, October 31, 1973, *Ellison v. Rock Hill Printing and Finishing Company*, pp. 124–25.

54. Brown interview.

55. Subhead quotation comes from Chambers interview.

56. Plaintiffs' Third Compliance Report Pursuant to Paragraph 37 [c] of the Amended Decree, December 1, 1981, *Sledge v. J. P. Stevens*, pp. 2–6; Plaintiffs' Summary of Their Proposed Decree, and Memorandum in Support of Its Entry, February 23, 1976, ibid., p. 23.

57. Findings of Fact and Conclusions of Law, December 22, 1975, ibid., pp. 23–28.

58. Plaintiffs' Proposed Findings of Fact and Conclusions of Law, September 16, 1974, *Adams v. Dan River Mills*, pp. 6–7. These figures were for average pay rates of all hourly paid workers in Dan River's Danville division.

59. Ibid., pp. 8–10.

60. Ibid., p. 12.

61. Ibid. At J. P. Stevens, for example, only 25.3 percent of blacks who were hired with previous textile experience made more than $2.51 an hour in December 1975, compared to 59.8

percent of whites. Findings of Fact and Conclusions of Law, December 22, 1975, *Sledge v. J. P. Stevens*, p. 25.

62. Plaintiffs' Proposed Findings of Fact and Conclusions of Law, September 16, 1974, *Adams v. Dan River Mills*, pp. 13–16.

63. Exhibit Data, December 28, 1980, *Sledge v. J. P. Stevens*.

64. Plaintiffs' Proposed Findings of Fact and Conclusions of Law, June 11, 1980, *Lewis v. J. P. Stevens*, pp. 99–100.

65. U. A. Tull to Paul Swaity, December 19, 1966, Box 316, TWUA Papers.

66. Trial testimony of Robert Wharton, November 3, 1975, *Lewis v. J. P. Stevens*, p. 1516.

67. Trial testimony of James Roosevelt Williams, November 3, 1975, ibid., p. 1489.

68. Ibid.

69. Trial testimony of Theodore Rollinson, November 3, 1975, ibid., p. 1503.

70. Ibid.

71. Trial testimony, November 3, 1975, ibid., pp. 1490–1514.

72. Deposition of James Montgomery, March 11, 1970, *Adams v. Dan River Mills*, p. 17.

73. Transcript of Trial Proceedings, June 5, 1973, ibid., pp. 105–10.

74. Ibid., pp. 100–101.

75. Ibid., pp. 220–22.

76. As Smyka put it, "Well, drug operators I would say it's dirtier because a lot of different chemicals are around and a lot of different dye stuff is around, you have powder, dust and all, it's a lot of spills and so and so forth and they always wearing dirty cloths and rubber boots and most of the time rubber gloves but overall I would say the drug operator is a dirtier job than the machine operator." Transcript of Trial Proceedings, June 13, 1973, ibid., p. 90.

77. Deposition of Chris Brown, August 18, 1972, *Ellison v. Rock Hill Printing and Finishing Company*, p. 69.

78. Deposition of Charlie H. Ervin, November 1, 1973, ibid., pp. 5, 10.

79. The allegation of segregated jobs was a major complaint in *Hicks v. Cannon Mills*, where workers complained that "the Company contrives to depress all wages by the process of assigning white employees to 'white jobs' and Negroes to 'Negro jobs' and paying them the lowest wages possible under the circumstances." Charge of Discrimination, April 16, 1970, *Hicks v. Cannon Mills*.

80. Complaint, March 3, 1972, *Ellison v. Rock Hill Printing and Finishing Company*, p. 5.

81. Deposition of Leroy Ellison, August 17, 1972, ibid., p. 25; Deposition of Leroy Ellison, October 31, 1973, ibid., p. 49.

82. Deposition of Waco Meeks, November 1, 1973, ibid., pp. 6–7.

83. Deposition of Jerry H. Williamson, November 1, 1973, ibid., pp. 7–9.

84. Plaintiff's Memorandum in Support of Motion to Certify Class Action, March 17, 1978, *Seibles v. Cone Mills*, pp. 2–3; Order on Final Pre-Trial Conference, September 29, 1978, ibid., pp. 4, 6; Consent Decree, May 22, 1981, ibid.

85. Harry Slade, who had worked in the company's drug room for thirty-two years, testified in 1973 that "it was always a black job for the thirty-two years I know of. . . . Never a white man worked in the drug room as a drug room operator." Transcript of Trial Proceedings, June 6–7, 1973, *Adams v. Dan River Mills*, pp. 283, 295. Similarly, fellow drug room worker Charlie Smith described how "I don't work with white. We just colored work in the drug room." Deposition of Charlie Smith, January 23, 1970, ibid., p. 33.

86. Deposition of Joseph Graves, February 9, 1970, ibid., pp. 17–18, 21.

87. William C. Barksdale, for example, who worked in the "all Negro" dyeing department, complained in 1969 that "Dan River Mills maintains segregated work departments and job classifications on the basis of race." EEOC Charge of Discrimination of William C. Barksdale, March 30, 1969, ibid.

88. Transcript of Trial Proceedings, June 5, 1973, ibid., pp. 70–71.

89. Transcript of Trial Prodeedings, June 6–7, 1973, ibid., p. 285.

90. "Compliance Report—DSA 1966" folder, DRMC Papers; R. M. Gardiner to M. A. Cross, February 23, 1970, "Affirmative Action—Correspondence February 1970" folder, ibid.; Data in "Adams v. Dan River: Correspondence 1973 Folder Number 3" folder, ibid.

91. Findings of Fact and Conclusions of Law, December 22, 1975, *Sledge v. J. P. Stevens*, pp. 38–39; Findings of Fact and Conclusions of Law, November 10, 1975, *Sherrill v. J. P. Stevens*, pp. 21–29; Deposition of Paul Gene McLean, October 8, 1973, ibid., pp. 23–24.

92. Transcript of Trial Proceedings, June 5, 1973, *Adams v. Dan River Mills*, p. 97.

93. Deposition of Joseph Graves, February 9, 1970, ibid., p. 8; Deposition of Charlie Smith, January 23, 1970, ibid., p. 29.

94. In *Sledge v. J. P. Stevens*, the company's attorney Whiteford Blakeney gave a good description of the way that departmental seniority often proved to be discriminatory for black workers in nonproduction departments: "The blacks, say, were in a warehouse, a heavy number of blacks in a warehouse. That's a low-paying job. The blacks had a right to leave the warehouse and seek another opening in another department, but he would lose seniority if he went over there. Therefore, it was a handicap on him to get out of the warehouse. If he went somewhere else in another department, he would go in there without any seniority; and therefore, departmental seniority was a disadvantage to him in the sense of mobility." Hearing of February 24, 1976, *Sledge v. J. P. Stevens*, pp. 58–59.

95. Jonathan Wallas to Robert W. Hemphill, October 15, 1980, *Ellison v. Rock Hill Printing and Finishing Company*.

96. Deposition of Leroy Ellison, August 17, 1972, ibid., pp. 26–27.

97. Deposition of Bobby Johnson, August 9, 1972, ibid., p. 20. Similarly, Waco Meeks supported the suit because "if you would get a transfer you would lose your seniority." Deposition of Waco Meeks, August 9, 1972, ibid., p. 10.

98. "Textile Plants in the South Now Woo Negro Workers Seeking Better Jobs," *New York Times*, May 19, 1969, p. 42.

99. R. M. Gardiner to R. C. Gourley, June 4, 1970, "Affirmative Action—Correspondence 1970 March–July" folder, DRMC Papers; R. M. Gardiner to R. M. Stephens, July 1, 1969, "*Adams v. Dan River* Correspondence 1969 January–October" folder, ibid.

100. Robert T. Thompson to R. M. Stephens, November 30, 1970, "Affirmative Action Correspondence 1970 October–November" folder, ibid.; R. M. Gardiner to W. C. Jackson, June 25, 1970, "Affirmative Action—Statistical Information on Black Employment, Promotions, etc., 1968–1972" folder, ibid.

101. "Problems with Respect to the Affirmative Action Program," November 5, 1970, "Affirmative Action Correspondence 1970 October–November" folder, ibid.

102. Ibid.

103. Handwritten notes, "*Adams v. Dan River*: Correspondence 1970 January–March" folder, ibid.

104. "Problems with Respect to the Affirmative Action Program," November 5, 1970, "Affirmative Action Correspondence 1970 October–November" folder, ibid.

105. Deposition of Robert W. Hereford, January 22, 1970, *Adams v. Dan River Mills*, pp. 51–54.

106. Deposition of Dillard P. McDowell, October 10, 1973, *Sherrill v. J. P. Stevens*, pp. 1–8, 18–20.

107. Long interview.

108. Little interview.

109. Lucion Waller report, May 1968, Reel 163, SRC Papers.

110. Deposition of Chris Brown, November 1, 1973, *Ellison v. Rock Hill Printing and Finishing Company*, pp. 15–16.

111. "Exhibits in Support of Plaintiff's Opposition to Defendant's Motion for Summary Judgement; Oral Argument Requested," August 13, 1990, *Woods v. Fieldcrest-Cannon*.

112. Complaint, April 1, 1983, *Patrick v. Cone Mills*, p. 3; Complaint, *Lindsay v. Cone Mills*, September 13, 1976, p. 3.

113. In *Arnold v. Cone Mills*, for example, a black spare hand was sent home for two days and replaced by a white former employee. The plaintiff's complaint stated that "at least part of the reason for plaintiff's being denied the opportunity to work in January 1974 was his supervisor's animosity for his having talked to several white female employees." Order on Final Pre-trial Conference, August 30, 1978, *Arnold v. Cone Mills*, p. 2.

114. Deposition of Lovett R. Bean, March 9, 1972, *Bean v. Star Fibers*, pp. 24–25; Complaint, November 30, 1971, ibid., p. 3.

115. The lead plaintiff in the *Ellison* case, for example, recalled that at Rock Hill Printing and Finishing Company, one of the reasons that black men in the shipping department were not allowed to take inventory was that this would have brought them into contact with white women. Plaintiff's Memorandum in Opposition to Defendant's Motion to Dismiss, October 6, 1972, *Bean v. Star Fibers*, p. 2; Ellison interview.

116. Bennett Taylor, a black worker who started at J. P. Stevens in Roanoke Rapids, North Carolina, in 1965, explained, "Our women have been exploited for years because supervisors, you know, say what they want to say, and some of them try to talk our women to doing whatever they want them to do just to get different jobs." Taylor interview.

117. Mordecai Johnson to Jean Fairfax, January 1968 report, Reel 163, SRC Papers, p. 5; clipping entitled "Textile Group Says Hiring Is Not Biased," in ibid.

118. George Perkel to Henry Woicik, August 5, 1975, Box 2, ACTWU-SRO Papers; Moody interview; Clayton interview.

119. EEOC Charge of Discrimination of Timothy Harris, June 20, 1974, *Sledge v. J. P. Stevens*; Si Kahn to Joel Ax and Scott Hoyman, December 14, 1977, Box 58, ACTWU-SRO Papers.

120. Deposition of Leroy Ellison, October 31, 1973, *Ellison v. Rock Hill Printing and Finishing Company*, pp. 42, 73–74; Ellison interview. Similarly, plaintiff Johnnie Archie remembered that "all blacks were considered nonskilled labor regardless of whether they drove a fork truck, a dump truck, worked in the power plant, whatever they did, in the mail room. We were all in the same classification." Archie interview.

121. As plaintiff Waco Meeks explained, in his job in the late 1960s, "I was doing just about any and everything. I wasn't supposed to be doing but one thing. . . . I was driving a squeeze lift job and driving a big pick-up truck back and forth to different warehouses doing everything he wanted me to do." This system worked to the company's advantage and meant that management prevented blacks from receiving promotions because they preferred to use them for a variety of different jobs. Deposition of Waco Meeks, August 9, 1972, *Ellison v. Rock Hill Printing and Finishing Company*, p. 23.

122. Deposition of Oscar Gill Jr., November 1, 1973, ibid., pp. 11–12.

123. Typewritten complaint letter of Donald Ray Hicks Sr., n.d., *Hicks v. Cannon Mills*; Complaint letter of Albert Simpson, ibid.

124. Robert J. Lenrow to Eugene T. Bost, May 10, 1977, Box 79, Cannon Papers.

125. Plaintiffs' First Compliance Report Pursuant to Paragraph 37 [c] of the Amended Decree, December 31, 1980, *Sledge v. J. P. Stevens*, p. 4.

126. The case of *Wilson v. Fieldcrest Mills*, for example, a class action suit brought by black textile workers in Columbus, Georgia, began in 1978. The Columbus workers complained that many areas of the mill were still segregated, and that only black workers were required

to perform "menial and servile tasks" such as sweeping. Indeed, the case showed that blacks had made very little progress into higher-paying jobs in this major southern textile company, as black workers claimed that "in many cases when a task requires great physical exertion or where the job is unpleasant, blacks are exclusively assigned to perform these menial tasks." Complaint, September 15, 1978, *Wilson v. Fieldcrest Mills*, United States District Court, Southern District of Georgia, 1978, pp. 2–3.

127. E. T. Kehrer to Don Slaiman, January 25, 1967, Folder 10, Box 2857, AFL-CIO Papers.

128. Ferguson interview.

Chapter 6

1. See Hall et al., *Like a Family*, pp. xiii, 67–72; Hall, "Disorderly Women," pp. 355–56; Janiewsksi, *Sisterhood Denied*; and Frankel, "Southern Textile Women."

2. Transcript of EEOC Textile Forum, January 12–13, 1967, Part 2, Reel 2, LBJ Papers, pp. 47–50.

3. Trial transcript, November 6, 1972, *Sledge v. J. P. Stevens*, pp. 4–5.

4. Findings of Fact and Conclusions of Law, December 22, 1975, ibid., pp. 25, 30. At Dan River Mills the pay differential between white and black women who worked on hourly paid jobs in April 1973 was twelve cents an hour. At the same time, the pay differential between male workers was forty-one cents an hour. Plaintiffs' Proposed Findings of Fact and Conclusions of Law, September 16, 1974, *Adams v. Dan River Mills*, pp. 6–7.

5. Betsy Brinson to "My Colleagues in the South," August 15, 1977, Box 33, ACTWU-SRO Papers; "Unionization of the Textile Industry: A Case Study of J. P. Stevens," *Backgrounder*, August 3, 1977, p. 13, clipping in Folder 886, Andrews Papers; "Fact Sheet Cannon Mills Company," Folder 565, ibid.

6. "The Textile Industry and Negroes in Western South Carolina," TEAM report, Reel 163, SRC Papers, pp. 1–3.

7. Transcript of EEOC Textile Forum, January 12–13, 1967, Part 2, Reel 2, LBJ Papers, pp. 6, 22–23.

8. "A Statement on the Textile War Goods Shortage," n.d., Reel 67, SRC Papers.

9. Transcript of EEOC Textile Forum, January 12–13, 1967, Part 2, Reel 2, LBJ Papers, p. 33.

10. "The Textile Industry and Negroes in Western South Carolina," TEAM report, Reel 163, SRC Papers, p. 4.

11. At Columbia Mills in Columbia, South Carolina, for example, 59 black men were employed in September 1965 out of a total male employment of 485. Only 5 black women were employed out of a total of 205. EEO-1 form of Mount Vernon Mills, Columbia division, September 2, 1965, copy in Box 316, TWUA Papers.

12. EEO-1 form of Rock Hill Printing and Finishing Company, January 29, 1966, copy in ibid.

13. EEO-1 form of Courtaulds North America, February 27, 1966, copy in ibid.

14. Archie interview.

15. 1966 EEOC Summary Sheet for Bibb Mills, Folder 49, Box 12, Wharton Papers; Purnell interview; Freeman interview.

16. Seals interview.

17. Cobb, *The Selling of the South*, p. 119.

18. Plaintiffs' Proposed Findings of Fact and Conclusions of Law, June 11, 1980, *Lewis v. J. P. Stevens*, p. 7.

19. Plaintiffs' Proposed Findings of Fact and Conclusions of Law, September 16, 1974, *Adams v. Dan River Mills*, pp. 79–82.

20. Plaintiffs' Supplemental Statistical Tables Drawn from the Exhibits of Record, September 30, 1981, *Lewis v. Bloomsburg Mills*, pp. 7–23.

21. Introduction to Plaintiffs' Proposed Findings of Fact and Conclusions of Law, *Sledge v. J. P. Stevens*, p. 61.

22. Ibid., pp. 62–64.

23. Complaint for Injunctive and Other Relief, April 3, 1973, *Lewis v. Bloomsburg Mills*, p. 4.

24. "Workers Win Battle against J. P. Stevens," *News and Observer*, February 18, 1995, p. 1.

25. Plaintiffs' Proposed Findings of Fact and Conclusions of Law, September 16, 1974, *Adams v. Dan River Mills*, p. 5.

26. Transcript of EEOC Textile Forum, January 12–13, 1967, Part 2, Reel 2, LBJ Papers, pp. 47–49.

27. Hall, "Disorderly Women," p. 356. The activism of black women in the civil rights movement, especially in protesting against segregated accommodations and public facilities, has been documented. See, for example, Crawford, Rouse, and Woods, *Women in the Civil Rights Movement*.

28. Findings of Fact and Conclusions of Law, July 29, 1969, *Lea v. Cone Mills*, p. 9.

29. Annie Calhoun deposition, April 26, 1973, *Lewis v. Bloomsburg Mills*, p. 17.

30. Findings of Fact and Conclusions of Law, July 29, 1969, *Lea v. Cone Mills*, pp. 3–4.

31. Trial transcript, September 17, 1968, ibid., p. 58.

32. Deposition of Romona Pinnix, October 20, 1966, ibid., p. 10.

33. Defendant's First Amended Proposed Post-Trial Findings of Fact and Conclusions of Law, December 14, 1981, *Lewis v. Bloomsburg Mills*, pp. 11–12; Trial transcript, August 19, 1980, ibid., p. 145.

34. Plaintiffs' Answers to the Defendant's Second Interrogatories to them, May 5, 1975, ibid., p. 13.

35. Trial transcript, July 8, 1975, *Lewis v. J. P. Stevens*, pp. 322–26.

36. Deposition of Sallie Pearl Lewis, April 26, 1973, *Lewis v. Bloomsburg Mills*, p. 14.

37. EEOC Charge Form of Eatherene Brown, *Lewis v. J. P. Stevens*.

38. Trial transcript, September 17, 1968, *Lea v. Cone Mills*, p. 75.

39. Deposition of Romona Pinnix, October 20, 1966, ibid., pp. 12–13.

40. Trial transcript, September 17, 1968, ibid., pp. 26, 35, 52.

41. Ibid., pp. 58, 68; Deposition of Annie Tinnin, October 20, 1966, ibid., p. 19.

42. Deposition of Janie Belle Ashmore, May 24, 1973, *Lewis v. Bloomsburg Mills*, pp. 6–12.

43. Deposition of Thelma J. Edwards, April 19, 1974, ibid., pp. 18–19.

44. Deposition of Annie Calhoun, April 26, 1973, ibid., pp. 10, 17.

45. Deposition of Thelma J. Edwards, April 19, 1974, ibid., p. 19.

46. Deposition of Sallie Pearl Lewis, April 26, 1973, ibid., pp. 9–10, 11–13.

47. EEOC Charge of Discrimination of Gracie Childress, July 28, 1969, *Adams v. Dan River Mills*.

48. EEOC Charge of Discrimination of Josephine Jennings, June 23, 1969, ibid.

49. Statement by Clifford L. Alexander Jr., Chairman, EEOC, before the Subcommittee on Administrative Practice and Procedure of the Senate Judiciary Committee, March 27, 1969, copy in Reel 163, SRC Papers, pp. 7–8.

50. Hearing of February 24, 1976, *Sledge v. J. P. Stevens*, p. 97.

51. Deposition of Loretta Harris, January 22, 1970, *Adams v. Dan River Mills*, pp. 9, 16; EEOC Charge of Discrimination of Loretta Harris, January 7, 1970, ibid.

52. Pattie Kearney to J. Rich Leonard, February 19, 1981, *Sledge v. J. P. Stevens*.

53. Back Pay Questionnaire and Claim Form of Ruby V. Ward, February 14, 1980, ibid.

54. Back Pay Questionnaire and Claim Form of Annette Hawkins, May 13, 1981, ibid.

55. Back Pay Questionnaire and Claim Form of Denise Johnson, April 12, 1981, ibid.

56. Back Pay Questionnaire and Claim Form of Hattie F. Lewis, February 14, 1981, ibid.

57. TEAM's records highlight the resistance of textile companies to employing African American women as well as the determination of the women to overcome the barriers of opposition. The civil rights agency was approached by many black women who asked for help in their seemingly endless search for a textile job. In September 1968, for example, TEAM reported: "At one of the committee meetings one lady stated that she had been to 8 companies recently and was told that there was no jobs for people who did not have experience." Project Report for Year Ending September 1968, September 12, 1968, Reel 163, SRC Papers, pp. 58–65.

58. Deposition of Marian Louise Epps, February 23, 1970, *Adams v. Dan River Mills*, p. 18; Deposition of Elizabeth Millner, February 25, 1970, ibid., pp. 30–32.

59. Deposition of John S. Crenshaw, February 25, 1970, ibid., p. 17.

60. Introduction to Plaintiffs' Proposed Findings of Fact and Conclusions of Law, *Sledge v. J. P. Stevens*, pp. 53–55.

61. Plaintiffs' Proposed Findings of Fact and Conclusions of Law, September 16, 1974, *Adams v. Dan River Mills*, pp. 6–7.

62. This analysis concluded that "compared with the showings of discrimination made at trial, the situation has become substantially worse for black males, and has become better for black females." Plaintiffs' First Compliance Report Pursuant to Paragraph 37 [c] of the Amended Decree, December 31, 1980, *Sledge v. J. P. Stevens*, p. 4.

63. Some interesting work has been carried out on black women who worked in tobacco, one of the few southern industries to hire black women before 1965. See, for example, Janiewski, *Sisterhood Denied*.

64. Lincks interview.

65. Blanche and Kay Willis interview, tape G8/G9, Uprising Papers, pp. 1, 8.

66. Trawick interview.

67. Peddaway interview.

68. Harrison interview.

69. Peddaway interview.

70. Corine Lytle Cannon interview in Byerly, *Hard Times*, p. 151.

71. Blanche and Kay Willis interview, tape G8/G9, Uprising Papers, p. 5.

72. Trawick interview.

73. Harrison interview.

74. "A Consultation on the South: The Ethical Demands of Integration," December 27–29, 1962, "Merit Employment Program Conference: Ethical Demands of Integration" folder, "South-Eastern Regional Office, 1960 to 1962" box, AFSC Papers.

75. Ibid.

76. Trawick interview.

77. Ibid.

78. Blanche and Kay Willis interview, tape G8/G9, Uprising Papers, p. 16.

79. Harrison interview.

80. Gordon interview.

81. Ibid.

82. Peddaway interview; Blanche and Kay Willis interview, tape G8/G9, Uprising Papers, p. 5; Seals interview.

83. Johnny Mae Fields interview in Byerly, *Hard Times*, p. 137.

84. Rogers interview.

85. Seals interview.

86. Crittenden interview.

87. Plant visit to J. Richard Walton of West Point Pepperell, July 14, 1969, Folder 18, Box 13, Wharton Papers. Riegel Textile Corporation claimed that they wanted to hire more black women "since they appear to be more reliable than men and better workers." Plant visit to H. D. Kingsmore of Riegel Textile Corporation, n.d., ibid.

88. Glover interview.

89. Dan River rewarded its best employees the least, while those with the least education and lowest performance held the best jobs. Indeed, in 1972 white males with three years of education earned an average hourly wage of $2.55, while black women with the same education earned only $2.03. These figures say much about the inefficiency of the segregated labor system that characterized southern textiles up to the 1960s, a system that virtually excluded black women from the mills and reserved high-paid jobs for white men. When black women did gain entry to the mills, they were determined to hold on to their jobs and prove that they were good workers. R. C. Gourley to R. M. Stephens, May 1, 1970, "Affirmative Action—Statistical Information on Black Employment, Promotions, etc., 1968–1972" folder, DRMC Papers.

90. Katie Geneva Cannon interview in Byerly, *Hard Times*, pp. 38–39.

91. Blanche Willis interview, tape G8/G9, Uprising Papers, p. 17.

92. Kelly Alexander to Horace F. Hill, August 10, 1966; Kelly Alexander to Frank D. Brannon, August 10, 1966, both in Folder 11, Box 28, Alexander Papers.

93. Charge of Discrimination, April 16, 1970, *Hicks v. Cannon Mills*, p. 2.

94. Affidavit of Sallie Pearl Lewis, September 16, 1970, *Lewis v. Bloomsburg Mills*.

95. Project Report for Year Ending September 1968, September 12, 1968, Reel 163, SRC Papers, p. 22.

96. Gordon interview.

97. Alice Gallman to Mordecai C. Johnson, August 25, 1968, Reel 163, SRC Papers.

98. Pope interview.

99. Harrison interview.

100. Carter interview.

101. Rogers interview.

102. "Jones Family 'Pulling Out' of Poverty; Industry Helps," *Greenville Piedmont*, June 1, 1968, clipping in Reel 163, SRC Papers.

103. Glover interview.

104. Ibid.

105. McCutchen interview.

106. June interview.

107. Deposition of Otto A. King, May 11, 1967, *Lea v. Cone Mills*, pp. 26–27.

108. Deposition of Anderson L. Hinson, May 11, 1967, ibid., p. 29.

109. John Bagwill, a vice president of Cone Mills in charge of industrial and public relations, explained this point: "The positions in the textile industry are pretty well established by years and years of tradition. A loom fixer is a loom fixer from one end of the textile industry to the other; a slubber tender is a slubber tender, and a card tender is a card tender, a weaver is a weaver, and a spinner is a spinner. They may work on different types of fabrics, but the basic nature of the job is many years old and substantially the same with minor variations in the entire industry." Deposition of John W. Bagwill, May 11, 1967, ibid., p. 10.

110. Deering-Milliken plant visit, n.d., Folder 18, Box 13, Wharton Papers.

111. Juanita Harrison, "My Activities with TEAM," Reel 163, SRC Papers, p. 1.

112. Mordecai Johnson to Jean Fairfax, report for January 1968, ibid., p. 5.

113. Lucion Waller report for May 1968, ibid.

114. Staton interview.

115. EEOC Charge Form of Ida Mae Caldwell, April 27, 1969, *Hicks v. Cannon Mills*.

116. Mrs. Crowder to Judge Stanley, March 24, 1970, *United States v. Cannon Mills*.

117. Mary J. Black to Judge Stanley, March 5, 1970, ibid.

118. Trial testimony of Willie Sue Johnson, August 19–September 26, 1980, *Lewis v. Bloomsburg Mills*, pp. 523–24, 531–32.

119. Trial testimony of Luella Gunter, August 19–September 26, 1980, ibid., pp. 645, 646, 651.

120. EEOC Charge of Discrimination, *Adams v. Dan River Mills*; Deposition of Leroy Johnson, March 31, 1969, ibid. , p. 37.

121. Deposition of Henry Wilson, February 10, 1970, ibid., pp. 25–26.

122. Deposition of Janie Hunt, February 10, 1970, ibid., pp. 5, 11, 16, 18.

123. Alice Gallman to Mordecai C. Johnson, August 25, 1968, Reel 163, SRC Papers, p. 6.

124. Back Pay Claim Form and Questionnaire of Marion Brown Mason, February 14, 1981, *Sledge v. J. P. Stevens*.

125. Back Pay Claim Form and Questionnaire of Lena Harris Dowtin, February 11, 1981, ibid.

126. Debbie Tedder, "Why a Woman Should Be for the Union," News Area 3, Box 58, ACTWU-SRO Papers.

127. Harold McIver to Henry Woicik, January 9, 1976, ibid.

128. EEOC Charge of Discrimination by Fayetta Kendrix, October 26, 1975, Box 4, ibid.

129. Back Pay Questionnaire and Claim Form of Evelyn Annette Pearson Ward, February 16, 1981, *Sledge v. J. P. Stevens*.

130. Back Pay Questionnaire and Claim Form of Doris Jean Lee Lynch, February 21, 1981, ibid.

131. Trial testimony of Mary Coleman, August 19–September 26, 1980, *Lewis v. Bloomsburg Mills*, p. 935.

132. Mary J. Black to Judge Stanley, March 5, 1970, *United States v. Cannon Mills*; Mrs. V.M. to Sir, April 3, 1970, ibid.

133. EEOC Charge of Discrimination of Anna F. Bethea, August 20, 1976, Folder 8, Box 25, Alexander Papers.

134. Rachel M. Houston to Clerk, United States District Court, February 3, 1982, *Hicks v. Cannon Mills*.

135. Mary Boyd to Sir, August 24, 1978, *Galloway v. Fieldcrest Mills*.

136. EEOC Charge of Discrimination of Elaine McCree, March 11, 1970, *Hicks v. Cannon Mills*.

137. EEOC Charge of Discrimination of Eva Blackman Rice, March 11, 1970, ibid.

138. Trial testimony of Mary Coleman, August 19–September 26, 1980, *Lewis v. Bloomsburg Mills*, p. 573.

139. Trial testimony of Luella Gunter, August 19–September 26, 1980, ibid., pp. 645–46.

140. Back Pay Claim Form of Cathy Lou Long, n.d., *Sledge v. J. P. Stevens*.

141. Trial testimony of Phyllis Dunlap, August 19–September 26, 1980, *Lewis v. Bloomsburg Mills*, pp. 579–81, 584.

142. Trial testimony of Paretha Clinkscales, August 19–September 26, 1980, ibid., p. 622.

143. EEOC Charge of Discrimination of Johnny Mae Wilson, July 27, 1969, *Hicks v. Cannon Mills*.

144. EEOC Charge of Discrimination of Ruth B. Leazer, March 26, 1971, Box 79, Cannon Papers.

145. Deposition of Mae Crews, January 7, 1970, *Adams v. Dan River Mills*, p. 20.

146. EEOC Charge of Discrimination of Erma Garland, March 31, 1969, ibid.

147. Deposition of Erma Garland, February 9, 1970, ibid., pp. 20–23.

148. EEOC Charges of Discrimination of Helen Crews and Mae Crews, both dated March 30, 1969, ibid.

149. Trial testimony of Mabel Floyd, August 19–September 26, 1980, *Lewis v. Bloomsburg Mills*, p. 592; Trial testimony of Fannie Mae Williams, August 19–September 26, 1980, ibid., pp. 606–7.

150. Trial testimony of Josie Mae Johnson, August 19–September 26, 1980, ibid., p. 677.

151. Deposition of Gracie Childress, February 9, 1970, *Adams v. Dan River Mills*, p. 23.

152. Application for Issuance of Order to Show Cause Why Defendant Should Not Be Held in Contempt, n.d., *Equal Employment Opportunity Commission v. Cannon Mills*, Box 79, Cannon Papers, p. 3.

153. Affidavit of Jay Campbell, November 11, 1975, ibid.; Memorandum in Support of Application for Issuance of Order to Show Cause Why Defendant Should Not Be Held in Contempt, n.d., ibid., p. 4; Appeal of the Regional Director's Refusal to Issue a Complaint, June 20, 1975, *Cannon Mills v. Textile Workers Union of America*, Box 79, Cannon Papers, pp. 2–4; EEOC Affidavit of Daisy R. Crawford, June 5, 1975, Box 79, Cannon Papers.

154. Deposition of Gracie Childress, February 9, 1970, *Adams v. Dan River Mills*, pp. 24–31.

155. Addie Jackson quoted in *Social Justice*, no. 23 (Summer 1979): 2, copy in Box 33, ACTWU-SRO Papers.

156. "Fact Sheet for Press: The Oneita Knitting Mills Strike," n.d., Pope Papers.

157. Pope interview.

158. Hoyman interview.

159. Sol Stetin to TWUA Local Unions, Joint Boards, and Staff, July 23, 1973, Pope Papers.

160. For the support given the J. P. Stevens campaign and boycott by women's rights groups, see Betsy Brinson to "My Colleagues in the South," August 15, 1977, Box 33, ACTWU-SRO Papers; Boycott Report, n.d., Box 58, ibid.

161. "Steinem, Rustin to Join Textile Workers' Demonstration at J. C. Penney Tuesday P.M.," TWUA Press Release, April 30, 1973; Sol Stetin to "Friend," March 22, 1973; Scott Hoyman standard letter publicizing boycott, n.d., all in Pope Papers.

162. George Perkel to Sol Stetin, August 2, 1973, ibid.; Rustin quoted in *Contract, Contract*.

163. Laura Ann Pope and Glora Jean Robinson quoted in *Contract, Contract*.

164. Scott Hoyman letter publicizing Oneita boycott, n.d., Pope Papers.

165. Sol Stetin to "Friend," March 22, 1973, ibid.

166. Sol Stetin to TWUA Local Unions, Joint Boards and Staff, July 23, 1973, ibid.

167. Pope interview.

168. Ibid.

169. Ibid.

170. "Fact Sheet for Press: The Oneita Knitting Mills Strike," n.d., Pope Papers.

171. Pope interview.

172. McCutchen interview.

173. June interview.

174. McCutchen interview.

175. Flyer reprinted from *Textile Labor*, March 1973, Pope Papers.

176. Rustin commentary to *Contract, Contract*; McCutchen interview.

177. Mary Cox in *Contract, Contract*.

178. Pope interview.

179. Mary Cox quoted in *Contract, Contract*.

180. Carmela McCutchen quoted in "A Talk with the Oneita Strikers," *The Call*, June 1973, pp. 12–13; Carolyn Ashbaugh and Dan McCurry, "On the Line at Oneita," in Miller, *Working Lives*, pp. 205–14, quote on p. 213.

181. Raynor, "Unionism in the Southern Textile Industry," pp. 90–91.

182. Ashbaugh and McCurry, "On the Line at Oneita," pp. 206, 210–11; unidentified black striker in *Contract, Contract*; Raynor, "Unionism in the Southern Textile Industry," p. 91.

183. Hall, "Disorderly Women," p. 355.

184. Ibid., p. 356; Jameson, "Imperfect Unions"; Thompson, "Women and Nineteenth-Century Radical Politics"; Humphries, "The Working Class Family"; Turbin, "Reconceptualizing Family"; Dublin, *Women at Work*; Tax, *The Rising of the Women*; Strom, "Challenging 'Woman's Place'"; Janiewski, *Sisterhood Denied*.

185. Much of the best material on women textile workers before World War II has been written by Jacquelyn Dowd Hall. See especially "Disorderly Women" and "Private Eyes, Public Women." Frankel, "Southern Textile Women," covers the years between 1900 and 1960; Roydhouse, "Big Enough to Tell Weeds from the Beans," concentrates on the first thirty years of the twentieth century.

186. Pope interview; Transcript of EEOC Textile Forum, January 12–13, 1967, Part 2, Reel 2, LBJ Papers, pp. 99–100.

Chapter 7

1. Norrell, "One Thing We Did Right," pp. 65–67.

2. Community studies of large southern centers include Corley, "The Quest for Racial Harmony"; Rogers, "Humanity and Desire"; and Beifuss, *At the River I Stand*. Studies of smaller communities outside the Piedmont include Greene, *Praying for Sheetrock*; Norrell, *Reaping the Whirlwind*; Colburn, *Racial Change and Community Crisis*; and Salter, *Jackson, Mississippi*. Chafe's excellent *Civilities and Civil Rights* is an exception to these studies because it focuses on the Piedmont community of Greensboro, North Carolina, and covers the attitudes of businessmen to integration.

3. J. Mills Thornton quoted in Norrell, "One Thing We Did Right," p. 75; Chafe, "The End of One Struggle, the Beginning of Another," p. 147.

4. "Information on Efforts to Reduce Racial Discrimination and Create Equality of Job Opportunity in the Southern Textile Industry," January 30, 1969, Reel 163, SRC Papers.

5. Project Report for Year Ending September 1968, September 12, 1968, ibid., pp. 1–2; Jean Fairfax to Mordecai Johnson, August 7, 1967, ibid., pp. 1–4.

6. Project Report for Year Ending September 1968, September 12, 1968, ibid., pp. 4–6.

7. "Agencies Unite to Increase Textile Industry Employment," *The Afro-American* (South Carolina edition), clipping dated November 4, 1967; clipping entitled "New Civil Rights Organization Aims at Opening Job Opportunities in S.C.," dated October 27, 1967, both in ibid.

8. "Agencies Unite to Increase Textile Industry Employment," *The Afro-American* (South Carolina edition), November 4, 1967, clipping in ibid.; Project Report for Year Ending September 1968, September 12, 1968, ibid., pp. 13, 27.

9. "The Textile Industry and Negroes in Western South Carolina," ibid., pp. 1–5.

10. Mordecai C. Johnson to Louise Moss, May 10, 1968; Mordecai C. Johnson to the editor of the *Greenville News*, May 27, 1968; clipping entitled "TEAM Official Says Negro Needs Unmet," dated May 13, 1968, all in ibid.

11. "Equal Employment in the Textile Industry of South Carolina," Workbook for Community Leaders, November 1967, ibid.

12. Project Report for Year Ending September 1968, September 12, 1968, ibid., p. 5; "Textile Jobs for Negroes Sought," *Spartanburg Herald-Journal*, October 22, 1967, clipping in ibid.

13. Project Report for Year Ending September 1968, September 12, 1968, ibid., p. 17.

14. Minutes of TEAM Board Meeting, March 8, 1968, ibid., pp. 2–3; Project Report for Year Ending September 1968, September 12, 1968, ibid., p. 12.

15. Four Months Activity Report of Robert M. Ford, September 1968, ibid.; Project Report for Year Ending September 1968, September 12, 1968, ibid., pp. 12–13, 15, 25.

16. Interview with Tom M. Georgian, personnel director, and Bill Price, Equal Employment Officer, Abbeville Mills, Abbeville, S.C., February 27, 1968, ibid., p. 3; Project Report for Year Ending September 1968, September 12, 1968, ibid., pp. 15, 25.

17. Project Report for Year Ending September 1968, September 12, 1968, ibid., p. 54; Minutes of TEAM Board Meeting, March 8, 1968, ibid., p. 3.

18. Mordecai Johnson to Jean Fairfax, September 22, 1967, Reel 164, ibid.

19. William Patrick Flack Report, August 31, 1968, ibid.; Minutes of TEAM Board Meeting, August 16, 1968, ibid.; Project Report for Year Ending September 1968, September 12, 1968, ibid., pp. 18, 52.

20. Alice Gallman to Mordecai C. Johnson, August 25, 1968, ibid.; Minutes of TEAM Board Meeting of August 28, 1968, ibid., p. 4; Minutes of TEAM Board Meeting, March 8, 1968, ibid., p. 6.

21. Minutes of TEAM Meeting, August 28, 1968, ibid., p. 1; "My Activities with TEAM from Juanita Harrison," ibid., p. 4.

22. Project Report for Year Ending September 1968, September 12, 1968, ibid., p. 21.

23. Lucion Waller to Mordecai Johnson, August 1968, ibid.

24. Project Report for Year Ending September 1968, September 12, 1968, ibid., p. 29; TEAM—Summary of Activities, October 1968, ibid., pp. 7–8. TEAM never achieved the coordination it desired with federal agencies. One summary report, for example, claimed: "We have had perhaps a little less than half of the performance we had hoped for, and sometimes promised, from government agencies." Generally, TEAM aides complained that the federal machinery was too slow to give confidence to African American workers to file charges. TEAM Summary Report, September 1968, ibid., p. 5.

25. Project Report for Year Ending September 1968, September 12, 1968, ibid., p. 33.

26. Ibid., pp. 15, 17, 37; Minutes of TEAM Meeting, August 16, 1968, ibid., p. 6.

27. Mordecai Johnson to Constance Curry, September 9, 1968; William Patrick Flack, report of August 22, 1968, both in ibid.

28. Project Report for Year Ending September 1968, September 12, 1968, ibid., pp. 32, 37, 69; report of TEAM aide William Patrick Flack, week of August 19–22, 1968, ibid. The children of TEAM aide Alice Gallman were subjected to abuse "on the school bus going to the white school." Project Report for Year Ending September 1968, September 12, 1968, ibid., p. 69.

29. Reports of William Patrick Flack, August 22, 1968, and August 24, 1968, ibid.

30. Project Report for Year Ending September 1968, September 12, 1968, ibid., pp. 61–62, 65.

31. Ibid., p. 53.

32. Report of William Patrick Flack, August 31, 1968, ibid., p. 3.

33. Project Report for Year Ending September 1968, September 12, 1968, ibid., p. 27.

34. Report of William Patrick Flack, August 31, 1968, ibid., p. 2.

35. Report of TEAM aide William Patrick Flack, July 15–19, 1968, ibid., p. 1.

36. Alice Gallman to Mordecai C. Johnson, August 25, 1968, Reel 163, SRC Papers, pp. 3–6.

37. Project Report for Year Ending September 1968, September 12, 1968, ibid., pp. 23–24, 37–39.

38. Ibid., p. 52.

39. Ibid., pp. 2–4, 70; TEAM Summary Report, September 1968, ibid., pp. 2–3.

40. Project Report for Year Ending September 1968, September 12, 1968, ibid., pp. 67–68.

41. Ibid., pp. 48–52.

42. TEAM Summary Report, September 1968, ibid., p. 3.

43. Alice Gallman to Mordecai C. Johnson, August 25, 1968, ibid.

44. William Patrick Flack report of August 31, 1968, ibid.

45. "TEAM Makes Presence Felt Here; High Level Jobs Not Forthcoming," clipping from Greenville newspaper, November 9, 1968, in ibid.

46. Solomon Barkin to William Pollock, April 5, 1961, "Equal Employment Opportunity 1961" folder, Box 316, TWUA Papers; "Negro Job Curbs in South Charged," *New York Times*, July 7, 1961; "Panel Criticized on Negroes' Jobs," *New York Times*, January 9, 1964; "Tactics Planned on Job Bias Fight," *New York Times*, July 20, 1968.

47. "Packard's Accord on Job Bias Called 'Sellout' by Rights Aides," *New York Times*, March 20, 1969; Hill interview.

48. NAACP Legal Defense and Educational Fund Docket Report, September 1966, Folder 6, Box 2, Alexander Papers; Memorandum from Ruby Hurley to North Carolina Branches, November 22, 1965, Folder 15, Box 28, ibid.; Memorandum in Support of Application for Issuance of Order to Show Cause Why Defendant Should Not Be Held in Contempt, n.d., *Equal Employment Opportunity Commission v. Cannon Mills*, Box 79, Cannon Papers, p. 5; Petition for Rehearing and Suggestion for Rehearing En Banc on Behalf of Plaintiffs-Appellees in No. 76-1988 and Plaintiffs-Appellants in Nos. 76-2150 and 76-2303, *Sledge v. J. P. Stevens*, copy in Box 22, ACTWU-SRO Papers, p. 1; Complaint, August 22, 1973, *Galloway v. Fieldcrest Mills*, p. 8; Brief for Plaintiffs, n.d., *Lea v. Cone Mills*, p. 40; Bloomsburg's Statement of Defenses in Response to Court's April 8, 1980, Order, *Lewis v. Bloomsburg Mills*, June 14, 1980, p. 42; Defendant's Discovery Deposition, March 29, 1966, *Hall v. Werthan Bag*, first unmarked page; Complaint, *Ellison v. Rock Hill Printing and Finishing Company*, p. 8; Complaint, October 24, 1969, *Adams v. Dan River Mills*, p. 6.

49. Statement of Southeastern Region V National Association for the Advancement of Colored People on Employment, Montgomery, Alabama, March 19, 1977, Folder 11, Box 18, Alexander Papers; Trial testimony of A. C. Sherrill, August 28, 1974, *Sherrill v. J. P. Stevens*, pp. 88–89.

50. 1965 Annual Report, Southeast Region NAACP, Folder 24, Box 17, Alexander Papers, pp. 21–23; 1967 North Carolina State Conference of Branches, NAACP, Twenty-Fourth Annual Convention, November 24, 1967, Folder 11, Box 23, ibid., p. 17.

51. Transcript of EEOC Textile Forum, January 12–13, 1967, Part 2, Reel 2, LBJ Papers, pp. 105–6.

52. Ferguson interview.

53. Ibid.

54. Chambers interview.

55. Brief in Support of Defendant's Motion for Summary Judgement, November 19, 1971, *Broadnax v. Burlington Industries*, p. 3.

56. Comments of John Bolt Cuthbertson in deposition of Leroy Ellison, August 17, 1972, *Ellison v. Rock Hill Printing and Finishing Company*, p. 46.

57. Ellison interview.

58. Deposition of Mae Crews, January 7, 1970, *Adams v. Dan River Mills*, p. 14; Brief on Behalf of Defendant, December 20, 1968, *Lea v. Cone Mills*, p. 20; Trial testimony of Shirley Lea, September 17, 1968, ibid., p. 35; Gordon interview.

59. Moody interview.

60. These letters are discussed in Chapter 5.

61. Transcript of Trial Proceedings, June 5, 1973, *Adams v. Dan River Mills*, pp. 72, 73, 85.

62. Transcript of Trial Proceedings, June 6–7, 1973, ibid., pp. 235, 241.

63. Ibid., pp. 228–29.

64. Deposition of Paul Gene McLean, October 8, 1973, *Sherrill v. J. P. Stevens*, p. 10.

65. Deposition of Robert H. Costner, October 8, 1973, ibid., pp. 2–4, 11, 50, 55, 56, 62, 73.

66. Transcript of Trial Proceedings, June 5, 1973, *Adams v. Dan River Mills*, pp. 1–6.

67. Deposition of Jerry Williamson, August 18, 1972, *Ellison v. Rock Hill Printing and Finishing Company*, pp. 92, 97.

68. Deposition of Chris Brown, November 1, 1973, ibid., p. 25.

69. Deposition of Leroy Ellison, August 17, 1972, ibid., pp. 89, 91–92.

70. Fairclough, "State of the Art," p. 393.

71. "Negro Youths Invade RH Lunch Counters," *Rock Hill Evening Herald*, February 12, 1960, p. 1; "Lengthy Trial Seems Sure in Test Case," *Rock Hill Evening Herald*, March 24, 1960, p. 1; "Visiting Negroes Stage Weekend Demonstrations," *Rock Hill Evening Herald*, February 13, 1961, p. 1; "Demonstrators Arrested in R.H.," *Rock Hill Evening Herald*, January 31, 1961, p. 1; "Human Rights Group Hears Visiting Sit-in Leaders," *Rock Hill Evening Herald*, February 7, 1961, p. 2; "How Will Rock Hill Be Judged?" *Rock Hill Evening Herald*, February 13, 1960, p. 4; "Let Law and Order Prevail," *Rock Hill Evening Herald*, February 8, 1961, p. 4.

72. "Citizens' Council Leader Urges Law, Not Violence," *Rock Hill Evening Herald*, February 17, 1960, p. 1; "Citizens' Council Formation Outlined," *Rock Hill Evening Herald*, February 22, 1960, p. 1; "600 Hear Gressette Push Citizens' Council," *Rock Hill Evening Herald*, February 26, 1960, p. 1.

73. The records of the North Carolina Advisory Committee on Civil Rights, for example, contain a large clipping file that shows there were many civil rights protests in Piedmont communities, often directly concerned with employment. See, for example, *Greensboro Daily News*, February 8, 1959, p. A9, and *Grifton Times*, July 20, 1961, clippings in Employment Clipfile, North Carolina Advisory Committee on Civil Rights, held at the Southern Historical Collection, University of North Carolina at Chapel Hill.

74. "Negroes Conduct Orderly Segregation Protest Here," *Greenville News*, January 2, 1960, pp. 1–2; "April 1960—Demonstration By Negro Groups in South Carolina," "South Carolina Voter Education Project April 23, 1958–April 14, 1965" folder, Box 87, Congress of Racial Equality Papers, Martin Luther King, Jr., Center for Non-Violent Social Change, Atlanta, Ga.

75. SNCC Fact Sheet, Folder 26, Box 105, SNCC Papers; "Dr. King Steps Up Danville Protest," *New York Times*, July 12, 1963.

76. Ivanhoe Donaldson, "Danville Report," September 1963, Folder 26, Box 105, SNCC Papers, p. 1; "News from Danville Christian Progressive Association," July 15, 1963, ibid.; "100 Foes of Segregation Picket Virginia Concern's Local Office," *New York Times*, July 18, 1963.

77. "An Overall Proposal," Folder 26, Box 105, SNCC Papers; SNCC Fact Sheet, ibid.; Ivanhoe Donaldson, "Danville Report," September 1963, ibid., pp. 1, 3.

78. "Danville, Virginia," SNCC Pamphlet, August 1963, copy in ibid.

79. White, *Black Leadership*, pp. 126–27.

80. "Danville Method Studied in South," *New York Times*, August 11, 1963; *Newsweek*, March 1, 1965, pp. 28–29.

81. Ivanhoe Donaldson, "Danville Report," September 1963, Folder 26, Box 105, SNCC Papers; Testimony of Robert M. Gardiner, January 11, 1974, *Adams v. Dan River Mills*, pp. 340–42; SNCC Progress Report, Danville, Virginia, Folder 26, Box 105, SNCC Papers.

82. SNCC Progress Report, Danville, Virginia, ibid.; Interview of Rev. L. W. Chase by Avon W. Rollins, National Executiveman, SNCC, ibid.

83. Plaintiffs' Proposed Findings of Fact and Conclusions of Law, September 16, 1974, *Adams v. Dan River Mills*, p. 53.

84. Deposition of Edward Crews, January 6, 1970, ibid., p. 40.

85. Deposition of Helen Crews, January 7, 1970, ibid., pp. 20–21.

86. Deposition of Mae Crews, January 7, 1970, ibid., pp. 14–17.

87. Trial testimony of Julious Adams, June 6–7, 1973, ibid., p. 214.

88. Deposition of Donald R. Aichner, September 19, 1973, ibid., pp. 72–75.

89. Aichner quoted in Reply Brief for Defendant, February 27, 1975, ibid., p. 77.

90. Minutes, Employment on Merit Committee, March 24, 1964, "Minutes High Point Regional Office 1964" folder, "Regional Office Minutes 1964" box, AFSC Papers.

91. Mayes Behrman, "A Presentation of Employment on Merit," "Merit Employment General 1959" folder, "Southeastern Regional Office 1957–1959" box, ibid.; Plant Visit to Archdale Hosiery and Machine Company, November 17, 1959, "Southern Program, High Point Regional Office, Employment on Merit 1959 Community Relations File" folder, "American Section 1959 Community Relations—Southern Program" box, ibid.; Summary of Visits Received in Philadelphia Office—March 1 to 30, April 2, 1956, "Job Opportunities—Summaries of Visits Made by National and Regional Office Staff Project Section 1956" folder, "American Section 1956 Community Relations" box, ibid.; American Friends Service Committee Merit Employment Programs: A Summary, November 19, 1957, "Southern Program—General Employment on Merit Reports, Civil Rights File" folder, "American Section 1957 Community Relations—Southern Program" box, ibid., pp. 1, 4–5.

92. These efforts are described in greater detail in Chapter 1.

93. "Negroes Conduct Orderly Segregation Protest Here," *Greenville News*, January 2, 1960, p. 2.

94. Eric Morton, "Proposal for a SNCC Project in North Carolina," May 30, 1965, Folder 3, Box 105, SNCC Papers; "The 2nd Congressional District," ibid.

95. Fairclough, "State of the Art," pp. 392, 398; Meier, "Toward a Synthesis of Civil Rights History," p. 212.

96. Ward and Badger, *The Making of Martin Luther King*, pp. 1–2.

Chapter 8

1. Wilton E. Hartzler to Edwin C. Bertsche, May 3, 1967, "College Program: Conference on Textile Workers' Rights, Southeastern Regional Office 1967" folder, "Southeastern Regional Office 1967" box, AFSC Papers.

2. Halpern, "Organized Labor," pp. 359–60, 382; Letwin, "Interracial Unionism," pp. 520–22.

3. Truchil, "Capital-Labor Relationships," p. 231. A further merger in 1995 saw the union change its name to UNITE! (Union of Needletrades, Industrial, and Textile Employees). ACTWU's ACWA heritage has meant that it has generally been more supportive of black worker inclusion than the old TWUA. The 1995 merger saw ACTWU incorporate the needletrades union, and UNITE! has had recent success among black apparel workers.

4. "Staff Meeting in President Pollock's Office," December 21, 1966, Box 90, TWUA Papers; Statement of the Textile Workers Union of America at the EEOC Textile Employment Forum, January 12–13, 1967, Box 316, ibid., pp. 4–6.

5. For the two-year period ending on February 28, 1966, for example, the TWUA lost eleven elections in the Carolinas and won only four. George Perkel to Richard S. Bunce, September 6, 1966, ibid.

6. Southern Union Staff Training Seminar, n.d., Folder 19, Box 1278, Via Papers.

7. This order required all government contractors to hire and promote without regard to race.

8. William Pollock to Pat Eames, July 7, 1961, Box 638, TWUA Papers.

9. Inter-office memorandum, "For Mr. Pollock's Use," May 5, 1961, ibid.

10. Solomon Barkin to John Chupka, May 12, 1961, Series 3, Box 316, ibid.

11. George Baldanzi to Members of the International Executive Council, August 27, 1962, Folder 3, Box 960, United Textile Workers of America Papers, Southern Labor Archives, Georgia State University, Atlanta.

12. Johnnie E. Brown to George Baldanzi, September 4, 1962, ibid.

13. CORE Report on North Carolina, December 10, 1964, Series 5, Box 17, Congress of Racial Equality Papers, Martin Luther King, Jr., Center for Non-Violent Social Change, Atlanta, Ga.

14. Southern Union Staff Training Seminar, n.d., Folder 19, Box 1278, Via Papers.

15. "Notes on Statements and Observations Made by Julius Fry, TWUA, at SRC Labor Conference, March 14," Folder 14, ibid.

16. "Continuation of Report of Via's Trip to South Carolina, North Carolina, Virginia, and Washington," Folder 17, ibid.

17. "Pro-Segregation Groups in the South," Southern Regional Council Report, January 28, 1957, Folder 13, ibid., p. 9.

18. Local Union Questionnaire, Granite Local 1113, Folder 11, Box 1277, ibid.

19. Local Union Questionnaire, Columbia Local 253; Local Union Questionnaire, White Oak Local 1391, both in ibid.

20. Local Union Questionnaire, White Oak Local 1391, ibid.

21. Organizing Drive Questionnaire, Burlington Mills, Chattanooga, Tennessee, Folder 8, ibid.

22. Local Union Questionnaire, TWUA Local 325, Clifton, South Carolina, Folder 11, ibid.

23. Charles Auslander to Boyd Payton, August 27, 1956; Wayne L. Dernoncourt to Boyd Payton, September 12, 1956, both in Folder 12, Box 1278, ibid.

24. These were riots that occurred in 1956 following attempts by a black student, Autherine Lucy, to break the color barrier at the University of Alabama.

25. Local Union Questionnaire, United Steel Workers of America, Birmingham, Alabama, Folder 4, Box 1277, Via Papers.

26. Local Union Questionnaire, United Rubber Workers of America Local 361, ibid.

27. Local Union Questionnaire, Communication Workers of America, Montgomery, Alabama; Local Union Questionnaire, Street Railway Local 765, both in ibid.

28. David Terry to H. S. Williams, April 24, 1961, Box 638, TWUA Papers.

29. Plant Visit to Celanese by Richard Rowan, July 28–29, 1969, Folder 18, Box 13, Wharton Papers; "Citizens' Council Leader Urges Law, Not Violence," *Rock Hill Evening Herald*, February 17, 1960, p. 1.

30. Staff Meeting in President Pollock's Office, December 21, 1966, Box 90, TWUA Papers.

31. Summary of Southern TWUA Staff Survey, December 12, 1966, Series 3, Box 316, ibid.

32. "Antidiscrimination Provisions in Major Contracts, 1961," Bureau of Labor Statistics, June 1962, copy in Box 655, ibid., p. 1.

33. Replies from Fairey Finishing Plant and Durham Hosiery Mills, Southern TWUA Staff Survey, December 12, 1966, Series 3, Box 316, ibid.

34. Summary of Southern TWUA Staff Survey, December 12, 1966, ibid.

35. Jean Fairfax to Mordecai C. Johnson, August 7, 1967, Reel 163, SRC Papers, pp. 18–19.

36. Raynor interview. For a good illustration of how a local textile union actively resisted integration, see Brattain, "Making Friends and Enemies."

37. Builder interview.

38. Gaines interview.

39. Carter interview.

40. Thomas Pharr, who worked at Rock Hill Printing and Finishing Company in Rock Hill, South Carolina, remembered being subjected to racial abuse from white union members when he tried to get elected to the local union committee in the 1970s. Pharr recalled that he only suffered from severe racial abuse after he became active in the union. He felt that his activism in the union had caused "a lot of resentment from the white towards me basically because I was black, because I am black." Pharr interview.

41. Local union officials, in particular, seemed to be willing to ignore black workers' grievances even though this apparently put them at risk of suits under their duty of "fair representation." I found no evidence of such suits being brought, however. Beck interview.

42. Deposition of Chris Brown, August 18, 1972, *Ellison v. Rock Hill Printing and Finishing Company*, pp. 47, 66–67; Deposition of Chris Brown, November 1, 1973, ibid., p. 25.

43. Deposition of Leroy Ellison, August 17, 1972, ibid., pp. 17–32.

44. Deposition of Jerry Williamson, August 18, 1972, ibid., pp. 88–89.

45. Deposition of James Barnes, August 18, 1972, ibid., pp. 109, 123, 127.

46. Beck interview.

47. Deposition of Leroy Ellison, October 31, 1973, *Ellison v. Rock Hill Printing and Finishing Company*, pp. 65, 86–88.

48. Archie interview; Brown interview; Deposition of Willie A. Simpson, August 17, 1972, *Ellison v. Rock Hill Printing and Finishing Company*, p. 21.

49. Deposition of Henry Wiley, August 17, 1972, ibid., pp. 19, 20, 36, 37.

50. Ellison interview. As Chris Brown put it, "If you stayed in the union you did have somebody to come and fight for you against the bossman. If not, they could just tell you to go home and that was it; there was nobody to fight for you." Brown interview.

51. Black worker Henry Wilson, for example, claimed that when black workers tried to file grievances with the union about not securing promotions, the union always told them, "We'll see what we can do. That's all. That's it." Deposition of Henry Wilson, February 10, 1970, *Adams v. Dan River Mills*, p. 11. Black worker William Still described how the union never helped him in his efforts to receive a promotion: "I would go and tell them there was an opening, that I knew this fellow was going to leave or that man is going to leave and he would say I'm going to look into it—then the next thing I knew the job was filled." Transcript of trial testimony, June 5, 1973, ibid., p. 7.

52. Deposition of Tommy Lewis Hairston, October 13, 1971, ibid., p. 6.

53. EEOC Charge of Discrimination of Edward Crews, March 30, 1969, ibid.

54. Deposition of Leroy Johnson, March 31, 1969, ibid., pp. 6–7.

55. Moore interview.

56. Plaintiffs' Response to the Defendant's Memorandum on Area "Labor Force" Statistics and Related Matters, May 20, 1976, *Sledge v. J. P. Stevens*.

57. McGhee interview.

58. Rogers interview.

59. Little interview; Broadnax interview.

60. Builder interview.

61. *Philadelphia Inquirer*, July 21, 1986, quoted in "Ball and Chain for African-American Workers?: An ACTWU Report on B & C Associates," ACTWU Civil Rights Committee Publication, July 1994, pp. 6–7.

62. Adkins interview.

63. Gaines interview.

64. Moore interview.

65. "Current Campaign Status, November 6, 1978," Box 48, ACTWU-SRO Papers.

66. Application for Issuance of Order to Show Cause Why Defendant Should Not Be Held in Contempt, n.d., *Equal Employment Opportunity Commission v. Cannon Mills*, Box 79, Cannon Papers; Order to Show Cause, n.d., ibid. The union described Crawford in these terms: "There is no person working at the Company who is more outspoken concerning the need of a Union at the company than Daisy Crawford. She openly talks for the Union in and out of the plant and attended Union meetings. In addition to being an active Union person, she is active in civil rights matters. Mrs. Crawford will be a witness in a civil rights suit involving the company that is now pending in United States District Court." Appeal of the

Regional Director's Refusal to Issue a Complaint, *Cannon Mills v. Textile Workers Union of America*, June 20, 1975, Box 79, Cannon Papers, p. 2.

67. Bayard Rustin, for example, wrote a biweekly column about the campaign that was published in black newspapers across America. "Report of Activities on J. P. Stevens Publicity Campaign Week of December 15–21, 1975," Box 22, ACTWU-SRO Papers. In March 1977, the Southeastern Region of the NAACP gave its formal support to the J. P. Stevens campaign. "Statement of Southeastern Region V National Association for the Advancement of Colored People on Employment, Montgomery, Alabama, March 19, 1977," Folder 11, Box 18, Alexander Papers.

68. "Fair Employment Practices in Cone Mills," May 15, 1961, Box 638, TWUA Papers, pp. 5–6.

69. "Recommendations for an Expanded Southern Organizing Program," June 4, 1970, Box 652, ibid.

70. Report on Kenlon Mills, September 17, 1970, ibid.

71. Hoyman interview; "N.C. Textile Firm Finally Unionized," *Washington Post*, September 2, 1974, pp. A1, A9.

72. Bush interview.

73. Paul Swaity, Report of Organizing, Southern Region, July 23, 1970, Box 652, TWUA Papers.

74. The National Interreligious Committee, for example, a group composed of more than forty religious organizations, visited Roanoke Rapids in 1980 to express its support for the Stevens workers. The committee noted that J. P. Stevens had been found guilty of racial discrimination and argued that "intertwined intimately in the struggle for justice through collective bargaining is the desire of women and minorities for equal rights and opportunities [such as the right to hold higher paying jobs], and the right to vindicate constitutional rights such as free speech." Statement from National Interreligious Committee Visit— Roanoke Rapids, N.C., September 9, 1980, Box 2, ACTWU-SRO Papers.

75. Sol Stetin to William E. Pollard, January 17, 1978, ibid.

76. Testimony of Michael Russell before House Subcommittee on Labor Management Relations, October 17, 1979; *Southern Fight-Back* (SOC Newsletter), January 1977, both in Box 33, ibid.

77. Statement of Principles and Purpose, Southern Organizing Committee for Economic and Social Justice; *Southern Fight-Back*, May 1978, January 1977, all in ibid.

78. White worker Donald Tifton quoted in "Special Issue: Southern Textile Workers," *Mountain Life and Work*, September 1978, p. 13, copy in Box 58, ibid.

79. Builder interview.

80. Reese Cleghorn, "The Mill: A Giant Step for the Southern Negro," *New York Times Magazine*, November 9, 1969, p. 142.

81. Paul Swaity to President Pollock, June 29, 1970, Box 652, TWUA Papers.

82. Peter Brandon, "A History of the Cone Textile Strike," in Reel 163, SRC Papers, p. 1.

83. Quinney, "Textile Women," p. 72.

84. Builder interview.

85. Ibid.

86. ACTWU organizer Joe Gaines remembered one example in Mobile, Alabama, where the white leadership used a capable black vice president because "they knew he could get things done. . . . He got to go to bat to try to get a lot for the other workers. . . . He was an effective person plus they knew he would pool the majority of the black votes . . . so basically what they saw was a guy that could get the job done and that they would have some type of steering power over, and by the same token they would have the membership behind them." Gaines interview.

87. At Fitzgerald Textile Mills in Fitzgerald, Georgia, for example, workers elected an African American woman, Esther Lee Davis, as president of their local union in 1970. Davis had also been active in the local NAACP before becoming president. Despite this, a TWUA representative noted that "interestingly, there is no resentment among the white employees of Davis being president." Patricia Eames to William Pollock, August 18, 1970, Box 90, TWUA Papers.

88. The *Washington Post* reported that blacks had voted overwhelmingly for the union because "while white mill workers had through generations been instilled with a tough independence, Blacks have been much more inclined toward banding together." "N.C. Textile Firm Finally Unionized," *Washington Post*, September 2, 1974, p. A9.

89. Taylor interview.

90. In February 1971, for example, the TWUA reported that workers at Keller Dye and Finish in Rome, Georgia, had walked out on strike when the company had fired two leading black union members during contract negotiations. The strike was supported by many white members who were anxious to ensure that the contract was renewed successfully. Scott Hoyman to William Pollock, February 24, 1971, Box 90, TWUA Papers.

91. Gaines interview.

92. Ibid.

93. Builder interview.

94. Moore interview.

95. Lincks interview; Waldrep interview; Hoyman quoted in Earle, Knudsen, and Shriver, *Spindles and Spires*, p. 303.

96. Atkins interview.

97. Truchil, "Capital-Labor Relationships," p. 231; Ed McConville, "Two Years After Union 'Victory': The Southern Textile War," *Nation*, October 2, 1976, p. 294.

98. Terrill quoted in Zieger, "Textile Workers and Historians," p. 36.

99. For an overview of historians' treatments of the failure to organize the southern textile industry, see Zieger, "Textile Workers and Historians." For the way that economic fluctuations and the structure of the industry could hold back unionization, see Flamming, *Creating the Modern South*, esp. pp. 199–204, and Minchin, *What Do We Need a Union For?* For analysis of the failure of particular union efforts, see Salmond, *Gastonia 1929*; Hall et al., *Like a Family*; and Griffith, *The Crisis of American Labor*. On the 1956 Darlington mill closure and the ensuing legal battle, see Arthur, "The Darlington Mills Case."

100. This argument is explained in greater detail in Minchin, *What Do We Need a Union For?*, especially pp. 69–98.

101. Hoyman interview.

102. This strike is examined in detail in Chapter 6.

103. Scott Hoyman to Sol Stetin, December 31, 1974, Box 22, ACTWU-SRO Papers.

104. Hoyman interview.

105. Atkins interview.

106. Minchin, *What Do We Need a Union For?*, pp. 37–44. For the way that racial propoganda was used during the Operation Dixie campaign of the 1940s, see Griffith, *The Crisis of American Labor*, pp. 62–87.

107. Raynor interview.

108. Henry P. Leiferman, "Trouble in the South's First Industry: The Unions Are Coming," *New York Times Magazine*, August 5, 1973, pp. 25–26; Peter Kovler, "New Fight in the 'New South': Unionization," *Los Angeles Times*, August 5, 1979.

109. Raynor interview.

110. "J. P. Stevens Workers Meeting," June 27, 1978, Box 46, ACTWU-SRO Papers.

111. Seals interview.

112. Testimony of the Textile Workers Union of America before the House of Representatives Committee on Education and Labor, Subcommittee on Labor-Management Relations, March 15, 1976, copy in Box 51, ACTWU-SRO Papers, p. 5; Paul Swaity to Charles Buff, February 21, 1974, Box 22, ibid. The best historical account of the Stevens campaign is Hodges, "J. P. Stevens and the Union." The Stevens campaign also received a great deal of coverage from journalists, and two of the best accounts are Gloria Emerson, "The Union vs. J. P. Stevens: Organizing the Plantation," *Village Voice*, July 16, 1979, and William M. Adler and Earl Potter, "A New Day in Dixie," *Southern Exposure* 22 (Spring 1994): 16–27.

113. J. P. Stevens letter to All Employees, April 25, 1973, Box 22, ACTWU-SRO Papers.

114. Ed McConville, "Two Years After Union 'Victory': The Southern Textile War," *Nation*, October 2, 1976, pp. 294–99, quote on pp. 295–96.

115. "Current Campaign Status, November 6, 1978," Box 48, ACTWU-SRO Papers. From a Stevens campaign in Montgomery, Alabama, it was reported in an organizing probe that around 60 percent of the mill was black, but that there were "still a relatively large number of older white females that would prove our weakest point." W. E. South to Harold McIver, July 27, 1973, Box 22, ibid.

116. ACTWU Staff Organizers Weekly Report for Vonnie Hines, week ending October 14, 1978, Box 56, ibid.

117. ACTWU Staff Organizers Weekly Report for Vonnie Hines, weeks ending August 23, 1980, and October 25, 1980, Box 50, ibid.

118. ACTWU Staff Organizers Weekly Report for Robert Ross, week ending May 10, 1980, Box 55, ibid.

119. Mel Tate, "Using Social Services to Build a Local Union in Tifton and Milledgeville," Box 48, ibid.

120. Paul Swaity to President Stetin, April 24, 1974, Box 22, ibid.

121. Purnell interview.

122. "Ball and Chain for African-American Workers?: An ACTWU Report on B & C Associates," ACTWU Civil Rights Committee Publication, July 1994, pp. 5–6.

123. Ibid., p. 35.

124. Ibid., pp. 20–21.

125. Ibid., pp. 10, 12, 14, 27.

126. Ibid., pp. 16, 32, 35.

127. Ibid., pp. 20–21.

128. Ibid., p. 6.

129. In *Sherrill v. J. P. Stevens*, for example, black workers described how the company's first black supervisor had been placed over their predominantly black department. Black worker Ray Lewis McDowell described his supervisor as black, "but he takes his orders from them." Similarly, union organizer Joe Gaines remembered that when companies started to hire black supervisors in the 1970s, they usually put them over black workers: "Still, once they put them into the position, they had very little or no authority to direct the white workforce. They could only deal with the black workforce. . . . You never would see them promoted over whites." Deposition of Miles Luckey, October 24, 1973, *Sherrill v. J. P. Stevens*, p. 31; Deposition of Ray Lewis McDowell, October 10, 1973, ibid., p. 42; Gaines interview.

130. Builder interview; Gaines interview. Macy Adkins, a militant black worker and local union leader at Fieldcrest-Cannon in Columbus, Georgia, was fired five times by white supervisors and reinstated each time through arbitration. On the sixth time, however, he was fired by a black supervisor, which, Adkins remembered, made it much more difficult to convince the arbitrator that the discharge was discriminatory. In fact, Adkins was not rehired and had to leave the mill. Adkins interview.

131. Builder interview; Adkins interview.

132. Minchin, *What Do We Need a Union For?*, pp. 180–81.

133. Bush quoted in Ashbaugh and McCurry, "On the Line at Oneita," p. 210.

134. Raynor interview; Gaines interview.

135. Halpern, "Organized Labor," pp. 359–60, 382; Letwin, "Interracial Unionism," pp. 520–22.

136. Halpern, "Organized Labor," pp. 362–64, summarizes this debate.

137. Atkins interview.

Epilogue

1. R. M. Gardiner to R. C. Gourley, November 17, 1969, "Affirmative Action—Statistical Information on Black Employment, Promotions, etc. 1968–1972" folder, DRMC Papers.

2. Ibid.; R. C. Gourley to R. M. Stephens, May 1, 1970, ibid.

3. Coles interview.

4. Long interview.

5. Halpern, "Organized Labor," p. 374; Raynor interview.

6. On resistance to pioneers in school integration, see Douglas, *Reading, Writing, and Race*, pp. 63, 274, and Curry, *Silver Rights*, esp. pp. 23–43.

7. George Waldrep Jr., a vice president of Burlington Industries, asserted in 1995 that "it would have took longer but eventually it would have happened purely on the basis of supply and demand." Waldrep interview.

8. For a summary of the debate about the relationship between the federal government and the civil rights movement, see Fairclough, "State of the Art," pp. 395–96.

9. Ibid., p. 387.

10. Alston interview.

11. Transcript of EEOC Textile Forum, January 12–13, 1967, Part 2, Reel 2, LBJ Papers, pp. 94–95.

12. Zieger, "From Primordial Folk to Redundant Workers," pp. 289–90.

13. Bluestone, "Deindustrialization and Unemployment," pp. 7–8.

14. Norrell quoted in Goldfield, *Black, White, and Southern*, p. 204; Bonham, "Robotics, Electronics," p. 165.

15. Zieger, *The CIO*, pp. 348–49.

16. Peddaway interview.

17. Ibid.

18. Tarver interview.

bibliography

Manuscripts

Andrews, South Carolina
  Laura Ann Pope Papers (private collection of Laura Ann Pope)
Atlanta, Georgia
  Martin Luther King, Jr., Center for Non-Violent Social Change
    Congress of Racial Equality Papers
    Southern Christian Leadership Conference Papers
    Student Non-Violent Co-Ordinating Committee Papers
  Southern Labor Archives, Georgia State University
    AFL-CIO Southern Area Civil Rights Department Papers
    Amalgamated Clothing and Textile Workers' Union—North Carolina Joint Board
      Papers
    Amalgamated Clothing and Textile Workers' Union—Southern Regional Office
      Papers
    United Textile Workers of America Papers
    Uprising of '34 Papers (tapes and records accompanying *The Uprising of '34*, a
      documentary film about the 1934 general textile strike)
    Emory Via Papers
Cambridge, England
  Cambridge University Library
    Civil Rights during the Johnson Administration Papers (material microfilmed from
      the Lyndon Baines Johnson Library, Austin, Texas)
Chapel Hill, North Carolina
  Southern Historical Collection, University of North Carolina at Chapel Hill
    Mildred Gwin Andrews Papers

Samuel Ervin Papers
Southern Oral History Project
Charlotte, North Carolina
University of North Carolina at Charlotte
Kelly Alexander Papers
Clemson, South Carolina
Strom Thurmond Institute, Clemson University
Strom Thurmond Papers
Columbia, South Carolina
Modern Political Collections, University of South Carolina
William Jennings Bryan Dorn Papers
Danville, Virginia
Dan River Mills
Dan River Mills Company Papers
Durham, North Carolina
Perkins Library, Duke University
Cannon Mills Papers
East Point, Georgia
Federal Records Center
Legal cases are listed in alphabetical order by company name.
Class action cases:
Sallie Pearl Lewis et al. v. Bloomsburg Mills
Case No. 73–324
United States District Court, District of South Carolina, 1973
Donald R. Hicks et al. v. Cannon Mills
Case No. C-115-S-70
United States District Court, Middle District of North Carolina, 1970
Patricia K. Price et al. v. Cannon Mills
Case No. C-84-1012-S
United States District Court, Middle District of North Carolina, 1984
United States of America v. Cannon Mills
Case No. C-65-S-69
United States District Court, Middle District of North Carolina, 1969
Equal Employment Opportunity Commission v. Cleveland Mills Company
Case No. SH-73-36
United States District Court, Western District of North Carolina, 1973
Shirley Lea et al. v. Cone Mills
Case No. C-176-D-66
United States District Court, Middle District of North Carolina, 1966
Millard Galloway et al. v. Fieldcrest Mills
Case No. C-275-G-73
United States District Court, Middle District of North Carolina, 1973
Graniteville Company v. Equal Employment Opportunity Commission
Case No. 68–723
United States District Court, District of South Carolina, 1968
Leroy Ellison et al. v. Rock Hill Printing and Finishing Company
Case No. 72–405
United States District Court, District of South Carolina, 1972
Norman Youngblood v. Rock Hill Printing and Finishing Company
Case No. 79–992

United States District Court, District of South Carolina, 1979
Charles Brown et al. v. Southern Dyestuff Company
  Case No. 2250
  United States District Court, Western District of North Carolina, 1967
United States of America v. Southern Weaving Company
  Case No. 68–10
  United States District Court, District of South Carolina, 1968
Sallie Pearl Lewis et al. v. J. P. Stevens
  Case No. 72–341
  United States District Court, District of South Carolina, 1972
A. C. Sherrill et al. v. J. P. Stevens
  Case No. 73–12
  United States District Court, Western District of North Carolina, 1973
Other cases:
Betsy Ann Broadnax v. Burlington Industries
  Case No. C-160-G-71
  United States District Court, Middle District of North Carolina, 1971
Ethel Marie Edmonds v. Burlington Industries
  Case No. C-136-G-73
  United States District Court, Middle District of North Carolina, 1973
Jerdean A. Mark v. Burlington Industries
  Case No. 77-390-G
  United States District Court, Middle District of North Carolina, 1976
Daisy R. Crawford and Ruth B. Leazer v. Cannon Mills
  Case No. C-76-113-S
  United States District Court, Middle District of North Carolina, 1976
Patricia K. Price v. Cannon Mills
  Case No. C-82-540-S
  United States District Court, Middle District of North Carolina, 1982
Edward Arnold v. Cone Mills
  Case No. C-77-32-G
  United States District Court, Middle District of North Carolina, 1977
Geraldine Lindsay v. Cone Mills
  Case No. C-76-487-G
  United States District Court, Middle District of North Carolina, 1976
Daisy Ruth Patrick v. Cone Mills
  Case No. C-83-287-G
  United States District Court, Middle District of North Carolina, 1983
Robert Seibles v. Cone Mills
  Case No. C-77-13-G
  United States District Court, Middle District of North Carolina, 1977
James E. Woods v. Fieldcrest-Cannon
  Case No. C-89-372-S
  United States District Court, Middle District of North Carolina, 1989
Judy Brown v. Fieldcrest Mills
  Case No. C-74-96-G
  United States District Court, Middle District of North Carolina, 1974
Robert H. Foster v. Fieldcrest Mills
  Case No. C-77-119-G
  United States District Court, Middle District of North Carolina, 1977

Shirley H. Freeman v. Fieldcrest Mills
  Case No. C-80-26-G
  United States District Court, Middle District of North Carolina, 1980
Samuel Millner v. Fieldcrest Mills
  Case No. C-86-190-G
  United States District Court, Middle District of North Carolina, 1986
Jesse E. Harris v. Golden Belt Manufacturing Company
  Case No. C-76-636-D
  United States District Court, Middle District of North Carolina, 1976
Lovett R. Bean v. Starr Fibers
  Case No. 71-1191
  United States District Court, District of South Carolina, 1971
Robert Hall v. Werthan Bag Company
  Case No. 4312
  United States District Court, Middle District of Tennessee, 1966
Madison, Wisconsin
  State Historical Society of Wisconsin
    Textile Workers Union of America Papers
Philadelphia, Pennsylvania
  American Friends Service Committee
    American Friends Service Committee Papers
  Federal Records Center, Philadelphia
    Julious Adams et al. v. Dan River Mills
      Case No. 69-C-58-D
      United States District Court, Western District of Virginia, 1969
  University Archives and Records Center, University of Pennsylvania
    Wharton School's Industrial Research Unit Papers
Raleigh, North Carolina
  United States District Court, Eastern District of North Carolina
    Lucy Sledge et al. v. J. P. Stevens
      Case No. 1201
      United States District Court, Eastern District of North Carolina, 1970
Washington, D.C.
  National Archives, Manuscripts Division
    National Association for the Advancement of Colored People Papers
    Southern Regional Council Papers (microfilm)

Author's Interviews

Adkins, Macy. Columbus, Ga., January 24, 1996.
Alston, Sammy. Roanoke Rapids, N.C., February 9, 1996.
Archie, Johnnie. Rock Hill, S.C., January 30, 1996.
Atkins, Nickolas. Atlanta, Ga., November 22, 1995.
Beck, Fletcher. Rock Hill, S.C., January 29, 1996.
Boger, Jake. Rock Hill, S.C., January 30, 1996.
Boone, James. Roanoke Rapids, N.C., February 9, 1996.
Boulware, Reese. Columbus, Ga., January 17, 1996.
Broadnax, Roosevelt. Columbus, Ga., January 18, 1996.
Brown, Chris. Rock Hill, S.C., January 30, 1996.
Buck, Billy. Opelika, Ala., January 26, 1996.

Builder, Nick. Atlanta, Ga., February 5, 1996.

Bush, Clyde. Roanoke Rapids, N.C., February 9, 1996.

Cannon, Corine Lytle. Kannapolis, N.C., March 11, 1996.

Carter, Joan. Atlanta, Ga., November 20, 1995.

Chambers, Julius. Durham, N.C., June 28, 1996.

Clark, Susan. Columbus, Ga., February 3, 1996.

Clayton, T. T. Warrenton, N.C., March 12, 1996.

Coles, Anthony. Eden, N.C., February 7, 1996.

Collins, Alton. Columbus, Ga., February 3, 1996.

Crittenden, Reverna. Columbus, Ga., January 25, 1996.

Davis, Clinton. Columbus, Ga., January 19, 1996.

Dawson, Mae. Tarboro, N.C., July 28, 1995.

Deal, Elboyd. Kannapolis, N.C., March 11, 1996.

Ellison, Leroy. Rock Hill, S.C., January 30, 1996.

Etheridge, Spencer. Tarboro, N.C., July 20, 1995.

Ferguson, James E., II. Charlotte, N.C., June 14, 1996.

Freeman, Robert. Kannapolis, N.C., March 11, 1996.

Gaines, Joe. Opelika, Ala., January 25, 1996.

Gill, Oscar. Rock Hill, S.C., January 30, 1996.

Gill, Robert Lee. Kannapolis, N.C., March 11, 1996.

Glover, Sammy. Andalusia, Ala., February 2, 1996.

Golden, Mamie. Columbus, Ga., January 25, 1996.

Gordon, B. J. Andrews, S.C., April 11, 1996.

Griggs, Luvon. Columbus, Ga., January 24, 1996.

Griggs, Retha. Columbus, Ga., February 3, 1996.

Harrison, Bobbie. Columbus, Ga., February 3, 1996.

Hedgepath, Maurine. Roanoke Rapids, N.C., March 12, 1996.

Herbin, Sarah W. Greensboro, N.C., December 4, 1995.

Hill, Herbert. Madison, Wis., November 16, 1995.

Hines, Vonnie. Chapel Hill, N.C., February 20, 1996.

Hoard, Leroy. Columbus, Ga., January 16, 1996.

Hoyman, Scott. Summerville, S.C., November 6, 1995.

Jackson, Frank. Phenix City, Ala., January 16, 1996.

Johnson, James. Andrews, S.C., April 1, 1996.

June, Charlene. Andrews, S.C., April 11, 1996.

King, Jimmy. Columbus, Ga., January 18, 1996.

Latham, Mary. Opelika, Ala., January 26, 1996.

Lincks, Robert B. Greensboro, N.C., July 17, 1995.

Little, Jacob. Columbus, Ga., January 18, 1996.

Long, Willie. Columbus, Ga., January 18, 1996.

McCutchen, Carmela. Andrews, S.C., April 11, 1996.

McGhee, James. Andalusia, Ala., February 2, 1996.

McGill, Eula. Birmingham, Ala., January 23, 1996.

McKissic, Patsy. Opelika, Ala., January 26, 1996.

Moody, Joe P. Roanoke Rapids, N.C., March 12, 1996.

Moore, Earl. Columbus, Ga., February 3, 1996.

Peddaway, Louise. Tarboro, N.C., July 20, 1995.

Pharr, Thomas. Rock Hill, S.C., January 29, 1996.

Pope, Laura Ann. Andrews, S.C., April 1, 1996.

Purnell, Jettie H. Roanoke Rapids, N.C., February 9, 1996.

Quarles, Calvin. Smiths, Ala., January 18, 1996.
Raynor, Bruce. Greensboro, N.C., July 28, 1995.
Rogers, Angie. Columbus, Ga., January 24, 1996.
Seals, Ollie. Columbus, Ga., January 24, 1996.
Smith, Ora Lee. Tarboro, N.C., July 20, 1995.
Staton, Lottie. Princeville, N.C., July 28, 1995.
Suggs, Theodore R. Tarboro, N.C., July 20, 1995.
Suggs, William. Princeville, N.C., July 28, 1995.
Tarver, Nellie B. Columbus, Ga., January 25, 1996.
Taylor, Bennett. Roanoke Rapids, N.C., February 9, 1996.
Trawick, Gladys. Andalusia, Ala., February 2, 1996.
Waldrep, George C., Jr. Summerfield, N.C., July 24, 1995.
Young, Sydney. Rock Hill, S.C., January 19, 1996.

Newspapers and Journals

The Afro-American
Backgrounder
The Call
Charlotte Observer
Christian Science Monitor
Columbia *State*
Greensboro Daily News
Greenville News
Greenville Piedmont
Mooresville Tribune
Mountain Life and Work
Nation
New Republic
Newsweek
New York Times
Philadelphia Inquirer
Raleigh *News and Observer*
Rock Hill Evening Herald
Southern Fight-Back
Spartanburg Herald-Journal
Wall Street Journal
Washington Post
Winston-Salem Journal

Trade and Union Journals

America's Textile Reporter
Daily News Record
Southern Textile News
Textile Hi-Lights
Textile Industries
Textile Labor

Books, Articles, and Dissertations

Arthur, Bill. "The Darlington Mills Case: Or 17 Years before the Courts." *New South* 28 (Summer 1973): 40–47.

Badger, Tony. "Segregation and the Southern Business Elite." *Journal of American Studies* 18 (April 1984): 105–9.

Beifuss, Joan T. *At the River I Stand: Memphis, the 1968 Strike, and Martin Luther King, Jr.* Memphis: B & W Books, 1985.

Bluestone, Barry. "Deindustrialization and Unemployment in America." In *Deindustrialization and Plant Closure*, edited by Paul D. Staudohar and Holly E. Brown, pp. 3–16. Lexington, Mass.: D. C. Heath, 1987.

Bonham, Julia C. "Robotics, Electronics, and the American Textile Industry." In *Hanging by a Thread: Social Change in Southern Textiles*, edited by Jeffrey Leiter, Michael D. Schulman, and Rhonda Zingraff, pp. 163–80. Ithaca: Cornell University Press, 1991.

Brattain, Michelle. "Making Friends and Enemies: Textile Workers and Political Action in Post–World War II Georgia." *Journal of Southern History* 63, no. 1 (February 1997): 91–138.

Brown, Douglas Summers. *A City without Cobwebs: A History of Rock Hill, South Carolina.* Columbia: University of South Carolina Press, 1953.

Butler, Richard J., James J. Heckman, and Brook Payner. "The Impact of the Economy and the State on the Economic Status of Blacks: A Study of South Carolina." In *Markets in History: Economic Studies of the Past*, edited by David W. Galenson, pp. 231–346. Cambridge: Cambridge University Press, 1989.

Byerly, Victoria. *Hard Times Cotton Mill Girls: Personal Histories of Womanhood and Poverty in the South.* Ithaca: ILR Press, 1986.

Carlton, David L. *Mill and Town in South Carolina, 1880–1920.* Baton Rouge: Louisiana State University Press, 1982.

Chafe, William H. *Civilities and Civil Rights: Greensboro, North Carolina and the Black Struggle for Freedom.* New York: Oxford University Press, 1980.

———. "The End of One Struggle, the Beginning of Another." In *The Civil Rights Movement in America*, edited by Charles W. Eagles, pp. 127–48. Jackson: University Press of Mississippi, 1986.

Cobb, James C. *The Selling of the South: The Southern Crusade for Industrial Development, 1936–1980.* Baton Rouge: Louisiana State University Press, 1982.

Colburn, David R. *Racial Change and Community Crisis: St. Augustine, Florida, 1877–1980.* New York: Columbia University Press, 1985.

Conway, Mimi. *Rise Gonna Rise: A Portrait of Southern Textile Workers.* Garden City, N.Y.: Anchor Press/Doubleday, 1979.

Corley, Robert G. "The Quest for Racial Harmony: Race Relations in Birmingham, Alabama, 1947–1963." Ph.D. diss., University of Virginia, 1979.

Crawford, Vicki L., Jacqueline Anne Rouse, and Barbara Woods, eds. *Women in the Civil Rights Movement: Trailblazers and Torchbearers, 1941–1965.* Bloomington: Indiana University Press, 1990.

Cross, Malcolm A. *Dan River Runs Deep: An Informal History of a Major Textile Company, 1950–1981.* New York: The Total Book, 1982.

Curry, Constance. *Silver Rights: The Story of the Carter Family's Brave Decision to Send Their Children to an All-White School and Claim Their Civil Rights.* San Diego: Harcourt Brace, 1995.

Douglas, Davison M. *Reading, Writing, and Race: The Desegregation of the Charlotte Schools.* Chapel Hill: University of North Carolina Press, 1995.

Draper, Alan. *Conflict of Interests: Organized Labor and the Civil Rights Movement in the South, 1954–1968.* Ithaca: ILR Press, 1994.

Dublin, Thomas. *Women at Work: The Transformation of Work and Community in Lowell, Massachusetts, 1826–1860.* New York: Columbia University Press, 1979.

Earle, John R., Dean D. Knudsen, and Donald W. Shriver. *Spindles and Spires: A Re-Study of Religion.* Atlanta: John Knox Press, 1976.

Fairclough, Adam. "State of the Art: Historians and the Civil Rights Movement." *Journal of American Studies* 24, no. 3 (December 1990): 387–98.

Fink, Gary M. *The Fulton Bag and Cotton Mills Strike of 1914–1915: Espionage, Labor Conflict, and New South Industrial Relations.* Ithaca: ILR Press, 1993.

Flamming, Douglas. *Creating the Modern South: Millhands and Managers in Dalton, Georgia, 1884–1984.* Chapel Hill: University of North Carolina Press, 1992.

Frankel, Linda. "Southern Textile Women: Generations of Survival and Struggle." In *My Troubles Are Going to Have Trouble with Me: Everyday Trials and Triumphs of Women Workers,* edited by Karen Brodkin Sacks and Dorothy Remy, pp. 39–60. New Brunswick: Rutgers University Press, 1984.

Frederickson, Mary. "Four Decades of Change: Black Workers in Southern Textiles, 1941–1981." In *Workers' Struggles, Past and Present: A "Radical America" Reader,* edited by James Green, pp. 62–82. Philadelphia: Temple University Press, 1983.

Garrow, David J. *Protest at Selma: Martin Luther King, Jr. and the Voting Rights Act of 1965.* New Haven: Yale University Press, 1978.

Glass, Brent D. *The Textile Industry in North Carolina: History.* Raleigh: North Carolina Division of Archives and History, 1992.

Goldfield, David R. *Black, White, and Southern: Race Relations and Southern Culture, 1940 to the Present.* Baton Rouge: Louisiana State University Press, 1990.

Graham, Hugh Davis. *The Civil Rights Era: Origins and Development of National Policy, 1960–1972.* New York: Oxford University Press, 1990.

Greenberg, Stanley B. *Race and State in Capitalist Development: Comparative Perspectives.* New Haven: Yale University Press, 1980.

Greene, Melissa Fay. *Praying for Sheetrock: A Work of Non-Fiction.* London: Secker and Warburg, 1992.

Griffith, Barbara S. *The Crisis of American Labor: Operation Dixie and the Defeat of the CIO.* Philadelphia: Temple University Press, 1988.

Hall, Jacquelyn Dowd. "Disorderly Women: Gender and Labor Militancy in the Appalachian South." *Journal of American History* 73 (September 1986): 354–82.

———. "Private Eyes, Public Women: Images of Class and Sex in the Urban South, Atlanta, Georgia, 1913–1915." In *Work Engendered: Toward a New History of American Labor,* edited by Ava Baron, pp. 243–72. Ithaca: Cornell University Press, 1991.

Hall, Jacquelyn Dowd, James Leloudis, Robert Korstad, Mary Murphy, Lu Ann Jones, and Christopher B. Daly. *Like a Family: The Making of a Southern Cotton Mill World.* Chapel Hill: University of North Carolina Press, 1987.

Halpern, Rick. "Organized Labor, Black Workers and the Twentieth-Century South: The Emerging Revision." *Social History* 19, no. 3 (October 1994): 359–83.

Hodges, James A. "J. P. Stevens and the Union: Struggle for the South." In *Race, Class, and Community in Southern Labor History,* edited by Gary M. Fink and Merl E. Reed, pp. 53–64. Tuscaloosa: University of Alabama Press, 1994.

———. *New Deal Labor Policy and the Southern Cotton Textile Industry, 1933–1941.* Knoxville: University of Tennessee Press, 1986.

Honey, Michael K. *Southern Labor and Black Civil Rights: Organizing Memphis Workers.* Urbana: University of Illinois Press, 1993.

Humphries, Jane. "The Working-Class Family, Women's Liberation, and Class Struggle: The Case of Nineteenth-Century British History." *Review of Radical Political Economics* 9 (Fall 1977): 25–41.

Jacoway, Elizabeth, and David R. Colburn, eds. *Southern Businessmen and Desegregation.* Baton Rouge: Louisiana State University Press, 1982.

Jameson, Elizabeth. "Imperfect Unions: Class and Gender in Cripple Creek, 1894–1904." In *Class, Sex, and the Women Worker*, edited by Milton Cantor and Bruce Laurie, pp. 166–202. Westport, Conn.: Greenwood Press, 1977.

Janiewski, Dolores E. *Sisterhood Denied: Race, Gender, and Class in a New South Community.* Philadelphia: Temple University Press, 1985.

Korstad, Robert, and Nelson Lichtenstein. "Opportunities Lost and Found: Labor, Radicals, and the Early Civil Rights Movement." *Journal of American History* 75 (December 1988): 786–811.

Letwin, Daniel. "Interracial Unionism, Gender, and 'Social Equality' in the Alabama Coalfields, 1878–1908." *Journal of Southern History* 61, no. 3 (August 1995): 519–54.

Meier, August. "Epilogue: Toward a Synthesis of Civil Rights History." In *New Directions in Civil Rights Studies*, edited by Armstead L. Robinson and Patricia Sullivan, pp. 211–24. Charlottesville: University Press of Virginia, 1991.

Miller, Marc S., ed. *Working Lives: The Southern Exposure History of Labor in the South.* New York: Pantheon Books, 1980.

Minchin, Timothy J. "'The Union Was Our Only Voice': African-American Textile Workers in Danville, Virginia, 1944–1957." *Odense American Studies International Series*, no. 17 (August 1995).

———. *What Do We Need a Union For?: The TWUA in the South, 1945–1955.* Chapel Hill: University of North Carolina Press, 1997.

Nathan, Richard P. *Jobs and Civil Rights: The Role of the Federal Government in Promoting Equal Opportunity in Employment and Training.* Washington, D.C.: U.S. Commission on Civil Rights/Brookings Institute, 1969.

Newby, I. A. *Plain Folk in the New South: Social Change and Cultural Persistence, 1880–1915.* Baton Rouge: Louisiana State University Press, 1989.

Norrell, Robert J. "One Thing We Did Right: Reflections on the Movement." In *New Directions in Civil Rights Studies*, edited by Armstead L. Robinson and Patricia Sullivan, pp. 65–80. Charlottesville: University Press of Virginia, 1991.

———. *Reaping the Whirlwind: The Civil Rights Movement in Tuskegee.* New York: Alfred A. Knopf, 1985.

Northrup, Herbert R. "The Negro in the Automobile Industry." In *Negro Employment in Basic Industry: A Study of Racial Policies in Six Industries*, edited by Herbert R. Northrup, Richard L. Rowan, Carl B. King, William H. Quay, and Howard W. Risher, pp. 43–126. Philadelphia: Industrial Research Unit, Wharton School of Finance and Commerce, University of Pennsylvania, 1970.

———. "The Negro in the Paper Industry." In *Negro Employment in Southern Industry: A Study of Racial Policies in Five Industries*, edited by Herbert R. Northrup, Richard L. Rowan, Darold T. Barnum, and John C. Howard, pt. 1. Philadelphia: Industrial Research Unit, Wharton School of Finance and Commerce, University of Pennsylvania, 1970.

———. "The Negro in the Tobacco Industry." In *Negro Employment in Southern Industry: A Study of Racial Policies in Five Industries*, edited by Herbert R. Northrup, Richard L. Rowan, Darold T. Barnum, and John C. Howard, pt. 3. Philadelphia: Industrial Research Unit, Wharton School of Finance and Commerce, University of Pennsylvania, 1970.

Northrup, Herbert R., Richard L. Rowan, Carl B. King, William H. Quay, and Howard W. Risher, eds. *Negro Employment in Basic Industry: A Study of Racial Policies in Six Indus-*

tries. Philadelphia: Industrial Research Unit, Wharton School of Finance and Commerce, University of Pennsylvania, 1970.

Pride, Richard A., and J. David Woodard. *The Burden of Busing: The Politics of Desegregation in Nashville, Tennessee*. Knoxville: University of Tennessee Press, 1985.

Quinney, Valerie. "Textile Women: Three Generations in The Mill." *Southern Exposure* 3, pt. 4 (1976): 66–72.

Raynor, Bruce. "Unionism in the Southern Textile Industry: An Overview." In *Essays in Southern Labor History: Selected Papers, Southern Labor History Conference, 1976*, edited by Gary Fink and Merl E. Reed, pp. 80–99. Westport, Conn.: Greenwood Press, 1977.

Rogers, Kim Lacy. "Humanity and Desire: Civil Rights Leaders and the Desegregation of New Orleans, 1954–1966." Ph.D. diss., University of Minnesota, 1982.

Rowan, Richard L. "The Negro in the Textile Industry." In *Negro Employment in Southern Industry: A Study of Racial Policies in Five Industries*, by Herbert R. Northrup, Richard L. Rowan, Darold T. Barnum, and John C. Howard, pt. 5. Philadelphia: Industrial Research Unit, Wharton School of Finance and Commerce, University of Pennsylvania, 1970.

Roydhouse, Marion W. "'Big Enough to Tell Weeds from the Beans': The Impact of Industry on Women in the Twentieth-Century South." In *The South Is Another Land: Essays on the Twentieth-Century South*, edited by Bruce Clayton and John A. Salmond, pp. 85–106. Westport, Conn.: Greenwood Press, 1987.

Salmond, John A. *Gastonia 1929: The Story of the Loray Mill Strike*. Chapel Hill: University of North Carolina Press, 1995.

Salter, John R. *Jackson, Mississippi: An American Chronicle of Struggle and Schism*. Hicksville, N.Y.: Exposition Press, 1979.

Sitkoff, Harvard. *A New Deal for Blacks: The Emergence of Civil Rights as a National Issue*. New York: Oxford University Press, 1978.

Strom, Sharon Hartman. "Challenging 'Woman's Place': Feminism, the Left, and Industrial Unionism in the 1930s." *Feminist Studies* 9 (Summer 1983): 359–86.

Tax, Meredith. *The Rising of the Women: Feminist Solidarity and Class Conflict, 1880–1917*. New York: Monthly Review Press, 1980.

Thompson, Dorothy. "Women and Nineteenth-Century Radical Politics: A Lost Dimension." In *The Rights and Wrongs of Women*, edited by Juliet Mitchell and Ann Oakley, pp. 112–38. New York: Penguin, 1976.

Truchil, Barry Elliot. "Capital-Labor Relationships in the United States Textile Industry: The Post World War II Period." Ph.D. diss., State University of New York-Binghamton, 1982.

Turbin, Carole. "Reconceptualizing Family, Work, and Labor Organizing: Working Women in Troy, 1860–1890." *Review of Radical Political Economics* 16 (Spring 1984): 1–16.

Ward, Brian, and Tony Badger, eds. *The Making of Martin Luther King and the Civil Rights Movement*. London: MacMillan Press, 1996.

White, John. *Black Leadership in America: From Booker T. Washington to Jesse Jackson*. London: Longman, 1985.

Woodward, C. Vann. "What Happened to the Civil Rights Movement." In *The Burden of Southern History*. Rev. ed. Baton Rouge: Louisiana State University Press, 1968.

Wright, Gavin. "Economic Consequences of the Southern Protest Movement." In *New Directions in Civil Rights Studies*, edited by Armstead L. Robinson and Patricia Sullivan, pp. 175–83. Charlottesville: University Press of Virginia, 1991.

Zieger, Robert H. *The CIO, 1935–1955*. Chapel Hill: University of North Carolina Press, 1995.

———. "From Primordial Folk to Redundant Workers: Southern Textile Workers and Social Observers, 1920–1990." In *Southern Labor in Transition, 1940–1995*, edited by

Robert H. Zieger, pp. 273–94. Knoxville: University of Tennessee Press, 1997.

————. "Textile Workers and Historians." In *Organized Labor in the Twentieth-Century South*, edited by Robert H. Zieger, pp. 35–59. Knoxville: University of Tennessee Press, 1991.

————, ed. *Organized Labor in the Twentieth-Century South*. Knoxville: University of Tennessee Press, 1991.

index

Anderson, S.C., 63, 120, 208, 212, 214, 215–16, 217, 218

Andrews, S.C., 62, 104, 180–81, 184, 185, 186, 196, 197, 198, 202, 270

Apparel industry, 9

Archie, Johnnie Franklin, 7, 56, 57, 113, 165, 243, 300 (n. 120)

Armstrong, Robert W., 84

Arnold v. Cone Mills, 300 (n. 113)

Asheboro, N.C., 19, 20

Asheville, N.C., 40

Ashmore, Janie Belle, 170

Atkins, Nick, 254, 256, 263

Atlanta, Ga., 18, 22, 49, 85, 102, 128, 130, 157

Attorneys: importance of, 29, 207, 220

Augusta, Ga., 26

Auslander, Charles, 238

Automobile industry, 8

B & C Associates, 260–61

Babbit, Thelma, 94

Bagwill, John, 304 (n. 109)

Baker, Ella, 225

"Ball and Chain for African-American Workers?," 260

Barksdale, William C., 298 (n. 87)

Barlow, D. B., 90

Barnes, James, 242

Bean v. Star Fibers, 157

Beck, Fletcher, 54, 113, 242

Behrman, Mayes, 94

Bell, Tartt, 93

Bemis Company, 145–46

Bethea, Anna F., 192

Bibb Mills, 26, 49, 85, 92

Bibb Recorder, 92

Birmingham, Ala., 239, 270

Black, Mary, 189

Black Awareness Coordinating Committee (BACC), 218

Blakeney, Whiteford, 37, 71–72, 74–75, 85, 87–88, 91, 299 (n. 94)

Bloomsburg, Pa., 169

Bloomsburg Mills, 46–47, 109, 171

Boger, Jake, 14, 60

Boggs, Emanuel, 27–28

Boone, James, 35, 123, 269

Boyd, Mary, 192–93

Brenton Textiles, 107

Bristol, Tenn., 21

Broadnax, Betsy Ann, 221

Broadnax, Roosevelt, 32–33, 246

Broadnax v. Burlington Industries, 221

Brown, Charles, 296 (n. 18)

Brown, Chris, 60, 141, 148, 156, 158, 242, 313 (n. 50)

Brown, Johnnie E., 107, 236

Brown, Robert J., 260, 261

Brown v. Board of Education, 23, 237, 238, 239

Brown v. Southern Dyestuff, 296 (n. 18)

Buck, Billy, 118

Buffalo Mills, 217

Builder, Nick, 123, 246, 250, 251–52, 253, 261–62

Burlington, N.C., 76, 114

Burlington Industries, 10, 11, 30, 41, 219, 238, 258; and Title VII litigation, 4, 36, 221; and reluctance to integrate before 1964, 22, 92–96; integration at, 45, 46, 47, 50, 51, 100, 105, 106–7, 110, 116–17, 121–22; and opposition to Civil Rights Act of 1964, 76; correspondence with Dan River Mills, 79; and executives' fears, 84, 85; complaints of black workers at, 103, 133, 221; and hiring of black women, 176, 179, 188

Burnette, David L., 137

Bush, Clyde, 54, 124, 249, 262

Butler, Richard J., 46

Bynum, N.C., 116

Caldwell, Ida Mae, 188

Calhoun, Annie, 169, 170

Calhoun, Joann W., 109

Campbell, Jay, 195

Campbell, Lawrence, 227

Cann, Robert L., 69, 72

Cannon, Charles, 81

Cannon, Corine Lytle, 53, 178, 269

Cannon, Katie Geneva, 183

Cannon Mills Company, 16, 56, 76, 81, 105, 120, 260–61; entry of black workers into, 3; and Title VII litigation, 4, 11, 36, 61, 247; hiring of black women by, 53, 176, 178, 180, 181; and segregated housing, 103, 134; complaints of black workers at, 113, 133–35, 158, 159; complaints of black women workers at, 188–89, 192–93, 194, 195–96

Carmichael, Stokely, 90, 274 (n. 4)
Car ownership: effect on textile South, 44
Carrboro, N.C., 251
Carter, Dell, 112
Carter, Jimmy, 9
Carter, Joan, 14–15, 185, 241
Cauthen, John C., 49–50, 87
Cedar Falls, N.C., 20
Celanese Company, 106, 240
Chafe, William H., 206
Chambers, Julius, 29, 39–40, 52, 62, 107, 143, 220
Charleston, S.C., 23
Charlotte, N.C., 18–19, 39–40, 81, 233
Charlotte Observer, 34, 79, 121, 128
Chattanooga, Tenn., 47, 90, 238
Cherokee County, S.C., 63, 70, 188, 213
Chicago, Ill.: civil rights campaign in, 206
Childress, Gracie, 171, 195, 196
Cisson, Fred, 117
Civil Rights Act of 1964, 2, 4, 16, 18, 25, 29, 33, 39–68 passim, 75–92 passim, 97, 102, 107, 137, 149, 150, 159, 167, 168, 220, 268–69, 296 (n. 18); Title VII of, 2, 29, 37, 39, 46, 48, 58, 59, 60, 61, 78, 97, 157, 167, 191, 220, 231, 268–69; as cause of integration, 42–62 passim, 75, 231, 269, 283 (nn. 43, 55), 284 (n. 70); impact on black workers, 55–56, 268–69; as cause of black activism, 56–58, 103, 130–37, 167–68, 268–69; opposition of executives to, 76–78, 81, 90–91, 97, 102–3; opposition of white textile workers to, 107; noncompliance with, 149–51, 159–60, 166–74
Civil rights leaders: target textile industry, 28–32, 183–84, 186, 204, 206–7, 208, 219–21, 270, 275 (n. 10); support Oneita Knitting Mills strike, 197–98; support J. P. Stevens campaign, 247, 314 (n. 67)
Civil rights movement: interpretations of, 1–2, 5–6, 205–6, 268, 274 (n. 1), 285 (n. 99), 302 (n. 27), 307 (n. 2), 317 (n. 8); and impact on black textile workers, 202–3, 246–47; and protest in textile communities, 225–29, 230, 269, 310 (n. 73); and impact on white textile workers, 250–52; textile executives' use of, 260–61
Clark College, 12, 21, 53, 128

Clayton, T. T., 57, 135, 158
Cleghorn, Reese, 280
Clerical jobs: obstacles to black entry into, 110, 184, 193–94, 214, 286 (n. 34)
Clifton, S.C., 238
Clinkscales, Paretha, 194
Clover, S.C., 112
Cobb, James, 166
Coleman, Mary, 192, 193
Collins, Alton, 53–54
Collinson, Noyes, 18, 120
Columbia, S.C., 107, 120, 238
Columbus, Ga., 13, 14, 15, 26, 33, 53, 63, 101, 103, 104, 105, 124, 156, 166, 181, 182, 185, 191, 245, 246, 247, 254, 257, 271, 300 (n. 126)
Columbus Towel Mill, 14, 101, 182, 246
Comer Mills, 26
Concord, N.C., 23
Cone, Herman, 93, 95
Cone Memorial Hospital: integration of, 93
Cone Mills, 11, 76, 114, 153, 187, 237, 251, 304 (n. 109); and Title VII litigation, 4, 36, 52, 109, 149; and black employment before 1964, 12, 16–17, 19–20, 24, 92–95
Congress of Industrial Organizations (CIO), 263
Congress of Racial Equality (CORE), 225, 226, 228, 236
Consent decrees, 39, 59, 61, 110, 112, 113, 149, 293 (n. 61); opposition to, 112–14
Contract, Contract, 198, 201
Conway, Mimi, 295
Cornelius, N.C., 253
Cornell University, 96
Costner, Durwood, 14
Costner, Robert, 89, 224
Cox, Mary, 201, 202
Crawford, Daisy, 195–96, 247, 313 (n. 66)
Crawford and Leazer v. Cannon Mills, 195
Crenshaw, John S., 173–74
Crews, Edward, 139, 244
Crews, Helen, 194, 229
Crews, Mae, 222
Crittenden, Reverna, 63, 182
Crocker, Boyce E., 72
Cross, Malcolm, 51, 80
Crothers, Edward, 96
Crowder (Cannon Mills worker), 188–89

313 (nn. 41, 51); attitude of black workers toward, 241–47, 313 (n. 50). *See also* Textile Workers' Union of America; United Textile Workers of America
Lane, S.C., 197
Lanett Mill, 26
Latham, Mary, 115
Laurinburg, N.C., 192
Law, Dexter, 133
Lea, Shirley, 170, 269
Leaksville Woolen Mills, 82
Lea v. Cone Mills, 31, 52, 58, 59–60, 168, 169–70, 187, 220, 221, 222
Leazer, Ruth B., 194
Lee County Manufacturing Company, 177
Leesburg, Ga., 177, 178
Leiferman, Henry P., 9
Leshner Manufacturing Company, 54
Lewis, Hattie F., 173
Lewis, Sallie Pearl, 169, 171, 184, 269
Lewis v. Bloomsburg Mills, 46, 48, 60, 109, 166, 168, 169–71, 184, 189, 192, 193–95, 220
Lewis v. J. P. Stevens, 37, 59–60, 69, 72, 86, 145, 147–48, 166, 168, 169
Lexington, N.C., 133
Lichty, Joseph S., 93
Like a Family, 161
Lincks, Robert B., 45, 50, 85, 116–17, 122, 176
Lindsay, Geraldine, 109
Lindsay v. Cone Mills, 109
Litigation: importance of, 4, 58–62, 112, 219–25, 231; major cases, 36–40
Little, Jacob, 13–14, 101–2, 156, 246
Little, William C., 51
Long, Cathy Lou, 193
Long, Willie, 63, 103, 104–5, 124, 156
Lorillard Company, 60
Louisiana, 231
Love, J. Spencer: attitude regarding black employment, 93–95
Love, Sadler, 49, 128
Lowenstein Mills, 38
Luckey, Miles, 117–18
Lucy riots, 239

McCain, James T., 225
McCorkle, Thomas, 118
McCree, Elaine, 193
McCutchen, Carmela, 186, 200, 201, 202

McDowell, Dillard, 155
McDowell, Ray Lewis, 89, 316 (n. 129)
McGhee, James, 104, 245
McIntosh, Carrie, 169
McIver, C. Almon, 76
McKinsey, Jerry, 75
McLean, Paul Gene, 152, 224
Macon, Ga., 26, 92
Madison, N.C., 221
Management. *See* Southern textile executives
Marable, Joe, 140
March on Washington (1963), 236
Mark, Jerdean A., 110
Marshall, John H., 119
Mason, Marion Brown, 191
Mayfair Mills, 78
Mebane, N.C., 46, 83
Medlin, Boyce, 121
Meeks, Waco, 149
Memphis, Tenn., 146, 260
Middleton, Mary Lee, 201
Migration of blacks to the North: role of textile integration in stemming, 33–34, 186–87
Milledgeville, Ga., 259
Miller, James B., 71
Milliken, Roger, 9–10
Millner, Elizabeth, 173
Mobile, Ala., 173, 314 (n. 86)
Mondale, Walter, 30–31
Montgomery, James, 107, 139–40, 148
Montgomery, Ala., 23, 173
Montgomery bus boycott, 237, 239
Moody, Joe P., 57, 157–58, 222–23
Moody, Mable, 222
Moore, Earl, 105, 245, 247
Mooresville, N.C., 24
Mooresville Tribune, 24
Morton, Eric, 230
Mount Gilead, N.C., 19, 24, 39
Muscogee Mill, 15, 105

Nashville, Tenn., 63, 76
Nation, 258
National Association for the Advancement of Colored People (NAACP), 6, 29, 60, 91, 111, 131, 183–84, 195, 199, 204, 214, 220, 226, 237, 238, 270, 315 (n. 87); Legal Defense Fund, 39, 206–7, 214, 219–20,

231; importance of, 207, 219–23, 231; criticisms of, 215–16
National Labor Relations Board (NLRB), 77
National Urban League, 206
Neisler Mills, 76
New England, 9
Newsweek, 79
New York, N.Y., 198; migration to, 33, 186–87
New York Times, 9, 30, 34–35, 36, 45, 81, 219, 228
Nixon, Richard, 9, 30
Norrell, Robert, 270
North American Free Trade Agreement (NAFTA): impact on textile industry, 270
North Carolina, 36, 236, 237, 246, 276 (n. 13); importance of textile industry to, 9–10, 29, 31–32; AFSC in, 18; integration in, 48; civil rights workers' assessment of, 230
North Carolina Agricultural and Technical State University, 129
North Carolina Central University, 40
North Carolina Good Neighbor Council, 31, 121
North Carolina State University, 73
Northrup, Herbert, 44
Norton, J. J., 77

Office of Federal Contract Compliance (OFCC), 31, 67, 207
Old Hickory, Tenn., 239, 240
Oneita Knitting Mills, 62, 248, 270; integration of, 180–81, 184, 186–87, 294 (n. 104); 1973 strike at, 196–203, 204, 255–56; 1963 strike at, 197
Opelika, Ala., 115, 118–9
Opelika Manufacturing Company, 115, 118–9
Orange, James, 247
Orange County, N.C., 168
Osburn, Donald, 28

Pacific Mills, 79, 107, 120
Packard, David, 30
Pacolet Mills, 77
Pamplico, S.C., 258
Paper industry, 8, 43, 44

Payner, Brook, 46
Peddaway, Louise, 32, 176–77, 178, 181, 271
Perkel, George, 198
Pethel, Norman, 195
Pharr, Thomas, 33, 53, 60, 312 (n. 40)
Philadelphia Inquirer, 246
Pinnix, Romona, 168, 169–70
Pioneer black workers, 4–5; experiences of, 99–114, 175–83, 290 (n. 5); hiring and promotion requirements for, 100, 116–22, 294 (n. 104)
Politicians: target textile industry, 28–32
Pollock, William, 235, 250
Poor People's Campaign, 218
Pope, Laura Ann, 185, 197, 198, 199–200, 201–2
President's Committee on Equal Employment Opportunity, 219
Price, Edward, 102, 132, 138
Progressive Era, 204
Purnell, Jettie, 15–16, 122, 259–60, 283 (n. 55)

Quarles, Calvin, 13

Race strikes, 27–28
Racial disparities: in workloads, 62–64, 155–56, 158, 187–90, 194–95; in hiring, 72–73, 135–37, 161–74; in pay, 141–46, 157–58, 297 (n. 61), 301 (n. 4); in discharge of workers, 156–57, 195, 221; in discipline, 195–96, 300 (n. 113)
Randolph Mills, 19–20
Rankin, Ed, 4
Raynor, Bruce, 202, 203, 240, 241, 257, 262, 267
Resistance: of white workers to integration, 100–114
Reuther, Walter, 237
Reverse discrimination: allegations of, 90–91, 113–14
Rhyne, C. A., 70
Rice, Richard R., 86
Rich Square, N.C., 24
Riegel Textile Corporation, 49, 115, 118, 211, 291 (n. 30), 304 (n. 87)
"Right to manage": textile companies' belief in, 77–78
Riverview Mill, 26
Roanoke Rapids, N.C., 3, 13, 36, 39, 53, 57,

for labor unions, 196–97, 199–201, 241; historical writings on, 203–4

Woods v. Fieldcrest-Cannon, 156

Woodward, C. Vann, 65

Woolworth's, 225, 260

Workloads: and complaints of discrimination, 62–64, 187–90

World War II: integration during, 25–28

Wright, Gavin, 3, 274 (n. 6), 275 (n. 14), 281 (n. 2)

Yelton, Carrie, 116

York County, S.C., 222

Young, Sydney, 62, 64

Youngblood v. Rock Hill Printing and Finishing Company, 113–14